# The
# Long Way
# HOME :

## The Testimony

Book #1

ODELL RICHARDSON JR.

BLUEPRINT PRESS
INTERNATIONALE

## DEDICATION

This book is dedicated to my Lord and Savior Jesus Christ.

Thank You LORD and GOD bless everyone!

# Table of Contents

# INTRODUCTION

"Home"; an internal or godly place of rest on earth which includes love, peace, purpose, passion, patience, prosperity, humility, humanity, joy, accountability, spirituality, intelligence and wisdom.

The journey of life shall bring forth many challenges, leaving us with many questions to ourselves. How did my life end up here? Why did I respond to certain situations in this manner? How was I able to hurt others without realizing it? These are just a few many of us will encounter before finally discovering the answer to the most important question of them all: Who am I? Today, I have the answer to these and others, but many still do not. With this story, I will share real life messaging to help others counter many of their inconsistencies with the hope of promoting a better standard of living. I believe this body of work can assist with growth for all people who are simply in need of encouragement.

Welcome, my name is Odell Richardson Jr. I'm an African-American author from Baltimore City, Maryland. My zodiac sign is Cancer. I love to write or express creative ideas on paper; I enjoy reading, occasionally drawing or sketching, and I enjoy watching professional basketball, football and boxing. I'm a proud father of three. I have a subtle but strong sense of humor. I'm a saved man; a humble man. I'm single, yet I've learned through experience what it takes to truly give and receive love properly. I'm pretty compassionate: a true people person who often considers the collective not just individual elevation. All this seems fairly normal, right? Well, not when it takes a man more than thirty-four years to fully grasp it all. Throughout most of my life, I've lived with absolutely no guidance or direction while in the tough city streets of B'MORE. It is my desire, now that I'm found, to help others achieve the same by escaping or surviving the same ideas of darkness I dwelled in for many years.

In this story, ALL of the names of everyday people, with the exception of my own, have been altered or changed to false names. However, there are several familiar names, and appearances by celebrities and/or stars in this story, you all will recognize throughout. These individuals DO NOT have any ties to any plots or themes throughout the entire story. These good people had absolutely NOTHING to do with the trials I've endured throughout my entire life. All appearances of any film or television stars, athletes, singers, rappers, or political figures were solely coincidental. I DO NOT know any celebrities personally! NONE of these celebrities know me personally. NONE of them knew of my background or of anything involving my past.

This truth-based story or novel began in the inner city of my hometown, Baltimore, Maryland. This story about my life will allow the readers to journey with me throughout this city and abroad. Today, my life is planted in better soil, therefore I must carry out the duty to share these experiences with the masses to influence positive change. Before I continue, I would like to thank all of the readers for taking the time to become one of the most important forces of my dream. The ultimate goal is to bring this message and true story to the silver screen. This is the honest prospective of a young African-American male from the inner city. I truly hope that I'm successful with informing the entire nation about the facts of this life, but from a very different angle. I love to express myself through writing. Since a young man, I've always been a writer at heart! This is what I do! This is who I really am! I'm reaching out with my testimony to follow my dreams, and simply because I have a genuine love for everyone; I know this is what I am supposed to do.

This evolution of my mind and spirit was long in coming. I've finally mastered my way of thinking. I'm now a man of integrity. I will breakdown the mentality of the streets in detail while displaying how our choices shape our future. As I do this, I hope to help and inspire others to make the necessary changes or adjustments in their lives, before it's too late. This story is filled with information based on many of my past experiences. Many will learn just how diverse or complex my people can be. We all are not the same. Still, we are beautiful people. To those who may lack insight; we are not all bad seeds, or the so-called, "throwaway." We may periodically attend the same party, but that does not mean we are all dancing to the same tunes.

This urban literature, narrative non-fiction story is not designed as a vehicle to disrespect those who are still trapped or engulfed in a world full of negativity, lies, and deceit. However, this could serve as a warning to anyone who will hear this cry. I wish to speak to everyone, including those who are just as stubborn as I in the past. I realize there are so many individuals in the world who need help and desire to live a more secure and peaceful existence. Some do not struggle with drastic illegal issues, but maybe these individuals could use a little help in other areas mentioned throughout my story. There are many! Much love to those folks who abide by the laws of the land! I'm now fit to join you all, yet I could really use your support with this message. I'm still plugging away in my own journey, therefore I do not have all of the answers. Still, I'm quite confident this message can help many understand what decisions not to make.

Cleansing my soul or burying the past is also an important factor behind this creation. Writing has been in my heart for over four decades. This story alone should have been told at least seven years ago. The world had such a tight grasp of my soul, I was not able to focus on positive things like peace, or the following of a dream. Where I'm from there are no true dreamers. To do such a thing, believe it or not, was often viewed as a sign of weakness. I was caught up for sure, yet I was blessed with grace and mercy to stay an exception to the infamous rule about street life and death.

In this story you will discover an unfamiliar landmark to many. Although Baltimore, Maryland is a fairly large city, the core setting is virtually unknown. Even relative hit television shows like, The Wire, The Corner, and Homicide (Life on the Streets), just to name a few, overlooked this small but interesting area. The setting of Roc (1991-1994) on Fox, was based on the exact location of this novel's premise. This unique place and its occupants were truly mind-blowing from many different perspectives. As I carefully walk you through my story, things will get quite disturbing and graphic folks. However, it is mandatory not to lose focus on the bigger, more important subject matter of this story; making changes for a better existence.

Praising God and creating positive change are the main driving forces behind this movement. This makes it crucial for me to express this to more than one particular audience or genre. This is a positive movement for all mankind. This story is designed to touch everyone. From the streets, to the athletes, doctors, lawyers, firefighters, correctional and police officers, and other professionals alike; this message is relevant. These personalities and others play significant roles throughout my journey. I've encountered a lot, yet I've always tried to hold on to a kind spirit. I'm not a thug or an ex-kingpin even, nor did I ever care to be. My journey was not exactly a pleasant one, but it was designed for me by God, ultimately with a positive outcome in mind. This is my story, and I feel obligated to promote my resources for the advancement of myself and my fellow men and women across the globe. I'm an extreme optimist. I hardly ever complain about anything. I don't point fingers, I'm incredibly patient, and I'm not big on excuses. Every wrongdoing in my life I've acknowledged, suffered, and repented. I've found peace and that's all I will ever need. However, there is a deep desire for me to follow this dream, and to help make a difference by promoting positive change, if even for a single soul. This, along with glorifying the Creator, promotes this material you can now take part in. Maybe by the time you reach this story's end you'll be better equipped to make a needed change in your life, or to promote change in the life of a friend or loved one. Perhaps with your help and my testimony, you, or someone you know or love, will not have to take THE LONG WAY "HOME."

# Chapter 1

# ENTERING AN EXIT

I, Odell Richardson Jr., entered this world on June of 1972 on the 29th day. I weighed in at exactly 7 pounds 15 ounces. I was my dad's first-born son. As for my mom, Denise Alexander, I was her second born child. This meant I was also the newborn baby brother of my four-year-old sister, Gina Alexander. Shots fired from a police officer's revolver explains the difference in our last name. Gina's dad Jean was killed in the streets of Baltimore City during the summer of 1970. Ironically, my sister's dad and I share the same birthday. After Jean's death, my mom then met my dad Odell Richardson Sr. Two years later, I was born in southeast Baltimore at then City Hospital. Today, the same location is named Johns Hopkins Bayview Medical Center. Despite the early tragedy endured by my sister and mother, the possibility to have a normal family upbringing still remained intact. So there I was, a healthy baby boy with an above average sized head, all set to start my journey in this game we call life.

My original residence was 1913 Kennedy Avenue located in east Baltimore. Not long after I was born, my immediate family and I moved to a house approximately three miles away. A three bedroom on Asquith Street slightly further east, would now be called home for myself, my sister, mom and dad. Both mom and dad were in pretty good health. My dad, ten years my mom senior, was an employee as a commercial truck driver for The Coca-Cola Company. My mom also worked at The Coca-Cola Company as a receptionist. Their place of employment was within five minutes walking distance of our new home.

On the surface, my dad appeared fine but was a chain smoker of Pall Mall cigarettes and a heavy drinker of dark liquor. My mom stayed far away from both. She was an extremely humble and responsible young lady. My mom was only sixteen years old when she had my sister Gina; only twenty when I arrived. Still, she was prepared to be a great mom. She was also an artist at heart. She loved creating handmade picture frames and stuffed animals from nothing more than cotton balls and colorful pieces of cheap fabric. Out of my two parents, my dad was certainly the more outgoing. My mom was very mild-mannered and soft spoken; a God-fearing woman despite having two children out of wedlock. By her early-twenties, she already understood what it takes to be a good mother and an even better person. My mother was a mom in every sense of the word. She made sure we ate three meals a day, stayed away from too many sweets, and got plenty of rest. My dad was already a father, but early on, there was no trace of other siblings. As time moved along, this age gap and my dad's imperfections would slowly begin to alter our plans to live the normal existence we all crave.

In 1975, as The Vietnam War drew to its end, claiming countless Americans, I was three years old learning how to gain full control of a normal stride. This is likely the age where I'm able to go back or visualize a few specific details about my childhood. I can recall certain events that took place inside of my household. I remember being forced to eat my spinach during dinner time. I despised spinach very much as a kid; my mother knew it. Still, mother would never use ignorance or violent tactics to get an important message across to me nor my sister. Instead, she would use her creativity. She would always say to me, "Odell, if you eat all of your spinach, you'll be as strong as Popeye." Mother knew Popeye was my favorite cartoon character at the time. I loved the sailor man so much, this statement worked on me with all of my veggies. Well, with the exception of Brussel sprouts.

At home, I also remembered not-so-pleasant instances like being punished for breaking the record player, and for pushing an innocent little girl down our red brick steps outside, apparently for no reason at all. I still don't understand what drove me to do such a stupid thing. Still I like to believe I was an average kid growing up in the early seventies. Life was just getting underway for my sister and I, yet we would soon be exposed to one of life's most certain facts.

As time moved on I began to develop a bit of my mom's personality and my dad's keen sense of humor. I also recall being pretty close to my sister at four years of age. We even took baths together, believe it or not. I enjoyed having a big sister. She definitely looked after me. Every time I hurt myself or did something I had no business doing, my big sis was there to help out. Gina was actually the first person to arrive on the scene when I nearly ate dog poop. That's right! At three years old, I nearly ate a piece of old dog mess. I had mistaken the white chalky substance for a piece of powdered doughnut. I've always loved cookies, pies, cakes, and doughnuts. Gina really saved me from this act. I was kneeling on the ground with the poop in my hand, when Gina suddenly arrived and yelled out at me from the front porch.

My sister Gina was there for me from the start. She was also the first to support me with my infamous reoccurring nightmare. Every so often, I would have this intense nightmare about Big Foot. It seemed like every other night, Sasquatch would drop in to visit me inside of my bedroom. Normally, during these nightmares, I would hold fast until the giant hairy fellow left from the foot of my bed, but one night he made sure I would respond to his presence. In the midst of these nightmares, I would periodically take peaks from out of one eye. I would do this until the creature disappeared. He always seemed to vanish right before I felt the need to yell out. Well, on this night I was forced to react. Just as I cracked my left eye for the third time, I found myself staring directly into the hairy brown chest of the beast. Big foot was on Asquith Street, in the heart of Baltimore City in my bedroom kneeling directly over top of me.

This nightmare seemed so real I thought I could actually feel its breath and its coarse brown fur brushing up against my skin. I remember looking directly into the yellowish eyes of the beast. My heart rate soon tripled as I struggled to scream as loudly as I could. "HELP, HELP, MOMMY, HELP, HELP!" I screamed. I continued to yell until I saw any kind of change in anything. It was not until I noticed the brightness from underneath of my own eyelids, I realized I was safe. My entire household rushed to my aid, but my sister was there first, out in front. After leading an extensive search party for the eight-foot creature and coming up short again, I regained my normal heart rate and was able to recover a normal sleep pattern. Memories like these and others, such as my mom's patented call for bedtime, never left me. As a youth, it was clear I was an individual who hardly missed a thing. No matter if it was good, bad, or if it meant anything at all, from this point forward I would likely remember.

Midway through my fourth year of life, I would gain even more knowledge about my dad. He never mistreated me in any way. Yet, I can slightly recall a few intense outbursts of his. I had no clue at this point what sparked them, but I do vaguely recall a few instances of him yelling and breaking things around the house. Childhood living for me was still normal as I saw it, but I was not yet five years old. My dad, I believed had done enough good by me to gain my total confidence. My sister kept her distance from my dad. I guess she refused to replace the dad she had lost when she was two or three years old. That was the only way I believed a four-year-old could comprehend my sister's vibe towards my dad. I really didn't know much, I was still too young. Therefore, I continued doing all I could to find my way and to simply be a kid.

As my fifth birthday approached, I would get a chance to really interact with my close relatives. My mom Denise was the second youngest of five children. She was one of two females brought into this world by my grandma, Alma Alexander. We all simply called her "Mama." I recall visiting my grandmother's house as I grew a bit more. Grandma's house was where the rest of my immediate family resided. This three- bedroom home sat to the right, off of a road named North Avenue. This row home rested directly across the street from today's March Funeral Home. Grandma lived at 1913 Kennedy Avenue. My visits there were a pleasant change of scenery. There, I also got to spend time with my grandfather, Edward Alexander; "Daddy," my three uncles, BoBo, Frank, and Marie's partner, Montell, who was like family as well.

My grandparents also had a dog named Deal. Don't ask! Deal was a female Alaskan Malamute puppy. She was the first dog, of any kind, I had ever encountered. With all this, it was none of these figures who kept me excited during these visits. My constant enthusiasm came from my six year old cousin Shawn. Shawn was an only child, the son of my aunt Marie. Marie was my mom's younger sister and quite a personality. My aunt was the exact opposite of my mother. She was more outgoing, louder, and much more animated. My lovable aunt had my cousin Shawn when she was just fifteen years old. She was now twenty-one, and had been with the same man for the last several years, but Montell was not Shawn's biological dad. That previous relationship fell through by my cousin's second birthday. Despite it all, the more I visited Kennedy Avenue, the more I knew I had found a partner for a lifetime.

Weekends became my most important days of all. My home on Asquith Street was becoming a place where I only slept for the most part. Even on some weekdays I would find a way, or my cousin would, to pull the necessary strings to get any of my uncles to bring me to 1913. All of my uncles were quite different from one another. "Uncle Bo," or "BoBo," we all called him, was grandma's youngest son. BoBo was a menacing six-foot, two-hundred eighty-pound student of Frostburg University. He had just started working for a local Nationwide Insurance office as a Claim's Adjuster. Uncle Bo was the guy grandma used as the disciplinarian, of the physical variety; "the ass kicker," if you would.

BoBo was the person who made sure the laws grandma laid down were enforced. Montell, a school teacher, was nothing more than a man we all respected who had charisma, good looks, and stacks of Bruce Lee magazines. Then there was our only married uncle Tony, who did not live at 1913. He usually kept a distance from his younger siblings, for some odd reason. He really only seemed to be concerned with his mom and dad; that was it. Under our uncle Tony was my uncle Frank. Uncle Frank was the friendliest of them all, not really by choice. My uncle was mildly handicap from a beating he received as a teen. Frank once lived life as a free-spirit similar to his sister Marie. He allowed himself to fall victim to the street lifestyle. Frank was severely beaten by a host of police officers as he made an attempt to defend my grandma from being treated rudely by these same officers; by his accounts. Details were sketchy surrounding the incident. However, my uncle's background was not. My uncle Frank was a bully and a drug dealer.

My uncle's chosen profession was not a concrete reason for him to be beaten senseless. We all know today, it was common during those days for authorities to do so to anyone, mainly blacks, and simply get away with it. My uncle spent a few years in prison after this beating, only to come home a completely changed human being. My uncle is prescribed medicine to take regularly in order to sustain control of his mental and emotional state. Since this unfortunate incident my uncle has had trouble controlling himself. Fortunately for the family, it's all harmless. Whenever my uncle fails to administer his medicine correctly, he has uncontrollable outbursts of laughter. Yep, that's right! Frank would laugh so loudly and long during these breakouts, all Shawn and I would do, most of the time, was join in. It probably didn't help my uncle's cause that he was a heavy drinker and smoker like my dad. He spent quite a few afternoons drinking his monthly disability check away with his buddies up on North Avenue.

Shawn and I simply loved our uncle. As kids it's always cool to have an impartial grown-up around. My uncle's situation still baffles me today. I can still recall most of the story grandma shared with me about the time when my uncle Frank was being released from prison after a few years. Grandma said she and her mom were called to pick up Frank from the prison facility. Months leading up to his release grandma had already grown suspicious about her son's behavior. She mentioned while my uncle was in jail the letters he regularly sent home had become quite peculiar. Frank began his prison stay by speaking on becoming a better person and moving on with his life. Over time, grandma indicated the content of these letters had changed drastically. Before long, all uncle Frank cared to discuss with mama were characters from Marvel and D.C. Comics; Spiderman and Superman, to be specific. My grandma, my uncle BoBo, and my great grandma, who was deceased before my birth, all picked my uncle up from jail after his release. For the first time, they all got to experience one of his patented outbursts. My uncle BoBo drove the car with my late-great grandmother in the passenger seat. My grandma sat in the rear with her freed son. Immediately after entering the vehicle, Frank would burst into laughter. Great grandmother quickly turned, looked over her shoulder, and yelled out to her daughter, "Yeah, he's gone!"

My immediate family of my sister, three uncles, an aunt, a cousin, grandma, granddad, and a puppy all stuffed into this three-bedroom home on Kennedy Avenue. There was more than enough attention to go around for Shawn, my sister Gina and I. Before long, my home on Asquith Street was an inconvenience for me. I didn't care about anything other than hanging out with "Buster." That's what our grandfather called Shawn. He called me "Bumble Bee," because I always seemed to accumulate at least one or two bee stings in a week's time during the summer months. Kennedy Avenue quickly became my home again away from home. Gina and I still stayed under the watchful eye of our loving mom, but it was clear Shawn and I needed to grow up together. There was a need for us to be around each other, certainly in the warmer months. We really loved the outdoors. We meshed immediately with the other kids in the neighborhood. We raced our "Green Machine" big wheel vehicles up and down Gorsuch Avenue with a controlled recklessness. We also made strong attempts to mask ourselves as superheroes. Well, if you call large and small bath towels costumes. That was the best we could do to become the ghetto's version of Batman and Robin. I was the youngest, therefore I was Robin. I loved my cousin Shawn so much, it was an honor to take a back seat to him.

Shawn, at only seven years old somehow managed to take my sister's place as protector. I no longer felt the need to be around my sister as much. I actually became a little frustrated when I had to be. I loved my sister, but at the age of five-and-a-half, all I had on my mind was fun. My cousin was the only one I felt a need to be around as a kid. Even when school was back in session, Shawn and I found ways to have lots of fun. Early on we attended separate schools. Shawn attended Cecil Elementary School, just minutes away from 1913. I attended Coldstream Elementary, about the same distance from our home on Asquith Street. I was a kindergartner. Shawn was in first grade. We loved our lives in east B'MORE. Fun, friends, toys, frozen cups, snowballs, sticky apples, and the delightful music whistling from the Good Humor Ice Cream truck was more than enough for us all. What more could a child ask for? Times could not have been more pleasant for me at this point. Life was too perfect for me to realize what loomed slightly ahead. The summer of 1977 was going great. We hardly experienced any precipitation all summer long. This gave my cousin and I plenty of time to run wild. I had no idea a storm was about to hit; both in east Baltimore and in my heart, changing my world forever.

One stormy summer night, my cousin Shawn and I, along with my sister and the rest of the family stayed huddled closely inside of grandma's house. The thundering rain pouring down the window panes was so intense, it actually felt like something more was coming; perhaps a blackout or a hale storm. If there was ever a place to be during a time like this as a kid, it was here, in big mama's hands. There's no presence like the one a grandmother possesses. On this night, my mom was the only immediate member of our family who was not present. My mom and dad were out attending a wedding reception somewhere in the county. My mom and dad were not married, although at the time many believed they were.

My sister and I were supposed to stay on Kennedy Avenue until the reception ended. Soon, the clock struck ten and the rain continued to pour as if God Himself had forgotten to turn off the faucet that showered the earth. Everyone sat relatively quiet, playing card games or painting their fingers and toes. I was drawing a picture of Superman. I'd inherited my mother's passion for quiet artistic creativity. It was only evident whenever I sat still long enough to zone in or focus on a specific topic of interest. I guess you can say I was trying to become the next Stan Lee. Like Mr. Lee, I never just liked pictures whenever I picked up a book, a pad, or a pencil. The dialogue did for me what the illustrations would, even more so at times. I felt the dialogue or conversations in a comic book really made the characters come to life. I loved this idea as a kid. That's why I would hardly ever draw without writing, and I almost never wrote without drawing. However, on this night in August, as I did my best to perfectly define Superman's bicep muscles through cramped, five-year old fingers, I was unintentionally interrupted.

The phone rang just as I rose to change my positioning on the chilled wooden floor. "Hello," "What?" my aunt Marie yelled into the phone attached to the kitchen wall. "What the hell are you saying?" she asked in a panic. "What's wrong with my sister?" she asked with an uncontrolled anger. By this time my #2 pencil had become a dormant object in my right hand. The rest of the household, including my sister, were now growing in concern. Suddenly, I was hearing at least six different voices all at once. I could not fully understand what was taking place, but I was doing fine reading everyone's body language. From where I was sitting, things did not look nor feel very promising. All I truly knew was that it was pouring down raining, there was a phone call, my aunt only had one sister, something was wrong, and everyone was seemingly upset. My conclusion as to what was going on was not a positive one. Minutes later, I learned two things of opposing circumstances. One, I can comprehend pretty well for a five-year old, and two, what I just figured out was my worst nightmare. This was turning out to be even more frightening than all of my many Big Foot encounters, combined.

On that stormy night, my mom and dad left the reception and were headed back to 1913 to retrieve my sister and I. On the way, my dad lost control of the vehicle and rolled the car over several times before landing it in a large drop-off. It was said my parents and the two others who accompanied them were hurt pretty badly. Of course, at this time details were sketchy. As my sister and I sat innocently at our grandparent's house during the rain storm, our mom and my dad remained traumatized in an overturned vehicle, apparently badly injured while awaiting assistance. My world was changing drastically as I stood still, fully unaware as to what life was all about. At only five years old, my first major lesson in life was already underway.

At five years old I was baring witness and learning a valuable lesson in life. I was learning that life is not all about fun and games, and that pain and grief is a part of it all. I didn't understand why, but I was able to understand the huge difference between laughter and crying. For a child, it's quite intense to observe several grown-ups sobbing. This indicates to a kid just how severe a situation may be. We all know, if adults are at a loss, then the child to a certain degree is at an even greater one. I began to realize there was a large cloud hanging over my family; much larger than the one responsible for producing the storm outside on that evening. My family was now in a state of emergency. As my family pulled together and headed for the hospital to check on my mom's condition, my sister and I, along with Shawn, stayed back with our grandparents. It was time for my family to get to the hospital. There were four badly hurt passengers in the sedan on this rainy night. All were injured seriously, yet we soon learned one of the worse injured was my mom.

As the days passed by, details of the accident began to surface. Starting with my dad; it was said he had suffered severe injuries to his back and to one of his legs. One of the rear passengers was actually his younger brother, an uncle I don't remember much at all. He was doing a lot worst than my dad, but was said to be in stable condition. The status of the other passenger, a female, was not disclosed initially by my family, yet she too was stable. My mom was the primary concern for my family. Being only twenty-three years old placed the family in a higher state of worry. My mom's condition from the accident was very critical. My mom suffered massive head trauma, several broken ribs, both legs were broken, and she had major damage to her face. My mom's face smashed into the vehicle's dashboard, causing her to lose most of her front teeth. We all knew things were not making sense when we learned my mom was not wearing a seat belt. This was something she practiced religiously.

It was said my mother had to be pulled out of the wreckage through the front windshield of the late-model sedan. My mom also received multiple internal injuries to her kidneys, liver, and stomach. It had taken surgeons quite some time to get the bleeding under control. My mother's 23 year old, 125 pound frame was in shock and being put through a severe test. A crying shame, everyone thought. Toxicology reports confirmed my mother was the only occupant in the car who did not have a single drink on that evening.

Details continued to pour in about the horrific incident involving my parents. My dad's near-paralyzing emergency back surgery was a success. His condition stabilized and he would soon be able to return home and back to work in the near-future. His brother Curt was just as fortunate. He too was released just days after the accident. His female companion was treated and released with manageable injuries as well. My mom's condition slightly improved, but she still was in a bad way. Evidence of my dad's blood/alcohol level placed a dramatic spin on the entire situation back at 1913. He was a pretty heavy drinker and reports of his behavior prior to leaving the reception indicated irresponsibility on his part. Rushing to and from the event also may have played a large role in the matter. Groceries were found on the roadway and inside of the trunk of the mangled vehicle. My mom had rushed through grocery shopping to make it to the reception on time. My parents felt they did not have enough time to drop off these purchases at home before heading out. These factors along with the severe weather and alcohol spelled trouble from the very beginning. In my family's eyes, my father was the man and the elder, therefore he would have to shoulder the blame, and become the target of their intense backlashes.

As my mother fought for her twenty-fourth birthday, my dad paced the earth upright for the first time since the horrific accident. After returning back to work as a driver for The Coca Cola Bottling Company, one of the first places he visited after work was Mama's. My dad hurried to see me for the first time since the accident. Because of my mom's slight progress, the "jury" was still out in regards to my dad's character. With hopes of my mom recovering, the focus mostly remained on me and my sister. My dad arrived at 1913 without my knowledge. I was upstairs, still somehow managing to be a kid. I knew my mom was in some kind of blameless trouble, but I guess the family did all they could to assure me I would be reunited with her soon. Shawn and I were upstairs hanging out when I received a called from grandma downstairs. "Odell, come down here boy! Your father is here," she yelled enthusiastically. "Oh," I replied excitedly. I hopped up quickly and rumbled down the winding stairway.

I was excited to say the least, yet I had no clue as to what I was running into. As a kid, have you ever found yourself running in the direction of something, full of excitement, only to find out what you were running to was the exact opposite of what you imagined? Well, that's just what happened to me as I entered the kitchen of my grandma's home. It was as if I had anti-lock brakes in my Converse sneakers when I observed my dad awaiting with outstretched arms. All I saw was an unfamiliar man smiling at me with his arms extended. Both of my dad's eyes were bloodshot and his voice was a bit distorted as well. I quickly made the sudden turn perhaps he should have made just several days prior. I hurried quickly over to the security of my grandma's huge left leg. As my dad made repeated attempts to reel me over, I planted my grill deeply into mama's flowered one-piece housedress. "Go ahead boy," she yelled down at me while smiling in embarrassment. "Go say 'Hi' to your father boy!" "No, no, no, I don't want to," I replied back while simultaneously peaking out from her dress. I was wondering if my real dad would suddenly appear. Nope! He didn't, therefore I proceeded to try to run and hide within the brush of the landscape printed on my grandma's garment.

I spent the next twenty minutes treating my dad as if he were a complete stranger. Suddenly, it seemed like the Big Foot encounters had never existed. The big hurry fellow had quickly slipped into third on the "Scare the Hell Out of Odell" list. Experiencing my family melt away due to the accident, and now observing a "red eyed monster" wearing a Coca Cola cap, was likely enough for me to pay a visit to a shrink for toddlers. During this very weird encounter, I remember vividly my dad's transforming facial expressions. He had gone from having a relentless smile as he pleaded for my embrace, to a look of disgust and frustration.

Nevertheless, nothing worked for my dad on this day. I didn't stop my uncontrollable yelling until he left the house all together.

A short time later, I would again be at a loss with my parents. It was now time for me to visit my mom at the hospital. Her condition was still very shaky, but she was slowly showing improvement. My sister Gina and I, along with the rest of the family, all headed over to Union Memorial Hospital in east Baltimore, located on 33rd Street. This was my first visit to any hospital. This idea alone made me a bit uncomfortable as we all entered this facility. The prep talk I was given by my grandma made me excited to see my mom. It had been awhile since I'd last seen her reassuring bright smile. I did not know the severity of her injuries at this time. Therefore, I was excited and very optimistic about this visit. I still struggled with getting passed just how weird my dad appeared. I had hoped for a more delightful experience with my mom. However, I was only five. I was unable to fully discern how different injuries could alter my parent's appearance in many different ways. I was not totally aware that one could be hurt much more than the other during the same incident. I was too young to understand why my dad was home and why my mom was still in the hospital. I did not understand the seriousness of this situation. As things progressed I became more lost and distant, and the terrible ordeal I had just gone through with my dad was about to worsen.

We all entered the room where my mom stayed. My sister immediately ran over to a "woman in a wheelchair." That was the title my mind forced me to use while referring to my mother when Gina rushed over in excitement. There was no way of convincing me the woman in the blue and chrome wheelchair was my mom. I watched my sister with uncertainty, trying to figure out why she was so cheerful about the battered individual in the light-blue hospital robe. As my mom finished greeting the rest of the family, I could slowly see her eyes coming around to meet my own; which had never left hers the entire time.

Before I could even blink, I found myself listening to the same phrase and observing the very same gesture my dad used earlier; outstretched arms from a "stranger." As my mom's arms drew closer as she leaned forward, I quickly glanced behind, making sure I was near the same large leg that bailed me out of the ordeal with my dad. Again, I ran to my grandma who ironically just happened to be making a similar statement to the one she had made earlier. "Boy, go over there and give your mother a hug," she insisted this time around. Everyone seemed to be repeating themselves, so I followed suit. "No, no, I don't want to," I yelled. There was only one difference between these two incidents. Instead of just my dad getting frustrated by my response, the entire family grew tired of my refusal to cooperate. As a kid I was more attached to my mom than my dad. However, I had a hard time truly believing the battered woman I was observing was the person everyone was claiming. My mom appeared much darker. She had lost an enormous amount of weight. And, I'd never seen her hair in braids going backwards before, so that was weird as well. My sister braided my mom's hair during a previous visit. This was my first and things were simply too difficult to grasp. Although my grandmother was leading the plea for me to advance over towards my mom, she was the only person I felt could protect me at this time. I'm not sure about all of the details involved with this visit, but I'm very sure the outcome was the same as it was with my father. I never went over to greet my mom.

Today, I still struggle with the lack of compassion I displayed towards my mother while she was in the hospital although I was just five years old.

I was afraid. I managed to get better at dealing with my mom's physical features as time continued. As her condition improved, talks of her being allowed to visit home periodically began to surface. My mother's condition had stabilized well enough for doctors to reluctantly agree to a few trial runs for her to periodically spend some time at home again. This allowed my family to breathe a temporary sigh of relief. This great news allowed me to once again settle back into a normal existence. For as tense as life was surrounding the accident, things seemed to be returning to old form a bit. My sister and I were back at home on Asquith Street with my mom and dad. Although they were banged up, we all were back together. The sun was shining brightly again and things were looking upwards. It was now time for my sister and I to continue on with just being normal kids in the inner city of Baltimore.

A month passed by, and it appeared as if my mom was going to be allowed to finally come home for good. She was only allowed to spend time with us a few days out of the week. My dad was almost back to normal, therefore he continued to work full-time to support the household. My dad and I had found the magic of old, thanks to his looks returning to form. My mom still showed signs of serious damage from the wreck, yet her condition showed gradual improvement. My uncle Frank spent a lot of time with us overseeing his younger sister. He was the only relative that never seemed to have a negative vibe towards my dad during this tough time. By this time, all of the others had all but dismissed my dad as a member of the family. Many heavy "darts" were thrown by my family towards my dad, but at this point they were all subliminal or subdued.

As the summer came to an end so would something much more. My mom was resting inside one day and a knock on the door alarmed me and awakened her. My sister was on her way home from Coldstream Elementary School. The people at the door were nurses from the hospital. They came unannounced, upsetting my mom quite a bit. Although she was better, she was far from being out of the woods. Still, at home she enjoyed her peace not knowing this peace would be forever interrupted.

After the physicians entered, my mom immediately began to resist their orders to get set to return to the hospital. Something in my mom's hospital files forced the hospital to react quickly and hurry to Asquith Street. I can recall two women in scrubs, pleading with my mom to not fight with them. "Come on, lets go Denise," a nurse insisted animatedly. "No, I don't want to go," mother yelled in fear. This phrase seemed to be genetic. "I know, but you have to, you're very sick," the other nurse said in a pleasant tone. "No I'm not, I'm fine," my mom replied fearfully. As the two nurses tried desperately to calm my mother down, a third person, a doctor also dressed in scrubs, entered through the front door. "Is everything alright?" he asked calmly. Just then, my sister entered the house from school and my mom began to cry. This set off a domino effect around our living room. Well, except for my uncle Frank. I never saw him shed a tear unless he laughed himself into tears. "I don't want to go," mother continued to shout. The representatives from Union Memorial Hospital continued to quickly pack up my mom's things for her to be escorted back to the hospital. As they did so, I cried with stares between my mom, these physicians, and the frantic red lights popping from the top of the ambulance that awaited just outside. Mother repeatedly tried to resist. "Frank, tell them to leave me alone!" mom yelled. Frank, usually short on words complied, "Let her stay, leave my sister be now," he shouted. My mother then held onto her brother's trousers with all the might within her battered little frame, but to no avail.

As my sister and I sat through yet another dramatic scene, my mother was taken away from the house for what would be the last time. Obviously the hospital knew more than they cared to share with us on this day. A few days later, my sister Gina was called upstairs frantically by our grandma as we found ourselves back at 1913. "Gina, Gina, come here," Mama yelled emotionally from upstairs after receiving a brief phone call. My sister entered the room to our broken-faced grandma who suddenly screamed outwards, "YOUR MOMMY JUST DIED!" My mom's injuries eventually won her over. Too much internal bleeding was the culprit. I was unaware of all of the details, but I knew what death meant. My inability to describe the exact moment I learned about my mom's death, to me, is an indication that I was likely in shock and severely heartbroken. At the tender age of five, my mom was no longer with me. I was now motherless! I had just received one of life's most fearful but certain facts; life must end whether we want it to or not. Just like that, she was gone forever. My beloved mother, Denise Alexander had passed away. She was just twenty-four years old.

# Chapter 2

# A Fresh Start

My mother's death devastated the entire family and all who were close. Initially, my sister remained emotionally neutral. She stated when grandma first broke the news she didn't feel a thing. Disbelief, along with just how much Gina loved spending time at grandma's house temporarily postponed my sister's grieving period. Gina stated it took an entire month or so for her to finally break down. Gina said as time went on her four most frequently used words were, "I want my mommy." Despite suffering this tragic moment, I still continued to be a normal kid. I was saddened by the death of my mom, and I was still haunted by her post-accident physical appearance. The impact of the void left behind was strong, but would almost fill immediately. Being around my cousin Shawn and my aunt Marie made things feel better but was confusing for me at such an early age. I did not have it all figured out, yet I did realize a few things. Shawn was as close to me as any member of my family, yet he had a mom, and I no longer did. This really hurt at times. My cousin noticed my mood changes. He even told me once, "O, don't worry, we can share my mom," just after observing me sitting in the vestibule with my head down. Thank God for family and thank God Shawn was there for me throughout this tragedy. I still had a sister and a host of aunts and uncles, yet I had just lost my mom, but in Shawn I felt I had recently gained a brother.

Situations revolving around my dad, my mom's possessions, and my well-being continuously would be the topic of discussion on Kennedy Ave. There were first talks of my sister and I staying on Asquith Street along with my dad. However, this all changed around the time my family was making arrangements for my mother's funeral. My mom was set to be put to rest at March Funeral Home on North Avenue in east Baltimore. If you've ever been to the heart of east Baltimore, you've probably driven passed March Funeral Home several times. There are several locations today. However, during the time of my mother's death, the owner, Mr. March, an old friend of my grandfather, had not yet expanded his business to the funeral home's present locations. March Funeral Home was originally down a couple of blocks on the right-hand side of North Ave. going westward; 928 to be exact. A home owned by Mr. March. That address would later be converted into an establishment in memory of the late great Dr. Martin Luther King Jr. Mr. March held funeral sessions for the beloved in this brick row home on the corner of North and Cecil Avenues. This was the place where my mom was laid to rest, not even five minutes from where she grew up.

My mother's very quiet demeanor or personality resulted in a pretty quiet funeral arrangement. Her personality also nearly prevented my family from ever discovering a piece of vital information about my father. As my mother's very private but emotional ceremony came and went, conversations about where my sister and I would now live revisited. It truly appeared as if my sister and I would be returning to Asquith St. with my dad, but the asking of one question changed everything. As preparations to try and return to normalcy proceeded, my grandma had a sit-down with my suddenly frightened sister Gina. The conversation was in reference to my dad's behavioral pattern on Asquith St. The conversation ended with an all too familiar question. My grandmother asked my sister if there was ever an instance where my dad "touched" her in any way. To my grandma's surprise, my sister responded with a reluctant nod, YES!

This realization added fuel to an ongoing raging fire. My sister explained to our grandma; my dad had touched her several times in an inappropriate manner. However, on the days when no one was home besides my dad and Gina, he would do the unthinkable. My sister told my grandma that my dad would follow her through the house while feeling on her buttocks. She would always hurry to her bedroom and lock the door to try to keep him away. Whenever my sister was not able to seclude herself my dad would become aggressive toward Gina. She assured grandma that my father never had actual sex with her of any kind, but the disturbing information forwarded was more than enough. Mama had heard all she could stand. After making her very quick decision to become our legal guardian, grandma immediately held a family meeting. Besides grandma, this was a men's only meeting. The only participants were my uncles Montell, BoBo, and yep, Tony. As I stated before, the only time we were going to hear from my uncle Tony was if Mama needed something. Well, as far as she was concerned, this was a definite need.

My uncles were furious about the death of their younger sister. Now they were learning of more disturbing news from their mother. My uncles, along with my granddad, all began to focus in very closely on my dad. He was now viewed as the man who destroyed our family. To them, every negative situation at this time surrounding our family had my dad's fingerprints on them. It took my uncles a week or so later to approach my dad. My father was coming to pay me a visit when he was violently cut off in the hallway immediately after entering the house. No one saw a thing. My three uncles quickly took my dad into a separate room and closed the door. The encounter lasted for about fifteen minutes. No one truly knows what really happened behind that door. With only a little noise there was hardly any evidence of violence. Still, this would be the last time my dad would ever set foot in 1913 Kennedy Avenue.

After the apparent threat given by my uncles my dad tried to lash back. Hours later, my grandma received a call from a neighbor on Asquith St. It seemed as if my dad had become so irate about what had transpired during the short encounter, he decided to take out all of his frustrations on several of my mom's prized possessions. The neighbor, a woman, stated my dad was throwing all of my mom's creations and pictures out into the backyard. It was a rainy day, therefore the woman offered to retrieve and store the possessions until someone could pick them up. However, just afterwards my dad took the items back after he calmed down. As all of this was taking place, I was clueless. I progressively believed my dad was the best person in my life other than my grandma and my cousin Shawn.

I simply didn't know about any of this.

Instead of being fed more bad news, I was allowed to play and have fun with all of the other kids in the neighborhood. After all of the turmoil, Shawn and I returned to the "bat cave" and found our groove as fun-loving children again. One moment we were burying my mom, the next we were engulfed in rock-throwing battles against the neighborhood bullies. We all had to know how to throw rocks and how to handle aluminum trash can lids in the hood, or else. During this same period, I also found pleasure in playing with insects for some strange reason. My cousin hated bugs, but I could not resist taking a closer look them. As you could imagine, I was usually alone during these moments. Needless to say, my cousin and I were usually "joined-at-the-hip."

Despite the tragedy, fun was at an all-time high for us at this point.

The penny candy, the toys, and I could never forget the evolution of television in our lives. Out of all of the kids on Kennedy Ave., I was placed in charge of the "T.V. Call." This meant I had to let all of the other kids in the area know when an "important" program was scheduled to air. I did fairly well. The job required lots of running in and out of the house, to my grandma's dismay, yet I still got it done. I became a host for the hood, especially when it came to my favorite show at the time. "The Incredible Hulk" on CBS, NBC (1978-1982) was, in my eyes, television's greatest creation. Right before the broadcast would air my call would go something like this: "Go in the house y'all, The Incredible Hulk is about to come on." This show, and the distant second, "Six Million Dollar Man" series ABC (1974-1978) was television at its finest for me. There was a reason the cooler Steve Austin (Lee Majors) fell second to Dr. Bruce Banner (Bill Bixby). The bionic man just so happened to invite my "old pal" onto his show. You all guessed correctly, yep, Big Foot. If everyone could have seen how my eyes were glued to the screen for these episodes, I believe people would still be in stitches today. However, even with the fright, it was clear early on, the world of television and film interested me tremendously.

Fun was at an all-time high, and I was surrounded by a heartbroken but loving family. Shawn and I felt we could not be coming up in a better place. Yes, we were being raised on the east side of Baltimore City, but I can't recall one incident in our hood during this time that made us feel differently. However, soon our feelings about 1913 Kennedy Avenue would not matter much at all. The time eventually came when our grandparents decided we indeed needed a better or larger place. I believed having nine people living in a three-bedroom house may have played a role in this decision as well. We needed more space! "Time goes on," they say, and after two years of living with my grandparents on Kennedy Ave. our days there were now numbered.

We tried to petition the move but it was all for nothing. We all hated the idea of relocating but we were just young kids. Initially, we didn't even consider the possibility of liking our new neighborhood. It didn't matter where it was located, we already hated it. Putting up a fight about moving was a waste of time for us kids. As the time drew closer, we felt we had no choice but to grasp the idea of starting over. Of course, at the ages of five and six, Shawn and I didn't have much say so. However, it was Gina who had the most difficulty with saying so long to her old friends. Despite it all, it was time to move on and adjust to a better and larger place in a better area in the city. With my mom's death and this move, I was learning fairly quickly that all good things really do come to an end.

The new neighborhood we were on our way to was approximately, a fifteen-minute drive north of Kennedy Avenue. Walking would not be recommended. This was east Baltimore! This new section we were headed to was called Govans; a community located in northeast Baltimore. The street we were headed to was named McCabe Avenue. Our new address would be 731. After creating so many fond memories at 1913, we were forced to hope for much of the same here, yet we ventured into our new residence short on optimism. However, our lack of enthusiasm was something we kept pretty much to ourselves. As kids, we had enough tough love instilled in us not to complain too much about anything. We were not the sweetest kids in the world, but we were not bad seeds.

731 McCabe Avenue came with a fourth bedroom, a larger basement, which still needed more work done, a larger bathroom, and a bigger backyard. We also would get to enjoy the benefits of a front porch. All the row homes on the block had them. This we actually liked a lot. It gave us all an extra option whenever behavioral punishment would be administered. No one wants to sit in a vestibule, peaking through a mail slot while trying to get perks during punishment. On Kennedy, we would all simply have to suck it up and carry out the entire sentence from inside. After arriving to McCabe, it must have taken the family about a full week to settle into our new humble abode. It was time to create new memories as a loving healing family. We were not well off by any sense of

the idea. We would be considered lower class, but were hardly ever noticed. That's because the love gleaming from our grandma was usually able to overshadow every lacking we may have had. I guess you could say we were upper-lower class, if that makes any sense. At this time, the one thing all of us kids truly understood about life was family. We all felt it; no matter what situations surfaced we would still have each other. That was all we really needed to know.

My sister Gina adjusted to the new neighborhood earlier than expected. It didn't take very long for the pretty young girls of the neighborhood to be knocking on our front door, inviting my sister outside to join in on their fun. My sister and I really don't share much of a resemblance. She looks more like her dad's side of her family. She has a softer grain of hair than I, and she has a much lighter skin tone. She's pretty. Her transition was so smooth on McCabe, we all virtually lost track of her. It was almost like she disappeared or something.

For Shawn and I things were a bit different. The confusion began when we noticed something we had never observed in person before. Our arrival to this new part of town gave us a lot more exposure to Caucasian people. I still recall the look on my cousin's face as we observed two little white girls, skipping along, down the street. It was priceless. Shawn was upset the two looked nothing like the runny-nose participants we faced off with during the rock-throwing battles just days prior. He was not a huge fan of change. I observed the two girls in the exact same way I viewed Laura Ingles (Melissa Gilbert), the character from the show (1974-1983), "Little House on the Prairie," another one of my favorite shows at the time. We had seen the white doctors and nurses from the hospital during my mom's ordeal, but they still did not appear to us as "regular" people. "Regular" meant Black! I was curious to know where these "different looking" people came from. I knew whites existed only from watching the television shows. I realized Dr. David Banner, Steve Austin, Bruce Wayne, Dick Grayson, and Fonzie were all white; 'The Egg Lady' was white. Still that was television; this was McCabe Avenue, in Baltimore City, Maryland. I was not sure as to what the future held, but we understood clearly that we were now at a much different location. For better or worse still remained to be seen.

After getting passed the fact that African-Americans were not the only race in real life, Shawn and I would turn our attention over to the other kids in the neighborhood. All of the others were African-American, yet we still would proceed with caution. It's always a bit weird meeting someone for the first time when you're a child. You're not sure if you should play tough or be nice. These two ideas could either get you a new friend or a new black eye. Being two inner city kids who believed we were superheroes and expert marksmen with rocks anyway, we both decided to take the tough guy approach when introducing ourselves to the first, new neighborhood kid on McCabe.

At 731, we had the prime location of all the row homes. Our house rested smack in the middle of the block. This made it quite easy for my cousin and I to sit in our bedroom window and watch the entire neighborhood's way of living unfold. So, after choosing the first guy we would approach, it was time to put on our costumes and transform into something we really weren't; tough guys. We walked down the street towards a guy who was apparently standing out in front of his home, but just across the street. We watched the slightly smaller kid exit from 714 McCabe. As we approached, he began to stare in our direction, seemingly in concern. The closer we approached, the more menacing our expressions became. We came to a stop directly in front of the guy, with the number one silliest question asked by kids who seek trouble for no reason. "What are you looking at?"

Those were the words violently shouted out of my cousin's mouth. Not, "What's your name?" or "How old or you?" You know, normal questions asked by kids with good sense. The boy, to our surprise, answered the question with a resounding "YOU, THAT'S WHO!" The kid's response startled us both, but my cousin was one who actually liked a little mischief every now and then as a kid. I was never afraid to fight, just from being around my cousin, but I had yet to get into a real scuffle. Shawn didn't mind fighting, but usually with reason. He would jump in quickly whenever I had to listen to "Your Mama" jokes thrown my way by other kids. Although most of them did not know my mom was deceased, this still hurt. Situations like this would give Shawn just enough of an excuse to violently respond; he wanted to see how good he was. With this new kid, things were a bit different. Shawn would attempt to strike him before he could even take his hands from his pockets. Shawn swung at the kid, missing by just inches. Although I pretended to be a bully as well, I was surprised by this. I just stood there looking stupid. I was trying to show Shawn I was with him in one regard, while simultaneously trying to feel sorry for the guy he went after. How was I supposed to do that?

As Shawn awaited the boy's next move, I looked around to see if anyone in the neighborhood was getting a good look at the two idiots who just moved onto the block; us. Before I turned back to observe from the front row, we heard the words, "I'm going to tell my brothers," come from the kid's mouth as he quickly took off towards his front porch. I believe this kid felt we would "bank" him or jump him, two on one. This statement was indeed enough for us not to chase after him at all. Shawn and I turned to each other and took off running ourselves. Although we didn't say a word, it was clear we both were focusing in on the letter "s" at the end of the word "brothers." This was our way of getting our feet wet on McCabe Avenue. We immediately decided we both liked my sister's transition and approach a lot better.

We never came back outside on this day. We took our positions back at the window of the bedroom. We watched with lumps in our throats, four much older guys blast from the front screen door of 714. The kid Shawn hadjust threatenedran and informed his brothers of the attempted assault. In just minutes, we had gone from bullies to two guys who now wished this kid's relatives would not come over and share this with our grandparents. More importantly, we were hoping the guy's brothers would not beat us up too badly once we gathered the confidence to return outside. Luckily for us, nothing came out of this situation. By the time we came back outside the very next day, things were cool again. As a matter of fact, Elroy, the kid we troubled, became our first friend on McCabe. His older brothers never responded to us after that day. Elroy said his brothers actually scolded him for telling. Thank God. From this point forward, it became clearer to us, Elroy's brothers were not choir boys by any stretch of the imagination.

Elroy had four older brothers. They all seemed to carry something unstable on their shoulders. Elroy and his family were new to the neighborhood as well. These brothers also shared a sister. From youngest to oldest; first, there was Tie. He was the kind of young man that would actually try to rob a bank as a teen. He was the type that just felt wrong by almost everyone. Whenever he was around, you felt trouble was close by. At the time, nothing seemed to go wrong on McCabe, but if there was a fight or a small altercation around, Tie was usually said to have started it. Next there was Chuck. Chuck, along with Elroy, was the closest to being normal. Well, if normal was being as silly as my cousin and I were. Chuck and his younger brother were the only two of their mother's children who still attended school regularly. Even Elroy's older sister Rebbie hardly attended school at an early age. She had already been dating for a few years despite being just fourteen years old. She was seeing a much older guy from a block named Beaumont Avenue; the next street over from McCabe. Guys in the street called him K-POX. Elroy's next older brother was Steve. He was a "piece of work." Steve or "Half," which they called all of the brothers, was the most delightful of all of Elroy's older siblings. The nickname they all shared came from them all having oddly shaped heads. It really seemed as if half of their heads had been sliced off. Not their hair, their actual heads.

Steve was the most outgoing of them all. He was the type of individual who would be difficult to keep in a box. You may be successful in placing him there, but keeping him there was another issue once you actually met him. He was too complex for that. This was the type of brother I was slightly intrigued by. Steve had the ability to make everyone laugh, including the grown folks. He also had a serious side that many did not care to see. However, he never seemed to seek out trouble. It just didn't seem to interest him very much.

The next-to-the-youngest of the brothers was the exact opposite. Nardo was what every neighborhood had at least two or three of; a bad seed. He was the type of guy who simply did not give a damn about much of anything. You could hardly ever get him to smile. He was the type of guy who would challenge the toughest and oldest tough guy on McCabe, or in any other neighborhood. He was the guy other thugs would seek out if there were any signs of trouble, simply because they all knew he would be more than ready. I can recall several accounts when I saw Nardo lose his temper. He blew up regularly during dice games. No matter how much money was involved, if he was losing, the dice were going on the roof. Then he would challenge any and everyone to a confrontation. I can only imagine just how many pairs of dice were on Mr. D's corner store rooftop.

Mr. D's was a black-owned corner store we all loved. Dice games usually took place just behind the store. Nearly every game would be interrupted with a loud, "Fuck y'all niggas, all y'all, and I dare any one of you bitch ass niggas to try me," as the dice would be tossed into the air. The older guys chuckled, but they all knew Nardo was dead serious. Multiple shouts would also come from the other players, trying to calm down the menace. Shawn and I were too young at this time to truly pay much attention to what the "big boys" or hustlers were doing, but an ingredient of negativity was noticeable from the start. We all witnessed these interactions as we passed by chasing a misdirected ball or something. Still, we were too young to entertain things like drugs or serious violence, but that does not mean it was not there. We all were just somewhere else mentally and emotionally; somewhere much more innocent, for now.

All of Elroy's older brothers except Chuck were drug dealers, but at this time we were clueless to what a drug dealer really was. We were too busy meeting more and more new neighbors. It was something to witness the new people move onto our block. Our excitement came from the fact; all of the new neighbors were black, and had sons. Soon Shawn and I were considered veterans to the other kids. The neighborhood was changing into one like the place we had left behind just months ago. I noticed the changes when I would watch from the living-room window. Nardo was yelling at someone on one corner, while the whites were loading up U-Haul trucks up the street. We were learning McCabe Ave. was not a bad place for us to live although most of the people there were not exactly what you would call good.

We all were adjusting fine, but my uncle Frank still struggled with the move. He would actually take that not recommended walk I spoke about earlier. He would walk all the way back down to Kennedy Ave, every other day, just to hang out on North Ave. with his old drinking buddies. This is no less than an-hour-and-a-half walk. Shawn and I would soon forget all about our previous address. The rest of us simply stayed put on McCabe and made more and more friends as time passed by. Soon we met a guy named Evan and several of his family members. Evan had what we thought of as, "The Perfect Family." At the time, we did not realize they also had something missing within the confines of their households; fathers. Many of them lived just two doors up from Elroy. Evan's family had always been a residence of McCabe. Recall my sister's appearance; she shows a resemblance to Evan's entire family. It seemed as if they were another nationality or something. We knew my sister inherited her complexion from her dad. With Evan's family we felt, just like with the whites, we were being exposed to another kind of race, but we were not. Evan's family is really African-American. They appeared to be from a different culture. Shawn and I were young but not stupid. I was old enough to understand; if my sister is a very pretty girl, and now there are replicas of her just across the street who are not related to us; this must be a good thing.

Evan's grandmother and every other female in his family were pretty, and there were plenty of them. Evan had two younger sisters and a host of cousins as well. Even the guys were "pretty" for real. You all know what I'm talking about. I'm talking about the guys of the world who resemble stars like El Debarge, Rick Fox, Christopher Williams, Al B. Sure, Special Ed, Boris Kodjoe, Shemar Moore, and so on. "Pretty boys," they all were called in the streets. Guys who resembled these celebs were most successful with the ladies in the 80's. I actually thought it was sort of cool for a guy to attract the opposite sex strictly because his hair was curly. That's great! I was never even close to having it that easy, but I cheered the guys on who were as fortunate. Evan's sisters and female cousins were so pretty, we all didn't even realize our Matchbox toy cars had run out of gas. We felt obligated to interact with the females at this point. Fantasizing about Evan's relatives became a lot easier as the school year of 1980 approached. Thanks to another family's arrival just next door, we would be as close as possible to the girls. So, what if we were too afraid to say much of anything to them!

Tee and Troy moved in between Evan and Elroy a-month-and-a-half before the school year would begin. They were looked after by their moms; two sisters. Both were single parents trying to give their sons an environment to grow up in they both could live with. These two kids were similar to Shawn and I in a few ways. They obviously were first cousins as we were. Troy was brown-skinned like me and Shawn was darker like Tee. Troy liked a degree of trouble like Shawn, but Tee rather do without any confusion as I preferred. There's more! Troy's birthday is May 24th1971. Shawn's landed on May 25th 1971. My birthday is June 29th 1972. Tee's is June 15th 1972.The 15thof June is also the exact same birthday as my aunt

Marie. Needless to say, we all clicked immediately. This meant it would take these two new guys no more than a week before they would join in our 'tongue wagging' contest, as we would stare at Evan's relatives religiously.

Before long, we all became a group, not a gang. We were simply young kids with no dreams or aspirations to become anything. Sad really, but it felt fine at the time. Becoming a police officer, a lawyer, a doctor, or planning to have any kind of stable, well-paying career was never instilled in any of us as kids. None of our parents had great careers or high paying jobs. Hell, some of our parents didn't have jobs at all. During this time, I'm not sure if we even cared. We were too engulfed with being kids. The flaws of our loved ones or the mentalities of the older guys in the streets played small roles, if any, in our lives at the time. All we thought about during this time were things like the admission into a new school, toys, 'shell head' Adidas sneakers, Jordache or Lee jeans, Izod shirts, girls, and sports. If you were in a selective group as Tee and I were, drawing and writing as well.

Soon, all of us would have a chance to meet the girls in Evan's family. Evan was not really a part of our circle early on. He had a few years on most of us. You would not have known this by how tough his mom, Ms. Julie, was on him and his sisters. Although Evan was older than us all, he had tougher rules to follow. In the summer months, if we had to be in the house by 11 pm, this meant he probably was in the house three hours prior. We all were eight to ten years old. He was twelve or thirteen. He was the oldest child therefore we found this to be a bit weird. I know today it was us who were offbase with that assumption. As young guys we never formally met the females in the neighborhood. We used the homemade street games to break the ice. Games like 'Its' or 'Tag', 'Hide N Seek', 'Skillet', and the infamous '7-11.' Yeah, 7-11! That's the game when you get to feel on, kiss, and 'dry hump' or rub pants with the females after chasing them down. We were always anticipating playing this one with a disgusting eagerness, as you may have imagined.

Evan's family of females reluctantly joined in with us on the fun and games. Whatever games played, that's right, they won. We were willing to do whatever it took to keep the girls close to us as often as possible. Especially Evan's cousin named Cristina. She was thirteen years old and very pretty. From the very first moment I saw her, I didn't care to run a race or play at all. I could feel just from the sight of her, my legs were not functioning correctly. The others were cute as well but none like her. I hardly cared what the rules were for attaining a girlfriend, or even if she was handing out "applications." All I knew was from the moment I saw her, I had a girlfriend, whether she knew it or not.

As school approached, I never received an answer from Cristina about going steady. Well, I never asked either, but we all did manage to score with the girls by playing "7/11." For those who are unfamiliar with the game or rules to "7/11," I'll share some context. "7/11" is a flirtatious game where the guys literally chase after the girls like a cat chases a mouse. Unlike "It's," it does not end the same when you catch or touch the person you're chasing. Instead, once you catch up to the female, you automatically are given an option to kiss the girls seven times or rub pants up against her eleven times. Some call it "dry humping." I always chose to kiss Cristina seven times. Sex was not an option for any of us mentally at the time. And, rubbing pants was not an easy task to perform without being embarrassed. Catching or running Cristina down was not very easy. She could run extremely fast. Luckily for me, I was fast too. So, I would track her down after getting passed my initial nervousness. We all were just crazy little kids. That was life for us at this point. We had lots of fun and we stayed out of trouble for the most part. We got away with things like interacting with girls at too young of an age. We also weresurroundedby some suspect characters. Yet, somehow it all felt just fine. None of us had a care in the world. Whenever I was not having flashbacks about my mom, I was having the time of my life in our new neighborhood.

The next two years on McCabe Avenue would be far more exciting than any of us could have imagined. My sister, Shawn and I experienced our very first block party. Theevent was produced by a neighborwholived directly across from our home. Everyone took part in this extravaganza. All of Evan's relatives attended therefore you know Shawn and I tried to display our finest dance moves. My sister was out there having a great time with her friends as well. The party also allowed us all to develop even more friends. Shawn and I soon met a kid named Tray at the party. Tray was a young and mischievous neighborhood thief and a low-scale drug dealer. He stole goods from every "mom and pop" store in the neighborhood, just for kicks. Local supermarkets, sneaker outlets, and toy stores were all in heavy rotation for Tray's sticky fingers. Whatever any of us wanted from any store, Tray vowed to snatch it up for us with ease. For as crazy as Tray was, we all were also very impressed with his dancing skills. He had moves not consistent with being a klepto and trouble maker. Tray didn't seem to care much for the pretty girls in the area. He simply liked controversy, but he was a good dancer and he also liked to play basketball.

The block party gave us a detailed description of how the older teens and adults lived on our block. We learned more about style and music, as we would get our first up-close and personal look at hip-hop culture. Several local acts performed during this event. We all knew early on, this great form of expression originated in the streets of New York City. Baltimore City was known more for a club or house music vibe. There were a couple of locally known rap groups from B'MORE, specifically, "The We Rock Crew," but they never made it to the big times or the national spotlight. Shawn and I loved hip-hop music from the start. The club music we heard plenty of was simply something neither of us could get fully into. Still, all of these unique tunes were displayed at the block party of 1982. By mid-summer we all began to understand; we were in a special place filled with lots of complex individuals. Some were drug dealers. Others were thieves and armed robbers. Yet, at the time everyone seemed to love one another. McCabe Avenue was a small, slightly hidden neighborhood filled with dozens of people, but nothing mattered because we all treated each other like family.

The block party of 1982 was a huge success although Shawn and I had to enjoy the evening portion of the gathering from inside of the house. Well, not exactly from inside! As the party continued passed our curfew, we were forced to go in the house. My sister Gina found this to be funny. "I ha, I ha, that's why y'all have to go in the house," she said with her tongue stuck out in our direction. "So, what," I yelled through the lyrics; "Boogie Nights/ Got to keep on dancing/ keep on dancing." Shawn simply looked at my sister and friends in anger and shouted, "SHUT UP!" However, Shawn's disappointment would soon produce positive results. He came up with the idea for us to pretend to be asleep in our bedroom to throw off our grandparents. Then, he suggested we exit the window and post up on the roof of the house. There, we could enjoy the rest of the party from an elevated position. We did just that. Talk about club level seats. As I stated, 731 McCabe Avenue was smack in the middle of whatever action would take place in the neighborhood. We sat on the roof until 1 a.m., until the party nearly ended. That was my cousin in a nut-shell. If he wanted to do something, he was going to do it. These were the good times; we shared plenty of them as kids on McCabe, and we were just getting started.

As the summer fun continued, we found ourselves in neighborhoods other than our own. At least once a week, we all would find interesting places to venture off to in the surrounding areas. It usually would be about nine or ten of us. We would ride anything from big wheels to bicycles, skates or skateboards to get to our destination. I normally traveled with my Sizzler skateboard. There would normally be a few females sprinkled around within our group. We always included the girls in everything. We simply were little guys who always enjoyed the company of females. During these road trips, we usually would end up in the upper-class neighborhoods of northeast Baltimore. There, we would be in amazement while getting a chance to see just how much greener the grass really was a little further up York Rd. York Road is a main artery that runs from the inner city to the suburbs of Baltimore County.

"Seven Lakes" community was one of the neighborhoods my friends and I ended up in as we would journey throughout the area. In this neighborhood, all of the grass appeared to be cut by the same groundsperson. The houses seemed to be a concoction of hundreds of family members all living in the same community. We paraded through this neighborhood in awe, cautious of how loud our tones were as we chatted. We understood the name of the community as we really counted carefully, all seven of the lakes, each separated by yards of perfectly groomed grass. This place was so quiet we could actually hear each other breathing. We loved the appearance of this unique neighborhood. We had never been in an area this nice. It reminded us all of "OZ." Like our home it appeared as better; it was safer, cleaner, and quieter. Perhaps this was why we stayed in this area for hours examining every detail. Surprisingly enough, not one homeowner would ever come out to inquire as to why there were ten little black children creeping around in their community.

No nosy people! That was a change of pace from McCabe Avenue. Evan's family was always viewed as being too nosy back home. If there was a scuffle or altercation of any kind taking place, the entire block would be more frustrated with the onlookers instead of the actual situation. I heard the statement, "They some nosy ass muthafuckas," more than once. Not here at Seven Lakes. This place was foreign to all of us, and there were no folks present to be nosy. We knew after discovering this area we would return one day soon. Not only was the scenery pleasant, there was also wildlife. Here, we ran across something else we'd never seen before; Crayfish. Every pond or lake in the area was filled with large gold fish and all sizes of Crayfish. I've always enjoyed wildlife. I knew right away I was going to take a few of these shelled fish back to the block.

Pulling Crayfish out of the water with a small tree branch and catching gold fish with thread, a hook, and a tiny piece of bread was a new experience for us. So was touring other areas in the same region. Tray would supply enough goods for us to have a great time when we would venture outside of the hood. We also would head off to places like the campus at Loyola College, or a small park in the Northwood community, nearby. We made a living by going to Tray's front door for assistance. "Tray, we need you buddy!" Shawn would say often. Shawn and Tray really liked each other. To be honest, they were one in the same to a degree. Tray was doing all the things you could clearly envision Shawn doing at any given moment. It was just as if Shawn was not quite there yet. Of course, at this time and in the midst of all of the fun, and being very young, for now this was a non-issue.

There were not many kids during this time who were considered to be degenerates. At the time only a few, including Tray, had all but given up on the idea of attending school. School was not really a good option in Tray's mind, yet he was always prepared to go to a store to shoplift. For him to hardly ever attend school, he had a pretty vivid memory. He never used a pencil to jot down the requests of at least six or seven people, yet he always completed the orders. We all would usually walk to the preferred store with Tray. Then we would all head around a corner and wait as Tray would casually enter into these establishments. Tray usually wore a baseball cap and very large sweat gear. We often wondered if the clothing he wore was his own or his two- hundred-ninety-pound brother.

Normally it would take Tray no more than fifteen or twenty minutes to complete his shoplifting mission. He simply loved the rush of taking things undetected. He would always give a report of each place he visited. He'd say, "Man, that spot was tough!" He would often come running around a corner where we would be awaiting; laughing. "Man, that shit was too easy," he would state. If a place was too risky, he was smart enough to pass on it. He would just go elsewhere. It was unbelievable to see how he could store so much merchandise underneath his clothing, yet it appeared as if he had nothing. Tray would have everything from burritos, chips, candy bars, small juices and cookies.

Helping the elderly with their groceries at the local markets, or performing chores around the house allowed us to have a few bucks from time to time. Still, with guys like Tray in the area, we always had things, money or not. Although the rest of us would not indulge in the actual shoplifting or other illegal activities ourselves, we were still usually pretty close by when it all went down. I guess you can say we fell somewhere in the middle. Although we did pretty much what we wanted when we were outside, we knew not to do anything illegal. We somehow figured, as long as we were not the ones stealing the goods, it was ok to use them. Besides, Tray didn't want a thing for his services. Looking back, I realized this was his way of being unique or gaining self-worth from his peers. He also just liked taking things. Why else would a kid enter a sneaker store, try on his favorite pair of shoes, and simply walk out of the store, leaving his old shoes in the box the new shoes came in.

Picnics, small house parties, street boxing matches, girls, sports, writing or drawing, and junk food were all in heavy rotation in my life at this point. My friends and my dad, who began to show up a lot more, often put a smile on my face. My family cared a lot. Especially my grandma; she was an angel. She loved me unconditionally. I knew it. I could tell from the look in her eyes whenever she would gaze in my direction. Perhaps that's why in the midst of all the fun and games, there would always come a time for me to retreat. I always got in a mood where I simply desired to be alone. Even during the summer months, I would find time to get away. I liked the idea of being away from it all. I spent most of this alone time writing, reading a little, or drawing. I was the only person in my immediate family who enjoyed these things. Still, as a twelve-year old kid, I would have to say I was pretty normal. I was involved with the same activities as everyone else. Yet, I was also the kid who just needed his space. I often had a need to be in the midst of quietness. This was me as well, and I loved this part of myself, but I hid it for some odd reason. This was the age when I became aware; I AM NOT ONE THING! I am not in a box.

Being a multifaceted kid can confuse a lot of people. One minute, I would be secluded in my bedroom writing excessively long love letters and stories to my self-made comic books. The next, I would be competing in tongue-kissing contests with the others. That's not all. After chasing the girls around and regaining control over our pre-teen erections, you could also periodically catch me hurrying to the house to check for a bloody nose, from our no-weight class, boxing matches. I guess one could say I was the same, yet different. I don't really know what folks saw in me. I just seemed to make an odd impression on the much older folks in the area. At twelve years old, I would be repeatedly approached or called over to socialize with the older women. They would be gathered on a porch, smoking marijuana most of the time. "Hey little boy," Lisa would smoothly yell as I passed by reluctantly observing. "C'mon, hurry up," she followed. As I approached, I would always get an intense fluttering sensation in my chest. There would be a strong smell of "weed," and five very pretty faces of much older women, but not as old as my aunt. Most of these young ladies were friends of my sister. For as nervous as these encounters were, I was never too scared to act on the phrase, "Give me a kiss!" So, there I was, kissing a very pretty, twenty-year old directly in the mouth, at the tender age of twelve. She put her tongue in my mouth too! I still remember the taste of smoke she left me with. "Go head, you and your cute ass self," she whispered. I left the porch that day, struggling to keep my balance from the intense feeling an older woman's tongue gave me. Occurrences such as these seemed to come my way more often than not. For some strange reason, I rarely cared to share any of them with my friends. All I would do was use these situations to be more assertive with the females in my own age bracket. My confidence grew, but perhaps this would ultimately prove to be one of my very first poor decisions.

By the end of summer, things began to gradually change. The era of self-made games and adventures were beginning to lose ground to a world of sports, movies, music, dance, and yes, drugs, sex, and money. The block party seemingly marked an era dominated by peace, love, respect, fun, and good spirits. Even the air had a more positive smell to it at the time. Togetherness and love would override any other presence during this time. As my first year in middle school approached, myself, my cousin, and friends somehow came up with a plan to finish out the summer strongly.

Well, more like finishing in idiotic fashion. I, along with Shawn, Tee and Troy decided to push the envelope a bit. We all believed it was time to take things a step passed the kissing and rubbing pants stages with the females. We all were spending far too much time thinking with the wrong body parts. We were very confused kids trying to grow up way too quickly.

By August, a month before school was set to begin, our little entourage had increased a bit. Across the street from 731 we received more new neighbors; a brother and sister pair, watched over alone by their mom. Kizzie and Karl were fourteen and thirteen years of age. They moved in a newly built townhouse on the corner after the home of the host of the block party was destroyed. Both were caramel in complexion, with jet black curly hair. Actually, they too could have passed for distant relatives of Evan. We all became friends quickly and began to hang out at their new townhouse. They were the only kids on McCabe Ave. who did not always have an adult inside of the home. Their mother, Ms. Kay, worked long hours as a short order cook at a restaurant in the county. It did not take long for us to realize this would be the landmark or the headquarters for much of our foolishness.

My cousin Shawn had somehow masterfully promoted this careless act perfectly. This was his thing. Earlier during this summer, Shawn composed a plan for us to watch Cristina and Evan's two sisters exit the shower from their bedroom window. A large tree rested in their backyard which led directly up to this window; one they often left wide open. One night, Tee, Shawn, Troy, and I climbed this tree. Shawn and I hit the jackpot right away, but Tee and Troy, slightly larger guys, were too heavy to get further up the tree. After minutes of watching and giving the other two guys the "play-by-play" of what we saw, Tee made too much noise trying to get closer. The girls suddenly realized they were being watched and quickly alarmed the rest of their family. Just like that, we were caught.

Seconds later, Evan and his entire household was out in the backyard yelling at us. Evan was holding a pot of scolding hot water while threatening us all to come down. Tee and Troy surrendered first. I hesitated, but soon followed in embarrassment. I was instantly upset for not knowing how to climb downwards as well as I could upwards. Shawn, he was never caught. He was an excellent climber. He climbed further up the tree, where the thin branches were, passed the length of all the homes. He was too far up in the tree for anyone to detect, even with their flashlights. I still remember seeing my cousin in the tree from nothing but the moonlight, hugging the thin limb while slowly swaying back and forth.

Shawn finally made his way down and out of the tree, and laughed at us all for hours that night. The situation was extremely funny. Shawn's ability to escape embarrassment impressed us all, although his plan had partially failed. He was more successful just days before this episode. Shawn learned Elroy had a place on his roof where you can see clearly into the bathroom. He spotted this when he used Elroy's restroom one day. Before you knew it; me, Shawn, and Tee were observing Elroy's older sister Rebbie taking a nice slow bubble bath. I guess it was fair to say, we were all young master perverts.

For the end-of-summer secret gathering, Cristina and Evan's sister Dena agreed to meet us at Kizzie's. We were there first of course. Before sneaking off, we all grabbed our baseball equipment as if we were headed to Dewees Playfield, about two miles north. This was all a cover-up. We all quickly made a detour into the alleyway, hurrying through Kizzie's back door. So, there we sat, periodically peeking out of the window to see if the girls were really going to come. I was extremely nervous at this point. I'd never had sex before. Suddenly, I was more comfortable with the earlier encounters with the older women. There, I knew I was not going to ever actually have sex with them. Hell, I had never touched a naked girl in my life. Well, my sister, but that was accidental contact when I was five years old in the bathtub.

During this time, the closest I had ever been to touching a naked woman was using the peak hole Shawn and I drilled in the bathroom door in our own home. We took turns with a screwdriver to create the hole. We wanted to view all of Gina's friends while they were sitting on the toilet. We made sure the hole was just low enough for us to stare directly towards a female's private area. Stop laughing! As we waited for the girls at Kizzie's, you probably can imagine how hilarious this scene was. I was extra nervous, Tee and Troy thought it all was funny, and Shawn was all business. He impatiently stood by the window, peaking outwards like Malcolm X, or as if he was the owner of a major company restlessly waiting for an important client. "By any means necessary," was the theme, but without the focus of a true leader for his people. Shawn made himself our leader, and his approach to pulling this off was very serious. Adolescent sex was the topic, still he was focused on making this situation a huge success.

While the neighborhood would proceed with its normal routine of displaying loud music, "pretty young things," Suzuki Samurai SUV, Toyota Cressida, Nissan Maxima vehicles, and Honda scooters, we were set to indulge in one of the worse acts any twelve- or thirteen-year-old kids could think of. The sad part about it; no one had a clue where we were or what we all were up to. For us, it was easy to hibernate undetected. Just as my nerves began to calm down and Shawn's pressure began to rise, there was a tap on the door. Shawn bolted to the door, snatching it open. "Bout time!" he stated in frustration. The girls ignored his slight attitude and entered with perfect smiles. After fifteen minutes of small talk, we all decided to venture upstairs. The closer I got to a bedroom, the more nervous I grew again. This was actually the very first time in my life I would be inside of a bedroom with a female I really liked.

The choice to hangout in Ms. Kay's room was made because of the king-size bed she slept in every night. Shawn and I sat at the foot of the big bed beside Dena and Cristina. Tee and Kizzie grabbed a blanket and found a spot on the floor to sit. Troy's partner never showed. He left in a frantic rage. Shawn, he was something! He negotiated with Kizzie well enough to get her to take the floor inside of her own home. I knew Shawn like the back of my hand. He really liked all of the girls, Kizzie and my girlfriend Cristina included. Fifteen more minutes of small talk came and went. A minute or two later, Shawn and I were side by side watching the comforter move like the waves of an ocean as the girls undressed beneath. There were training bras, Izod polo shirts, Jordach and Sasson jeans, along with those canvas military belts all being ejected from underneath the covers. I hardly remember taking my clothes off at all. That's how nervous I was. By the way, where were the condoms? Oh, that's right, there were none present. Talk about recklessness!

The positioning my cousin and I were in was similar to the one we held just days prior. However, this was far more complex than a street race in the middle of McCabe Avenue. Here, we were rested motionless on our hands and knees, draping over two of the more attractive girls from the area. Shawn and I looked across the bed at each other, then back, staring downward. Shawn soon said in excitement, "Y'all ready?" The two girls nodded simultaneously.

I briefly looked over to my right to check on Tee, but he was fine. He and Kizzie were already buried under the covers on the floor. "O, O, you ready?" Shawn asked. "Um yeah, I'm ready!" I responded. I elevated my torso, temporarily causing the comforter to fall from our shoulders. I had to adjust my blue and red Spider-Man UnderRoos down around my ankles. I was not comfortable enough to get fully undressed like my cousin. Just seconds later, Shawn started counting down. "Get ready, get set go!" he said in a deep tone. So, there we were, on top of the girls, imitating moves we had seen on our grandma's favorite show, "The Young and the Restless." Shawn appeared to know what he was doing. I was having a more difficult time. I continued to push and squirm, but I could not get in or comfortable. I was determined to gain the same motion Shawn and Tee had found. Little did I know, my time was running out, and fast.

After about five minutes or so of poking around, I began to feel extremely weird. I would jump up, lay back down, and back up again. Suddenly, I rose, observed my property, and was surprised to say the least. I looked at Cristina in shock and said, "What the fu ?" She replied, "What?" surprisingly smiling. I hopped up as fast as I could. "What's wrong?" Shawn asked with a glaze of sweat on his forehead. Tee's head resurfaced to be nosy as well. "Nothing, I have to go," I said in embarrassment. I pulled my superhero attire up as quickly as I could. If we were competing to see who could put their clothing on the quickest, perhaps then, I would have been more of a superhero. I surely was not thus far. If I were, it was clear at this point, "coochie" was my arch nemesis. If I were a superhero, I would have been The Flash.

After repeatedly missing and bolting from Kizzie's, I found myself at home, upstairs examining my property. My royal blue briefs were now sticky enough to hold together a massive school project. I needed some answers. No one warned me about this feeling or the leaking mess I was now washing away with a washcloth that was not my own. After a few minutes, I managed to calm down, but I continued to scrub aggressively. I tossed my Spidey-draws away, but I held on to the shirt, because I thought it was the cooler of the two anyway. After I exited the bathroom, I hurried to my room window to see when the others would exit the house. I wanted to see the guys act as if they were really at the playground. I sat at the window still trying to figure out why, and what went wrong with me across the street. I was embarrassed more than ever. I was already wondering what kind of an excuse I could use to help my cause. As I conjured up my lies, my thoughts were disrupted by a woman outside. She was walking up the street, dressed in all white with food stains on the thigh portion of her one- piece uniform skirt. It was Ms. Kay, arriving home from work two hours early. Immediately, I saw a benefit in my "minute-man" routine. Ms. Kay was not one of those pushover types at all. Let's just say Kizzie was about five minutes away from spending the rest of the summer indoors, soaking her ass in alcohol.

I was worried about Shawn and Tee, but there was something in me that found what was about to unfold very funny. I watched Ms. Kay enter her front door, which happened to be directly below the stairs. I began to laugh as Ms. Kay's key entered the lock to the front door. No longer than three seconds later, I could see a pair of white Adidas exiting the top story window. I smiled immediately. I knew it was Shawn before his body ever cleared the window seal. I shook my head from side to side, as I watched my cousin extend himself as far as he could from the window, then let go. As I watched my cousin drop from the house, I immediately felt fortunate to have such a cool big cousin. Shawn's landing from the very long drop was flawless. The impact caused him to squat as far as the human body could, but he kept perfect balance. He then slithered along the side of the house, only to cross the street as if he was coming from the corner store.

Shawn entered the house, exploded upstairs in tears, laughing. I was just as amused. "Man, I saw you make that great escape like a real superhero," I shouted in excitement. "Yeah, I had to, fuck that," he replied. "Ms. Kay would have come right over here and told Mama, and she would have told BoBo," He said in a concerned tone. "I know," I followed. "What are y'all two doing up there?" came from Mama downstairs as Shawn and I conversed with excitement. "Nothing Ma!" we both yelled. "Yeah right!" she replied. "Did the hang-jump hurt at all?" I whispered as we both hurried back to the window to see the aftermath of the situation. "Not really, my feet just burn at the bottom," he replied while squinting his face in discomfort. Together we sat and watched from the window, the "caught-in-the-act" expressions on the faces of Tee and the two girls. We quickly assumed what happened to Kizzie, and we were right. We knew she would be placed on punishment for the duration of the summer.

After laughing at Tee from the window, Shawn turned to me and asked, "What happened in there, O?" "I don't know," I said while hunching my shoulders. "Ha," Shawn expressed. We both knew what had taken place, but neither chose to elaborate. "That was the first time I have ever done that," I replied. "Oh yeah, it won't be the last, I'll bet you that," he ended with a confident smile.

During this time, I believed I was far too young to experience what happened at Kizzie's place. Although my cousin gave me reassurance, I still didn't like the way the entire situation made me feel. I also despised the way my stomach fell when Shawn asked me about the details of what took place when Cristina and I were close. Although this was the very first time, I had ever tried something like this, I knew I was unsuccessful. This was actually a good thing considering how reckless we all were. Therefore, I quickly put away any ideas of future troubles surfacing. That was until the entire neighborhood got a hold of our little event a few days later.

As I fell back into a kid's place and reconnected with my G. I. Joe action figures and my Matchbox cars, I would periodically hear people saying, "I heard one of Evan's little female cousins is pregnant." At first, I thought to myself, "So what, Evan has dozens of female cousins." As time went on and school time approached, the rumors intensified. Before long, it was said in nine months, I could possibly become a DAD! "WHAT?" I thought. "I'M TWELVE!" I suffered for nearly a month wondering about the rumors. I still felt strongly in my mind things were fine, but I still was not completely sure in my heart. I did allow quite a bit of semen to rest on her belly button. It did not take long before I began driving myself crazy, and the humiliation was still there. Now I was ashamed to confront the fourteen-year-old beauty at all. As September rolled in and my one-hundred-forty-pound frame shrunk, I grew tired. I had to know before I began the 7th grade; was Cristina even ready?

I finally gathered up enough confidence to ask Cristina about the matter. We all were at the playground; for real this time. At Dewee's we all played sports together, the girls and the guys. We loved playing baseball, whether in an alley or on a playing field. We still raced each other regularly too, just to see who was the fastest. We also played football with the females. Yes, we took it light on them a bit. However, tackling females for hours at a time never got old for us. At the baseball diamond, I waited for the perfect time to ask Cristina the million-dollar question. Dena had just hit a triple, sending the others into the outfield in an uproar. She was stronger than the average female in all of the sports we played. Dena could hit and throw a lot further than several of the guys as well. Thank God I was not one of them.

Anyway, as Dena exploded around the bases and a friend chased the hardball into center field, I slid next to Cristina as if we had just met. I couldn't bring myself to ask her about the event, therefore I started talking about nothing. After ignoring half of what I said, she then made a move. "C'MON let's walk over here," she offered. I felt good the ice was broken once again. I felt a sense of anxiousness, not knowing what was next. "Have you heard what everyone is saying around McCabe?" I asked. "No, what?" she replied with a smile. "Everyone is saying you are pregnant." She quickly fell into heavy laughter before replying, "What?" "Are you?" "Are you pregnant?" I asked with a slightly relieved smile. "No boy; is that why you haven't been talking to me lately?" she stated. There I was, once again, looking and feeling extra stupid.

Cristina asked me this with one eyebrow lifted higher than the other. "Well, I thought you were mad at me, and I was scared as shit." I said as I nodded. "Well, are you ok now?" she asked. "Hell yeah, I'm fine," I shouted. "I'm about to go hit me a 'homer' now!" Needless to say, we made up with a kiss and a hug. That was it though. I was now set to return to Winston Middle School in a week. Cristina, she was already in high school. She attended City College High School, a respectable college-prep establishment near 33rdStreet on the eastside. As far as sex was concerned, after that very close call, I knew a long time would pass before I would ever try to get close to some "nookie" again.

Back to school symbolized a host of new ideas for my cousin and I. We were indeed excited about the upcoming school year. For me, I was happy the school itself was a lot closer. Winston Middle School was approximately a twenty-minute walk from 731's front door. The last day of school of the two previous years had ended with the words, "You barely made it!" At Walter P. Carter Elementary school and my first year at Winston Middle were tougher than they should have been for me academically. My focus was too much on females, creating exciting stories and drawing. The elementary school was also in walking distance, but in a peculiar area we were clueless about the significance of at the time. It was not until my ears picked up on harmless conversations between my sister and her boyfriend at home, I began to learn more about the history of our hood and other neighborhoods close by.

One night, before school was set to start, I sat in my room drawing and overheard my sister sharing a story with her new boyfriend, Freddy. Freddy; Shawn and I really liked. Unlike my sister's previous boyfriends, he had class. He was always calm. Even in the dice games where Elroy's brother Nardo lost it, Freddy kept his cool. We also liked the fact that he dressed well, and worked for the sneaker outlet, Shoe City at the Alameda Shopping Center. The conversation I heard was about my sister being approached in a restroom at Eastern High School, previously located on 33rd Street. Today, this establishment is called Johns Hopkins University at Eastern. During its high school years, my sister was cornered by a notorious female bully in the restroom of the school. The previous Eastern High School was the same school our mom had attended in the 70's. The original all female school periodically held its reputation over the years despite becoming co-ed. "Yeah, this girl approached me in the restroom, asking me if I was I one of those bitches from McCabe Avenue," she said. The student-body immediately assumed an altercation was taking place inside of the school between my sister and the husky bully named Boog, but they were inside ironing out wrinkles. Gina said the conversation began threatening but ended in peace. The more disturbing news came a week later. Old York's, Boog was found in an alleyway completely naked strangled to death. She had been beaten and raped, and speculations surfaced that someone from McCabe Avenue may have known the details or even shouldered the blame.

Shawn was asleep as I continued to write, sketch, and listen. "I'm getting really sick of this McCabe and Old York Road shit," Gina said. Old York Road was less than five minutes away from the elementary school I had attended for four years. I could hear in my sister's tone, there was a unique history between the two landmarks. I never witnessed my sister in such a distressed state while conversing. Well, once. Awhile earlier, my sister was caught shoplifting at Woolworth's department store at The Alameda Shopping Center, in the neighborhood. This was the same shopping center Freddy was working. The security guard called Mama, and Mama called BoBo. I sat and watched my sister get the ass whipping of her life by our uncle. He beat her so hard and long, I started crying. His words to me were, "Shut up, before you get your ass whipped too." Needless to say, I shut right up. That was the only time, until this, I knew of danger being near my sister. For some strange reason, I didn't hold on to the things said by my sister on this night. I was too excited about meeting new friends and beginning 7th grade. I was about to return to middle school, and life for me, my sister, and my cousin Shawn was about to get even more interesting.

# Chapter 3

# BREAKIN THROUGH

It's been said it's better to accept accountability for your actions than to avoid them. Shortcuts will often make things worse; may even push you further back, forcing you to ultimately take the harder way to recovery; the long way. I believe going through implies progress, while going around, avoiding, or taking the longer route, usually indicates stagnation, uncertainty, or even digression. In life, we must choose a path to travel on and be willing to deal with the aftermath of that choice. Looking back, I realized I was never taught how to choose wisely, therefore I practiced both ideas; and this usually leads to uncertainty or instability. My life as a seventh-grader began on an eighty-degree morning in September. Myself, Tee, Shawn, Evan, Troy, and three others, all walked up McCabe Avenue towards Winston Middle School. We were on our way to discover as middle school was midway complete, the energies all around us were also changing.

Of course, we all relished in sporting our new gear. Grandma always made sure we had at least a week's worth of new clothing to wear back to school. If possible, we all followed the trends of the older guys in the neighborhood. The females did the same with the older sisterhood. As in prior years, we all had the colorful Lee jeans, or those from Jordache, Sergio Velente, and other popular fashions. I occasionally would be able to wear what the older guys wore whenever my dad decided to show up. When this would happen, then I would be seen wearing the $100 sneakers. Grandma, she was not having that over-priced sneaker mess. Superstar Adidas or "Shell-Top" or "Shell-Head" Adidas, they were called in the streets, once cost us $45 and some change. Grandma would normally give us the base amount. If we came up short or if the taxes were more than anticipated; well, we would still be seen at the local supermarket assisting senior citizens with their groceries. We often got the things we wanted and always received what we needed. I guess that was a direct result of knowing our limits. As kids we watched the television show, "Different Strokes" regularly. We knew we were not as fortunate as characters, "Arnold" and "Willis," therefore we knew to keep the asking for things at a minimum. As long as we passed all classes in school, took good care of our possessions, and practiced having manners and respect for others, we were fine.

The first day of school was an instant success. Tee and I learned we were in a few of the same classes, so that was cool. Shawn passed to 8th grade. Evan also passed although he had failed once before. Everyone was stunned when they learned Evan was once held back. With his strict home schedule and all, no one could picture him not being focused enough to pass every grade in elementary or middle school. Shawn and I could not have imagined not passing a grade at the time. We had enough trouble trying to get passed feeling guilty about bringing home a few satisfactory report cards.

With all of this said, school was proving to be a pretty good experience. There were plenty of new people to meet from all parts of the city. We immediately observed the cute girls from other nearby neighborhoods. We knew very early, the girls from around the block would soon be distant memories. School was a blast, if that makes any sense at all, but I still found time to relax, write, and draw. My bedroom, whenever my cousin was not in, became a sanctuary for me. It was the place where I would speak to God. I began talking to God after I was old enough to understand how serious it was for someone to lose a parent. Most single parent family households in the inner city are dominated by mothers, not fathers. Praying and talking to God every so often helped me cope with any negativity I seen or felt around me. I also believed my mom could hear my prayers or conversations with God; I still do. This allowed me to still try to have a positive outlook on all things, no matter what happened.

It was not until Evan started chatting with me about the sport of basketball; I decided maybe I should try out something new. The frequent street games had slacked a bit. The rugged football games we played almost produced a blown-out knee. This completely pushed me away from playing the sport. I had already broken my right arm from a skateboard fall, which I was still slightly traumatized from. There was a bit of good that stemmed from this fall. I learned how to write lefthanded pretty well. I proceeded through most of that school year as a lefty. Still, I struggled to get the picture out of my head of how contorted my forearm was from that fall. It actually looked like a small bridge. I broke both bones (Radius & Ulna) in my lower-right arm. The sound and the pain I endured as the doctor squeezed the bones back into place, before placing a cast over my arm, periodically returned to haunt me.

A few months into the 7th grade, my personality strengthened. I became a more outgoing and vocal young man. Meaning, it was not always my cousin Shawn carrying most of the conversations in our small group. My popularity was now rising in middle school. During after school hours, I was still putting Evan off on his offer to teach me the game of basketball. Still, I took good notes while watching the other guys play. I liked basketball a lot, but no one in my family ever played. Montell was the only adult I was close to who could play a little. This unfamiliarity allowed me to continue with making excuses not to join Evan on the court. He had several cousins who knew and played the game very well. My sister's boyfriend Freddy could play also. So could a few others from the neighborhood. As a younger guy, Freddy was once a close pal of two very good local players. Their names were David Wingate and Reggie "Truck" Lewis.

Many new ideas began to surface as the school-year headed towards the winter holiday season. I had just started having girls on the brain again. This actually took place a lot quicker than I had anticipated. And, I was finally inching towards playing ball with Evan against some pretty good competition. I had picked up a ball a time or two at this point, but my confidence was not where it needed to be in order to compete with the more seasoned street-ball players around town. Rap music also began to intrigue my peers and I more and more. Run-DMC was on fire in the city and all over the country. Michael Jackson was like God to all African-Americans and millions all over the world. Michael Jordan sneakers had just altered my list for Christmas, early, and New Edition had me singing, "Delicious" until midnight to any pretty girl who decided to look me in the eyes on that day.

Times began to gradually change for the worse. A few more fights than normal, an unexpected pregnancy popped up every now and again, and arrests would occur more frequently; thanks to marijuana, now being sold on every corner. All of these situations were circulating in one very small area. However, love was still a strong presence on my block. The good music continued to play, and the smell of fried chicken still dominated the air. Hot dogs, baked beans, Kool-Aid and frozen cups still headlined all of our cravings. Good times were still present in the midst of change. Nothing was more evident of this fresh new era than the emergence of a phenomenon called "Break Dancing."

"Break Dancing," for those aliens who are not too familiar, was a unique dance craze created from the world of hip-hop. This style of dance, just like rap music, also originated in the city streets of New York. To explain further, "Breakin" is a complex style of dancing; self-expression, creativity like rapping and graffiti, but more physically demanding. This artform landed in B'MORE in the early 80's. It fully grabbed our attention by the mid-80's. I believe it made it to east Baltimore first, then a little later, up to McCabe Ave. Several kids from the east and west sides of town had brought the craze inside of the schools. Before long, the dance had all but taken the place of most students' school work. Students now only did just enough work to get by. The rest of their time was spent on trying to become the best dancer, or on becoming a member of the best dance group. Students would often get hall passes to supposedly go to the restroom, just to find dance contests. All one had to do was see a dancer quickly walk by their classroom, and at least four hands would rise. Contests would break out around the clock in the hallways during school hours.

Although girls and sports were still in heavy rotation for us young black males, it was clear at this point; if one was not either dancing or trying to rap, you were considered "a nobody" in the streets. Well, unless you were actually really in the streets. Meaning, you were a hustler or you sold drugs. For as much as we tried to ignore the "big boys," or the hustlers, it was very evident to us who ran things in the streets. These guys were for real. No time for dancing, no joking around all the time, no singing, no rap music, just doing what they felt they had to do; MAKE MONEY, at any cost, PERIOD.

It was true the hustlers were in charge, but we were too busy dancing our hearts away to care. The planet was rocking everywhere you turned. Schools, recreational centers, movie theaters, playgrounds, and even on the street corners where the older guys hustled. I guess watching us dance gave the hustlers more of an excuse to be on the corners. We loved making an impression on the older guys. Besides, they threw good money our way. Break Dancing was a new and exciting way for us to stay positive, stay fit, and learn something new. Unfortunately, not all of my buddies found the craze interesting enough to participate. Evan, Tee, Troy, nor Elroy found the dancing interesting enough to join in. Shawn and I loved it. So did Karl. Still, we never severed ties with any of our original friends. We all still hung out together. These few just didn't take part in the actual dancing.

Back at home my grandmother even received word about the dancing. She was fine with it. As long as we were not doing anything illegal, Mama would tolerate almost anything. Well, she never found out about the fiasco we had at Kizzie's place, but that too was not illegal, just plain stupid. Shawn and I had a good thing going with the dancing. To form an entire group, we circulated the surrounding neighborhoods to see who the best dancers were. Most neighborhoods had a dance crew. Kirk Avenue, Poplar Grove, North Avenue and Pulaski Street, and of course, Old York Road. I believe Old York's dance crew was called, "The Seekers." There were also dance groups nearby in the Northwood and the Alameda communities.

Eventually, Shawn and I soon would have to dig deep and find five young good dancers who were not afraid of leaving their neighborhoods or being observed by onlookers. "In the spotlight," we once called it. Some guys were good at a lot of things, but didn't care to be out in certain elements. Since my cousin and I were from McCabe, we felt we never had to worry about a mishap. Although our street was small, its reputation was respected on the east side well enough during this time to relieve us of possible trouble from other nearby neighborhoods. Living on McCabe Avenue had its perks. We were a close-knit street and neighborhood. It simply was not very easy to be there without resistance if you did not live there or very close by.

Meaning, most would certainly have to live on McCabe Avenue, or one of the four connecting streets in order to hang out. Those blocks were Alhambra, Ivanhoe, Craig, and Ready Avenues. People from other streets really were not accepted during this time. These were not my words or rules. These were the codes of the street of McCabe's frontrunner, Benny McGirt.

After Shawn and I were finally able to gather up five guys to join the four concrete members we already had, we set off to really make the most out of our interests. Our new members were guys from different areas in the city. There was Antmo, a five-foot-two, compact-built dancer who could also do back flips for an entire city block without stoppage. He also attended Winston Middle. The other students thought we were related because we both wore matching blue, lambskin coats with the hats and gloves to match, during the winter months. Those were very hot items in the 80's. There was also Richard, a soft-spoken honor-roll student from City College Prep High School where Cristina still attended. He lived up the street on one of the alienated blocks I mentioned. Then, there was Eddie. He was a strong personality, but an introvert. However, he could flat out dance. We would often hear his name come up in several conversations about dancing in the streets. Shawn used his people skills to give Eddie the confidence he needed to step off of his porch. The last two guys were interesting. Not for their dancing skills, but where they were from. Marcus and Mickey both lived off of Old York Road.

No matter how much I tried to bypass this area, these three words continued to pop up during conversations time and time again, 'Old York Road.' "What's the deal with this place?" I said to myself often. No matter where I would be, something about this neighborhood would surface. When I was in the house, my sister had a story a night about this place. Out in the streets, Benny would shout, "Fuck them punks down there on Old York Road." School was the same. I drew the conclusion that McCabe Ave. and Old York Road had a suspicious history long before we arrived on McCabe Avenue in late-1979.

School, dancing, girls, drawing, basketball, and creating small stories were my interests as we entered the end of the year. As Christmas approached, I had placed my order for Castle Grayskull (He-Man/Masters of the Universe) toy collection, and the 255 Computer Command vehicle; a toy sports car you could program from under its hood to drive and turn corners on its own. Still, I was sure to find time to be extra nosy whenever my sister was engulfed in conversations with Freddy.

It was about 1 a.m. when I listened in on my sister as she, again, talked with her boyfriend Freddy. This time Gina was reflecting on a very intense situation she endured before she and Freddy became an item. I learned my sister used to date a guy from Old York Road. Humorously, his name was Romeo. I had seen him around a few times. Gina was sharing a story with Freddy about an afternoon when Romeo was shot. She said that she was only standing five feet away from him when he was hit multiple times. When I finally got a chance to see Romeo, I noticed the peculiar hitch in his walk. "I don't know how he's still living," she stated to Freddy. "If you could have seen the way he was shaking on the ground, you would understand what I'm saying." "I was scared as hell that day," she said. The guy responsible for the attempted murder was still in the area. It was crazy to hear who had actually pulled the trigger just four years prior. Just days before, while walking to Eddie's to make sure he was joining us for an upcoming dance contest, Shawn and I were admiring a black and silver Mongoose bicycle. The rider was K-POX. He and Elroy's sister shared a new born baby girl. He was pulling off the hottest stunts of any rider in the neighborhood. This was the guy responsible for shooting Romeo! He was showing off his skills, smiling, after nearly killing someone not long ago.

Suddenly, I was becoming aware of where we were growing up. As time passed by, all of the fun things of the past began to slowly fade away. Christmas came and went, and so did winter. We did manage to dance frequently at different venues throughout Baltimore City. There were times where we actually made a little money. However, it was hardly enough to disperse between nine members. Most of the time, we were just content with winning a battle. We won battles in west Baltimore, Towson; in Baltimore County, and downtown at the prestigious tourist attraction, The Inner Harbor. After dancing enough to raise the eyebrows of an aspiring, music and film manager and producer, things actually improved. Although the craze seemed to lack longevity, we still enjoyed the ride. We even solidified our group with a name. We called ourselves "Break Force." We strongly felt our dance group could compete with "The New York City Breakers," "The Rock Steady Crew," and the "Turbos" and "Ozones" of the world.

Looking back, today, I doubt if we would have won, but we were pretty good. That competition would have been interesting. Harmon, the aspiring CEO, believed this too as he observed us in action in his neighborhood on Montford Avenue, located in east Baltimore; or "down the hill," many call the area. He was so impressed he shared with us his own dream to produce a motion picture about Breakin' in the city of Baltimore. Originally, we thought we were dealing with a pervert of some sort, but we were wrong. Harmon gained our confidence when he produced scripts, books about the craft, and a pretty nice professional camera. I was not completely sold on the idea after reading some of the material. There were countless eras and the plot was weak or corny, but I respected his passion. Writing stories and scripts or books is NOT an easy feat. At ALL! Especially when resources are extremely low; trust me. Writing can be complex and it demands lots of focus and patience. Harmon was serious about his vision. He also helped us with our dance routines. He bought us all Russell Athletic wear, and suede Puma sneakers with the "fat laces" to match. After this, I was sure to share this information with my grandma. She totally opposed the connection in the beginning, but she trusted me a bit. She knew I was not going to befriend anyone of questionable character. Perhaps Mama should not have trusted the decisions of a confused thirteen-year-old, but in this case, it all turned out just fine.

Harmon turned out to be a decent human being, but his vision was not established enough to support the erratic, impulsive dreams of nine, young black kids. We all were insecure when it came to dreaming. We all felt real dreams coming true were not really for us; not here. Besides, as time progressed it became clearer, "Break Dancing" was only going to last for so long in our town. While the majority of the guys, especially Eddie, tried to hold on to the dream Harmon preached, I found myself chasing after a dark-skinned young lady named Kima. Still, I continued to join in on the contests. I was very excited and interested when I learned our next battle would be held on Old York Road, inside of an empty church. Meanwhile, Harmon continued to try to ignite a fire under us that was gradually burning out. Maybe it was due to the relationship he sparked with Eddie's mom, or perhaps he felt we had more potential within ourselves than even we realized. Whatever the case, after dozens of contests, a couple of videotaped routines at small venues, and a few trophies, it was clear, dancing in the city had lost quite a bit of its flare. We soon headed down to Old York Road, more excited about the place than the actual battle. It would be one of our last, but quite frankly, my most memorable dance experience.

On the way down to the battle we discussed our feelings about Harmon. Everyone thought I was lashing out towards him because I had grown tired of the same story. "Be patient and don't worry, the movie will get done." I've always been an optimist, but this just got old. I can admit it all appeared to be possible at times. Yet, I was the kid who grew irritated with things typical kids don't inquire about. "Has anyone ever wondered why Harmon has only met one of our parents, and he's screwing her?" "Excuse me E," I casually said as I looked at Eddie as we walked towards Old York Road. Shawn tried to cut in on me by saying, "O, Mr. H is cool, he's good people's man." "All I'm saying Shawn, is he's not able to do what he says, that's all." "What's wrong with that? It's the truth," I explained. No one wanted to hear what I had to say. I believe it was because we all were afraid to do one thing; grow up a bit more. Looking back, I also did not need that father figure Harmon presented, as much as my peers had, Shawn included. My father was not present as much as I needed him to be, but I had a dad. The others simply did not. On top of this, we all were scared to see ourselves in the future. We all had no clue as to what we wanted to do with ourselves. No one besides Richard was looking ahead with confidence. Our strength was in the dancing and the craze was losing steam, yet we still entered the empty building with our chests stuck far out ready for battle.

Actually, being on Old York Road was very intense for me. I was the only guy there who was really aware of the disturbing history between McCabe Avenue and the street we were about to compete on. Shawn had a clue, but I had details. I took my time when observing all of the guys from Old York Road. With the history shared between the two neighborhoods, I felt there was a good chance I would be seeing these guys regularly as time went on. Talent was evident during this contest and we certainly made our mark. There were so many people inside of the old church, I lost sight of my buddies. The contest lasted for over an hour. Shawn was excited because the person handling the tunes was playing all of the right songs. "Planet Rock," his favorite dance song, "Play It at Your Own Risk," and "Dominatrix Sleeps Tonight" all were blasting from the boom box.

We were eventually victorious to the dismay of over twenty young men from the Old York area. The loss they suffered caused tightness in the air. Tensions would spread and that's when things became much clearer about the growing rivalry. After only a few years, the dance craze was certainly dying out in our area. The music continued, but the spinning and flipping slowed drastically not long after our competition on Old York. Speaking of music, as we hurried to leave the building on this day, I was interested in checking out who was actually handling the tunes for the rival dance crew. I made eye contact with a guy standing near the radio. I was not sure if he was just the DJ or a dance member. We nodded in each other's direction. Minutes later, the guys of Old York Road had confirmed all of my sister's stories about the rivalry. They began to grow irritated with losing the competition and the bragging we displayed. They started yelling foul language at us, instructing us to leave their neighborhood. Before we knew what hit us all, we were being chased up Old York Road by dozens of participants and bystanders. Fortunately, no one was caught hurt. I'll never forget that dance battle. For me, it symbolized a change in time in northeast Baltimore City. Oh yeah, there was also a unique figure there on the rival's side on this day, but no one knew at the time. The guy I greeted without ever opening my mouth was a young kid named Tupac Shakur.

After experiencing our first encounter with the possibility of being involved in a serious and violent situation, we returned to normal form. The vibe on McCabe Ave. still seemed to be as pleasant as usual to us.

Lyrics such as, "Good times, These are the good times," continued to blast from stereo systems of the neighborhood. To all of us times were, in fact, good. I felt they were great actually, and getting better by the moment. As I approached my 13th birth-year, all sorts of new experiences were landing in my lap. The most important was a visit from a father I had not seen at all during the school year. Suddenly he was back as the weather improved and I was very receptive to his return.

After spending lots of time observing my buddies enjoy the luxury of spending life with at least one of their birth parents, I felt a strong desire to do the same. For as much fun as I was engulfed in with my friends, nothing felt as wonderful as the feeling I would get when my dad came to see me. He would always "bop" or strut straight down the middle of my block with his hat tilted to the side. All of the guys got a huge kick out of how cool my dad appeared. "Look at O's pops man," "O father slick as shit," they would yell out in laughter. And he ate it all up like a male model. I felt at home on McCabe for sure, yet every time my dad came to see me, for some odd reason, I still felt as if I was being rescued.

By the following summer, break dancing was almost a mere memory for my cousin and I. Break Dancing in the streets was now another definition for broke pockets. With so much attention paid to the dancing, Shawn and I barely advanced to the next grade. A bittersweet victory for us both as Shawn was set to soon enter high school. I would have to tackle another year at Winston Middle. Tee was still rolling with me step for step throughout school. Troy struggled more than us all. I also learned Tee and I would be joined by Evan as well. He flunked again. My buddy Evan was on his way to celebrating his 16th birthday, yet still in the 8th grade. Tee and I showed little compassion for Evan's misfortunes. We sort of liked the idea of us three sharing Grade 8 together. This all would come in three months. For now, it was time to enjoy another summer filled with even more fun than the previous two. Well, at least this was what we all believed.

Two weeks into the Summer of 1985, I learned I would be spending half of the summer vacation at my dad's place. My dad lived in south Baltimore in the Dundalk community. He shared a two-bedroom townhouse with his girlfriend in the O'Donnell Heights area. This was another bittersweet scenario for me. I was excited to have the opportunity to spend time with my dad, yet I loved just being around the guys, simply finding ways to enjoy ourselves. I figured I would be writing a lot more at my dad's. Although I still would have the chance to hang with my pals for the second half of the summer, I was not looking forward to being away from the company I felt the most comfortable around. I was aware the time spent at my dad's could very well turn out to be a lot like the time I spent in my room; in seclusion.

A few days before I got set to leave for "The Heights," it's called, I surprisingly managed to rekindle a flame with Cristina. I never really knew how much she liked me over the years, but I did feel she understood me, and felt she was attracted to my uniqueness. Cristina was a very smart young lady, to go along with her beauty. In the midst of growing romantically, I also managed to do something even more fulfilling at the time. For the first time, I would dunk a basketball. Pretty impressive we all thought. Out of myself, Tee, Evan, Shawn and Troy, I was the youngest. I only stood at 5'9". Dunking gives you a great feeling. It separates you from the other players dramatically. It also seems to make the other players a little jealous. However, no one felt this towards me, because I still had major ball handling deficiencies, and I shot a jumper with both hands. I was far from being the next Michael Jordan, but I still was proud to become a member of the area's very small slam dunk fraternity.

The day had arrived for me to venture off to a foreign part of the city with my dad. I sat and waited for my dad in the living room with my grandma. I was a bit nervous, but not enough to lose sight of how happy and fortunate my sister and I were to have a grandmother who loved us unconditionally. Grandma's smile would always coat my heart when we would gaze into each other's eyes. I could see how proud she was of herself for how I was turning out. I was not the best student, but I was showing signs of being a very good one, and I was always a positive-spirited person. To my grandma, there was not a school or a sum of money in the world that could offer a good spirit. She felt only God could instill a positive attitude in a person's soul. Even as a teen, it was not too hard to see, I was simply a very loving person.

My grandparents were far more focused on morals when it came to all of us. Neither of them finished high school, therefore their knowledge of the importance of school and obtaining above-average jobs as adults fell by the waste side to things like spirituality, attitude, and humility. The lessons were evident at 731, despite the approach. We all had plenty of freedom. Our grandparents were not outgoing at all. When I say "at all," I mean at all. They never exited the house, not even to go to church. I believe most of this stemmed from disclosed physical ailments, while more of it came from the fact that grandma felt she could do whatever she needed to do from indoors. If there were any physical problems, no one knew. Grandma was one of those elders, quick to tell someone "I'm fine" or "I'm not going to no damn hospital." She would always say, "When it's my time to die, I'll go." My grandma was never short on words. Despite her constant referrals to the Bible, being very blunt and using foul language, more often than not, came very easy to my grandma.

My dad would soon arrive in a 1980 Buick, pulling up directly in front of the house. At the time, it was still an uncertainty as to why my dad hardly ever came in to greet my wonderful grandparents. It seemed sort of peculiar, but I was too busy soaking in the bliss of having a dad show up in my life. I can't think of any of my close friends, Evan included, whose father came to visit them more often than my dad would, but only at times. After giving my grandma a big kiss on the cheek and hugging the other adults in the house, I hurried outside. Have y'all ever had that weird feeling when it seems as if the entire world is staring at you? Well, that's exactly how I felt as I walked towards my dad's car. All of my friends, including my comrade Shawn, were sending me well wishes from the corner. Shawn quickly ran over to greet my dad. He did this every time my dad came to visit. I loved the live shot of those two. It gave me a tremendous burst of emotion to see my dad and my cousin embrace. Shawn hardly knew his dad at all. We both probably had seen his dad the same number of times. I loved my cousin, and I wished I could have shared my dad with him, just as he had wished for me with his mom. As I pulled off of McCabe Avenue, I found it to be impossible to eliminate the lump from my throat. This would be the first time I would be away from Shawn or any of my friends since we met them all. I was interested in experiencing new things with my dad, but I was already missing my friends before I had even made it off of the block.

The Buick would reach its destination after a thirty-minute drive. The neighborhood appeared to be a tad nicer than where I lived but nothing like "Seven Lakes." My dad was smiling from ear to ear as if the place was new to him as well. "We're here buddy!" he said vibrantly. I smiled through my nervousness. I maintained my smile until my dad broke it with the words, "You ready to meet your mother?" I didn't respond outwardly, but those words passed through me like a sharp unknown object. "That's not my mother," I mumbled in anger to myself. I soon let that question go so I could give the visit the benefit of the doubt. The two-bedroom townhouse was nice, but considerably smaller than 731. I felt I could adjust to the place well enough to live there for 3-5 weeks. After placing my bags into my new bedroom, I stepped out back to look the place over more thoroughly. As I stood on the top step, of a set of three, I observed about seven or eight kids my age running about. The feelings of uncertainty I once had on the first day I set foot on McCabe had returned. This feeling was not the direct result of me, once again, relocating. These feelings returned because every kid I observed in the area was white.

Now it was inevitable that I would get plenty of opportunities to interact with kids who were not black. I often wondered what made me different than the other kids I knew. I realized most of my friends would be very upset at this point. I asked myself, "Why am I not upset?" "Why is there an anxiousness boiling inside of me to meet people from different social and ethnic backgrounds?" "Why did I feel right at home, despite not seeing another black person other than my dad's attractive girlfriend Sherry?" I was clearly in another world, yet it all felt right; like back home. These questions remained unanswered, but my comfort level never wavered. Not even around my dad's woman-friend, Sherry. Sherry was black, and as close to perfect as one could have as a possible, future stepmom. She was cute, pleasant, patient, and quite generous. Perhaps I still needed the void left by my mom's death filled, but it all felt genuine. It had been nearly eight years since my mom had passed. Yet, it was still far too early to know if Sherry would prove to be the next best thing. Within the first few days of spending time at my dad's place I was sure I had, at the very least, met an awesome person in Sherry.

Being surrounded by a ninety-percent white population had little effect on how I approached my summer vacation in O'Donnell Heights. I had paid enough attention to my grandma, and in History class, to understand that there was a tremendously disturbing history between whites and blacks years ago, and that the residue may remain forever. This was far more disturbing than the seemingly senseless feuding unfolding in northeast Baltimore. However, I also believed in God enough to feel we were all put here on earth together for a positive reason. I had trouble believing it was to treat each other like crap forever. I would not buy that; I just couldn't. Therefore, I stepped out on the faith I hardly knew I had, and made myself a part of an all-white group of kids, socially, just having harmless fun.

This fun was no less exhilarating than the fun I was exposed to on the eastside of Baltimore City. The only difference was no girls, no violent sports like boxing or football, and a different shade of skin; that's it. I knew early on as a teen; I was not going to let race hold me back or give me an excuse not to try new things and/or be a decent person. My take on it was as simple at this time, just as it is today. I feel there's so much more to do besides allowing a bad past to give birth to a bad future. Early on in life, and during this vacation, I virtually mastered how to co-exist with both whites and blacks almost equally. Of course, my heart rested with my cousin, and the friends I had since 1979. I was only thirteen-years old, but I still did not have a clue about what I wanted to become in life. There were no dreams or visions within me, like a few of my friends had. My dad was still a tractor-trailer driver for The Coca-Cola Bottling Company, but that field hardly interested me as a kid. I loved writing and drawing, but I was simply too embarrassed to share that vision with anyone.

Where we were from, everyone seemed to be trying to follow David Wingate's path to Georgetown University with hopes of entering the NBA Draft. That was not a vision of mine either. I understood I was "a late bloomer" in reference to hoops. Most kids from B'MORE started playing ball at ages five or six. I was already thirteen years old, and I only had less than a year of shooting around under my belt. Yeah, I was trying to dunk from the free throw line, but that was just for kicks. Did I pull it off? No, but I did come closer than one would believe a few times. Nevertheless, I felt I had great social skills, but I lacked direction, therefore I tried to ignore where my life would be in the next few years and just have fun.

This problem never entered 731's doors, nor did any questions about my future ever exit my dad's mouth. My dad was crazy about me, yet it appeared as if he felt it was more important for him to impress me, rather than teach me. He would buy me any and everything I desired. Luckily for him, I was never a kid who felt very comfortable asking for things. I believed had I been, I may have gotten a car from my dad at fourteen or fifteen. I had all the latest apparel worn by the older guys in the city. I already had all of the hottest Matchbox cars as well. That's sort of funny, right? I was a thirteen-year-old kid, playing with Hot Wheels toy cars and G. I. Joe action figures, while wearing a $200 Le Coq Sportif jogging suit, and a pair of $150 royal blue and white high-top Forum Adidas. I was living in both worlds successfully, and never really paid much attention to it at all. I did not know at the time, because of how I dressed, my name would come up on the street corners during casual conversations as guys bragged about their own pricey gear. This period, I believe, is what made me much different than any of my peers in O'Donnell Heights and on McCabe Ave. I had what all my friends had, and also what they may have never gained. This was the ability to peacefully and productively connect with anyone, at any time, in any place, if given the opportunity.

My stay with my dad was filled with new experiences throughout. I was having a blast on a daily basis. I was looking forward to wearing all of the latest fashions my dad had bought for me to wear back to school in September. However, here, there was no need to dress impressively. No one there cared what the other person was wearing. All they cared about was having a good time and enjoying the weather. I loved to wear nice things, but I never let material things control my attitude. Still, I was continually spoiled out of my mind by my dad and his lady. I don't recall how many Baltimore Orioles' home games I attended with my dad. Back then, The O's were a pretty good squad. They were coming off of two stellar years, making it to the World Series in1977, and again in 1983, in which they won the title. Hopefully, they'll get another soon. I loved the ball park at Memorial Stadium on 33rd Street. I remember trying to get my uncle to bring Shawn to the stadium, just so we could smile at each other and shake hands for a second or two. I was having the time of my life, despite never catching a fly foul or homerun ball. Still, the white O's batting glove, on one hand, and the outfielder's glove on the other, made a strong fashion statement.

I learned a little bit of everything during my stay with my dad and his significant other. Whenever my dad would be at work, I would often spend time with Sherry. She was such a cool-spirited woman. She helped me appreciate the beauty and class of a good woman. Sherry was a bit older than the women who flirted with me on McCabe, but she presented the same sense of grace. Sherry seemed to be the only woman around, so I studied her closely. I learned how to read females more through interacting with her. Sherry allowed me to see what makes a woman tick. Things like soap operas, music, certain perfumes, flowers, compliments, pretty colors, painted toe nails, a new hairdo, seafood, and handbags are just a few of the extras that are very important to some females. All of these things and much more seem to penetrate a woman's essence. I would often watch General Hospital or Days of Our Lives with Sherry and observe secretly, the look in her eyes. I understood from situations like these and so many more; most women want nothing more than attention, or to be loved by a man to the fullest, every single day of their lives.

I was not sure if my dad was taking care of all Sherry's emotional needs. I loved my dad, but my guess would be negative. He spent most of his time talking about someone else; HIMSELF! Somehow, I just don't believe he read Sherry that deeply. I did, I couldn't help it. She was cute and she was not very old; just much older than me. Her age could not persuade me to look away when she would pick the remote up from off of the floor. I would get frequent looks down the front of her many colorful summer dresses. Remember, I was a teen, therefore, "her friends" were by far, the largest I'd had seen at the time. Like I said, I can co-exist everywhere, and O'Donnell Heights was alright with me. With that said, my stay at my dad's would begin to wind down. The offer for me to move in permanently with my dad would soon be put on the table. I knew I would miss Sherry and my dad once I left, but not as much as I would have missed Shawn and my grandma if I had elected to stay. The decision to do away with this idea was an easy one to make. Despite my interesting experiences, I was almost ready go back home, and one situation would soon arise in just enough time to push me over the edge.

There's an old saying my grandma and other wise elders would say as they would get into their evangelistic moods. "Make the most of your time here son, because nothing in life lasts forever." Perhaps, this was why as time began to slip away from me in Dundalk, I could see the flip side of things. My dad had suddenly started a few senseless arguments with Sherry, the Orioles were, surprisingly, on a losing streak, I ran out of KIX cereal for the first time, and I was in desperate need of a haircut. Grandma couldn't stand to see my hair uncut. "Got damn it," she would say in frustration as see brushed away with a painfully coarse brush; often brushing into my forehead. "Look at it. It beads right back up soon after you fuckin brush it." This was her mild approach. If she were already pissed off about something, she would just say, "Boy, leave me alone, you 'beady head sap sucker.'" At the time, I was not sure what that creature looked like! I know now! It's a small bird; a woodpecker from North America that gets its food source; sap, from trees. Funny grandma! In reference to leaving Dundalk, none of these small sad incidents were enough to make me tired of this pretty successful getaway. Really, the deciding factor came in the presence of this white kid; a fifteen-year-old, pudgy bully named Jeramy.

During the first several weeks at my dad's, I managed to stay clear of negativity; no fighting, stealing, nor using foul language. All of the kids in the neighborhood were friendly towards me. Yet, we all know, in every neighborhood there's at least one idiot. My favorite place during this time was McCabe, and there were at least ten known idiots there. I just happened to be cool with them all. Well, in Dundalk, this two-hundred pound, oddly shaped, trouble maker was not looking for any new friends. Jeramy was away on a vacation, similar to my own, when I had arrived in Dundalk. Well, he was back, and he desperately needed to know why were all of his "yes kids," now being entertained by a newcomer, and a black one at that. This was unacceptable to Jeramy; therefore, he wasted no time to make sure I understood "the rules," and that they were all his.

Jeramy's approach was weird. I had participated in a couple of stare downs with the guy for at least two minutes each time. I believed this placed him in a state of concern. Not worry, but uncertainty. Like most chumps, he was comfortable only when knowing how he would make out in a situation well before getting deeply into it. Even after our usual stare downs, I would see him violently slap a much smaller kid in the head. Other than the stares, I would ignore the tactics of this guy. Sometimes you can ignore a person so well, he or she may just go away; out of your sight and mind, but this didn't work for me in this situation.

One sunny summer afternoon, five of us played quietly in the next court south of where I stayed. We were making dirt tracks for the several small toy cars we had. This was something I took part in with the kids from back home as well. My pal Evan was great at making dirt roads with one half of an ice cream stick. It took us all an hour to nearly complete the landscape. However, before we could fully complete this project, I found my Matchbox silver Corvette parked next to a size ten, Jack Purcell. A "Smiley," I thought, was blocking the entire entrance to my make-pretend condo. I don't know what irritated me more, the "Smiley," or the big shoe print smearing a portion of our project. I really never cared much for the look of that shoe. None of this mattered as the next course of events taught me a lesson, we all must encounter at least once in our lifetime.

Before long, I found myself looking directly up at an abnormal-sized green booger, partially hanging from the nose of this neighborhood bully. I stood up slowly making sure not to look away from Jeramy. McCabe taught my buddies and I to never give a possible threat a free shot at your face. The mood was dark even in the bright sunlight. It was so quiet, I thought I could actually hear passengers yelling from our toy cars, arguing over the four large shoes blocking the roadways; mines and Jack's. I could feel the other four kids staring at me as if they felt sorry for what was coming my way. I never wanted to give them eye contact. I believed this would have confirmed their suspicions. "C'mon y'all, let's go," one kid uttered. "Shut up you!" Jeramy yelled. We all started walking back towards my dad's house after retrieving our possessions. Jeramy continued to stay very close to me, staring and walking closely. I knew he was extremely close, because I could smell his bad breath even as I walked straight ahead. By the time we reached the top of a thirty-step walkway, I'd had enough. I stopped, looked at the much larger, much taller white kid and said, "What do you want, ha?" The unthinkable then happened. Jeramy never said a word. Instead, he sucked up the visible booger and all of the snot that created it, widened his eyes, and spit it all directly into my face.

I would really like to be more specific about what I felt other than shock, but I can't. I guess I just blacked out. I don't remember any sounds outside or what the others may have said at the time. I don't even believe they were still around. All I remember was the horrible smell of the enormous amounts of the halitosis fluid that was all over my face. It was dripping from my chin as if I had done the spitting myself. Immediately afterwards, Jeramy seen The Omen's Damien-like expression on my face, and he took off running. That's the only explanation I have to explain as to how all of my small cars were now driving in six different directions. After I dropped my case, all I could focus on was Jeramy's backside. This proved to be the bully's worse move since his return. I quickly ran up on the severely slow teen at the top of the steps, and gave him the hardest shove my entire body could muster. Jeramy's body took flight just as a 747 would. I did not stick around to witness "The Jeramy Airliner" depart, run out of fuel, and crash. I immediately panicked and took off in the other direction. Running away quickly still would not prevent me from hearing his violent landing. The ground seemed to shake, and a frightening scream followed. The scream then gradually lessened as Jeramy's body continued down all thirty of the concrete steps. I continued to run directly passed my own toys, thinking, it's definitely time for me to go the hell back home.

I quickly ran into the townhouse in a delirious state, immediately trying to explain to Sherry what had just happened. "Slow down Odell, tell me what happened?" Sherry said in concern. I eventually calmed my nerves down well enough to give Sherry the details before, during, and after the incident. I told Sherry everything while dealing with the smell of bad breath turning my stomach every time I inhaled. After scrubbing my face and neck area for nearly five minutes, Sherry first took me to retrieve my things. This only took a minute, as the others graciously took the liberty to gather up every single car of mine, neatly placing them all back inside the case nicely. I guess this was their way of thanking me for standing up to the neighborhood bully. Sherry and I then observed the blood trail on nearly all of the steps where the altercation had taken place. "Oh my God Odell," she said nervously. I hope he's not hurt too badly. I was hoping for the same, but all I could do was look stupid.

This was the first time I had faced a situation such as this and I hated how I felt. I never intentionally would hurt anyone, but this time I felt I had no choice. All I had to go on from a positive stance was the fact that Jeramy's body was not there. Neither were the paramedics or the sound of any. By day's end, we all learned he was going to be alright. He was still badly injured, and his family remained clueless about the details surrounding the incident. I later learned Jeramy had suffered a broken arm, a broken left ankle, a badly sprained right ankle, a bruised elbow, various scrapes and lumps, along with a slight concussion. Oh, and he lost his two front teeth as well. Jeramy told his parents he fell down all of the steps, but he never mentioned my shove or the assistance I gave him.

After feeling like crap for the next few days, it was time for me to go back home. I called home to share this story with my grandmother and Shawn. For once, they actually agreed on something. These two conversations were interesting to say the least. Grandma angrily shouted, "That nasty muthafucka spit in your face? That's exactly what his ass gets." "He should have gotten hurt more than that; a nasty bastard," she followed in anger. My cousin Shawn spent most of his time on the phone laughing at me and Jeramy. "I wish I would have been there, O," he said. "I would have run down the steps behind him while he was falling, then I would have stomped him in the head." "Don't worry O," he went on to say. "You did the right thing buddy." My family's views were not how I felt at all. I really felt an urge to apologize, but even my dad opposed my feelings. I was surprised no feedback or retaliation stemmed from this incident. I simply was never pointed out by Jeramy. I guess he did not want his family to know he spit in a black guy's face. Perhaps he didn't learn behavior like this at home. I usually tried to use this sort of thinking and my small but personal relationship with God to move pass issues like this in a constructive manner. This episode did not change my feelings about white people or the time I spent at my dad's. I still viewed my time in O'Donnell Heights as a huge success. I learned a lot in nearly six weeks. Although my time there ended on a pretty sour note, I still liked how I was able to step out of the box for a bit, try something new, and enjoy it.

I left O'Donnell Heights midway through the summer a much smarter kid. The stay gave me the opportunity to see things and people perhaps it could have taken me forever to see. The place I was headed back to was filled with individuals who had never been in the company of Caucasians. Well, only when they would decide to snatch an old woman's pocket book or stick a gun in someone's face for loot. Besides this, the only close scenario there involving whites would be a parole agent or probation officer. This experience told me in detail; there's so much more to life than McCabe Ave. Unfortunately, for Shawn and I, we felt this was the best place for us to be; forever if possible.

I returned to McCabe Avenue, eager to reunite with my pals. As I pulled up to the front of the house, I could see from a distance, all of my friends in a foot race, fighting for position to greet me first. They were jockeying for this position so fearlessly, Tee fell down. All eyes were on me as I exited the Buick. Even the older guys stopped to see what was happening. Having a father in your life was a very rare occurrence in my neighborhood. So was not having a mother. I guess you could say, in the inner city, the chances of you either having both parents in your life, or even knowing both were slim. I was really enjoying having my dad around during this time. I felt like a teen pop star stepping out of his car on that day. I was brand new from head to toe. I had $100 bill in my pocket for the first time ever, and I had a fresh haircut. It appeared as if I could have run directly across the street and joined in with Nardo and the others as they gambled. With all this said, I believed what really gave me the ability to attract was the fact that I really could care less about all of the possessions deep down inside. I guess my peers could see that I really didn't care about things. No matter what I would have or had on, I always wanted to be viewed as the nice kid who presents himself with class, not a well-dressed idiot.

After locking my cloudy eyes onto the rear of my dad's car as he drove off, Shawn and I carried all of my bags inside of the house. I greeted my grandma, giving her an extended hug and a kiss. I watched her roll her eyes in Shawn's direction as I pulled away. He chuckled and headed for the fridge. "That cousin of yours is something," grandma whispered. "What he do?" I replied back in a similar tone. "One of the neighbors said they saw him hanging out with them new boys down the street. They were on the porch smoking them drugs," she would say. "Smoking them drugs" was the best analogy Mama used when she made a reference to anyone who was getting high or smoking marijuana. My grandparents were so out of touch with the selling and the usage of narcotics; they never really knew just how deep my uncle Frank was involved with drugs when he was a teen. As she said these things to me, I glanced into the kitchen at my cousin, only to see his eyebrows rise up and down over a recycled, large 7 Eleven Big Gulp cup. "He's alright ma," I said gently. "That nigga ain't alright," she replied. "He's headed for trouble," she offered. I looked at my grandma rather unsure of what she meant. As Shawn approached with his red Kool-Aid grin, I decided not to go into further conversation on the matter. Things slowly were beginning to feel a bit strange. All my friends were still around and the weather was still beautiful, yet the mood on McCabe Avenue began to shift somewhat. Some kind of new energy was beginning to break through. The incident in Dundalk, I believe, allowed me to feel this oncoming change. Grandma obviously could feel the possibility of a new negative presence forming as well. My sister always knew of situations involving our neighborhood and we all knew they were not very positive. All we could do at this point was hope that our new intuitions were wrong.

# Chapter 4

# CHANGING WORLDS

The second half of Summer 1985, began almost as weird as the first half had ended. Tee had recently stated his family was considering moving away from McCabe Avenue. This bothered me tremendously. Tee and I were nearly as close as Shawn and I were at this point. He was not completely sure about when the move would take place, and he believed money played a huge role in the matter. Perhaps there were concerns about the neighborhood gradually unraveling. He and Troy despised the idea of leaving the area. We all could feel a change coming, and we were no longer strictly focusing on enjoying ourselves. Tee also shared another situation with me that I found quite peculiar. "O, while you were gone Cristina found a new boyfriend," Tee said with hunched shoulders. "Shit!" I yelled in disappointment. "Who is he?" I quickly asked. Tee then cut his eyes in my direction and slightly stuttered out the name, "Shhawn." "What? Are you sure?" I asked consecutively. "My cousin Shawn?" I added. "Yeah man, Shawn, your cousin!" he confirmed. "Are you mad?" Tee asked. "Nah, just surprised," I replied with a confused expression. "Knowing Shawn, he probably already had sex with her," I said with uncertainty. I don't think so, this just happened," Tee stated. "She didn't know when I was coming back, but why my cousin?" I wondered. "I don't know O, but if you want to get her back, we can?" Tee offered. This was a weird situation for me to come back to, but I never approached my cousin one time about it. However, I did send Tee to speak with Cristina. For some odd reason, I decided to still want to be around Cristina. We were not sexually active, but I still liked her a lot. Oddly enough, she accepted my offer to go steady again. I guess you can say this was my first experience learning how females are often just as confused as us guys. Surprisingly, Shawn and I never discussed this matter. I don't believe he even cared. He was too busy getting acclimated with some newer, yet older guys on McCabe.

As the new school year approached, I noticed more and more new faces sprouting up in our neighborhood. I didn't think much of it at the time. I was busy still writing a bit, and playing more and more basketball. I managed to add a few more slam dunks to my repertoire. I began to really impress Evan a great deal on the court at this time. After all, it was he who displayed tremendous persistence with me taking an interest in the sport. I was glad I did. Basketball gave me an outlet or an escape like no other game could. It kept me away from the suspicious characters who were in my age bracket. The basketball court was just ten minutes away, yet it seemed as if I was in another world there. I truly realized my neighborhood was digressing when I found myself actually looking forward to going to school during the summer months. This was unheard of a year or two prior.

Our original click managed to cling together through the beginning stages of this transitional period on McCabe. Playing "Skully" or "Skelly" was not what it used to be. "Tops" was a game played out on the blacktop or concrete. We would draw a large square board; approximately six feet (2 m) to a side, on the surface with chalk or spray paint. Fill plastic milk tops with asphalt or wax, and pluck or flick the tops around the board with precision to see who could complete the cycle fastest. You did this while simultaneously knocking others out or in back of the competition. This was another pastime B'MORE inherited from New York City; specifically, Manhattan during the 50's. Now, in Baltimore, the older guys were not even allowing us to play much. Whenever they did not dominate the board, they made it their duty to continuously walk through the middle of our games. Not all of the guys were "shit starters" or bullies, but there was a fair share of them on McCabe Ave. Thanks to Elroy, none ever really bothered us, although his brothers didn't pay us much attention. However, a few of Elroy's brothers' acquaintances made sure we knew who ran the neighborhood.

After examining the state of the neighborhood, now with a more mature eye, it was clearer we were no longer in a place where you could hear the birds chirping effortlessly, or even the tunes playing from the Good Humor ice cream truck. My neighborhood still appeared to be safe to us, but it was clear, there was more here than what met the eye. Our neighborhood was losing its neighborly ways and converting into a hood or ghetto. Let's define the term, ghetto; defined as a part of a city in which members of a minority group live, especially because of social, legal, or economic pressure. That's the dictionary's way of putting it. The "hood" is a place where all of the folks who are poor live. Money is extremely hard to come by honestly, and everything negative and detrimental to life is very easy to grasp. In short, it's a place very easy for minorities to be born into, but very hard for most to escape.

McCabe Avenue was gradually becoming "the hood," and the occupants of this place were not the type of individuals you would place unwanted responsibilities on. Here, you had a few dozen young men, who believed in their hearts that they could do whatever they wanted to do, whenever they felt like it. All of these guys were leaders of their own causes; answering to no one. All of them were making their own way by doing whatever they felt was necessary. Some were struggling, while others were relatively successful by street standards. Then there was "B-Mack" or Benny McGirt. Benny was the top representative for a large percentage of the illegal practices on McCabe Avenue. If there was a guy to go through, to deal with to make money, to be around, to fight with, it was Benny.

B-Mack, like other well-known kingpins, was not your typical street hustler. Shawn and I knew him from day one. He was always a good friend to my sister and Freddy. We saw him on a daily basis. He lived maybe a half a block up from 731, on the same side of the street. He had two brothers and two sisters, but they were seldom seen together. Benny was a hustler with a keen sense of humor, style, and insight. Everyone seemed to be his friend. They all would light up like fireflies whenever he surfaced. He and Elroy's brother Steve were the best of friends and shared similar personalities. Benny and Steve were the only two guys, other than Freddy, that would be able to enter 731's front door unannounced. My grandma was really beginning to get uncomfortable with the direction the neighborhood was headed in, but you would not be able to tell the moment Benny came by. He always helped my grandparents with their groceries. He would also come by to see if my grandmother needed anything regularly. Grandma would always be smiling from ear to ear whenever he would drop in. Mama loved Benny's vibrant energy. She hated the idea of illegal drugs, but for some strange reason, it seemed as if B-Mack received a moral pass from her.

Sometimes I would see grandma smiling, looking out of the window; I would then take a look for myself, only to see Benny headed towards the house smiling. He would enter the house as if he lived there most of the time. Gina would sometimes be on the phone or upstairs, if in at all, and he would still drop in. We all would usually be on the front porch or out and about most of the time. Benny would often be seen going inside of our fridge, looking for his favorite fruit or flavor of Kool-Aid. Different; he was that and more. The guy who would eat most of our sweet produce and goodies, was the same person who controlled a large percentage of the heroin trafficking on the northeast side of B'MORE.

Benny McGirt introduced heroin to our part of town in the early to mid-80s. Before then, dealing drugs meant you sold a decent amount of marijuana, in corn bags for a good profit. Back then it seemed as if "weed" was not really considered an illegal substance. Guys simply thought this particular "crime-for-pay" idea was cool and smart. Three reasons; one, the drug didn't seem to get the best of one's soul like cocaine and heroin were known to do. Two: the money came fast and easy. Three: it seemed to be the only drug you could actually sell and use, and not lose your way and fall completely apart. Finally: if you did happen to get pinched by the authorities, the penalty probably would only result in one having to piss in a cup once a month. Nearly every guy on the block sold marijuana. Even my sister's boyfriend Freddy made a killing selling weed. His Shoe City job was mostly for ethical purposes. Guys like Benny could care less about how he was viewed by outsiders. He was one of many guys on the block who simply believed he was born to hustle or sell narcotics.

While Benny's trafficking business began to expand throughout the city, my friends and I were getting prepared to head back to school. Tee shared a bit of good news with me at the ball court one day. He told us that his mom would definitely allow him to finish out middle school as a resident of McCabe Ave. This was good news especially because Shawn and I were not as close as we had been in the past. He was beginning to hang out with a couple of older guys during this time. Many of these older street guys took to Shawn immediately. The older dealers believed my cousin had a lot of heart, or more courage than the average fourteen-year old. These feelings gave Shawn a free pass to interact with the "big boys" without being bullied or disrespected for simply being afraid or too young. This was a frequent practice on our block. Guys like Todd and Craig were just two of the bullies that paced up and down the streets daily. The love was still evident in our neighborhood, no question, but it was not hard to see more negativity was inevitable.

The growing drug market influenced the bullies to intensify their antics also. I was not picked on much at all, but I knew I was not exempt either. A simple store run could go horribly wrong. The bullies hanging around the stores could have just lost a couple of hundred bucks in the ongoing dice game, only to then see an innocent teen approaching. You could be walking along, smiling with a $10 or $20 bill partially exposed from your grasp, never expecting a thing. Consider it lost. Any one of the several bullies in the neighborhood would have simply taken your money. And that would be on a good day. If your money would have been in your pocket, you would probably get tripped or punched in your arm so hard or with so much force, a golf ball-sized lump would protrude through your tee-shirt. We all called this a "frog." Ouch!

This was our hood, but all we were really concerned with was the first day of school. Although money was tight at times, I usually had a nice amount of new apparel to choose from. We may not have been spoiled as kids, but we were clean and particular. I made sure whatever I got from grandma; I was going to keep in good shape for as long as possible. This made her proud, to know I cared about how much money she spent, and how often. This way of thinking helped me accumulate over twenty- five pairs of good clean sneakers. Back then, for a thirteen-year-old kid, that was pretty cool. Dressing actually became another hobby I enjoyed quite a bit. Well, let's just say, I really like nice clothing. Mama always would say to me, "If you have to spend tons of money on something you can't even afford, it's not a hobby; that's lust." Lust was the theme that was spreading like a plague outside of 731's front door. The closer we drew to the first day of school, the more evident it was to observe. Fights began to break out more frequently. There were more arrests than normal. Then, the unthinkable took place just days before I was set to begin the 8thgrade. I partially witnessed a horrible event for the very first time ever; a murder.

By the end of August, my friends and I were all geared up and ready to embark on our last year in middle school. My cousin Shawn was beyond excited. He was entering his first year in high school. Elroy and few others would join him. We all were pleased with the realization we would be high school students the following year. As the summer ended and our enthusiasm for the unknown began, a dark cloud would hover over our neighborhood. Perhaps it was that same infamous cloud from 1913 Kennedy Ave. However, this particular presence came on a sunny day while everyone was out making the most of the last days of steamy weather. I just so happened to be standing on the porch alone. I was eating a cherry-flavored frozen cup, innocently observing the energy of the streets. I did this quite often. As I stated, my front door was at the center to all of the action. The neighborhood was becoming so busy, folks were almost on standby; people thought they would miss something if they were not paying attention for a moment. Still, in a thousand years, my eyes and ears were not ready for what would take place on this day.

While standing on my front porch, I had just made the mistake of puncturing clear through the Styrofoam cup with a metal teaspoon. The unique sound indicated that I had misjudged the depth of the center hole I created through my "freezy cup." Seconds later, I heard a weird but similar popping sound. It was not very loud, therefore no one outside panicked initially. It was one of those sounds you hear when one or two people look around and may say, "Um, what was that?" or they would simply ask, "Did y'all hear that?" Just as I looked up, I glanced back downwards immediately, but not for long. A second after shaking my head at the red juice stain on the bleached-white shoe laces of my fairly new sneakers, there was a loud scream. "Uuuh, Uuuh, Help! Help me!"

I could see right away; it was Wilbert, an older guy who lived just two doors down from our house. He continued to run towards his house with his left hand holding one side of his head. The violent screams persisted as he drew closer to his doorstep. My eyes followed his every step. I remember thinking, "Wow!" My heart sped as he drew quickly near his home. Wilbert surely was running fast for a nearly, three-hundred-pound man. Wilbert, also around six-foot-three, made it to his porch, but collapsed hard, falling through his front door, leaving half of his body on the front porch while his upper torso rested inside of the home. Wilbert was silenced, but terrified yells and screams immediately consumed the block. People were sprinting toward the incident from all angles. I stood just as still as Wilbert's body, wondering what in the hell was taking place.

Paramedics arrived sooner than later and carted Wilbert off to a nearby hospital. Details surfaced quickly as we all learned Wilbert had been running at top speed with a .22 caliber bullet enlarged inside of his head before crashing onto his porch. Rumors arose suddenly; he and Benny, who were close friends, had been seen disputing in an alleyway the night before. No one truly knew who was responsible or why Wilbert was shot. Everyone understood; this was Benny's show on McCabe in reference to hustling. If something was out of line on McCabe Avenue, Benny usually fixed it one way or another. However, this was new, especially to my peers and I; this was extreme violence. Wilbert would never get the opportunity to divulge his side of the story. No words would ever come from Benny nor the others. Wilbert died hours later in the hospital. I did not see the shot fired, but I witnessed a guy struggling right before his death for the first time. Scary! This was extremely difficult to discard mentally, but this was the direction my neighborhood was headed in. Just like that old 1982 hit song by "Madness," one that once played frequently at the time, the theme was becoming reality: "Our house, in the middle of the street."

Wilbert's death devastated the neighborhood. It also symbolized the huge negative change for our area. It was the first time since we had been living on McCabe that anyone had been murdered. I was in shock as if Wilbert was not really dead, just hurt. I asked myself for days, "Did I just witness someone die from a gunshot wound to the head?" "Did I really?" Wilbert was one of the many guys in the area my friends and I would ask for a quarter or a dollar bill over the years, but now he was gone, forever. The buzz of people moving from McCabe increased significantly. No such mention of moving ever entered our dwelling, but Tee, Troy, Evan, Karl and Kizzie were seemingly going to be the first from our list of friends to leave the area. Who could blame them really? A human being had just been murdered underneath of all our noses. I recalled the look on Freddy's face upon his return from Wilbert's funeral. At 13 years old, it's very strange to witness a grown man cry. Freddy was not the only person having difficulties withdrawing from showing emotions. Wilbert was one of those big lovable types. He usually made the entire block laugh.

Everyone seemed to be a friend of his. However, no matter how you put things in regards to Wilbert's personality, he still was a huge brother; physically menacing. No matter what hood you're from or what town you live in; mix in a lot of anger with being black in the ghetto, you will likely find an unhealthy outcome. Wilbert just happened to end up on the short end of things. He was just twenty-three years old.

On the first day of school, I found myself spending most of homeroom session daydreaming about how painful it must have been for Wilbert to run several yards with a bullet in his skull. I was also wondering how I managed to get to dreams like this, after first aspiring to be the next Robert Taylor, the young actor who played "Lee," the lead character from the hit motion picture, Beat Street is the New York City-based film covering the origin of hip hop. Now, Wilbert had passed away and the dancing was fading. It was not an everyday occurrence for a thirteen-year-old kid to watch a guy virtually die on his own front porch. Tee shared similar feelings. I caught him in a daze a time or two as well.

Despite the horrific tragedy, school had begun, and we only knew of one way to get passed the traumatizing situation with Wilbert; girls, girls, and more girls. One of the best things about school for us as teens was how it brought kids from all over the city to one small location. Young ladies from east Baltimore still tickled our fantasies. Somehow, we all felt they simply were more put together, physically, than the girls from our neighborhood. Most of the females from our block would dress pretty conservatively. So maybe it was the tightly fitting Calvin Klein or Guess jeans that had us all going. I certainly was ready to do whatever I could to get closer to these young beauties. I had not been involved seriously with any girls since my meltdown with Cristina. Negativity in the streets, different schools, and the two years she had on me, finally would pull our innocent union apart forever. I was ready to put that all behind me and dive into the world of promiscuity once more, even if it was going to cost me ten packs of "Now and Later" candies.

For as demanding as Grade 8 was for Tee and I, the sight of cookies and candy still had a profound effect on us as it had in the early 80s. In middle school, all anyone really had to do in order to get close to any type of female, was purchase lots of candy. Candy for kids in school was the equivalent to coffee for adults headed out for work in the morning. They all simply need it. Most teenage bombshells would spend countless hours at home, on their cordless phones, up all night, talking to a boyfriend or talking to a girlfriend about a boy. More than likely, they all would be dead tired the next morning. Tee and I were well aware of this. Candy was the remedy. So, in the morning we would purchase plenty. I never cared for candy much personally. I usually received a clean slate from the dentist for having no cavities after every visit. I've always been more into cookies, cakes, and pies. I've always been a very unselfish guy, but I did not play with my two for $1 cookies. For as generous as I was, cookies were the only thing I struggled to share. Once, my sister Gina crept up on me, from behind, as I was eating a pack of these cookies at the dining table. "Give me one!" she yelled as she snatched two of my vanilla creams from the pack of twenty. I hated sharing these cookies so much, I became outraged and threw the entire pack in the trash can immediately afterwards. I was probably the most considerate kid on the block, but it was simply illegal to ask me for a cookie. Candy however, I intentionally purchased to give it all away.

Our candy routine was quite simple. In the mornings, we all would take a shortcut to school through a wooded area surrounding one of the two basketball courts we frequently played on. Tee, Evan, myself and a few others would stop at a corner store on Winston Avenue. By this time Mr. D's was struggling, and the Koreans were dominating the "mom and pop" or corner store market throughout the city. Foreigners now practically owned every store in the area. Here, we would buy lots of candy and luscious, fresh "twister" doughnuts for a small fee. Back then, a five pack of "Now and Later" candies sold for ten cents a pack. I would usually purchase at least fifteen packs. I figured that would possibly get three or four girls to introduce themselves to me. The candy was nothing more than an "ice-breaker." It actually prevented the female from carrying herself like a "ball-breaker."

The candy plan took about a week to materialize. Before the first month of school had ended, all we had to do was arrive and stand in an elevated position where we could be easily seen. Girls would flock to me like I was a member of New Edition. New Edition is an R&B music group millions of young blacks grew up on. For us, the group was extra special simply because the members were close to us in age. New Edition, formed in 1978, originally had five members; Ralph Tresvant, Ricky Bell, Bobby Brown, Michael Bivins, and Ronnie Devoe. A sixth member, Johnny Gill was added in 1988, three years after the solo departure of Bobby Brown in 1985. Today, I'm happy the full group is still active. Whenever possible, when they are performing nearby, I'm there. Over the years, my family believed I favored Mr. Ronnie Devoe. I see it somewhat and he seems like a really cool dude. Tee was always there with me as we connected with our "candy girls," but he was more of a fan of candy than I. He clung to his sweets just as I had with the cookies. The females, of course, did not care for Tee's lack of generosity.

I now craved to be around females so much, I actually used "Now and Later" candies to give a life lesson on sharing. I used sweets to show the girls that giving is a beautiful thing and should be done with an effortless smile. Ok, I'll be honest! Tee and I were really hoping to score with the young ladies, now rather than later; the candy was the only gifts we could afford or had to offer. There were two females in particular, who were the most consistent in showing up with there pretty little hands out. Kima Bains and Caroline Johnson were two best friends, and next-door neighbors, from an east Baltimore Street named Windemere Avenue, near 33rd Street. Kima was a very dark-skinned, beautiful sister. Caroline was just the opposite. She actually reminded me of my sister Gina, at first glance. Tee was blown away by the beauty of Caroline. I quickly fell for Kima. "Y'all got any candy today?" Kima would ask. I would immediately give her five packs to start, placing Tee in a peculiar position. He would then reluctantly place a pack or two in Caroline's hand. To have more fun with Tee, because I knew it was killing him to give up the goods; I would give Kima another pack or two, bringing the total to seven or eight packs. That would be it for Tee. He would then begin struggling to open up a single pack, only to hand the beauty one or two separate pieces from the package. It would be hilarious to observe the expression on Tee's face. "I can't do it," he'd say while still struggling with the packaging. The candy game was fun, but it only produced mediocre results for myself. Kima had a boyfriend. No hard feelings. He spotted her first, and he was a more popular guy at the time.

For as interesting as school was for my peers and I, back home was much more intriguing. Word would spread throughout the hood that

Benny never pulled the trigger in Wilbert's death. However, it was stated that he may have still been responsible or aware of the details. A strange and new figure was seen with Benny during the days leading up to, and after Wilbert's death. He was rumored to be a hired gunman from the westside of Baltimore City. I actually brushed shoulders with the suspected trigger man on the ball court a time or two. Basketball was beginning to place me around the older guys a bit more than my peers who were not into the sport as much.

Greg could actually play ball well. He was a very quiet guy in his mid-twenties. He kept close to Benny, but only few made attempts to get to know him. I believe they all knew why he was around McCabe Avenue or Benny, but no one asked any questions. Only Etton Briggs, Benny's understudy, if you would, could be seen laughing and joking with the suspicious young man. The "Code of the Streets" is very real people. Although there were no true eyewitnesses, everyone in our neighborhood indirectly felt they knew who killed Wilbert, but would rather die a cruel death themselves before notifying any branch of law enforcement. Snitching is a state of mind that comes with the despair of the streets, and yet it simply is not tolerated there.

While the chattering continued and the neighborhood proceeded with watching Greg from the corner of their eyes, I was home doing homework. My cousin Shawn had forgotten what homework was. He was too busy hanging out with Etton's two younger cousins, Skippy and Devon. They were two drug dealers Etton brought around to get a piece of his new rising pie, one which was also vastly spreading throughout the entire city. McCabe Avenue used to be a market primarily dealing in marijuana during the late- 70's, although cocaine was already a theme here during the 60's, during a totally different regime. By the early 80's, only Benny was able to make the transition from weed to heroin on McCabe. By the time he had staked his claim and expanded his business, several other dealers began to surface and take more risks in becoming "heavyweights" or kingpins in their own right. The most popular drug of choice? Cocaine. This time in the hands of younger, more volatile individuals.

As the drug market began to negatively blossom on McCabe, my cousin Shawn and I grew further apart. He became very interested in some of the activities most of the older guys took part in. He was really becoming more impressed with the high-priced sneakers and the thick gold chains, than he had been in prior years. He now liked the smell of constant weed smoke and the company of females three to four years his senior. Suddenly, the idea of playing sports and performing above-average in the classroom had no true meaning with my cousin. However, what we once had was not totally lost. We still had our occasional, heartfelt one-on-one talks. The love was certainly still evident when he pulled himself away from the others; not very often. I believe he just had a void he needed filled. The $50 bills granddad would try to secretly slide Shawn were no longer enough. Grandpop would always give my cousin and my sister more money than he gave me. Every time my grandfather laid eyes on me, he saw my dad, the "spit and image" or "spitting image" of the man who mistreated and recklessly caused the death of his first-born daughter. I was never given $50 to get sick of.

Shawn's affiliation with the older guys soon began to raise eyebrows throughout our household. Grandma really began to feel uncertain about Shawn's future, although all of ours seemed a bit uncertain. I actually felt Shawn was fine. The hood had it right in their assessment of him. Shawn was a tough kid, a born "street soldier," or a leader from depressed circumstances. Immediately, he really never feared nothing or no one. He honestly believed, in the midst of all of those older hustlers and hard cases, that he was the coolest and the toughest. He told me he honestly felt he could win a "one-on-one" fight against anyone on McCabe Avenue. All of the guys could see this confidence in him. That's where the unity came from. They loved him. So, did I. So much so, I too would hang out at Skippy's pad on occasion. I felt I was not ready to exist without my big cousin. Especially knowing in a matter of months, I too would be entering high school. However, nothing seemed for certain anymore. So eventually, I would end right back up in my room, in solitary. I soon began writing again just to clear my head. Basketball helped as well, but all I really could do for true peace at this time was pray. I did this every night before sleeping. I could feel drastic negative changes taking place all around me. Still, I did the best I could do to adapt a positive outlook on everything.

At thirteen, I got the message that growing up in the city was not going to be very easy. Eventually, all things must change, and in 1985 and 1986, changes were rapidly passing through a place we all once felt great about.

"Nothing stays the same," they say. Home was now a place where you simply didn't really know what kind of negative situation would surface or unfold next; you just knew one would.

Halfway through the school year, I really began to feel good about my chances of being promoted to high school. It was a bittersweet scenario considering Tee's mom was adamant about moving away. She was set on her son attending the prestigious Dunbar High School, instead of Northern High School; our district's appointed school. Dunbar was easily the best scholar-athlete school in the city, and one of the best in the country. Tee's desire to play football was to be taken seriously. I really enjoyed the sport of basketball, yet my confidence level was not parallel to Tee's passion to play football. While we were all set on attending Northern High, a much better school in Dunbar made greater sense to he and his mom. Most of the best athletic talent the city had to offer was produced from Dunbar High. At this time, I hardly ever thought about competing against these guys on the basketball court. They were simply much better players.

This realization did not deter me from practicing and striving to be a better ball player. I never took the sport of basketball too seriously to lose sleep over, but I knew, sooner or later, I would have to compete with the better players. Even if these games were just for fun and bragging rights. As the 1985 school-year came to a close, my basketball talents would elevate, and so would my persistence with the females. I had reached Kima progressively despite her having a boyfriend. She always seemed to want to share her problems with me for extended periods, only to bail out of these conversations just as my interest grew. Still, I felt like we were making good progress. Her boyfriend ignored her emotions more than she could stand. However, she and I would lose contact before the school year would end. Soon afterwards, there were talks circulating around Winston Middle that Kima was supposedly pregnant, and was headed to a school in east Baltimore for pregnant teens. To make matters even more complicated for Kima, it was stated the unborn child she carried did not even belong to her current boyfriend.

Disturbing news about Kima bothered me, but not enough to affect my excitement about the upcoming summer. I was more concerned with playing basketball, writing more, and attending high school. My sister was twice as excited about the summertime, and her school career officially being over. She was scheduled to graduate in a matter of days. She also had another reason to be very excited and anxious. Once my sister graduated high school, she would immediately have access to over $25,000. My mom had set up a trust fund for my sister and I to receive, but only upon the completion of high school.

My family never shared this information with me until my sister was up for this money. Luckily for me, I did not fail a host of times or get expelled. Gina's enthusiasm, of course, would now be seen all over her face. Sometimes she would harmlessly take a minute to remind Shawn and I that she was going to have this money very soon. "Don't worry O, in four more years, you'll have some too." I never really thought about money much during this time. It hardly occurred to me at the time; in four years, I would immediately be entitled to over $40,000 cash. This was significantly more than my sister Gina had access to considering time and interest. Talks of money began to circulate throughout the household, just as more confusion began to materialize out in the streets. The weekend before school had ended there was a breakout of violence between the guys of McCabe Avenue and the rival crew from Old York Road. The incident occurred at Dewees Recreational Center. There were several reports of women also fighting and being stabbed and beaten during this brawl. The party was to celebrate graduation and the beginning of summer. All this managed to accomplish was getting both camps going, creating more of an explosive atmosphere for the new summer, and for down the road.

While my sister and her friends were running from knife-wheeling maniacs at a party, Evan and I were headed for a special treat from a local great. Evan somehow pulled the necessary strings to grant us the opportunity to play on a Division 1 collegiate basketball court. We were invited to play pick-up basketball for a few hours at Towson State University in Baltimore County. The university is located about fifteen minutes on York Road, north of McCabe Avenue. To make the situation even more exciting, we were going to be joined by David Wingate (NBA career from 1986-2001). David was a childhood friend of Freddy's, and was now a player for the NBA. David was enjoying life in the big times as a member of the Philadelphia 76ers. At thirteen years of age this was certainly a big deal for me. This chance of a lifetime had easily surpassed any baseball game, or seeing Jim Palmer passing by in his sports car. I'd witnessed the great pitcher a few times in the past with my dad. As my neighborhood was redefining the term turmoil, I was knocking down shot after shot with a local legend. David, by the way, went through the entire night only missing one or two shots in no less than five pick-up games.

David gave us all a firsthand look on just how talented one must be to make it to, or to become a great player in this prestigious league. David was rarely acknowledged for his offensive abilities on the pro level, but we saw the greatness he possessed. He allowed us to see through him, just how great guys like Michael Jordan and Magic Johnson really were. It also showed me I was not as bad a player as I thought originally. Playing with Dave made the game much easier. No one let their egos get in the way. What's the use, right? If we did this, we still would not be in the great position he was in. That night after shaking David's hand, I left Towson State a better, more confident player and person. To see a guy from the area make it to the pros was refreshing, especially considering how our neighborhood was falling apart at the seams. Unfortunately, I was still not able to see the possibility to follow in David's footsteps athletically. I got a late start playing the sport of basketball. Still, there were things to look forward to. I was almost as good as Evan, I was a decent student in school, and I had over $40,000 on the way. No one brought these good attributes to my attention, and I never really had the know-how to put it all together, alone, at thirteen. This way of living and thinking only allowed me to live a mediocre and pathless existence. I had no clue as to what I wanted to do with my life or what my next move would be to improve my life as high school approached. This question that many were asked never really came my way. I was relieved, because I did not have any answers to it. Despite the money I had coming, I was simply one of many city children, in a bad place, with no direction whatsoever.

The Summer of 1986 started similar to the previous two. Everyone seemed to be consumed with wearing their finest linens and chasing the pretty girls around all day. The drug trafficking was growing by the minute, and so were the pockets of many of the younger guys on the block. Benny still spearheaded the onslaught on how much heroin circulated in the area. The more money that poured through the hood, the more fights and patrol cars followed. My bedroom window soon would be synonymous with good seats on fight night. I would often get to see plenty of fist fights. "Oh! Ouch! Damn! He's about to get knocked out! He's out cold!" I would whisper these phrases to myself in the dark. I was usually alone when this took place. My cousin would have an even better seat. He would still be outside, near the action, despite his mother's wishes or instructions. Shawn and I were still close, but nothing like we were as kids. We made strides and plans to find the partnership we once had, but it was very difficult to see them through. I felt Shawn needed me in a sense. I was going to come into some money in a few years, which I felt could help us both possibly grow positively. He was struggling to stay out of trouble at home, and the same held true in school before it ended for the year. Shawn was participating in smoking marijuana with the older guys, and for the very first time, he failed a grade. As you may have imagined, he was not too thrilled with the realization of us sharing the same grade. My cousin was certainly heading down the wrong path, yet I still felt he was strong and smart enough to pull himself together. I never worried about Shawn at all until our grandmother made it her duty to remind us all regularly, "God does not like the ugly."

More emotionally mixed moments came and went in and outside of 731's front door. Made plans for our first King's Dominion trip produced excitement, while talks of my aunt Marie, Montell, Shawn, and his now, five-year old sister Monica or "Monnie," we all called her, moving dimmed the mood. I kind of understood their decision to move from my aunt's prospective. As Monnie grew, there simply was not enough room for the four of them on McCabe Avenue. Speculations of my aunt being pregnant again added on to this decision. It all just felt weird to me because Shawn and I had been living together since my mom passed. To me, whenever we were not together or interacting on some level, things just felt wrong. We were the perfect fit for one another. Leaders in our own right, yet, whatever he was, I was not, and vice-versa, and we both knew it.

Walking through the neighborhood in 1986 was far different than in 1981 or 1982. House basement parties with colorful light bulbs were losing ground to nightclubs like Godfrey's, and another ironically named, Odell's. Music blasting from porches was still evident. However, the content had changed from, "One of Those Nights" by Billy Ocean, or Michael Jackson's "Don't Stop Til You Get Enough," to "Rock the Bells," by LL Cool J or "It Takes Two," by Rob Base, or any song by Run- DMC.

McCabe Avenue was now filled with hosts of lost, horny kids; myself included, with nowhere to go and no dreams to follow.

As my 14th birthday approached, I received some good news when we all were informed my cousin and family would only be moving around the corner; not even five minutes away on foot. I don't know what it was with our family and this neighborhood. Every one of our friends, including Evan and his parents spoke on soon making a move, yet we never seemed to entertain relocating. Grandma could certainly feel the change taking place there, but the need or desire to stay put stayed the same. Shawn and I entertained a move, but we never panicked. We were too busy looking forward to returning to school. Shawn promised to return to his proper grade, despite his current lack of focus. My focus was not where it needed to be as well. I wanted to return to school to be around the pretty girls more than I wanted to succeed. We both were looking forward to the summer and our first trip to King's Dominion. Still, in the midst of it all, I periodically had my sights and mind totally locked in on the $40,000 I had coming in the Summer of 1990.

My sister and Freddy decided to treat Shawn and I to King's Dominion amusement park for the first time ever. We were excited to be taking a long drive away from the neighborhood. Shawn and I had recently talked in his new room about one day getting away from places like McCabe Avenue, and living in LA or in a New York City suburb. We still were clueless about how we would make it there. We periodically would take walks on the outskirts of the hood, just to talk and try to envision a decent future. It was hard to say these talks were about following passions. I believed we both wanted a good life, yet we could never come up with any professional ideas to achieve this way of living for ourselves. The closest we would come would be references to professional athletes. We really did not desire in our hearts to be as such. We were two teens who were good at sports; basketball for me, and in Shawn's case, football, but with the school we were attending and the late starts in these sports, we knew this was not to be for our lives. We were not the inner-city kids who had the backing or the folks in place who would make sure we participated in activities surrounding our interests. That was not our upbringing.

At the fun park, one may have thought differently. I made every shot I took on the basketball games played there to win souvenirs. An imitation sport's magazine photo Shawn and I took for the cover was quite convincing to the eyes as well. We actually appeared to be professionals on the photograph. I held the "round ball" as if I were the best player ever, while he tightly cradled the pigskin, characterizing a #1 leading rusher for a first-place team in the NFL. It was clear on this day we were still a two-man team. We needed each other more than we realized. King's Dominion was more than a fun-filled beautiful afternoon at a park. This day brought Shawn and I closer together again. There would be another interesting situation which would truly display our unconditional love for one another.

# Chapter 5

# TEN DAYS

McCabe Avenue quietly stumbled through another summer and fall on the heels of Wilbert's death. In the midst of the loss of a brother, a blessing emerged; confirmation of an addition to our family. My aunt Marie was, in fact, pregnant; due to have a beautiful baby boy. Shawn would soon have a little brother. News of the pregnancy lifted spirits, but the energy outdoors were worsening. In 1986, evidence of the hostility between my neighborhood and the Old York Road hood had begun to constantly surface. Altercations breaking out at the local nightclubs now seemed like a once-a-week occurrence. My sister Gina still shared her periodic horror stories on the situation. She spoke on the "beef" or feud as if she were a news reporter following an unfolding, increasingly negative situation. I was too busy wondering who was going to become my next best friend other than Tee or my cousin. As the 1986-87 school year got underway, for the first time I would be attending without my good friend Tee. His mom kept her word, and although Tee was still a resident on McCabe, he began his first day of school at Dunbar High. Still, I was excited to finally be in high school. I was even more tickled I had caught up to Shawn, who had flunked the previous year.

High school would symbolize a period of growth for my peers and I. It was also an era where unpredictable circumstances began to surface more often than not. High school and all that it entails, was just the beginning of where my life was going and how fast. As spring break rolled around, we all believed we were young men who better understood what living in the ghetto was all about. Whatever lessons were missed, I would be forced to process them during the next ten days.

Spring Break of 1987 came pretty quickly compared to the days of middle school. I guess spending multiple hours with your head on a swivel, checking out the females, helped time pass by faster. Unfortunately, I was enjoying the 9th grade a little too much. My grades quickly slipped to all-time lows. All I had on the brain was females. The older I became, the more I fell for more and more girls. I never really liked the idea of seeing more than one girl at a time, but I just could not help myself. I simply loved being around pretty young ladies. I've always tried to be in an exclusive relationship. It had taken me all of middle school to get close to Kima, but I finally persevered. I was surprised, out of the clear blue, by a phone call from Kima, yet I never gave her our home number. We talked one late afternoon. She went into detail about why and how she was less than two months away from conceiving her first child. Most of the information she provided I already knew from other sources. Although much of the info was deflating, I still wanted to show compassion and offer support to the expecting young, mom-to-be. Even back then, I had no problems with moral victories from time to time.

Despite the birth of an unexpected child, Kima and I were still able to grow very close. She had a beautiful baby girl named Shera. The presence of a baby altered nothing in reference to our union. It actually helped. It helped me understand motherhood more while showing Kima that she was not alone. I did all I could to make Kima's new life more comfortable. I would usually walk about five miles to her house to help her out with anything she needed. I would walk back home after sundown. I even picked up a summer job to help us out a bit more. I knew I truly cared for Kima once I found myself selling shoes at "PIC N' PAY," a shoe retailer known in the streets for mediocre quality products. I never really thought about working for a living before this situation. Nor did I ever imagine developing a relationship with a small child. There was just something about the innocence of this child that affected me early on. The feeling to care for a harmless child was simply too irresistible for me to look pass.

I love kids; unfortunately for Kima, I loved girls even more. High school, females, and the desire to be fly conflicted with my attempts to be a normal, hardworking, teen stepdad. After a while, there was no longer a need to pocket baby shoes from my job. I was not a noted thief, but I did impulsively grab a few pairs of baby shoes over a four-month period.

I know; stupid! The quiet and too advanced intimate nights were now interrupted by too many pick-up games of basketball, and my constant roaming eyes. My dad, who still came to visit on occasion, would even disrupt my peaceful situation. He once offended me one evening as he dropped in on Kima and I while we were watching television. I was shocked my dad was in our house, let alone upstairs. Perhaps the most troubling news was being able to be alone in my bedroom with Kima at 14 years of age. I excitedly introduced my dad to Kima, and immediately after waving to her with a fake smile, he pulled me aside in the hallway. I'll never forget the words he spoke to me. After staring at me like I was crazy, my dad asked, "Is she the only one?" "Yeah," I replied in disbelief. "What?" he shouted before instantly lowering his tone. "Son," followed by a giggle. "Look, you're never supposed to have just one girl, NEVER!" I was so stunned by my dad's comment; I can't even recall the rest of our conversation. After a while, I simply left my dad in the hallway, embarrassingly closing the door in his face. I truly believe those words stuck with me over the years. I tried hard in every union I was involved in, but this may have helped me form excuses to pry myself away from any fairly good relationship. Perhaps I still should have had sense enough to think with the appropriate body part. That may have helped here as well. Maybe then, I would have been able to see some of the other troubles ahead.

Another form of trouble would slowly materialize; disguised perfectly on one of the most anticipated nights McCabe Avenue had seen in previous years. The Easter holiday was supposed to be a time to get away from school work, get closer to the pretty girls, and enjoy the nicer weather. It was also the year where our city was fortunate enough to host a concert starring the hottest hip-hop group at the time; Run-DMC. The rap trio from Hollis Queens, New York, had a tremendous impact or influence on our city and neighborhood. Although there were never any images of the group indulging in illicit activities, their hardcore energy gave the guys in the area a sense of power, respect, rebellion, and a feel of confidence, even arrogance. We all could identify with the group. They were so hot they became the representatives or the ambassadors for the forgotten people of our ghetto.

Run-DMC, during this time, was hotter than Michael Jackson in the hood, because they were actually from a tough city. We were thrilled the Hollis Queens, New York super duo were their way to our town. We knew right away we would not miss out on this event for the world. Myself, along with Shawn, Evan, his sister Dena, Tee, and two or three others from the block, all decided to go to the concert. Troy was not going to attend. He too struggled in high school, and according to Tee, was ready to dropout. Like my cousin Shawn, he also began to hang around suspicious guys in the streets, but they were from another part of town. My sister Gina was nice enough to purchase tickets for Shawn and I. Now all we needed was our best outfits, $20 or $30 to spend, and roundtrip bus fare.

Instead of searching for the true meaning of the Easter holiday, we were preparing to go enjoy a rap concert. Growing up, we were never taught in detail, the true meaning of holidays like Easter, Thanksgiving, nor Christmas. I used common sense to know they all were affiliated with God in some great way or another, but the approach to teaching lessons to us kids was overshadowed by negativity, and a lack of focus by our older relatives. So instead of learning more about the Spirit, we were all getting dressed in new clothing to head downtown to Baltimore's Civic Center (1961-1986) (Also named 1stMariner Arena from 2003-2013). Today the establishment is named the CFG (Citizens Financial Group) Bank Arena. Everyone was scheduled to meet Shawn and I at 731. We all were excited about the concert, and with having the opportunity to ride the MTA [Mass Transit Administration] bus together for something other than school. To be able to ride the bus at night with the adults was a big thing for us back then. After we all got dressed in our best garments for the occasion, I kissed my grandma goodbye, and we all headed towards York Road to the #8 bus stop, which was our straight shot to Downtown B'MORE.

During the walk up McCabe towards the bus stop struck me as odd; the older guys did not seem interested in attending this huge event. Devon and Skippy never thought of going to the concert, and they actually thought they were the members of the rap group. It just seemed strange none of the older guys cared to take part in going to the concert. No one noticed this but me. Everyone else was too busy with their heads down, admiring their own new foot gear. New sneakers were huge for a ghetto teen's confidence during the 80's. Gold chains were as well. I loved receiving new sneakers as a teen. Thanks to Mama and my dad, I managed to have over thirty pairs of nice tennis shoes over a short span. Still, this did not stop me from hunting down the hottest shoe, other than an Air Jordan, to wear to the concert. My attire for this event was a royal-blue Russell sweatsuit with pockets, and a pair of royal-blue, orange and white, Patrick Ewing promoted Adidas. I figured, it's Run-DMC; it's a New York thing, so let me wear Knicks colors and have a good time. Grandma earlier refused to purchase the $120 shoes, but my dad didn't hesitate. When it came to providing wants, my dad was a specialist. He came through for me more times than not, financially. It felt good to be the only kid on the block with these shoes. It is crazy how something as small as a pair of shoes can create so much attention. This was what I experienced during the entire trip downtown to Baltimore Street where the venue is located.

Stepping out of the bus and onto Baltimore Street was surreal; it was like entering another planet on that evening. There were hundreds of people parading throughout, trying to enjoy the scenery filled with pretty cars and even prettier girls. Others were trying desperately to enter the arena to solidify their seats by beating the rush; folks were hoping not to miss any of the show. It was clear people were coming from all over the region. The entire east coast had landed in the heart of Baltimore City, and there we were; several little teens from a relatively unknown street in a small neighborhood.

Suddenly we found ourselves standing on a corner in the midst of droves of patrons. We were lost puppies, abandoned by the street guys who decided to stay back and take advantage of Baltimore City Police to watch over the largest rap concert the city had ever seen. With a bit of a struggle, we would finally reach our seats. Shawn and I, along with Tee, sat side by side while the others dispersed out to other nearby sections of the arena. We had pretty good seats, thanks to my sister's quick swipe of her new credit card. The others were not as prompt and were forced to sit upwards a bit in the stands. Nevertheless, we were in the best place to be on that warm spring night. The excitement over my first ever attended concert was all I thought it would be. The sweaty palms, the increased heart rate, or the unbelievable adrenaline rush were all in effect as the host introduced the trio. We all were in a world of fantasy as the words, "Now DJ Run's my name!" echoed throughout the facility as the group appeared. This was a dream come true for all of us, but I would soon become a participant to one of life's unexpected nightmares.

Run-DMC had Baltimore City in its palms. Fans were screaming and jumping about, repeating every word of the group's many hit songs. I was blown away by the power of this form of self-expression, hip-hop. I was amazed how freedom of speech can influence so many different people, in so many different ways. As the rap group celebrated and cemented the emergence and the significance of the culture, I was trying to picture myself one day making a similar impact. Not as a rapper, but as someone with similar significance; someone special.

The extraordinary show would come to an end around midnight, but outside intense energy carried over out into the streets. The commitment made before the concert was met. We all had made previous plans to reunite across the street, on the corner of Baltimore and Howard Streets after the show. From there, we planned to head back northbound on the #8 bus or the #36, which again, were the buses we rode to and from school during the week. Whatever one was to come first, we were going to take. Despite the party-like atmosphere outside, none of us were too interested in hanging around for long afterwards. It was clear to us from the start; most of the individuals prancing about in the streets after the show were much older than any of us. The uncomfortable feeling of displacement lived in all of us on this evening. We were like fish out of water, and the confirmation of this was more than we ever could have imagined.

As we all waited patiently for the bus to arrive, we observed a group of males and females frantically running in different directions. There were plenty of screams coming from the girls. These were not the shouts of approval produced by the hit song, "King of Rock" thirty minutes prior. Coming from a neighborhood where violence was climbing allowed us all to stand and watch instead of distancing ourselves from the possible disturbance. Minutes later, it was clear to see how this confusion took place. There appeared to be a large group of young black males stirring up trouble for those who came to celebrate or enjoy a growth in the hip-hop culture. In the city, it's not unusual for packs of people to hang around for long periods after a concert or major party.

In most towns, parties take place inside and outside of the venue. Those who hang around outside were probably never present during the actual event. To most, after the event was actually better than the event itself. These were the type of individuals we observed after the concert had ended. These teens certainly were not dressed in any newer clothing. They didn't appear to have haircuts, and right away, their facial expressions shunned any hopes of a peaceful encounter. They were strictly there to cause trouble. I could feel the negativity mounting as the group of at least twenty males made their way over to where we were. With no bus in sight, a weird quietness dominated our entire group. Their noisy group fixed its eyes on us, conjoining together in a larger mass with each step toward our direction. They quickly crossed the street with something wicked clearly in mind. Whatever that was, we quickly understood it was not an invite to a break-dancing challenge. That vibe was over with! Forty-five minutes after one of the best times of our lives, my friends and I were face to face with about twenty older guys. Little small guys from McCabe Avenue; meet Murphy Homes Projects.

Murphy Homes Projects was one of the most notorious housing projects in B'MORE city. Every inner-city neighborhood is familiar with its infamous exploits. We never felt we would encounter anyone from there, but on this night, that's exactly what happened. From just a few feet away these orphaned individuals gave us all intense stare-downs. Many of them appeared to be much older guys. They were sizing us all up. With hundreds of onlookers, we stood fast. The focus soon left all of my peers and shifted solely on me. My friends were so quiet I almost forgot they were standing behind me. I knew we were in for trouble from the expression on my cousin's face. Shawn usually welcomed trouble, but this was a lot more than any of us could have imagined. We were clearly outnumbered. Out of all the people downtown on this night, this group of guys managed to shift their focus towards me and my peers. All of this because of a pair of tennis shoes I wore that happened to be promoted by basketball legend, Patrick Ewing. That's right! I was spotted through hundreds of concert-goers because of a simple pair of sneakers.

As the intensity of being approached by dozens of unknowns from the projects mounted, I quickly realized the probability of me fighting my heart out was quite high. At 14, I had only been involved in a few meaningless and brief scuffles. I hardly felt prepared for an all-out fist fight against a flock of older dudes. However, for some strange reason, I was not scared; a little nervous maybe, but not terrified. It was a feeling of knowing what was certainly coming instead of guessing; that calmed me. Considering the large number of guys, running still was my first logical option, but they sort of had us all surrounded. Soon, one guy walked up to me angrily and stated bluntly, "What's up slim?" I stared back but gave no response. "What size shoe you wear?" he asked casually. "Why?" I replied. His expression then worsened. "What the fuck do you mean why nigga?" another guy shouted in anger. "That's right, you heard him chump, why?" Shawn yelled. "Look nigga, y'all already know what time it is," he continued. My frustration grew by the second. "I ain't goin ask you again nigga, what size fuckin shoe you wear?" "I wear a size ten," I replied with rippled eyebrows. It was now very clear. I was in trouble, big trouble.

The lead bully's next words were, "Take em off!" I stood and looked into his eyes while trying to plot my next move. All of my choices were poor, at best. First, I thought to just punch him in his face with as much force as I could, with hopes of scaring the others off, or just run and try and avoid getting jumped all over. I chose the latter. I thought fast, and slowly bent over to give these dudes the illusion of a guy in submission. I wanted these knuckleheads to really think I was going to give them my own shoes and just walk away. I was far from the toughest kid on McCabe, but I could not have lived with myself if I would have fully cooperated with these chumps. As the chattering intensified with Shawn adding words of opposition towards the bullies, I was performing a fake shoe unlacing routine, preparing for my own personal marathon. I knew I was the only one there who understood what I was up to, and that was completely fine with me. So as the commotion persisted above my head, I suddenly dashed out from underneath the gathering. "What the fuck!" I heard as I breezed passed everyone. One second later, I was already in full stride.

I ran down Baltimore Street as fast as I could. I was running so fast I could not see any onlookers clearly. Everything was a blur. The more I ran, the more I feared getting caught. Guys were hot on my trail, but I controlled a commanding lead. I was worried about my cousin as I ran. I was hoping I could draw the entire crowd of guys with me, eliminating the possibility of my friends having to fight over a pair of shoes I wore. It's crazy how there were no cops anywhere in the midst of this, despite the huge event which had just let out. Go figure!

As I continued to run, my lead suddenly got smaller, and my plan would prove to be short-lived. Although I had a slight chance at getting away, I did not. I learned at this very moment, I was living in an entire town where violence and despair was more commonplace than ever, even at times embraced. I may have been ahead of the initial crew of guys, but there were other people there whom actually wanted to see these guys catch up to me. These anonymous individuals decided to try and grab me as I quickly approached them. This slowed my efforts significantly. Now you had a very nervous teen trying to run from a group of older dudes, while simultaneously knifing through countless others. It's a crazy feeling to look behind and see so many angry people advancing quickly, all with intentions set on hurting you, badly.

Tired and now quite nervous, I stopped and began to swing at the closest guy. The onslaught quickly swallowed my punches as I found myself quickly on the ground covered up. Suddenly, I was the character, "Kleon," the leader of "The Warriors," the gang and fictional motion picture about a group of guys from where else, Coney Island, New York. Like I said, this night had New York City written all over it. These kids were using my body to create tunes which could only come from a great DJ like the late Grand Master Jay. As I made attempts to sneak in an occasional kick, I could feel the guys grabbing at my ankles. They were attempting to pull off "my Adidas." The more they tugged away at my feet, the more I tried to get up. I soon sprung up, not seeing where I was or who was assaulting me, swinging once again. I quickly found myself back on the ground, rolling about in some construction crew's unused gravel. I sprung up again and again, now with the heel of my foot smashing down on the back of one sneaker. As I was picked up off the ground again, I landed hard and lost my left shoe. I balled up again, for what seemed like the thousandth time. The kicks and rib shots continued and the tugs were now at my right foot. These idiots were one shoe away for completing their senseless mission. I was being beaten for so long, I almost became comfortable with it. All I could do at this point was attempt to get in one good shot. I hopped up once more, balled my fist closed as tightly as I could, temporarily peeped upwards, aimed and punched with all that was in me, at a pair of crusty lips.

With the lack of punching experience, the pain I felt from the clean punch I landed was far more excruciating than any blow I suffered during this attack. "Ahhhhhh!" I heard this as I was able to land a single forceful blow to the mouth of one of my assailants. Seconds later, my other shoe was off of my foot, and I was down again. I knew my punch had made an impact because the beating intensified and frantically continued. Being sure to cover my head, I grew tired of getting up, so I made my body out of a "human ball" and rode out the rest of the beating. The punches continued for a minute or two longer before I could hear sirens in the backdrop. The closer the sirens came, the fewer punches I felt. Minutes later, I was watching the backsides of at least fifteen guys running away, towards Light Street; a cross street off of Baltimore Street. Police arrived from all angles, but not directly to where I was picking myself up from. They were apparently called to the area to simply break up the crowds of lingering bystanders. I could have been knocked out or in the gravel dead, and these officers would have still taken some time to even notice me.

I was a bit dazed and embarrassed, but surprisingly, not seriously hurt. I only had one sign of bloodshed and that was on my right knuckles from the single clean blow I had landed. Although I was alright physically, I still had trouble grasping the entire ordeal. I believe a bit of shock had set inside of me. I made it to my bare feet and began to advance towards the many police cars I observed at the opposite corner. The beating may have been over, but a sad reality was just beginning.

I observed my surroundings as I advanced quickly to get some form of assistance. I took a quick look behind me only to see a mangled, single Adidas shoe on its side. I left it sitting right there. I was so embarrassed at this time; I could hardly even think straight. I felt as if I could have passed out before reaching the police. It's not common for a young teen to find himself smack in the middle of downtown Baltimore at night, barefoot. All of my other feelings until this point had an excuse. If I were sad or hurt in the past, it may have been the direct result of a death in the family to a distant relative or an illness. Even a severely sprained ankle gives you an excuse for pain or suffering. This was simply too hard to fathom. I didn't understand what was taking place, or why? Why me?

This concert evening ended up becoming one of the longest nights of my life. The police officers were just as bad as the guys I received the beaten from. They looked at me like I was crazy when I approached them. I could already read in their mannerisms; they labeled me as a corporate in the confusion that had taken place on this night. I do understand their positions with having a lack of knowledge, but this still should not come with rude assumptions. They offered no assistance, no ride, nor any shoes for my feet. They did not even ask me any questions. They made me feel as uncomfortable as walking the streets barefoot.

As I made my way back towards where I originally took off from, I could hear folks snickering or laughing. Many people made fun of me with humorous gestures. Onlookers and neighborhood funnymen simply used me as a comedic highlight reel for their evening. As I walked up Baltimore Street, I was the bud of every joke and wise crack the audiences had to offer. I had just gotten beaten up and I was barefoot! I pulled myself together enough to focus on the well being of my friends. They all had made it back to where the mess had started. Everyone was physically alright and that was most important. We almost appeared the same as before. The pricey sneakers were the only thing missing. This was a tough night for me to handle. In the hood, situations like this helped the streets to ultimately create the phrase, "getting the brakes beat off of you."

The embarrassment I endured from start to finish continued as my friends were all gazing at my feet in amazement. The look was actually similar to the look they all gave when they first observed the new Adidas. This time there was only partially white tube socks on display. Only Shawn seemed concentrated on my emotional state. He was furious. He quickly pulled me to the side while holding the right side of his face, nursing his slightly injured right eye. "O, those bastards all ran away, all of them," he shared in anger in reference to our peers. "They whipped my ass too, but I did ok," he said. Shawn wore a pair of $45 Shell-Head Adidas to the concert. That was likely the most common shoe worn there on that evening. Hell, even Run DMC themselves had on these sneakers. "O, they ran for dear life man." "They're not our friends," he followed. "I don't want cowards as friends," he offered as he used his shirt to dab his small wound. "Man, I ran too," I replied in their defense. "Yeah, but that shit was different," he emphasized. "They were going to bank you regardless O. So, you tried to do the smart thing," Shawn reassured. "They broke out on us though," he repeated in frustration. "I tried man, it was just too many of them fuck as cousin," I expressed while shaking my head in disappointment. Keep in mind, I was barely a teen. "I know you tried, I know O," he said with a slight smile while patting my left shoulder. "Let's get the hell out of here O," Shawn instructed. We all left the chaotic scene together, but Shawn had little desire to converse with the others along the way.

Our peers all carried the guilty look, but we knew if it all somehow happened again, they would probably pull off a repeat performance. However, I was not upset with anyone. I believe things would not have turned out differently if they would have helped. Shawn did not care, he just wanted them to try; he was even mad with the females. I've always tried to be a realist. Things will happen to us all, some good, some bad; that's just life.

We soon managed to get on the #36 bus downtown. I wanted to take this particular bus because it runs in the same direction as the #8, but on a scenic route, using multiple secondary roads. This would allow me to exit and get to McCabe Avenue virtually undetected without any shoes on. After hiding my feet by sitting beside my cousin near the window, we quickly exited the bus and made our way home. I've never wanted to get to my bedroom so badly in my entire life. I had more than thirty pairs of new sneakers, all lined up around the walls in my room, yet I was walking past my old middle school, barefoot. I pulled myself together enough to realize this accident was simply indicative of how our world and communities were turning. After taking a little time to consider a few of the recent incidents on the block, my situation did not seem too far-fetched. This bothered me in more than one way, but I dealt with it and moved on by the time I arrived on McCabe. I guess it was simply my turn to go through something like this.

As we drew closer to home, guys and females began to branch off, one by one, without ever saying good-bye. They all knew Shawn was very upset with them. Saying anything could have led to another fight. Shawn stayed close to my right, blocking everyone's view of me. "Go put your shoes on O, and come back out," Shawn stated in a low tone. "Alright, cool," I replied as I dashed in the house faster than I ran from those cowards. I returned home to my room and immediately dropped to my knees to give thanks; I immediately began to pray.

I was young and not very sure of what I wanted to become in life, but I was not too young or naive to know that there is a God, and that HE is always good. I immediately got down on my knees and thanked God for allowing me to make it back home. I guess I could have thrown a "pity-party" or whined and continuously asked God why, but I wanted to show appreciation for still being alive and well. From my bedroom window, I could already hear Shawn explaining to the entire neighborhood, everything that took place. I finished up my quick prayer, put on a pair of my new FILA sneakers, and sat on the end of my bed for a minute. I stared out into space for a second, then, surprisingly, I suddenly fell into a very loud laughter. I just felt a need to laugh. After I prayed, I realized; because this mess just happened to me, did not make it any less humorous. No one was seriously hurt, so after a little while, I simply found it all very funny.

While trying to control my laughter over the not-so-funny incident, the words, "Boy, what are you up there doing?" came from my grandma from downstairs. "Nothing ma," I replied, now almost in tears. It was Mama who told me, "Always be willing to take what you dish out, no matter what it is." Making fun of people can be funny, brutal or insensitive, all at the same time. She told me to always be aware of this before you decide to pick on someone else. "Don't ever leave yourself out of any equation," she would say. "This is what will give you humility and character; looking at yourself first." I headed back outside without ever telling my grandma a thing about the wicked situation. Mama did not ask to see my sneakers. She never really paid attention to them from the start, because she did not pay for them. I viewed it all as what it was; an ass whipping, a wake-up call, and a lesson. It depends on how deep one thinks. I reentered the block, leaving all of the embarrassment behind. Everyone was looking down at my feet to see if the new shoes were really gone; they were. After standing outside listening to the conversations and reading everyone's body language, I realized there was more to be concerned with than a pair of sneakers and lopsided scuffle downtown.

I truly appreciated the gestures of sympathy and concern from the guys, but I noticed something far more important. I was wondering why so many other people were holding on to this, yet I was already passed it. "Why don't I care very much?" I thought. My cousin was feeding off of the negative energy the older guys expressed. I heard every line from, "We should go bring those niggas a move," to "I need to fuck somebody up anyway," to "Let me know what y'all want to do." This line was uttered by Benny as he stayed concentrated on his turn at rolling the dice. I sat back and just observed everyone. Here we had a street full of young men, ready for war, but for no real cause. The love was real though. Regardless of how displaced it was, the older guys loved us younger kids. They cared if we went to school. They also got on us if we did something our parents were not pleased with. They truly loved us all to the best of their ability.

During this era, we just didn't get a thrashing at home when we went too far, we would also receive one from the hustlers if the news of our wrongdoings reached them. Love is the greatest emotion or presence in the world, in my estimation. Yet, when there's a lack of control of these emotions, love can also become a recipe for destruction. Just like money; loving emotions can be a gift or a curse depending on one's mindset. These instabilities were all materializing in my once, next-to-perfect neighborhood. There was too much love for all of the wrong things. The ten days of spring break came and went as fast as my Patrick Ewing sneakers had. In such a small amount of time, I learned so many of life's most valuable lessons. A new era of personnel was still constantly allowed to move onto the block. Despite the love, overall, it seemed as if everyone's way of thinking became more and more complicated or negative. Nearly every adult over age 20 in my neighborhood were dealing drugs, or using or abusing drugs and alcohol. Even inside of my own household the effects of alcohol began to make a negative impact. Shawn's affiliation with the older guys still alarmed our grandma. However, he did manage to line himself up to be promoted into his proper grade if he followed certain procedures. Life in our hood was uncertain at best. More turmoil and trouble often seemed easy to come by. McCabe Avenue was trying desperately to hold on to the little peace and genuine love left from the years past. After the break, I returned back to school with a new outlook on life. I realized we all would have to grow up a bit more and adjust to change. It was still clear there was a slight chance for restoration or maybe a return to normalcy, but no one, myself included, really felt things would.

# Chapter 6

# WHISKERS ON THE CHIN

J ust as facial hair began to slowly sprout from the faces of my peers and I, the excitement of high school picked up from where it had left off before spring break. Shawn and I somehow found the past partnership we grew up under. It was a great feeling to know we had not outgrown each other. We were back to enjoying our lives as a popular, "one-two punch" in the community. Although Shawn was trying hard to get promoted into his correct grade, we still found time to interact with our new school mates. Unfortunately, girls and basketball were the ideas I placed my focus on at this time. Writing short stories and drawing were now a distant third. This was about the time my cousin and I believed we could pretty much do whatever we felt, whenever we wanted, and not suffer harsh consequences. We were our own parents really. No matter what we were up to, we usually could pull it off without ever being seen or penalized. We didn't have the type of home environment where our parents or guardians would attend the PTA (parent-teacher association) meetings. We took it upon ourselves not to make fools out of our parents by doing just enough not to hang ourselves. This lack of guidance came with lots of freedom, but with a drastically declining neighborhood, and a school full of new pretty girls, things began to get testy for us all.

While Shawn was fighting with his promotional opportunity, I managed to achieve an exciting first accomplishment. I made the cut to play for Northern High School's junior varsity basketball team. The accomplishment caused me to feel excited, sad, nervous, anxious, and embarrassed, all at the same time. I was excited because this confirmed that a few coaches believed I could play ball in an organized setting.

I was not one of those kids who played religiously in the recreational organizations throughout the city. This realization created nervousness and an anxiousness inside of me. The embarrassment came from me being the only guy from a group of four, to strike out on making the varsity team. Evan, Ron, our 8th grade ex-classmate, and Travis, another ex-classmate from Winston Middle, had all made the varsity squad.

The four of us casually came up with a plan to resurrect a suspect basketball program at Northern High. Simultaneously, we really wanted to land our names in the local newspapers as a team with four promising starters. We were not very focused, but we all believed there was potential for us to possibly venture off into Division 1 collegiate programs someday. My elevating skill-set gave me confidence, but this still was not about a dream. This was more of a challenge. It was tough looking at the two separate lists of eligible players on the gymnasium's doors, only to see my name on a separate sheet from the others. I understood the others were involved with the sport much longer than I, but I was hoping the coaches would let me slide through with my peers. Despite my feelings about not making varsity, I still humbly prepared for the lesser squad. Ironically, a week after making the team, I had learned, out of us all, I would be the only guy eligible to play ball at Northern High. Evan, Travis and Ron all found out they were ineligible to play. They all failed for the semester.

I enjoyed moderate success in my debut as a scholar-athlete. The junior varsity squad would get the scrapings or leftovers from the varsity team's crowd, and I still struggled to make the transition from the playground to organized play. Poor decisions, quick fouls, and turnovers usually plagued me during these games. I got better as the year progressed, but I never felt I played my best when it counted. Still, we had a pretty good record. Much better than the team my friends failed to play for. My woes out there on the court gave me more determination to get better. I needed to figure out why I was able to play like Ron Harper on the playground, but like an amateur when the whistle blew. The Northern Vikings junior varsity squad finished second for the season. I averaged a measly 7 points per game, if that. I still enjoyed the experience. None of my family members would ever make it to any of my games, other than Shawn, but I still felt good about my progress on and off of the court. With the way things were turning out on McCabe Avenue, just to be in school made life more worthwhile.

The school-year would soon come to an end with me passing the 9th grade by a decent margin. Shawn also had some good news. By the middle of next year, he would be promoted to his proper grade; the 11th. He was relieved that he would still be able to look down at me from a grade above. Shawn and I were excited to be able to meet lots of new friends during the school year. We had lots of fun flirting with the pretty girls. We got plenty of satisfaction from running behind countless pairs of size 26 or 28 Tale Lord jeans, Calvin Klein, and Guess jeans frequently worn by these cuties. These pants we chased effortlessly were usually worn by the sexiest young ladies Northern had to offer. Jody and Joanna were two of many. Wherever these two beauties were, Shawn and I would not be too far behind. We never had much trouble socializing with these young ladies. The only bit of trouble in it all was the need to know why all of these girls were from the worst neighborhood possible, Old York Road.

Knowing many of our school's bombshells resided in hostile territory placed a wedge between them and us getting to know one another a little better. Tensions were spreading more and more between the two neighborhoods. More fights and more arrests were being connected to the rivalry. Most of them were drug related. Drug related activities now were spearheading the way things operated on McCabe Avenue and throughout Baltimore City. Benny was still running his very lucrative heroin business throughout the city. He called his product "Good and Plenti" or GP. The drug trade and the mentality behind it began to place strain on many of the households in the neighborhood and throughout the city. Mothers began to lose their jobs while fathers began to leave these same mothers alone with the children. Kids began to drop out of school more often, teen pregnancy and diseases increased, and even more people were getting hurt and killed. This was the direct result of the impact of illegal drugs in our town. All of this destruction was simply due to the love for fast money.

Drugs usually came to me as an afterthought. I realized they were a heavy part of our culture; I just didn't allow anything surrounding it to reach me too closely. I guess I had no love for lots of money like so many of the others. I had recently almost gotten killed for a pair of pricey sneakers, and I never cared to speak about the $40,000 plus I had on the way in a little more than two years. I rarely thought about money as a teen. I hardly realized it at the time, but I was already set up pretty good to have a decent start in life. Not being able to recognize it allowed me to follow Shawn and witness what this crazy street life entailed. During this time, it didn't take long for me to see this lifestyle simply was not my cup of tea.

Throughout the summer I would spend time at Devon and Skippy's house with my cousin. I guess I was very comfortable mainly because Shawn was. I sort of felt obligated to join him because he had always been there for me. I knew he loved it there and I wanted him to see, no matter where he was, I would be willing to join him to prove our union or bond could never be broken. This place was home to many situations most parents try to keep their kids away from. Gambling was there. So were the drugs and under-age sex. Artillery was there as well. It was no big deal for me to see pounds of marijuana, ounces of cocaine being packaged for sale, or five or six loaded assault weapons neatly spread across a small child's bed. I saw it all, yet none of it phased me in any way. It never alarmed me, nor did it entice me. I was sure I wanted no part of this lifestyle, yet, I was certainly not afraid to co-exist around it.

Shawn's affiliation with the older street guys was not a major concern for me, but it sure was for our grandmother. She began to speak very adamantly about how she felt in regards to my cousin's lifestyle and the company he kept. She really felt he was headed for self-destruction. I would usually downplay the accusations by reassuring Mama that Shawn was fine, and that he was simply enjoying his summer vacation. Although my tactics would manage to calm her down a bit, it was clear she could see something we all were missing. Grandma despised the idea of selling drugs. Although my uncle Frank took part in this years ago, grandmother was still a stranger to the details about this deadly game. She simply could not grasp the concept of it. It would not be until the turmoil entered 731's front door, grandma would understand further, and begin to really feel a need to panic.

The drug game was victimizing the Govans neighborhood more and more. At every turn there was someone either selling or buying drugs. There would usually be at least one guy on every corner. They may have been pretending to be just hanging out, but they were steadily at work; turning a profit on the souls of the sick. McCabe Avenue's entire landscape was changing. Police sirens were once non-existent. Now, they consumed the tunes coming from the nearly extinct, Good Humor Ice Cream vehicle.

People stopped cutting their hedges and mowing their lawns regularly. The music stopped playing from porch-fronts like they had a few years prior. Yells and screams now dominated the soundtrack of the streets. Guys were jockeying for position to get to addicts first. Instead of music, the block sounded more like the stock exchange. It would not take long for most of the parents in the neighborhood to get seduced. Living with your grandparents, more than likely, would lessen the chances of drugs entering your household. However, the epidemic still managed to touch other members of my immediate family.

While myself, my cousin, and our friends continued to try to enjoy the summer, many of the adults were giving in to the drugs and the street generals who supplied them. There was once a time when we hardly noticed a thing. We were kids simply pretending to be adults ourselves. Shawn and I would periodically steal my sister's car key to go joyriding. Shawn and I would take turns awaiting the perfect opportunity to "borrow" my sister's 1986 Nissan Sentra. Her boyfriend Freddy was not exempt from our mischief either. We stole Freddy's Honda Elite 250 scooter several times. For about two weeks, you could catch us speeding up and down Northern Parkway, a road near our high school, recklessly, with no protective headgear at 1:00 a.m. The growing negativity never interfered with our ability to have fun. It was not until a family member began to struggle, we learned just how real this drug epidemic is.

During the summer, Mama began to notice her youngest daughter's daily routine gradually changed. My aunty worked as a secretary at a multi-purpose center on York Road, just north of our home. Shawn and I would often take walks there if we were unsuccessful in getting money from one or both of our grandparents. By mid-summer, we no longer had this outlet. Before long, my aunt Marie would lose her job, and my grandma began to speculate drugs may have played a role. All Marie would do was sleep during the day. Every so often, I would hear a comment from grandma. "I think she's messing with that shit out there in the street," she'd say with frustration. My aunt's wardrobe had changed from classy business attire, to old shorts and sneakers. Although Marie tried desperately not to disclose any changes, grandma was convinced. She now had negative vibes from both Shawn and his mom. For as much as Mama preached on how we all should live and treat each other, she was experiencing a rude awakening, or a look forward to where our once decent neighborhood was headed. Morals, character, and substance no longer seemed to be very important here. As the 90's approached, all that seemed to matter was money, money, money, money. money.

Although Benny was still very much in control of the drug trade in the area, he did not specialize or concentrate most of his efforts on dealing cocaine. Etton was now handling the movement of the cocaine business on McCabe. Everyone began to notice his come up. Early on, Etton was not seen as one of the guys who stayed up on the trends or fashions as many others were. Now things were much different. He never wore the same outfit twice, and now the "steaks would compliment his beans and rice." He also purchased his very first car; a fully-loaded, 1987 Audi 5000. Etton, Devon, Skippy, and several others were making lots of money alongside Benny and his sidekicks. Knowing I had money coming, allowed me to not pay much attention to how successful all of the dealers were on my block. Shawn, on the other hand, was very interested. Although young, he felt qualified, if not more so, to be where several of the older guys were financially. It would not be until he learned of his mom's struggles that he would become even more confused and desperate.

While women, drugs, money, and cars seemed to be on the minds of everyone, at home my household was literally falling apart at the seams. While rumors would spread throughout our home about Marie and Montell's affiliation with drugs, I noticed even more. My uncle BoBo, a heavy drinker, was experiencing a significant amount of weight loss over the past few months. The 10th year Claim's Adjuster had slipped down to two-hundred-thirty pounds from being over three-hundred pounds, without a diet plan or exercise. He no longer posted the menacing presence he possessed during our younger years. Vodka was beginning to get the better of our uncle. His older brother Frank was not much better. He still was spending the majority of his disability check in liquor stores on beer and wine. This was if he made it there before his money would run out. Grandma usually would give Frank all of his money in cash; $900 monthly from his disability allowance. Frank must have loaned one or two of his friends some money, allowing the entire community of drunks to know when he received his cashed check. Knowing my uncle was mildly disabled, guys would simply walk up to him, ask for large amounts of money, and he would usually comply. In a couple of months, my uncle gave away several hundreds without ever knowing who he gave the money to. Situations like this and others proved my family was falling apart quickly, and so was the house itself.

When we arrived to McCabe Avenue the house was a spacious, clean, four- bedroom home. It was now a dwelling with more than enough problems. The house had bad ceiling leaks, and heating and insulation problems. Our basement was leaking so badly, everyone just pretended as if there was no cellar at all. For us, McCabe Avenue was like a troubled boat, slowly sinking, while floating out into the middle of a sea full of sharks. The windows were old, and we desperately needed new doors. To make matters much worse, our grandfather was not feeling very well. At seventy-four years old, a smoker and a drinker as well, his health slowly began to deteriorate over the summer. During this time, my sister Gina and Freddy were the only relatives who lived with the least amount of stress. They moved out. They were enjoying life, privacy, and comfort in a drug-free environment while shopping every other day. They obviously spotted the neighborhood's downfall early. Things were digressing by the minute, and as we passed the halfway point of the summer, situations surrounding my family would further worsen.

Shawn's affiliation with the older hustlers allowed him to gather more information about his mother's negative activities. He learned through several sources, Montell had been making several purchases of cocaine over the last few months. This news, along with my grandma's remarks, helped my cousin draw the conclusion that Montell was helping, if not solely responsible, for his mother's apparent decline. Shawn grew increasingly frustrated with Montell. He was also extremely embarrassed by the confirmation of his mom actually being a drug addict. We talked about this realization for hours and I could see for the first time, a serious hurt on his face I'd never seen before in previous years. I never remembered an instance where Shawn showed this much emotional pain. His attitude was normally driven by lust, anger or humor. "I'm going to get him O," he sadly stated. "How?" I asked. "I don't know yet. You know he knows some of that karate shit, so I have to plan this shit out," he explained. Montell received a belt for his studies in the martial arts during the earlier stages of his life. Shawn was one who had no issues with confrontation; he embraced it, but he was only 15 years old. Montell was in the prime of his life in his early 30s. However, some sort of confrontation was inevitable. Things would soon unravel quickly as summer's end approached. My cousin Shawn was officially losing control.

Before Shawn set out to get even with his stepdad for his mom's substance abuse issues, he first decided to take a closer look at her peers and the dealers who actually witnessed or dealt with his mom personally. Shawn was so well-liked on McCabe, he managed to get all of the dealers' attention by pleading with them to no longer deal drugs to his mom. This was a far-fetched effort, yet he felt he had their word. His next move was to tag or follow his mom and find out who all of her friends were. Before long, people would observe Shawn fighting grown-ups nearly everyday; male and female addicts were being assaulted by Shawn for using drugs with his mother. He slapped a woman in the face, punched an old man in his eye, and threatened to kill another guy. News of his actions soon got back to my aunt, but he hardly cared. His disappointment in his mom allowed him to ignore her plea for him to calm down. His approach however, would only produce temporary results, but would infuriate our grandma in the process.

After a few weeks of tormenting the neighborhood junkies, Shawn realized just how serious cocaine was. Actually, we both understood drugs like cocaine would not be something that would just go away. Times were turning for sure, and in a last effort attempt to help his mom, Shawn ultimately decided to go to the person he believed was initially responsible for his mom's introduction to this abuse.

Shawn tried to avoid Montell throughout this entire ordeal. He respected his stepdad a lot until this all occurred. Montell had been Shawn's only father since age six. He also was the father of Shawn's younger siblings as well. Physically harming Montell was a last resort for Shawn, yet he felt someone needed to make a strong stand before matters got worse. While I sat at home surprisingly writing small stories for a few days, Shawn was terrorizing the addicts in the neighborhood. He never shared with me specifically what he planned to do to his stepdad. I believed he wanted it to be a secret and not feed more off of an outsider's reaction. Making sense out of these recent situations was no easy task. Mama had been adamant about me distancing myself from Shawn. I usually listened to Mama speak on the matter of Shawn, but I felt this was an unrealistic request. I loved my cousin regardless of his actions. Although we were exact opposites at this point, we still stayed connected. Whether I stayed long was something different. Our grandmother reached a point where she could comfortably say Shawn was quickly headed towards his own death. She felt he would soon get himself into big trouble. "That fuckin boy will not make it, watch!" she yelled while looking out of her favorite window. "God does not like ugly, and he is ugly," she followed. "I seriously doubt if that boy lives to see twenty-one."

The powered certainty in Mama's voice gave me the chills as she spoke on the likelihood of upcoming troubles for my cousin Shawn. In my room, I dropped my pencil and surveyed the neighborhood from the top-story window. I was looking for Shawn. "That damn boy has lost his mind," I heard from downstairs. I knew I needed to speak with Shawn on this issue. Grandma usually knew what she was talking about, in my estimation. I figured, if I could catch up with him in time, I may have been able to calm him down and possibly save his next victim; Montell. I was too late. The two bumped heads inside their home when his mom was out. Shawn made his move on Montell by running up on him from behind and violently pushing him down all of the stairs in their home. I wondered if my cousin had picked this up from me telling him about my days on Aisquith Street. Montell suffered a severely bruised hip and other small injuries. Shawn executed all of these moves for the love of his mom, but in return, he would receive the exact opposite.

By the time Montell returned from Union Memorial Hospital in fair shape, Shawn's actions had the entire family in a panic. With grandma leading the way, the entire family was at odds with my cousin. Grandma had convinced the rest of the family that Shawn actually liked inflicting pain on others. I disagreed, but there was little I could do to change the minds of a house full of adults; one of them being his mother. Shawn retreated to Devon's house after the assault on Montell. He knew the last place anyone would come looking for him would be the home of two heavily-armed, drug dealers. However, I quickly made it over to the house to occasionally check on Shawn's emotional state. After arriving, I immediately realized there was only one idea left I could do to stymie my cousin's downfall; pray.

I had spent time at Skippy's house before, but after leaving my home to go there, I realized there was not much peace left in my hood. Everything seemed shaky. The inclusion of more drugs and outsiders would shift virtually everything from the past. My household used to be a safe haven full of love and fun. During the 70's and 80's we all would sit and eat as a family. Everyone would be sharing jokes and eating crabs while listening to greats like, Jeffrey Osborn and Aretha Franklin. Now, everybody was in an uproar about situations involving drug usage.

Across the street at Skippy's place, I found myself inside of a dealer's bedroom watching my cousin Shawn carry on as if the incident with Montell never took place. Everyone at Skippy's was playing around, laughing and joking with drugs and weapons sprawled all over the place. I was even given another class on firearms. "O, come here a minute," Devon asked after exhaling weed smoke. "What's up?" I replied while catching a slight contact. "Check this shit out!" Devon insisted. He pulled back the large plastic trash bag where there were at least seven automatic weapons inside. After handing his six-year-old, 150 pound little brother a "roach" or leftover marijuana cigarette to smoke, he would pull out one gun after another. These two brothers often exposed their little brother to drugs, foul language, and porn at just six years old. "O, this is an AK-47… This is a… a M-16, this one is a 12-gauge shotgun; this is a Desert Eagle pistol, this a Tech-9, and we got a few more too," he added. "Nice shit, right?" Devon asked smiling while returning the weapons to the large lawn bag. "Yeah, y'all got some Vietnam artillery hah?" I replied. "Yeah, we're ready for war for sure O," he assured. Afterwards, I touched bases with Shawn. It was clear he too was one of the guys passing marijuana cigarettes around. His eyes were reddish; I noticed his fingertips were slightly burnt when we shook hands. "You alright?" I asked while tightly grasping his hand. "Yeah, I'll be alright O man," he replied with his head partially down. "Cool, I'm out. I'll catch you later," I added. "What you doing, writing?" Shawn asked as I walked away. I turned, "Yeah, how did you know?" I replied with a grin. "That's just what I figured," he said with a slight smile of his own. After nodding, I hurried through the weed smoke to leave the residence. As I continued towards the exit, I realized, there were enough drugs and weapons there to put us all away for a very long time.

Tempers settled by the time I got back home from Skippy's. Everyone carried on with their normal routines. The only thing left from the intense discussion was the expression on my nana's face. I walked over to Mama and kissed her on the cheek. She smiled while disappointingly shaking her head from east and west. I headed upstairs to pick up on the writing before going off to the ball court with Evan. "I'm sure glad you're nothing like him," she stated in reference to Shawn. I paused in the middle of the stairway, turned, and smiled. "I gave that boy twenty-one years to live, but at the pace he's going, he may not even make it to eighteen," she explained. "Ma, don't say that please, he'll be ok," I replied calmly. "Alright, y'all don't see it," she insisted. The more Shawn showed off or would act out negatively, the more time grandma subtracted from his life span. Whenever I sat and took it all in, I realized grandma's inclination was sort of spooky. Over the years, I would never disregard or discredit the wisdom of the elderly. The way I saw it, they had to have done many things correctly in order to live as long as they have.

High school was now just weeks away. Shawn had alienated himself from the family, but he and I still found time to talk. I did the best I could to ease our grandmother's nerves by chatting with Shawn and letting her know he was alright. He usually seemed disinterested in talking about Mama, or the incident with Montell. I expressed my feelings to him about chilling out from frequently visiting Devon's house. He listened but made no comment. I also expressed my feelings about the future with my cousin. He was aware I was due to receive over $40,000. As we walked along York Road, as we had done regularly in the past, I told my cousin we could split the money down the middle. I wanted Shawn to feel like he too, did not need to sell drugs or live a life of crime to get by or ahead. Shawn held his silence, but I could see the sigh of relief on his face after I made him the offer. I loved my cousin; he knew it. He also knew he had inherited $20,000 for simply being my big cousin.

Our two-hour much needed discussion was all I needed to regain the confidence in my cousin like in past years. I trusted Shawn to make the necessary alterations with the way he handled things. I was sure he would take his time pulling himself away from being a regular at Skippy's pad. I felt he still required the attention of the older guys; that was cool. I liked being cool with the guys too. Make no mistake; they all liked me a lot as well, but on a different level. I was considered cool, but not really down. I was not classified as a nut, or a tough guy, in the streets like my older cousin. This was great for me out in society, but can be viewed as weak or soft in the hood. That was fine with me as well. My reputation was based on being calm, my ability to play basketball a little, mix in some book smarts, and my relationships or abilities with the young ladies; good enough. The guys were all impressed with my ability to hang out with a variety of beauties at no expense, and with very little effort. I've always believed some people are just naturally comfortable around the opposite sex or women of remarkable beauty. I'm simply one of these guys.

However true, attractive females were also my largest weakness. My interest was hardly ever about sex with myself and females, despite conventional wisdom. I simply love the company of beautiful women. Although sex seems to be an important piece to the puzzle for most relationships, the peaceful company is what matters most for me. During most of my experiences, fast sex was the mistake in it all. Throughout all my family woes, I was not off sitting alone in innocent land. I'd already paid two visits to Planned Parenthood for impregnating Kima. She got an abortion once. The other time was simply a delayed menstrual cycle, but she very well could have been pregnant for a second time. These were traumatizing experiences for us both, especially with a small child already factoring into things. To have dozens of anti-abortion protestors yelling at you, at 14 years of age, while entering and exiting the establishment scarred us both. Only Shawn knew about my slip-ups with Kima, just as I was the safe-keeper of his marijuana and drug secrets. We all were messed up emotionally to an extent. My entire household was dealing with some type of affliction. My troubles just happened to be female-related.

The weekend before the start of school was better than previous weeks. Shawn and I dug deep to find the resolve necessary to better ourselves as teens. We were looking forward to the start of a new year. Shawn swore to give the weed smoking a break, and to slow up with hanging out in compromising places. He still managed to lose another two years off of his life, according to our grandmother. Before Shawn made a promise to chill out, he took part in the growing fad of drinking Robitussin cough syrup, to get high. Many guys in the neighborhood took part in this. After being drug to my house from Devon's, myself and Elroy carried my passed-out cousin around the corner to his home. During a visit to his house the very next morning, Shawn told me his right eye momentarily went up into his head, while the left one stayed in its place. Drinking two bottles of cough syrup comes with an ugly price! This act of recklessness scared my cousin enough for him to finally reevaluate himself. Unfortunately, grandma happened to still be up on this night to witness the entire senseless act. I honestly felt Shawn was sincere in his approach to making a fresh start. I also believed he wanted to get back the confidence he had lost with our grandma. He was finally getting tired of hearing about when his life would end prematurely. By the time school began, grandma had my cousin's life ending at just 16 years old. In theory, this meant Shawn would only have less than a year to live. Of course, we both blew this off. We were too excited about sporting more fresh gear. Still, I had heard a time or two that old folks can see into the future. I'm not referring to the fortune tellers or psychics; wise elderly people. For Mama to be so sure and demonstrative with her claim was weird. Perhaps my grandma was actually one of these unique older wise individuals.

# Chapter 7

# THE PREDICTION

The first day of school temporarily filled my neighborhood with the positive atmosphere of the past. It was refreshing to witness a few stable parents remaining observe their young men and women as they ventured off for another challenging year. Early mornings were usually the most peaceful of days. Most of the hustlers would usually stay asleep or indoors until around one or two in the afternoon. During this time it was not far-fetched for a drive-by to also take place during the wee-hours. The rivalry with Old York Road was steadily increasing as we tried to focus on academics. For me, school was more of an escape, but even here there were vibes of uncertainty. It appeared no matter where I was, home or in school, I would be reminded about the other side.

"Odell Richardson!" These were the first words I heard as I entered homeroom of the 10th grade. My name slid from the angelic voice of the cutie named Jody. My heart immediately sunk yet I remained calm. Jody was totally in the dark about the huge crush I had on her. Running into her at school was something I was looking forward to. I had no idea we would be classmates for the entire school year. After forcing myself to casually speak to Jody, I sat down while simultaneously trying to dry my sweaty palms on my new blue jeans. The school year had just gotten off to a good start, despite the anxiety I was managing. Still, I was able to harmlessly get Jody's phone number. I also would get better acquainted with several other cool classmates. Ironically, Jody and another classmate, a male named Donny, were both from the Old York Road area.

Knowledge of this had little effect on my desire to converse more with Jody. I believed she was easily the cutest girl in the entire school; I checked.

Just getting to know her was more than enough. The older I became, the more severe my fetish for females grew. My ability to interact with the opposite sex still came very naturally despite the nervousness. Even my cousin Shawn began to ask me questions about certain attractive females. He would ask, "O, what should I say to Janet when I go see her away from school for the first time tonight?" Janet also attended Northern. He would also ask, "Should I talk the same way I talk around the guys when I'm around a girl?" "Hell no!" I replied to the question. Shawn was a humorous and sensitive spirit, but fearless, and talked lots of trash most of the time. Although I struggled mightily with my inability to concentrate on a single female at a time, I had an opposite approach. I did the best I could to be gentlemanly or courteous, respectful; I simply desire be a nice guy. My philosophy has always been pretty simple in reference to females. If you're really interested in a young lady, get to know her, and treat her the best way you know how. What's so hard or wrong with that?

I can admit, I spent the first month of school studying the chemistry between myself and these pretty young ladies. Shawn stayed more persistent with his school work as he was finally drawing nearer to his promotion into the proper grade. Nothing was going to interfere with him getting his academic situation back on track. Although he still mingled with the wrong crowds after school and on the weekends, he made sure he passed and turned in all assignments, and attended class everyday. Shawn's determination allowed us to spend more time together than we had the year before. At times, it was as if he was trying to be apart of two worlds at once. Shawn felt more in control of himself around me, Evan, and a few of the other original guys from McCabe, yet he always seemed to enjoy himself more around Devon, Skippy, and the other older dealers in the hood. I noticed the difference. As long as we continued to share the closeness of old, I remained neutral. I simply forced myself to look passed his uncertainties.

Whatever circumstances I allowed myself to let go, grandma would catch in the wind. She acknowledged Shawn's efforts in school, but she never stopped predicting his demise whenever he made foolish comments or decisions. It all became very weird. I also made bonehead or poor decisions, yet I never was told, "You are not going to make it boy," by our grandmother. Shawn continued to laugh most of Mama's suggestions off and carry on as normal. Grandma's predictions once bothered Shawn, but now they were all brushed off. This irritated Mama even more. During this time, we all tried hard to live life as normal human beings, but it simply was not to be; not here. As our grades increased, the moral values in our neighborhood continued its downward spiral. More talks of trouble brewing with the rivalry, and much more police activity circulated throughout the area. By mid-October, I witnessed three guys get arrested for selling drugs, and I observed at least seven brutal fist fights, all over money. One fight I witnessed involved a guy breaking a thick wooden stick over another guy's head, leaving him unconscious, in between two parked cars, for an hour.

These incidents were intense to watch, but hardly something one would want to get used to. Again, I would spend a little more time indoors. I picked back upon my ability to express myself through writing. I escaped by writing too-long, love letters to females who I felt were interesting. The majority of these letters never left my bedroom. Most of them ended up in the garbage. I would express myself, become liberated, only to feel embarrassed afterwards, so I would trash the letters; not because they were not constructed well. I just did not want anyone to one day get a hold of them and detect my inner thoughts and feelings. I usually felt like the kind of expression I took part in was just too emotional and weird for the people where I lived. I knew this way of expression was a positive idea, yet I also knew I would never mention it to any of my buddies or family members.

Some of the ideas I wrote down on paper did actually make it through the phone wires and into the ears of the young ladies. I finally decided to use Jody's phone number. I called her periodically. Her mother usually answered the phone, only to tell me she was not there. When we did chat in class, Jody spoke on having a boyfriend, but just like with the others, I hardly cared. In the hood, most of us learned: if a girl states she has a friend while simultaneously handing over her number, she probably has just about given up on the guy, or wants to. "Why should I care?" "She gave up the number!" I justified. This was how I thought at the time, because I was far too focused on females.

Eventually, I would get an opportunity to talk to Jody on the phone. The fact we shared the same homeroom meant nothing. She would hardly ever come to school. I housed empathy for the gorgeous young women who hardly attended class. I knew this usually meant they were seduced by the dealers out in the streets. When Jody did attend class, she was usually late; therefore, I would still hardly get to see her because we did not share any other periods. Perhaps this was why my heart played the same tune it did on the first day of class, when we finally conversed. She answered the phone in good spirits; she actually seemed content to hear from me. We talked for more than an hour about everything from basketball to movies. I even offered up a surprise to Jody. I confessed in reference to a wallet-sized photo of her I possessed, before she ever attended high school. Marcus, a member of our old dance group, showed me a picture of Jody he got a hold of from their days at Roland Park Middle School; a school near Old York Rd. She was baffled how the picture ended up in my possession. Mystified, she asked a couple of questions. After stating, "You don't have a picture of me boy!" Jody wanted to know what she had on in the photograph. "Here, you have on a light-blue Ivan Lindel tee-shirt, and your hair is in a mushroom style," I described. For those women out there, who are unfamiliar with ethnic hair styles, simply ask your aunt, a friend, co-worker, or older sister about a "Mushroom" hairdo. "Oh yeah!" she replied in laughter. "I know which one you're talkin bout," she continued. "You need it back?" I asked. "Nah, you can have it," she said quickly. "It's a pretty picture, thank you," I said graciously. I was cool enough to tell Jody about the innocent photo, but I would never discuss with her my source, or how many times I would serenade it to New Edition tunes.

The phone conversation between Jody and I was an intense rollercoaster ride, but just for me. Whenever she would ask me to hold on, so she could answer another call, I would drag out, only to be lifted by the sound of her active bath water once she returned. With confirmation of bathing, a cordless phone, and a photo, all I had to do was use a little imagination with a lot of testosterones, and I was able to get a much bigger and better picture. After coming out of a perverted coma from the sounds of swishing bubble bath, I finally got up the courage to ask Jody about her boyfriend. When I spoke on the subject, I was hoping she would discredit or change her mind about ever having a friend, but she didn't. "What is your boyfriend's name?" I asked. "Limon," she said vibrantly and as if she expected me to recognize the name. I did not, but I could tell by the tone of her voice, this guy was a part of her soul. "Never heard of him," I replied casually.

"That's his name," she confirmed. Although my emotional generator was blown, I still was pleased with how the conversation had gone. I asked Jody how were my chances if Limon was out of the picture, and she gave me a good response. However, she was clear about the impossibility of her and Limon ever parting ways. We talked a few times afterwards. I even made a poor decision by innocently stopping by her place months later, but she was not at home. Whatever chemistry I was trying to develop with Jody quickly diminished. Looking back, it's amazing this crush allowed me to senselessly walk alone to Jody's home, smack in the middle of Cator Avenue, off of Old York Road. I didn't really realize at the time; I could have literally walked myself to death.

I soon learned Limon was to Old York Road what B-Mack was to McCabe, in a sense. He was a pretty successful street dealer with his own band of followers. I had not yet seen Limon, but I was familiar with his younger sister, Mesha. She attended Northern High as well. I held on to the wallet-sized picture of Jody, but I soon would let go of the dangerous crush I had on her. I returned to reality. Meaning, I continued to chase other females and played basketball, while trying to figure out who I really was. Drastic changes continued and I was still without a solid destination. Unlike so many kids, I was never promoted to concentrate on the popular question, "What do you wish to become in life when you grow up?" For those who answered this question, I learned later, this was just an answer, but not a real one. Today, guys said they answered, "doctor," "lawyer," or "firefighter," just to give a decent answer. Like me, they all were clueless as well. However, the pressure of this question was real. Today, this is one of those questions I wondered why no one at home ever asked. Back then, I never thought about it much. Good thing; it was very hard for me to answer. I had no clue whatsoever, as to who I really was or what I ever wanted to think about becoming; none.

The notion of possessing over $40,000 in a couple more years, living in an unstable setting, and having too many crushes, allowed me to lead a life with excitement, but no direction. Later in the year, I learned Jody had left the school before the third quarter. Immediately, another beauty would instantly take the "crown" in the hearts and minds of every male, and apparently some of the females at Northern High. Her name was Victoria Hammonds. Everyone called her "Vikki." Ironically, she was an acquaintance of Jody and also a resident of the Old York Road area. As you can see, I had no personal problem with this neighborhood at this time. All the fine females were somehow connected to each other, this place, or both. Vikki stole the hearts of the majority of the popular dudes at the school. In short, most of the other females hated her. I liked Vikki, but I really began to take notice of a quiet, slim cutie who often wore a Hally Berry-like short haircut. Her name was Tracey. Tracey was the exact opposite of Jody or Vikki, but she was just as beautiful. Surprisingly, she was not from Old York. She lived in west B'MORE with her mother and younger sister. I truly didn't know what I was doing, but for the first time ever, I was thinking with the right body part with her, and things felt really different, better; right.

The decision not to pursue Vikki turned out to be a good idea for a few reasons. She, like Jody, was in a relationship with an older street hustler from Old York. His name was Frankie. This relationship explained the flashy brown and gold, Toyota Cressida Vikki frequently drove to school. Still, it was clear to see, Vikki loved receiving attention from more guys than just Frankie. All of the brothers who were considered to be slick, hip or flashy, or popular, liked Vikki in one way or another. Whether they would admit it or not was a separate issue. That's why learning she actually had a crush on an anonymous guy had the "chat lines" fully open. The news turned out to be very surprising. The guy Vikki wanted and was determined to land was my friend Evan.

When it came to females, Evan simply did not care too much at all. All of the ladies felt Evan was cool and very good-looking, but he simply did not care. Not wanting to chase women and have sex with multiple hotties can be a very great thing, but when you're in your late-teens, this decision strikes many in the hood as extremely weird. Many say my basketball mentoring friend was a virgin. Others immediately said he was gay. His decisions may have been slightly consistent with these claims, but there was never any real proof. He was one of my dearest friends. He is definitely one of my best friends today. He's certainly not gay. When I informed Evan about Vikki's crush, he did grow flustered. It scared him a bit. The nervousness I often felt during these encounters, he would express or display outwardly. Needless to say, this was not the response I'd hoped for with my pal. I was ready to either throw a party for my friend, or promise him a few thousand bucks to trade shoes with him at that very moment. He was extremely nervous when I gave him the news. Internally, my friend was immediately searching for the nearest exit.

Having fun with the females dominated our lives, just as the drugs and violence would consume our neighborhoods. This caused continuous concerns for our grandmother. She feared my cousin was in the midst of the increasing violence and drug trafficking, which now seemed to be an everyday, all-day occurrence on McCabe Avenue. I still tried to ignore it all. I was really just having too much fun in school. That sounds weird; fun in school. Anyway, one Friday afternoon, I spent thirty minutes or so, socializing with the most popular female in our high school. Vikki interrogated me to gather information about my close friend Evan. I used her as well; as a prop or "arm candy," to model my Friday school gear before all of the onlookers. I don't recall the specifics of Vikki's questions, because I was not really listening. I was more focused on how attractive she was. I was so excited about being in Vikki's presence, nervousness caused me to quickly forget her words. I told her I would set something up for her and Evan to meet soon. Vikki would state she had made several attempts to connect or "break the ice" with Evan in the hallways, but he resisted or ignored the beauty. The possibility of Evan being an 18 year old virgin excited Vikki tremendously. She definitely wanted Evan physically, in every way she could think of. With Evan, patience truly was going to be exercised. Still, it was only going to be a matter of time before her chance with my pal would present itself.

In many ways, I've always considered myself a leader although I never cared if my cousin Shawn controlled certain situations. Perhaps this was the direct result of not knowing where I was headed in life. The bus ride home gave me a chance to ask myself a question or two. I asked myself the question: "Why am I so hung up on females and not something more productive?" I understood there were things more important than chasing or thinking about women. I just struggled to focus on those other things. Somehow, I would never let the thoughts go far enough to answer the question. I would be too busy picturing myself in Evan's shoes whenever he and Vikki were to meet. I exited the #8 MTA bus on York Road, directly across from McCabe Avenue. I was awaiting the chance to dash across the road with the six, heavy text books I carried inside of my net bag. After crossing, I stopped for a brief moment to glance upwards at the green street sign with my block's name inscribed on it in white letters. I was interested in knowing the origin of the title of this street, but at the time I was not focused enough to look into it. Today, I know exactly WHO Mr. McCabe Avenue was; that's a part of another story. The top portion of McCabe Avenue always offered a different picture, much better than the block's southern sections. I was sure there were residences, here, on the hill that had no idea what took place just blocks below.

I began to advance south towards my home, down the very same stretch of asphalt I used to glide downhill on my Sizzler skateboard a couple of years prior. The block I was walking deeper into at this time was no longer a place for fun and games. People were still laughing and joking, but in pain, or for all of the wrong reasons. Here, people thought it was funny to see a guy get knocked out, a female to get slapped, or for a guy to get chased by the police. I proceeded to stroll through my neighborhood looking for my cousin. I simply wanted to touch base with him. I knew he was just one month away from being promoted into his proper grade; therefore I wanted us to celebrate early. I headed towards Skippy's house feeling this would probably be the best place to locate Shawn. Greetings from the residents, young and old, were always evident. I've always had a genuine respect for just about everyone, therefore I usually found myself speaking to lots of neighbors and everyday citizens. "Hey Tray, have you seen my cousin around buddy?" I yelled out as I passed by. "Yeah, earlier, he said he was going to chill out in the house for a while," he replied. "You ok O?" he asked. "Yeah, I'm cool!" I replied back. "Why?" I followed. "I guess you didn't hear about that shit that happened earlier today hah?" he whispered as he drew closer towards me. "I didn't, what's up? I asked attentively. "Some nigga got blasted down by Old York Road," Tray offered. "Oh yeah?" "Yep, some dude named Dee-Dee got smoked," he shared. "I heard the nigga got into it with B-Mack son, and lost apparently," he said. "Nigga got shot up! He's outta here!" Tray followed. "For real?" I added. "Hell yeah!" Tray added. "This could be the start of some bad shit buddy," I stated calmly. He followed my comment with, "Yeah, be careful, but I'm ready; I'm not worried about shit." During this entire feud, you did not have to be directly affiliated with the mess. If you were from one of the two blocks, or if you had family or close friends from the area; this usually meant, in one way or another, YOU and your family were IN.

After receiving the interesting news from Tray, I really felt the need to chat with Shawn and the others. B-Mack was a true legend on McCabe. Now, it appeared as if his freedom and run as a major supplier was in great jeopardy. He was accused of the assault on the young man from Old York. I walked by Skippy's, quickly asking him, "Yo, have you seen Shawn?" "Yeah, he went in the house O," he replied. I hurried over to 731 and entered. Shawn was sitting at the dining room table engulfed in information from his notebook. "Hey ma!" I said with a smile and a kiss as usual. "Hey daddy!" I offered with a smile to my grandfather as well. Granddad was still not too fond of me, but I still remained pleasant and respectful. "What's this mess I hear about B-Mack out there?" Mama asked. "Ma, I told you already!" Shawn yelled. "Ah boy, shut up, I don't believe shit you say," said grandma. "He said Benny got into a fight with those guys from that other neighborhood and somebody got shot or killed. Is that true?" she asked. "Yes ma'am, I believe that is true," I replied. "Oh Lord!" she replied before I could fully answer. "Some guy named Dee-Dee was apparently shot and killed. "Benny shot someone?" grandma asked. "I don't know that ma!" I replied. "NO!" Shawn yelled. "No, he didn't, somebody else did it," he said in an uncertain tone. "He doesn't know, he's a liar," Mama stated while looking in Shawn's direction. "I'm proud of him for his hard work in school, but he's bad as shit," she said while shaking her head with a tired smile. Shawn's slight grin followed. Despite the subject matter and difference in opinions, I was actually happy to see the two smiling in the same room for the first time in a while.

News of the murder would spread throughout the neighborhood quickly. Benny soon disappeared from the neighborhood, confirming all suspicions that he may have had some knowledge of the incident. After all of the ranting and fighting going back and forth between the two hoods, someone was now dead. In the streets, you could hear how people could just sense this was going to be the start of a long war between these two neighborhoods. Afterwards, I asked my grandma if she ever considered relocating to another neighborhood. She would simply say, "Boy, we're staying right here! We can't afford to move." Shawn and I both mentioned to grandma how we felt the negativity and violence would continue to grow in the area. However, the decision was made and it appeared if there were going to be many more battles fought, we were simply going to have to live through them.

By week's end, details had surfaced about the still unsolved murder of the 20 year old from Old York Road. My sister was familiar with Dee-Dee and mentioned he was simply a cool guy; a very nice person. It was told, the altercation took place near Old York, in broad daylight. Apparently, drugs were the motive, creating friction between the two participants. A fight ensued between Benny and Dee. It was said DeeDee attempted to land the first punch during the altercation. Then, Benny would produce a handgun; shooting Dee-Dee several times leaving him for dead in the street. These were all alleged accounts on this incident. Still, with several onlookers, Benny quickly became a wanted murder suspect. Police officers were now seen combing through McCabe and the rest of the city, with precision looking for Benny. Some suspected he may have fled the country, knowing just how much money he was able to accumulate during his four to six year reign. It was all good for Benny just weeks earlier, but it all was about to come to an abrupt end. He was wanted for the worst possible reason; murder in the first degree.

The tragic death of the youngster known to McCabe as "Dee-Dee" made headlines in the newspapers as well as on television. News of the homicide consumed area schools as well. Vikki confirmed just how upset the guys from Old York were about the loss of their friend. "Man, there is going to be some shit now. You better be careful boy," she stated in concern. "Who me?" "I'm cool... I don't fool around with that drug stuff, I'm cool," I replied. "I know that Odell, but you live around there," she stated. "I get what you're saying. I'll watch my ass, ok?" I offered with a smile. "You better!" she stated softly with a flirtatious tone. Vikki sure was attractive, and despite her interest in Evan, she would flirt with me periodically, but my heart was focused on Tracey. Still, Evan had no idea what kind of a treat was headed his way in just a short while.

The shooting incident seemed to be the topic of discussion for several upcoming weeks. The authorities were still in search of Benny. There were several tips confirming his whereabouts still being connected to the region. This baffled many of his associates on McCabe, myself included. It appeared as if Benny was still nearby, but why? While several pondered on this question, others prepared for retaliation. Coming home from school became quite interesting. I began to see groups of guys conversing about the incident and how things may escalate in the future. Before heading inside of the house, I would hear phrases like, "I pray those suckas get bold," or "We waiting for dem niggas," or "We should go down there first, before they even decide to retaliate," and even "I can't wait til they make a move." I felt trouble was certainly looming, but I focused on school and staying away from the negativity. It was not an easy task considering how closely it constantly surrounded me. The same armed guys who sought trouble were usually found sitting on our stoop, simply because our home was in the center of the neighborhood.

The negativity continued to increase. It was apparent to me during this time, in order for guys to make money selling drugs, they had to constantly go back and forth to jail. The trade off hardly made sense to me, but jail time never seemed to bother the guys enough to want to give it all up. I understood jail as a part of hustling, but guys seemed to relish in it, as if incarceration was actually a good thing. That, I could not understand. My close friend Elroy seemed to stay out of harm's way. He sold drugs for an up-and-coming, younger kingpin named Hubert. Hubert was a cool but quiet kid from the block Winston Avenue, a few blocks east of McCabe. Winston Avenue was the home of several hustlers and our middle school. Heavy drug activity existed atop of this street as well. I attended elementary school with Hubert. He was the type of kid no one talked to very much back then. As a kid, he always seemed to have limited gear, and his hair was not as neatly cut as the others. Hubert was now working his way to the top of the drug game in B'MORE, while everyone else focused on violence and the rivalry, along with the recent homicides. Elroy was the only guy from McCabe Hubert was willing to deal with, because of his decision not to indulge with the violence, and no one could resist my pal's crazy sense of humor.

Throughout all that was transpiring, I was sure to still make time to write, play basketball, and get to know Tracey a lot better. Most importantly, I would pray. I rarely would forget to pray to God. I could feel the problems in the area increasing. I periodically found myself looking over my shoulder for the first time in my life. I especially did this whenever I'd be alone, walking along a quiet, dark street. Prayer helped me cope with everyday life, simply because I felt I was the only guy doing it on a consistent basis. I believed there would be more confusion in the area, so all I would do was pray for my health or wellbeing; I prayed I would be still standing whenever it all ended.

The holiday season of 1987 was near, and all Shawn and I had on the brain were good report cards. This was the first time we ever cared about how high our grades were. We both worked hard, and for my cousin, this report card was special. This report card would symbolize his promotion into his correct grade, the 11th. There were only a few weeks of school left before the Thanksgiving holiday. How fitting? This was a tremendous blessing for my cousin Shawn to achieve on such a holiday. While the neighborhood was celebrating Benny's elusive capabilities against the authorities, Shawn and I were simply making the grade.

The celebration of achieving better-than-satisfactory report cards was short-lived. After Shawn realized his promotion was in the bag for the following year, he once again headed for Skippy's house for adult-like fun. His cravings for the unknown and the unconventional slowly began to drive him backwards. Suddenly, he began to do the things that originally hampered his life and school grades. Shawn loved me like a brother, yet it was clear he simply needed to be around the action. I preferred spending my time alone or with Tracey. Sometimes, I just loved simple things, or moments when the sun would hit my face through a window. It did not take too much for me to be content. Even today! I want a full life, but peace has to be the foundation. And I pray consistently for the ability to be able to separate my peace from the forces of this world. As a teen, the sun shining, or even a pack of Oreo cookies and a glass of milk, would often be more than enough to make my day.

Grandma once told me I had an old soul. She said this explains why I'm so patient, and why I almost never get upset. I guess that's also why I admire older folks so. I love to observe them walking a dog or watering beautiful plants. I was always intrigued by older folks like my grandma and others, who were even more better off. I wanted to know how they managed to own things; own stores, homes or cars. I was impressed how they had done things we as young people had not. These ideas, which often ran rapid in my mind, allowed me to realize I was not much like any of my peers. The things I thought about never crossed their minds, and I loved that realization. I loved knowing I was still the same, yet very different.

None of my friends or people in my age bracket noticed anything significantly different about me, but grandma did. She often would say, "No matter what's going on or what happens, you'll be fine." "I know it!" I never quite knew what she meant by this, but those words helped me believe more in a Higher Power, and allowed me to really enjoy my prayers. I guess Mama drilled me with these phrases because she was really beginning to feel the opposite for my cousin Shawn. Maybe she also felt her conditions changing personally. As much as I gave her hope, he gave her fear. The fear of knowing Shawn was seemingly headed for trouble really worried grandma, despite how she expressed her concerns. I always tried to console my grandma whenever I could. I felt like Shawn was having a little fun, but we were cool, therefore I never truly saw what she felt. The best I could do was give her a small report of the streets; I informed her of a few things that were bad, but not enough to lose any sleep over. I believed my explanations helped, but I was only a teen. Grandma was not about to change her mind, despite the information I forwarded. She understood how I felt about Shawn. She figured it right. I would have lied to her to help Shawn stay out of trouble. Not because it would have been right. I would have done it because he would have done the same for me. Although we spent less time together because of our differences, we were still, in many other ways, joined at the hip.

This difference in taste between Shawn and I placed us on separate buses to and from school. He usually took the # 8 bus home from school. This bus traveled along York Road. Shawn and several others felt there was always more action on the # 8. I usually took the # 36 bus. I guess I preferred this bus because it once served as a quiet way home for me during my horrible concert experience. It's safe to say, I like quietness! The little side of town this bus traveled on was naturally peaceful. Just around the corner from where I usually would exit the bus was where Cristina and her mom lived in a two-bedroom apartment. A few of Evan's relatives lived in the area at Winston Apartments. For as nice and peaceful as the small area was, it would serve as a landmark to a very interesting final encounter with a troubled pal.

One day after school, I exited the bus on an unseasonably warm, late-October day. Although this stretch of street was normally quiet, I realized I was the only guy exiting the bus at this stop. I was also the only person on the block itself, so I thought. As I began to walk towards the direction of my home, I heard a voice whispering, "O." I turned back and stopped to observe the only vehicle parked on the left side of Winston Avenue. The car was a tan, Nissan Stanza. I could see one person sitting inside of the car from its rear. The driver of the vehicle was signaling with his arm outside of the window for me to come closer. Not recognizing the car, I bent slightly to get a better view. I did advance slowly for some strange reason. I believe I felt a little more comfortable because the person called me "O." Only people from my block called me "O" at the time. I carefully made my way to the side of the vehicle and I noticed the driver. "What's up Rock? I didn't know that was you," I said calmly. Rock was one of the few older dealers left from McCabe. "Benny told me to call you over," Rock replied while thrusting his thumb back over his shoulder. I looked in the rear seat of the vehicle, and there he was, smiling. I smiled quickly and instantly began to look all around. Benny was grinning at me from ear to ear as he partially laid across the rear seats. He occasionally looked out of the rear window to see what or who may have been coming. After months of fleeing the authorities, the man wanted by police wanted for first-degree murder had found me.

"What's up O? How's the family? How's Gina? You alright?" he asked consecutively. "Yeah, everything's cool man," I replied with a grin. "O, I'm in big fuckin' trouble O, big trouble," he emphasized. "I know," I replied. "They after me O, like a muthafucka," he stated referring to police. "What are you going to do now?" I asked. "I don't know; run until I can't run no more, I guess," he replied casually. "That's the only way they're going to get me O, catch me," he stated while giggling. I slowly shook my head in silence, realizing this encounter may very well be our last. We never spoke on the crime Benny was apparently running away from. "O, I got to get ready to get outta here," Benny stated with this hand extended. "O, no matter what you do man; do not get caught up in this bullshit on McCabe; don't do it." There I was, clinching the same hand possibly used to claim a life just weeks earlier. "Remember O, don't get involved with that mess man. Stay out of trouble," Benny said seriously before sinking further into the back seats. I replied with a nod. I stood in the middle of Winston Ave. observing the Stanza slowly drifting forward toward the traffic light to make a right turn. Benny's head popped up momentarily to look back at me; he shared a silly grin. The Nissan Stanza's right turn represented the last time I would physically see B-Mack. He was apprehended by authorities just two days later, and charged with the first-degree murder of Daniel "Dee-Dee" Watkins. Benny was eventually given a 50-year prison sentence for the crime.

# Chapter 8

# CONFIRMED SEPARATION

News of Benny's extensive prison sentence really upset several of the guys in the neighborhood, despite the fate of "Dee-Dee." Before he was captured many had viewed the crime as a victory scored for our neighborhood. However, the length of this sentence erased any need to celebrate from those who found reason to. Some were saddened by Benny's arrest, while others in the neighborhood used Benny's absence as a way to catapult themselves to higher positions in the streets. With all of the interesting events taking place, I began to pay even closer attention to the ways of the streets. The break for Thanksgiving holiday was underway. Despite any uncertainties we endured in our hood, we all felt we still had plenty to be thankful for. Shawn's promotion was all but confirmed, and his mom, who had been doing much better, was concentrating on finding another job and taking good care of Shawn and her other two children. Shawn was very excited about having a little brother. This was quite evident when he would take a break from the streets. Both of Shawn's siblings loved him tremendously. At home during the holiday season felt like yesteryear. It appeared as if Benny's sentence had caused guys to "pump the breaks" or slow down a bit. I couldn't blame any of the guys for these feelings. Fifty years in jail; that's a very long time!

During the small vacation I managed to get out a bit more to shoot some hoops with my buddy Evan. We may have played more often if I would not have gotten on his nerves with this question: "So when are you going to hook up with Vikki?" "Man, you crazy O," he'd often say. "When you do, I want to watch," I said jokingly. Vikki was that fine in the eyes of everyone. Take Etton Briggs for example. He was Benny's understudy, and was apparently next in line to control the drug dealing in the area. He was already one of the main guys to connect with to purchase cocaine on the northeast side of town. He got a first look at Vikki when I was seen conversing with her near the school. After observing the two of us chatting, he began coming up the school almost every day to offer me a ride home in his nice, Audi 5000. I usually accepted, but I knew the real reason he came up to Northern High; Vikki. In his eyes, not only was she hot, she was also the girlfriend of a guy from the rival neighborhood. Etton, and others alike, loved taking advantage of any opportunity they could to score on the other side. Fast females, as Vikki was known to as, were fine but appeared slightly lost and blinded by the financial success of the hustlers. The dealers, regularly, would manipulate the women with materials, often using them to stir up even more confusion. Vikki was no exception.

The unfolding situation with Vikki was interesting, but Evan and I stayed more concentrated on the hoops. I continued to play basketball well enough to get noticed by several of the finer players from the inner city. I made my way to different parts of the city just to see how far my game had progressed. It's a good feeling to have guys who can play really well go out of their way to speak positively about your game. This gives you a scale as to how good you are, or how far you have to go to keep up. I really liked playing ball as a teen, yet I never loved the sport as much as the better players. Still, it hardly mattered who was playing me or who I was playing against. Growing up on McCabe Avenue and playing with those personalities gave me a sense of fearlessness on the ball court. Basketball courts were the last place for me to be afraid. I relished in the elite competition. Still, I was never in love with the sport. I simply loved to play the sport with the other better players; nothing more, nothing less.

Basketball was a must for us all year round, but the winter months also allowed my writing to pick up. While writing I often received a similar satisfaction or rush as I had when I played basketball. The beauty of writing; it gives you tremendous excitement, feelings of accomplishment, peace and quiet. I love that! Because of this, I began to do much better in English class. Before long, the creativity with the small stories would blossom as well. Ideas for movies and books constantly popped into my brain, forcing me to grab a pen and pad impulsively. Great ideas would come to me, only to leave very quickly if I was too slow with jotting it down. Even explosive rap lyrics would periodically come to me, but for some odd reason they never seemed to stick. As a teen, I was mostly interested in writing extensive love letters to beautiful girls I knew. I was not in love obviously; I just enjoyed being romantic, gentlemanly, and creative. The more I wrote, the more pleased I became with what I was saying in these writings. As a teen, I was always fascinated with the idea of love, but not the exclusive portion of it. Tracey would be the first to test me; to see if I could entertain the possibility of being in love with one female, at one time.

While my favorite cousin patrolled the streets recklessly, I became a much more laid-back personality with a romantic bug in his heart. Tracey's style and grace demanded respect. She possessed a quiet confidence I really connected with. This meant I would have to come with the charm of the Casanova types from the 50s and 60s. You all know who I'm referring to; Nat King Cole, James Dean, Elvis Presley, Frank Sinatra, Sean Connery etc. As a teen, I always wanted to be recognized by young women for how I treated them, not much else. So this was me; girls, basketball, and the literary arts. Not necessarily in that order. Although Shawn and I were still very close, it was quite evident our lives were now heading in opposite directions. I was trying to shoot everything other than guns, and write until my thumb hurt, while he was playing with guns, smoking weed, and holding drugs for much older dealers. Shawn always appeared to be in control, but I could still notice a slight struggle. I was not able to pay much attention to his problems because of my own, but I noticed insecurities. His problems stemmed from peer pressure, while mine originated from a weakness for pretty females. It was a bit easier for me to disclose my issues, because whenever I did something involving matters of the heart, the end result usually turned out alright.

So as my cousin Shawn lived by what he thought, I moved on what I felt. Interacting with a variety of pretty girls became routine for me. As I stated before, I rarely cared if we ever made it to the bedroom. All I needed to know was I could likely do so if I wanted to take things further. At times, I did just that, but more times than not, I passed. I was simply enjoying teaching myself about women and patience. I never had the typical, "Birds and Bees" speech addressed to me by a parent. No one took the time to talk to me about females. No one in my home seemed to know much about females. I lived with two grown uncles, and I've never seen neither of them with a woman. The rules at 731, we believed, were reasonable but pretty basic. Come home at a respectable hour, treat people decently; no drugs, do not make or have any children, and do well in school. Everything else was totally up to us. There was no one to determine where we hung out, if we had protected or unprotected sex, or if we did anything crazy. Moving forward the ability to discipline us vanished. As for our uncle, the older we became, the more weight he lost; courtesy of too much Smirnoff Vodka.

Concerns about my cousin's actions in the streets continued to intensify with my grandma, especially when my sister also brought his behavior to her attention. Gina had heard about a few disturbing things involving Shawn in the streets, and grew in concern as well. Both, my sister and grandmother shared their views with my aunt Marie. Full of hopes for a better future, she discarded any negative information forwarded about her oldest son. "Shawn's fine, ain't he Odell?" she added concerned. Just as I nodded positively, Marie yelled, "Shawn's just 'hardheaded' as shit." "Oh yeah, well 'a hard head makes a soft ass,' and that boy is well overdue," grandma stated angrily. "Mama!" yelled Marie. "Mama shit! I mean it," she yelled with widened eyes. Just when things would get out of hand outside, homelife improved, and when things calmed down on McCabe, the "war" would simply transfer behind closed doors.

These explosions took place regularly within the household. At times, my grandma was so blunt with her delivery, I actually found it funny. For as much as she spoke about God, she still used more profanity than any of the guys on the corners. Still, when it came to Shawn, Mama simply felt something wrong in her heart. She seemed to always have a premonition for Shawn, but he continued to laugh it off or disregard what was being said. Sometimes he would make fun at our grandma and her warnings by mocking her. I didn't know what to make out of these interactions. There were moments when I thought all was fine and other times I wanted to tell Shawn to listen closely to grandma. There was always something in my heart that said, "Mama is on to something."

As the holiday season approached, our household was again, a shell of its former self. The occasional sit-down dinners we once shared as a family were no longer in existence. The regular consumption of alcohol and drugs had made a huge negative impact on my family. No one really reached out to one another. Everyone seemed to have too many negative issues to deal with themselves to help others. The approach here was: If you messed your own life up, fix it. It was an "every man for themselves" mentality at 731, to an extent. Us kids, we virtually were making up our own under-developed minds. By late October, 1987, my grandparents were also beginning to slow down physically. My aunt and uncles were all addicted to some kind of drug or drink. My cousin was expressing his confusion with anger and reckless actions. Well, and I was wondering who I was, where my life was headed, yet often thinking with the worst body part. Only my sister proved she had a slight grasp on reality. Gina and Freddy usually stayed away from the McCabe Avenue household.

In the midst of this confusion, it was nice to still know we would still have gifts underneath the tree on Christmas Day. We truly were clueless about the details of the true meaning of the holiday at this point. I'll be totally honest, Christmas at this time meant I would soon own a pair of the new, Michael Jordan sneakers. At 14, I knew more about those sneakers than I did the true meaning behind the holiday. I prayed a lot and I've always believed in God, but that was as far as it went spiritually. I tried to express myself in a godly manner, but I often allowed females to distract things. Most of Shawn's actions would indicate a disinterest with spirituality. Still, we remained close. Shawn's spirituality was blocked by what head directly in front of him; pain. These images caused resentment in him. Shawn was very upset about how our neighborhood turned out, and how our family was now abusing drugs and alcohol, and yet he too was taking part in those things. He even went back far enough to say, "I told you O, we should have never moved around here; should have stayed down the hill!" "I hear you, but I got a funny feeling Kennedy Avenue is just as bad now, if not worst," I replied. The cocaine epidemic had a stronghold on the entire city of Baltimore. If anything, Kennedy Avenue fell well before McCabe Avenue.

Before long, the neighborhood we lived in had its teeth sunk deeply into my cousin. He really began to show erratic behavior with a consistent pattern of outbursts of disrespect towards any and everyone. School represented the only source of good or stability in both of our lives. My cousin became two different guys. In school, he was a hard worker with poise, charm, and flare. Back home he was a reckless, up-and- coming street general; a thug on the loose. The older guys added to Shawn's inconsistencies. They all took turns boosting him up, complimenting him for negative words and actions. In the middle of any foolish act committed, they would say things like, "Shawn, you're crazy son," "That boy a real nigga there," or "Shawn's a serious ass youngin." He still desperately craved the attention he received from the older guys. I was almost just as lost as my older cousin, but my troubles were more subdued. I also realized something he did not. All of the guys he looked up to and tried hard to impress were more lost than the two of us combined. Even here, both of us still had a chance at a good life. The others were older so time was running out. They were far more compromised by their poor decisions than Shawn and I. Not having a plan to follow was our biggest problem. We were young, but we still didn't have any true dreams to pursue or a clue about what we wanted to do with ourselves.

Life at home would digress further, and so would the neighborhood we lived in. Talks of retaliation and threats of murder surrounded our area. Meanwhile, my cousin and I, for the first time, began to really show signs of drifting apart. I noticed a greater change in him during our last conversation. Shawn once talked to me with a confidence and a big brother's swagger. During a conversation we had after an explosion he received from our grandmother, he spoke to me with an unsure and embarrassed presence. He realized I saw a weakness in him for the first time. The entire conversation was in a soft tone on both ends. He was calm, but made statements like, "I'm sick of this shit O, all of it," or "Fuck everybody," and "I hate it around here O," just to name a few. Most of what he said displayed a defeated attitude or brokenness within his spirit. However, Shawn's last words during the conversation we had just before distancing himself were, "I love you O."

Shawn's due promotion into his correct grade was the equivalent of him leaving the school all together. It suddenly became weird to even be around him. In school, he would see me and turn his back towards me as if he didn't. Back home, he stopped dropping in to touch base with me, or just to shake my hand like in the past. Even other students at school noticed the unexplainable new distance between us. One student asked, "What's up with y'all two?" "I don't know," I replied with hunched shoulders. That was the truth. Looking back, I guess Shawn felt he had to choose a direction to take. Maybe it was too stressful to live on both sides, and the side I rested on, was not the route he cared for or respected.

The neglect I was enduring from my closest relative was really eating away at me. I was hoping this phase would soon end, perhaps in a week or two, but I was wrong. For some strange reason, Shawn was sticking to his guns. So much so, grandma picked up on the vibes as well. "What's wrong with you two?" she asked calmly in concern. "Ma, I don't really know. He just doesn't really say much to me any more for some reason," I offered. "Oh God," she replied in disappointment. Leaning over the right arm of her favorite chair, she then yells out, "Hey, what's your problem boy?" to Shawn as he walked by. He pretended as if he never heard a word and slowly strolled out of the front door, slamming it as grandma spoke. "Ignorant bastard!" she yelled in anger as she quickly turned to observe Shawn through the living room window. "Don't worry ma, it will all work out," I said calmly. "I told you there's something wrong with that boy," she said as she looked in the direction of our grandfather. "That's right, your 'Buster' is an idiot," she followed. Granddad, never too big on words, just stared over at his lifelong partner with frustration.

After this weird sequence, I went out front simply to take a seat on the porch, observe, and take in some fresh air. I was debating whether or not I should go and write about things to feel a little better. I also pondered if I should go by Evan's to see if we could find a pick-up game of hoops. Dropping in on Tee, who was still around, was an option as well. I would periodically check in with him to see how things were going at Dunbar High. Tee and I were not as close during this time. It was clear he had made new friends at Dunbar High. That was understandable. Troy was long gone, and said to be on the wrong path as well. Tee's mom was over McCabe Avenue, and hardly allowed him to come outside at this point. He and his mom were just weeks away from moving across town.

I sat on the porch of 731, and for the first time, I felt a sense of loneliness. Before I could make up my mind on what to do next, I observed my cousin rushing back over towards the house. I thought for sure he was coming to either, start trouble, or talk about why he was acting so fickle towards me. Instead, Shawn leaped the first set of steps in one jump, only to dash passed me as if I were invisible. Now I'm pissed! I hopped up and quickly followed him inside. As he searched for cravings inside of the fridge, I asked, "Why are you acting crazy man?" He quickly replied, "Get the fuck out of my face O." "What?" "What's going on with you?" I asked in anger. "I wish all y'all leave me the fuck alone," he yelled after taking a quick sip of Kool-Aid and forcibly landing it on the kitchen table. "Hey! Watch your mouth boy," yelled our uncle BoBo. "What's your problem?" he asked Shawn. "Y'all my problem," he replied. "Leave me alone," he stated in a much softer tone. My sister soon entered the kitchen and put her two cents in. "Boy, you need to stop acting stupid." "Shut up!" he said to Gina. "That boy is nuts!" came from grandma seated in the front room. Before long, the entire family was a participating audience to Shawn's rants, or our domestic madness.

After being approached by our uncle and Gina, the phrase, "Man, y'all the ones crazy, not me," Shawn yelled out. "Y'all always fuckin' with me," he stated. "Boy, ain't nobody fuckin wit you!" Mama yelled. "I'm upset with you because you have been very disrespectful and ignorant," she yelled out. "Man... fuck that!" Shawn yelled. "Boy, you better watch your mouth," our uncle shouted. "Y'all always sayin shit to me," he insisted. "What about him?" he said while pointing in my direction. "What about me?" I stated with confidence. I knew there were things only Shawn knew about me, but I seriously doubted he would ever tell. "Y'all ain't know he had that black ass girl pregnant, did y'all?" he said in frustration. Immediately, it felt as if my heart had fallen through the floor, and down into our nasty flooded basement. "What girl?" grandma yelled as the entire momentum shifted my way. "Pregnant," my uncle stated in shock. I had told Shawn this in complete confidence. "What is happening?" I said to myself. The entire household was turning into the setting of a teenage stage play about stupid confessions. "Who's pregnant?" Mama asked. "No one!" I stated confidently. "Not now she got an abortion," Shawn added. My eyes slowly closed!

The pressure was still on me; I had to think fast to hold it together. "Abortion!" my sister and uncle yelled in anger. "Where in the hell did you get the money for a got damn abortion boy?" grandma asked. "You selling them drugs and shit?" she added. "No ma'am; and the abortion clinic did not charge us ma," I explained in embarrassment. I was extremely ashamed; it was time to try to pass the buck back to Shawn. Everyone in the house was looking at me with wrinkled eyebrows. "Well, at least I'm not out there smoking weed and holding drugs for dudes," I yelled out. I did it, and what a shame! We were both snitching. I managed to put the pressure back on Shawn, and this was a big one. The house would erupt with an array of yells and screams about Shawn's poor decisions in the streets, and my own between the sheets. Irony surfaced as everyone now seemed to show concern for how we were living, but was it too late?

Grandma was furious with Shawn and I. She could not believe I once had a baby on the way. After all the strings I pulled making sure Planned Parenthood would never call my house, Shawn just let the cat right out of the bag without even blinking. I immediately went over to grandma to offer her my deepest apologies. "Sorry Mama. I did make a couple of mistakes with females, but it will never happen again," I sincerely stated. "I think both of you have lost your damn minds," she replied. "Alright, well, at least you did the right thing by apologizing," she said. "Do you have any more girls pregnant?" she asked in concern. "Say it now while all this other mess is floating around in here," grandma stated sarcastically. "No ma'am," I replied. The room soon cleared with the members of our family walking away in disbelief over what had just transpired. Uncle BoBo stood around, but we no longer felt the fear of old. Shawn and I both sat there on opposite couches looking really stupid. "Like I said, at least you had the decency to apologize," Mama said while scowling at Shawn. "Look at him; he's just going to sit there, with his ugly ass self." That was our grandma. Like I said, she never held any punches. She was a true, "verbal knockout artist." After Shawn and I sat and listened to our grandmother's thrashing, we would again part ways. For the first time ever, I knew we were no longer friends. It hurt me tremendously to not be viewed as a friend in my cousin's eyes. I was very confused at this moment; I truly could not figure out why Shawn chose to let our relationship fall completely apart.

I pondered on the topic for weeks; making no significant progress. In the beginning, I attributed the tension he felt towards me came from the young ladies I dated. Shawn was a much more popular and outgoing teen than I in school and in the streets. Still, I always seemed to gain more attention with the nicer, more attractive females. I always dated more attractive girls than my older cousin, mainly because they were not as quick to have sex as the others, and that's what he desired from most females. I quickly discarded that notion, and began to think maybe this was about the $40,000 plus I had coming soon. This hardly made sense to me. I specifically told my cousin we were splitting the money down the middle, 50/50. Maybe he thought I was lying. I was not. I loved my cousin that much. Over $20,000 was his, whether he knew it or not. Ultimately, I drew the conclusion, neither of these ideas explained why Shawn alienated me from his life. I honestly believed he had an issue with me having the ability not to follow his way of living. He knew he was not living right. Instead of reconnecting with me and focusing more on school and the friends we both grew up with, he decided to play the streets and justify it by viewing me differently. I believe his pride told him that I felt I was a better person than he and his peers.

One of the finer qualities I possessed as a kid was my ability to always try to make a good impression on virtually everyone I came in contact with. I never displayed any signs of a poor attitude, anger, arrogance or traces of having an ego. I was never a fan of being out in front although I always liked the idea of leadership. In many aspects, I've managed to practice extreme selflessness; total unselfishness. The only time I did not mind receiving attention was from females, and on the ball court. With the ladies, I wanted to be seen as a good guy, and on the court, the same, one of the good players. At the time I wanted to be liked by everyone, yet I never thought I was better than anyone. I believe Shawn started wanting me to be more into the activities he was involved in. This would express more loyalty to him. I believe this was the mentality behind his decision to separate our spirits for the first time since 1977.

Getting over this situation was no easy task. I spent countless hours praying for a positive and peaceful resolution. My unanswered prayers produced several breakdowns when I was alone in my room. It took me about a week or two to toughen up and get on with my life by doing the things I loved. It was not easy to constantly see my cousin and know we were not going to speak nor look in the same direction of one another. No matter how much I moved forward, this bothered me equally every time. After awhile, I thought some things were just meant to happen a certain way. To make matters even worst, our dog died. "Deal," our Alaskan Malamute grew tremendously sick from complications from an earlier operation. Once again, the family gathered in the living room in pain. This was a period of rough patches we all go through in life. We know they're coming, yet the pain is not reduced on the notion. At this point, all I could do was stay positive, pray, and hope for gradual improvement.

A few weeks passed by and something finally came over me. It was now November, just weeks before Thanksgiving. The time I spent not socializing with Shawn allowed me to mature a bit. Suddenly I told myself, "It does not have to be this way O. And if it is, and there's nothing you can do, live with it." However, I believed there was something I could do to change or improve things. All I needed to do was be the bigger person and just break the ice between Shawn and I. I told myself, "This has been going on long enough." "Just go inside and playfully jump on him, or something," I mumbled to myself. I was free from all of the negative thoughts the turmoil originally produced. During the bus ride home from school I felt great about reconnecting with my cousin. I was pretty sure I would help fix things; I was already having good feelings as if things were great again. The sun was shinning brightly on the unseasonably warm, November afternoon, and the bus could not get me closer to McCabe Avenue fast enough. I hopped off of the #8 bus with hopes of running into my cousin quickly. I darted across York Road, in excitement, keeping a steady pace down my block, anxious to finally reunite with my best friend.

However, the closer I drew to the house I could, once again, feel the butterflies resurfacing inside of my belly. I stopped running about ten houses before I reached 731. I waved to Elroy's mom hoping to distract my own nervousness. A shortness of breath followed as I reached the porch. After holding my breath in for about twenty seconds and then releasing, I reached for the tarnished gold-plated doorknob, and turned. As soon as I entered the house the mood grew darker. It was unusually cold in the house to begin with. The massive flood we had in the basement destroyed the furnace, leaving us only with the option to heat the entire house with several portable heaters. I immediately observed Shawn sitting in the living room with our grandparents. Surprisingly, he was there with an old friend of ours from the Kennedy Avenue days.

Rosco, the only non-relative in the room, was Shawn's best childhood friend when my mom was still alive. Shawn sitting in the living room with grandma was a good sign, but his head never turning to acknowledge my presence, was not. Rosco spoke, but Shawn didn't. My plan to jump on Shawn was left out on the porch, or at the front door. I was inside flat-footed, trying to still feel things out. Shawn's eyes stayed locked on the 19 inch television, which sat atop a broken, 32 inch floor model. I advanced slowly from the hallway into the living room. I bent over and kissed our smiling grandma on the cheek. Shawn sat on the end of the glassless coffee table as I headed for the couch. As soon as I sat down, Shawn quickly got up. The air immediately left me and the room, as I dropped my head for a second and watched Shawn's backside turn the corner I had just entered from. Rosco took a quick glance backwards as he followed. I looked into Mama's eyes and we simultaneously shook our heads. "Don't worry, you two will be ok," she stated while observing Shawn and Rosco walking away from the house. I quickly joined her at the window. I leaned over my grandmother, staring at the two as they passed by the old, leafless tree in front of the house, until they were no longer visible. I slowly pulled away from the window and filled the same seat Shawn had just exited. I sat there contemplating my next attempt for reconciliation while periodically glancing at the tube. I can't recall what was playing on the set; I was staring clear through it with disappointment. Before I could complete my train of thought, from outside, there was the sound of a gunshot; POW!

The sound of the blast caused my grandmother to quickly thrust backwards, away from the window, while I dove onto the floor. While there, I watched my aunt Marie hastily skate down the stairs shouting, "What the hell?" "Are they shooting?" "Yeah, get away from the window!" I stated nervously now on my hands and knees. This singular blast was uncommon. Guns being fired were becoming a regular practice on McCabe. One evening, a bullet passed clear through our home, entering the window directly above where my grandma sat. The slug would exit the dining room window and out into the backyard, enlarging itself in a tree. It was a good thing grandma was not getting up to go check on the pot of greens! "Where's Shawn?" his mother yelled. "He just went outside," I stated quickly as I crawled back to the window, I had just left two minutes prior. "Oh God!" were the words I heard coming from Mama's shaken voice as I slowly began to peek upwards out of the window. Seconds later, I observed two guys running quickly towards the house. I knew for sure, one of the guys was Shawn, yet I could not make out the other person. All I knew, it was not Rosco. Panic set in as the two drew closer. Shawn appeared to be ducking downwards, and the guy seemed to be assisting him, or holding onto him tightly. Everything was happening very fast. Between the ranting inside and the confusion brewing outside, I could hardly think clearly. I finally lost the two for a split second just as they reached the front porch. Then, there was a huge crash. The momentum the two had built from running to the house violently carried them clear through the front door. The two knocked the door clean off its hinges and fell onto the floor in the hallway. The guy who smashed in the door with Shawn was Todd, one of McCabe's most noted bullies. His status in the hood would not be nearly as important as the words that instantly came from his mouth. "Help! He got shot!"

We all quickly realized my cousin Shawn was on the negative end of the blast we heard from inside. "What happened?" yelled Marie as she, my grandparents and I observed Shawn moving about, frantically, sprawled on the floor. "Call 911!" Todd screamed. I dashed to the phone doing just that. "What happened to my son?" my aunt screamed out in tears. "Somebody shot him!" Todd replied. "What?" Marie screamed. "Shaawn!" grandma yelled as my cousin squirmed about from the hallway into the living room. My uncle soon rumbled down the stairs from out of his sleep, also searching for immediate answers. With the ambulance in route, the atmosphere intensified. Shawn had been shot once in the chest area by some sort of handgun. The yells and screams continued to intensify inside and outside of our home. As Marie stumbled over her words, interrogating Todd, my sister and Freddy entered the house adding to the frightening scenery. In just minutes, the scene had become unbearably loud and gory. My cousin Shawn was apparently immediately up against the clock of life. After several weeks of silence between the two of us, and as Shawn's dark-red blood carpeted the living room floor, I broke our silence.

Through the unbelievable noise and panic, I could hear the sirens from the ambulance nearby. "Shawn, don't move!" I insisted. Above all the crying and screaming, I heard the words, "I can't breathe," from Shawn while down on all fours. Police quickly arrived as the sirens intensified. Pain and panic continued as Shawn made several attempts to stand upright. "Shawn, just stay down," Freddy pleaded along with Shawn's friend, Rosco, who had just entered. Grandma and BoBo also cautioned Shawn to stay down. Gina and Freddy had just purchased a bushel of crabs for the family. These shelled-fish laid in silence in a large wooden basket, but everything else was noisy and out of control. Even our granddad yelled out nervously, "Shawn!" Shawn's strength and stubbornness was still evident during this pivotal ordeal. As paramedics rushed up the steps, Shawn made it to his feet to everyone's dismay. "I can't breathe!" he uttered lightly. The darkened blood now consumed most of our living room floor. My cousin stood in a massive puddle of his own fluids, with the posture of a defeated fighter who had just been hit directly on the chin. It was not long before he would drop back to his hands and knees. As the paramedics entered and attended to Shawn, the world appeared to be spinning too fast. Everyone was still screaming and crying. Arguments and outbursts were taking place all around our house as onlookers displayed their concerns. All of our lives were changing before our eyes. No one saw this coming, or understood what was taking place. Well, except maybe grandma. Paramedics effectively slowed down Shawn's massive bleeding after cutting away all of his clothing. Then they placed him on a gurney and covered him with a sheet up to his neck. His eyes was closed, but I knew how strong Shawn was, therefore I tried to draw my own conclusions about the severity of his injuries. I stood and watched, in devastation, the paramedics take Shawn away. While Shawn was being rushed to Johns Hopkins Hospital, I went to join my desperate family members with their search for some much-needed answers.

Details about the horrific incident involving my cousin were sketchy immediately following. The police were questioning Todd on our porch. Onlookers held their positions. Some were there for support and concern, while others were preparing to use the material for gossip for their work week. I stood and listened to some of the interview between Todd and the police officers. Todd told police he and several others were standing on the side of the corner house, directly across the street; Karl's and Kizzie's home, when a brown car drove by and fired one shot into the crowd. Immediately, I thought Old York Road had decided to retaliate and Shawn was at the wrong place at the wrong time. After listening for a minute or so, I went inside, angry and confused. The expressions and tears pouring from the faces of everyone forced me to join in. I witnessed my grandfather cry for the first time on this day. I quietly sat at the three bottom stairs, fixated on Shawn's gradually drying blood, wondering what would come next. To my surprise, the answer was standing right in the doorway.

Police had finished their first line of questioning with Todd and left a number for the family to assist in the investigation. Suddenly, Skippy made his way over to the porch right after the authorities left. I went out onto the porch to share what I had learned with Shawn's buddy, but he was the one with the news.

Skippy was there during the shooting. "O, what that nigga tell the cops?" he asked with suspicion. "He said there was a drive-by with a brown, late-model vehicle," I replied. "Yo, that nigga lyin,' here's what happened," an emotion Skippy whispered. Skippy and I sat on my porch and talked about the moments leading up to the incident. Skippy, who happened to be on the corner when Shawn and Rosco left the house, indicated there was never any drive-by shooting. "Man, ain't nobody come through here shootin'," he said with twisted lips. "Who the fuck drives by and shoot one fuckin time?" he stated. Skippy stated, he along with his brother Devon, Rosco, Shawn, Elroy, and two others were leaning against the fence chatting. This was the very same home where we had our under-aged orgy years prior. "O, that muthafucka came around the corner and started pointing the gun at all of us," he stated. "What kind of gun was it?" I asked curiously. "He had a little automatic," Skippy indicated. "A.22 or a.25; a chrome joint," he added quickly. Skippy said Todd placed the small caliber handgun up against everyone's chest, one at a time. As Todd smiled at the sight of fear on each guy's face, he would move down the line to the next available guy. Skippy said some guys were terrified, and a few including himself, violently knocked Todd's hand away. My cousin Shawn just happened to be the last participant of this sick prank, and that's when the gun mysteriously discharged. "There was no drive-by O, he did it," Skippy assured.

Skippy left the porch immediately after that statement. I immediately tried to form a picture of what kind of look of fearlessness Shawn may have given Todd. As he awaited his turn, I'm sure Shawn gave Todd a look lacking in concern with the very stupid prank Todd was forcing on them all. If Skippy and Devon were two out of three, of the six or seven guys who were not afraid, I'd bet my life on it, Shawn was the third. Everyone on McCabe knew he feared nothing, even Todd. This notion forced me to ponder on the idea whether this incident was initially a mistake or not. Before my family and I could even calm down enough to visit my wounded cousin at the hospital, I was faced with plenty of unanswered questions. "Should I let the police figure this out first?" My word could only do so much. I was inside of the house when the shooting took place. Skippy may have told me out of respect for Shawn, but he would never go to court and testify; never. I also wondered if I should tell my family, but they were going through enough. I also thought about approaching Todd myself. These questions are commonplace in the hood after a tragic accident. Everyone's a possible victim. Todd was still in my sights as I sat on the porch. His demeanor was totally opposite than usual, but he was still there. My mind was spinning in every direction, but it was most important to go and support my family; all hurrying to Johns Hopkins Hospital.

The entire family from McCabe Avenue, with the exception of our elderly grandparents, rushed to the hospital to check on the condition of my first cousin. We had already learned Shawn's condition was quite serious. Shawn had suffered a tremendous amount of blood loss. Visiting the hospital alone was a blessing to us all. In Baltimore, consider yourself lucky if you experienced being shot and lived long enough for folks to visit you in a hospital. We quickly entered the prestigious establishment. We were soon escorted to the Intensive Care Unit. Everyone, with the exception of Marie, sat patiently in the waiting area. She, understandably, could not stop pacing back and forth, anxiously waiting to speak to a hospital representative specifically assigned to Shawn. I sat patiently in silence wondering, "How in the world am I visiting my shot cousin in a hospital?" This was the first time we had experienced an immediate family member being shot. All I could think about were the moments leading up to this bad situation. More questions plagued me. "Could I have done more?" "Was this all my fault?" "Is Shawn going to make it?" I needed answers; we all did, and Marie's patience had just run out.

My aunt's frantic pacing abruptly ceased with the words, "What in the hell is taking them so long?" "I know," Gina added. "I'll be back!" Marie stated while trying to decide on a direction to take. As my aunty took off running, we all nodded in silence. We all watched Marie as she sprinted down a hallway. Just afterwards I sat and watched two young boys exit the hospital with their mom. They were all smiling. I remembered when Shawn and I were this age. Those were the days when everything felt right. Those times now served as just a dream. Minutes later, my aunt returned but was not alone. Marie, dressed in her sweats and Reebok sneakers, was coming toward us clutching the right arm of an African-American male in scrubs; a doctor. "Here come Marie and a doctor now," I stated while turning towards everyone. The smile on Marie's face gave everyone a bit of confidence. We all were anticipating great news. She closely held onto the doctor's arm and stopped before us all. I was anticipating good news about Shawn's recovery, but there was more to share beforehand.

Marie looked at us with teary eyes and said, "Guess what y'all? This is the very same doctor I had fifteen years ago, when I gave birth to Shawn." Some of our eyes popped open, while others began to squint in confusion. The news was unbelievable and weird all at once. What are the odds of being delivered and operated on, due to an act of violence, by the same doctor, at the same hospital, 15 years apart? A dreary question for a scary situation, the answer was not very important. We needed to know how Shawn was doing and Marie wanted us to hear it together. Doctor Spencer drew closer and everyone fell into attention mode. "I know Marie family, so I'm not going to beat around the bush with this. Shawn is very critical, but there is a bit of hope," he stated seriously. "You all have to understand, first and foremost, that he is in a lot of trouble," he said with eyebrows raised. We all took an optimistic approach to the information shared by Dr. Spencer, but in a split second it hit me hard, "I'm losing my cousin as we speak."

The doctor soon confirmed the .22 automatic firearm used in the incident. He also confirmed Shawn was shot once in the left side of his chest. "The bullet had exited his body through his lower back, on his right side," the doctor stated. "The bullet exiting the body is good, but he has a lot of internal damage. That is not good, at all," he stated. "He didn't do himself any favors by getting up from the place of the initial shooting, then running over to the house," he indicated boldly. "And he would not stay still after he made it to the house," Gina whispered as we all listened. The bullet first entered my cousin's chest on the left side. He immediately fell to the ground. Scared, he hopped up immediately. Then, as he began to run towards 731, the bullet began to travel. "First the bullet hit a couple of his ribs, fracturing them," the doctor stated. "Then, the bullet destroyed his left lung, and finally pierced his heart before finding an exit." "The heart was the big one," he added. "This is why he bled so profusely," the doctor confirmed. As the gasps and tears increased from all of us, the doctor continued. "As I said before, the bullet exited the body, so that's good, but it did so much damage, so fast; as it often does," he emphasized. "I know this is tough, but this is where we are family," he said with compassion. "This is where we are, and here's what's ahead," Dr. Spencer suggested. All I could do was sit and listen, cry, and think, WOW!

The doctor was gracious and professional in how he handled my family with the negative details about our injured loved one. He continued to be thorough in explaining the operation and its intended purpose. Shawn had been unconscious since he was taken from the house. Still, the operation was a success considering all the damage he sustained. "It's hard to tell exactly when Shawn's going to regain consciousness," Doctor Spencer noted. "He loss a lot of fluid and that has to replenish," he added. "If all goes well family or everything falls into place, he could regain consciousness within forty-eight hours," the doctor stated with slight uncertainty. "If not, there could be a sign of brain damage." He added, "And that is never a good sign, but let's not jump too far ahead." To be completely honest, this doctor was good, but I had heard enough. I knew my cousin better than anyone. I needed to see for myself, the state of my beloved cousin.

After realizing all the scenarios surrounding Shawn's shooting, we were all ready to see how he was doing. We all wanted to observe his physical condition. I believed in spite of the details shared by the doctor, I would be able to determine if Shawn would pull through. No more than two or three relatives were allowed to see Shawn at once. My aunt Marie, her husband Montell and our uncle BoBo would go inside Shawn's room first. Myself, Gina, and Shawn's now eight-year old sister, Monnie were up next. While the adults went into visit Shawn, the three of us held hands and said a prayer for him. My eyes never closed and my palms saturated the hands of the two females on both sides of me. We all drizzled tears into the carpet with our heads bowed. I listened to the pleas and praise my sister freestyled to God, realizing we may be in the presence of the Lord, while simultaneously losing my cousin to a place we all grew to love just years prior.

The words, "Y'all can go back now," soon came from Montell just as our small prayer had ended. Marie was weeping again as expected, but the overall mood seemed hopeful. We walked past the others and I observed my uncle struggling to smile at me through the pain. The three of us soon entered my cousin's room to a bitter calmness; only hearing the soundtrack of the machinery used to assist in Shawn's possible recovery. The three of us slowly approached the side of his hospital bed, bringing tears and sniffles along with us. My eight-year-old cousin Monnie immediately left the room after a minute or two of seeing her big brother's condition. My sister and I stayed close, reliving the past in our minds about our mother's tragic death, also due to internal injuries. Gina began to slowly stroke the fluid induced, swollen hand of our favorite cousin. Stained blood was still visible around the cuticles of Shawn's fingers. "I love you Shawn," Gina said softly. I stood in silence and pain as my conclusion began to draw nearer. My sister slowly pulled back the bed sheet to view more of Shawn's body, only to release it and flee the room in tears. My sister got an up-close look at Shawn's entrance wound. The wound was profound, but I was taken aback by Shawn's overall appearance. He suffered a tremendous amount of blood loss; the fluid he was replaced with made him appear at least twenty pounds heavier. "This is not really my cousin lying here," I thought.

Everyone else could not stand the sight of the aftermath of this incident, but I felt I had to. So, I stood over my cousin, kissed his forehead, and said good-bye. I truly felt, at this point, my cousin was gone forever. "See you on the other side brother," I mumbled with tears. "I love you."

The family and I left the hospital to head back to 731, where our grandparents were awaiting an update on Shawn's condition. As we headed back northbound towards home, everyone seemed to be optimistic about Shawn's condition. "He'll be alright!" "He'll pull through!" "If he was going to die, he would have already," Montell offered. I was thinking to myself, "What?" I was sure to remain quiet throughout this particular conversation. I was hoping no one asked for my opinion. My heart, mind, and spirit were all telling me Shawn was not going to wake up. To me, he just appeared too traumatized by the incident. He was full of fluid and his eyes appeared to be nailed shut. So much so, I could not picture them ever reopening. With all of that said, I still hoped I was dead wrong.

We arrived home from the hospital about twenty minutes later. My sister and I, along with my two uncles, all tried to explain to our grandparents how Shawn was doing. Grandma asked, "How is he?" as soon as we entered. "Not too good," Montell softly stated while rubbing his palms together. Grandma immediately glared over at her partner and yelled, "Shawn's not doing too well. He may not make it!" "What?" granddad shouted in response due to his hearing problem. "I said, Shawn is in bad shape and he may not get better." Partially understanding his wife, he slowly leaned forward in his chair. "Shawn might die!" she impatiently yelled. The defeated look which suddenly appeared on granddad's face instantly broke my heart. As he sat back into his chair, I could see and feel the pain swelling inside of him. His face read the exact expression a child has when denied access to something by a parent. As daddy gazed emotionless, grandma pierced through the window observing the area where Shawn strolled into trouble. "These streets sure are getting worst; poor Shawn," she sadly stated. "That boy was bad as shit, but I love him so; I pray he pulls through." We all were huddled in the living room as before, but now under more humbling circumstances. We had no idea at this time, in the midst of all the pain, justice was still prevailing.

The Govans community was in unrest about what had transpired with my cousin's incident. Most of the parents in the neighborhood were outraged about how this all took place. Evan's family and Tee's mom were in search of more answers. They all had trouble believing the drive-by story Todd gave police. Skippy informed me and I believed him, but speaking about it at the time did not appeal to me. I learned early on, speaking too much is never a good thing in the streets. To put it in plain English, I did not truly know all of the facts. I believed Skippy's claims, but for me, it was technically still hearsay. Thankfully, after only twenty-four hours, the pressure from the neighborhood and good police work forced Todd to come clean about the details of the shooting. Apparently, the pressure and the guilt intensified, causing Todd to give up on his drive-by shooting theme. He had made an attempt to implicate Old York Road in the crime, but fell short. During this fabrication, he even stated, "The bullet went right passed me and hit Shawn." As my cousin continued to fight for his life, his assailant was now in custody, apparently for murder.

Police came by the house and shared bittersweet news with my aunt and the rest of the family. My family was more surprised than I thought they should have been. However, I realized they were never outside with my friends and I to actually witness how Todd constantly used intimidation tactics on the younger kids for fun. They were never at the basketball court to see him trip a guy as he attempted a lay-up, or how he would dare a guy to foul him on a shot attempt. Not only was this sort of incident not a surprise when it came to Todd, it would pretty much be expected. Todd finally told the authorities the shooting was a huge mistake. As much as I know the stupid game was not a mistake, I did believe Todd did not want Shawn dead. The fright I observed on Todd's face was something no one had ever seen; he too was scared during the incident. However, the fact still remained; his desire to simply be a bully placed our loved one in a tremendous struggle for his life.

Back home, my aunt continually called the hospital to check on the status of Shawn's condition. During these calls, despite my intuition, I was still hoping and awaiting a smile to appear on Marie's face. I never wanted to be wrong so badly. After more than twenty-four hours, Shawn's condition remained the same. I wondered how long my aunt would continue calling at this pace. She was really driving herself crazy. Meaning, she would get jacked up and excited to make the calls, only to quickly fall into a depressed state after hanging up with no change in the news. In a situation like this, I learned I could not have put my own views beyond the needs of others. It's like I felt what was coming, but I kept my opinions to myself.

The exhaustion from the course of events finally landed me inside of my bedroom for the night. Thoughts about the incident and how Shawn appeared in the hospital bed had drained me emotionally, mentally, and physically. It was a blessing to receive the support from the few classy people left in the neighborhood. They showed a lot of compassion towards our family. Now, I just needed time alone. I sat on the end of my twin bed and watched, from across the hallway, my sister and Freddy hug and cry over Shawn's situation. I believed my sister and I felt the same, but she was trying hard to increase her faith. At this time, I knew there was a God, and was learning life on earth will often be unpredictable at times, yet true religion still escaped us all.

After about ten minutes of watching my sister and Freddy crying, I walked across the small hallway to help console the two. Seeing tears rolling down Freddy's face brought back memories of his fallen friend

Wilbert. It was still a difficult sight for me to handle. Freddy was an intelligent, cool, street-smart guy my sister adored. The two fell in love and Freddy quickly became a vital figure in our lives. He showed us how to be cooler. He gave us a more refined sense of respect, style, and class. Make no mistake, Shawn and I were already very stylish young guys. We were a little ahead of our time, as far as the older guys were concerned. People outside of the neighborhood believed Shawn and I were much older than we were. I recall being asked if I were 16 when I was 12 years old due to my attire; Forum Adidas and an Adidas jogging suit. To put it all in perspective, Freddy, aside from our grandparents, may have been the best positive influence we had, and yet, he too sold drugs.

I sat up with my sister and Freddy all night talking about Shawn and the better days of McCabe. This gave us all a stronger sense of peace. Shawn's time-clock had reached its 40th hour, but we still made progress emotionally. The three of us pulled together and realized the situation was leaning more towards the negative in reference to Shawn's recovery. We were sure not to place our feelings and views on the others, but we had an idea about what would transpire within the next eight hours. The realization didn't cause the pain to subside, but the suspicions were nearly over. By early evening, around the 43rd hour, we received a call from Johns Hopkins Hospital about our loved one.

The phone call had been the first, although my aunt had placed at least ten to the critical care unit. Dr. Spencer was on the other line, but the smile on my aunt's face only lasted for a second. The family all huddled around Marie, making sure we came in contact with her physically for support. We all used her facial expressions to determine the type of news forwarded. Witnessing my aunt's face break apart was heart-wrenching. Her distressed reaction created a domino effect on the small, semi-circle around the phone before trickling into the front room with my guardians. Our worst fears were confirmed. The process with Shawn's recovery had turned the wrong way. Sometime after the operation, Shawn's brain suffered damage due to a lack of oxygen. He was brain dead, solely supported by a respirator. With a damaged heart, a non-functioning brain, and only one remaining lung, my aunt reluctantly made the logical call for her asthmatic son to move on. Marie ultimately agreed with Dr. Spencer and Johns Hopkins Hospital; it would be best if Shawn was taken off life-support and allowed to go

"Home." Just like that, my best friend and closest cousin was officially gone. Shawn Fernando Alexander was pronounced dead on a Saturday at 9:15 p.m. His body was laid to rest six days later at March Funeral Home, across from our old home on Kennedy Avenue on Friday the 13th of November, 1987.

# Chapter 9

# SEARCHING

Shawn's death immediately sent shockwaves throughout our northeast community. My cousin's very stubborn and sometimes rude attitude proved to have little effect on his popularity. He knew how to be a great friend to many, and how to make a great impression on those he cared for. His funeral was the first time I had ever witnessed so many young people in such a sad state. Hundreds of people came to lend their support. It was almost as if my cousin was a teen celebrity or icon of some sort. It was truly amazing to observe such a large turnout for a 15 year old kid. As everyone periodically would burst into tears, I sat quietly knowing Shawn was in a better place, but irritated about how things were between us during the time leading up to his death. The first few nights were as tough as it gets. I would wake up feeling as if this was all a nightmare, only to go downstairs and see small evidence of the truth. Traces of Shawn's blood could still be easily located in the crevices of the ashy, wooden living room floor. School was no different. For several weeks, I could feel masses of eyes locking in on my every move. I was a pretty popular kid in school, but I usually liked to stay relatively private. Shawn's death unintentionally introduced me to so many more people. I was not eager to meet any new friends, but the love being displayed was irresistible and actually may have been what I really needed, what I was internally searching for.

As things improved, I also became a bit more focused and mature. I began controlling whatever I could; things like my grades and my choice of friends. I had plenty of friends and could be seen with several different types of individuals throughout the course of a day. Still, I was quite lonely. I was trying to get a grasp on life and understand the frequently elusive question to myself, "Why?" I wanted and needed to understand, "Why was I the only kid around without a mother?" "Why was the closest person to me now gone?" "Why was there no plans for the forty-thousand plus I had coming?" There were others as well. I thought, "How am I supposed to get help or support from home when everyone there has serious issues of their own to overcome?" My grandparents did all they knew how to, but they were getting older. My sister was usually a blur. She usually ran the streets and enjoyed her life and freedom with Freddy. Marie, Frank, BoBo, and Montell were all involved with situations stemming from drug and alcohol abuse. This realization placed me in a peculiar position as a teen. I truly love my family, yet I was sure they could not do much for my growth in terms of becoming a man. Lost, lonely, but full of personality, I began to try and view myself as a grown-up. The largest disparity between myself and many other mature adults; working jobs but not enjoying the type of work performed. I was never a fan of the dead-end, nine-to-five. This was compounded by still not knowing what I wanted to be in life.

The very elusive question, "What would you like to become when you grow up Odell?" was still evasive. I continuously tried not to think about it much due to my uncertainty. I knew I did not want or need to sell drugs as the others believed they had to. Drug dealing, I could easily discard from my way of thinking. I felt going to jail was not for me, and I understood the resource I had coming would sustain me until I located a solid path. As I made attempts to come up with some structure or a plan of my own, I decided to stay concentrated on doing well in school. At this time, that's truly all I had of any substance.

After momentarily slipping academically following Shawn's untimely death, I began to, again, excel in the classroom. English, Social Studies, and Science were my favorite subjects in school. I was also great in Gym class, as most were. Basketball was still a preferred hobby. I played more as time passed. Basketball gave me an outlet from the world. As long as I played, I hardly thought about more important issues like school, family or social life, or even girls. I was quiet, but often effective on the court. Evan was still my hoops partner despite his recent move from McCabe. Tee's mom followed through on her promise to move as well. Kizzie and Karl soon followed. Shawn's death put a rush on these already confirmed decisions made by my friends' parents. As the new year approached, with the exception of Elroy, all of our childhood peers had relocated to other areas throughout the city.

Becoming an honor roll student as a sophomore was huge for me. I had proved to myself I could achieve something without much assistance. My grandma was excited for me, although she hardly monitored my progress. She had tremendous confidence in me and usually seemed to be content with allowing me to do things my way. My dad approached my progress in the same manner, but he was missing again during this period. My grandparents were very old fashioned. They had it rough back in the days of their youth. Education was not the main focus; my grandparents concentrated far more on raising us from a premise of love and labor. Neither of my grandparents reached their sophomore year in high school, and at this time, no one in my immediate family finished college.

The long days of healing continued, and every holiday during the end of 1987 was a complete drag. I could not seem to stop thinking about my cousin. Holidays simply were not the same without him. They were all sad reminders of how bad things had become. Everything seemed to be a negative first. On Thanksgiving, I was unable to eat all of my food; I had no appetite. On Christmas, I got up late instead of extra-early, and still didn't open all of my gifts right away. I missed having Shawn there to share in the moment with me. New Year's simply represented the notion, once someone has passed, they're gone forever. I sat in my dark room listening to dudes display their shooting talents by playing with guns; I was thinking this sounds a lot like any other weekend. The world was beginning to cave in around me. I could see the many changes taking place. Whether instances of frequent gunfire or behavioral changes within, the negativity was clear.

McCabe Avenue and Northern High became two opposing worlds. In school, I was this young inquisitive, optimistic teen with pretty good grades and zest for cute girls. On McCabe, I was this lost, worried, lonely and withdrawn kid with no direction. I was probably the only black, inner-city teen who liked school more than home. School was everything for me at this time. This was where the most support was, the prettiest females were, and where I felt the safest. I treated school like home, and used home as a place to write and spend time with my grandma. My grandmother quickly became my very best friend after Shawn passed. She was the only person on earth I felt comfortable talking to, about anything. I had always hoped for a mate to feel this way about. I sort of wanted what my sister and Freddy had. They shared a closeness in an era where going steady had lost its flare a bit. At times, my lonely moments felt too damn lonely. I knew lots of females, but only one seemed to fit with my personality. Tracey was the only girl whose style matched my persona. After many nights of swatting the butterflies, or contemplating with nervousness, I decided to approach Tracey with hopes of going steady in the near-future.

Tracey's sophomore status allowed the process of trying to go from being single to steady less stressful. Although I was a bit nervous, this gave me the opportunity to communicate with Tracey without saying a word. I would continuously make eye contact with her or speak to her nicely. I even used an old ice breaking tactic. I offered Tracey candy. I was convinced, "Now and Later" candies did not have an expiration date on its effectiveness. It did not take very long for Tracey and I to hit it off. We exchanged numbers, and from this point on, I felt no desire to interact with any other females in a flirtatious manner.

School was teaching me plenty. Maybe even a few things I should not have learned there. I would hear the stories about sexual encounters amongst students, which supposedly took place on school grounds. I witnessed a dice game or two with my own eyes on school grounds. I knew guys would occasionally spark up the weed in the restrooms. Elroy, the lone pal remaining, never attended school without his chrome .25 automatic handgun. I observed the gun one day during Gym class in the locker room. The whole Old York Road / McCabe Avenue rivalry usually had Elroy a bit paranoid. He and I were opposites. He usually felt comfortable on McCabe. I once felt this way. McCabe was probably the only place where I was not completely comfortable as a young teen. I guess this was what brought Elroy and I closer together. Well, the girls too. Like myself, Elroy loved females, but often played around too much to be taken seriously by the ones classified in the streets as "winners" or bombshells. In the streets folks would say a dude was "winning" if he made a lot of money or had easy access to the finer things in life. The same held true for women, but they usually got the nod or the "winner" label solely for being fly and gorgeous.

Elroy compromised his ability to interact with the beauties simply because he really enjoyed playing nasty or vulgar pranks for laughs. So, despite his financial victories, many only classified Elroy by the pranks he practiced. He'd fart close to people or belch extremely loud in someone's ear; or just play with peoples' ears. He was a hilarious, 16 year old; not a great school student, but extremely bright in other areas. All Elroy cared about was making $600-$1000 a day selling drugs, making folks laugh or frustrating them with pranks, and having tons of sex with the young ladies. I was his key to success with a few females, and he was my ticket to healthy laughs every five minutes. I needed to laugh and smile about something besides Tracey, and he gave me this. The drug money, I simply didn't need it.

As time passed, Elroy would offer me more than a cramped stomach. He also educated me on the streets, free of charge. I never asked to know all about what took place in the world of the streets, but I gladly listened. Although I was fixed on never participating with any illegal activities, I found the information interesting. Elroy spoke on how easy it was to make lots of money; how safe it was to hustle around McCabe Avenue. Wilbert's and Shawn's deaths were not enough to constantly see patrol cars surveying the area. What can I say? We were in the hood. There are several instances where a black man is killed, and there's simply no coverage on the local news, no intense follow-up by police, no arrests; nothing. It's almost like the individual never passed, or never even existed. Benny's arrest and conviction seemed to promote this lack of interest or aggression by police.

Benny was serving the second year of his fifty year sentence, yet he continued to play a vital role with my decision to stand clear of the foolery. Benny often called the house to see how everyone was doing. He was really bothered by Shawn's passing. The few moments of silence he expressed on the phone told the story. This amplified his desire to continuously drill me about flying straight or never getting involved with drugs. Whenever Benny would call, I normally would allow a guy or two from the neighborhood to come in and speak with him. This usually took place about two or three times a week. Mama really liked Benny, so she never complained about guys coming in to use our phone, and she always accepted Benny's collect calls.

After learning how Elroy was able to take $250, and easily turn it into $600, by selling cocaine with the assistance of baking soda, I realized large amounts of thinking and preparation goes into drug dealing. It's time consuming to fill several very small baggies with the substance. One has to be pretty accurate to complete the packaging process in a timely fashion. Elroy, considered slow by school standards, was anything but in the streets. He, and three, out of his four older brothers hustled in the area. By the time Elroy and I connected closer, he had already been arrested once for selling drugs. "Man, that was nothing, that was bullshit, a humble," he said while giggling. The "humble" charge means you were arrested, stemming from something defined as a surprise, or considered to be stupid or meaningless. A "humble" is a mistake arrest! So, there I was, learning the streets, getting more comfortable with my surroundings, elevating my level of play on the ball court, and falling really hard for a girl for the first time. I tried to remain a positive young man by doing well in school, staying active in sports, writing, and making sure I did not get too close to the neighborhood drama. Elroy spent plenty of time glorifying drug dealing, but I remained focused on positive ideas. "O, what kind of cookies you want?" he asked while in the school's cafe' lunch line. "Chocolate chip buddy, thanks," I replied as he opened the eyes of the school's cook with his own roll of bread. In his hand, was at least $700. He caught me looking at the large, neatly rolled money and jokingly asked, "O, what you want a stash or something?" Here, a "stash" are drugs fronted to the seller who will make a set percentage for moving the product. This is done with larger amounts as well, but the term "stash" is not really used there. There was one thing I learned on my own about my people from the hood: Usually, if they're offering something so freely, you can bet lots of trouble and pain will ultimately come along with it. "Nah, I'll never sell drugs homeboy," I replied while shaking my head frantically. Elroy cut his eye at me, and with a devilish grin he said, "Never say never!"

Drugs were an everyday occurrence on McCabe Avenue by the late 80's. It was no big deal to see nearly every young black male hustling on all of the many corners. No one seemed to even consider another alternative. School, to most, was simply a waste of time. "Why don't any of the guys just hustle for a few months, then quit and do something legal before they get caught and go to jail?" I asked Elroy inquisitively. "Man, shit like that only happens in the movies or on television," he replied while shaking his head. "You know it, a guy gets his shit together right before he dies n' shit," Elroy followed with laughter. "Not here buddy, niggas dyin' chasin' money," he followed. "You know none of us finished school O. What else is there?" he asked while shrugging his shoulders. I simply stated, "Go back to school." "Yeah right!" he replied with a giggle. "For real though; that shit you talkin' is what some niggas be planning to do," he said with certainty. "Let me make some money, get a job and chill out n' shit, but it never turns out that way," he added as we sat at a virtually empty table. "Oh yeah?" I mumbled. "I wonder why," I stated in disbelief. "Money O, greed, the shit is very addictive n' shit, just like using drugs O!" "We're too addicted to the cash flow for that slow working bullshit buddy!" "Look at these fuckin broke ass cooks in here n' shit O. They in this school cafe cookin for hardly no money. That is sad homie!" Elroy stared at the cafe workers with a shameful look in his eyes. "Niggas can never have enough money, that's why they don't do normal shit," he stated calmly. "Goin' to jail for years, or even being shot up or killed means absolutely nothing to a real nigga O." "They'll die and kill for the money."

Despite my struggles, I was elated not to have to think about money right away. I was learning a lot about the allures of society; what it does to folks is sad, but in some strange or weird way, I also find it interesting. The information Elroy shared was depressing, but the jobs average folks worked was impressive to me. The money I had coming in two years served as a security blanket. I was simply hoping by the time I received this money; I would also have a good path to follow. I frustrated myself quite often with not knowing what to consider for the future. My best counter for this problem was to forget about it all and enjoy myself. The vibe I got from the streets pushed me further away from that sadness. However, Elroy and I were gaining respect for one another and really enjoyed hanging together. I spent quite a bit of time with Elroy, but he was unable to participate in the things I liked most. If I played basketball, Elroy would hardly ever come. He was extremely uncoordinated when it came to basketball. Catching a football cleanly was a bit of an adventure for him at times as well, but he played that sport fairly well. Still, the ball would hit his chest and the ground, before his arms would come together.

In school, I only saw Elroy in Gym class and during lunch time. The students with learning disabilities were designated to the second floor. The rest of the students were instructed not to go there, and students on the second floor were not allowed on any of the other three floors, without specific reasoning. As for the writing and sketching I enjoyed, Elroy simply could not read well enough to feel very comfortable around literature. Still, we grew as friends and found ways to enjoy similar things. Movies, shopping, music, and the company of females, just to name a few. I was sure not to be insensitive and judgmental towards the guy who made me laugh and enjoy life under such testy circumstances. I'm not making fun of anyone! Read and comprehend the ENTIRE story and you will understand this! Here and throughout my story, I am just stating the facts of my testimony. Regardless of my pal's make-up, Elroy was the only dealer I felt close to. Elroy is a super cool dude; when not dealing, and even sometimes when he was, he was simply the funniest guy alive. He never cared for the image or stereotype other dealers craved to have. He did not need to be like the others who portrayed the hottest rappers. Tareek, a younger kid, and friend of Elroy's from a nearby neighborhood took another approach. He would assist Elroy on occasion. Elroy just loved money and wanted lots of it. During this time, it was really hard for me to view him as a bad guy. I felt he was my friend, and the fact that he sold drugs was simply not enough to interfere with that.

Elroy usually hustled alone due to the impulsive violent minds around him. Outsiders, meaning guys who were not from McCabe Avenue or its connecting streets, were not usually welcomed with open arms, but this concept was forever changing. Earlier, regardless of age, anyone from a distant neighborhood would catch hell from the others, especially if they were not accompanied by someone from the block. I would hear statements like, "Hey, don't bring your boy around here no more or we're going to fuck him up or take all his gear or money," or "Slim! Go back up on the hill where you from," or "You don't belong down here nigga." Benny was huge on this idea, but things were loosening up for newcomers.

Spring rolled around sooner than anticipated. I guess all those wonderful times I shared with Tracey helped. We were exclusive and one of the school's most promising young couples. Tracey was an entirely different level of girlfriend. My entire family took to her well and accepted our relationship with cheers. I would also meet her mom and younger sister. They were both receptive and very gracious towards me. I found a feeling I never had before. It was a feeling of normalcy, happiness, anxiousness, compassion, and fear all in one. My life was as complex and emotional as one could picture, but I hid it very well. With all I had going on inside emotionally, I was still searching for something real. Tracey was indeed real, but I could not determine if she was what I needed or if she was just a very good paint job on my beat-up-vehicle of a life. Nevertheless, I proceeded to go with the flow and just enjoy the feeling I received from the best relationship of my life at the time.

Tracey and I talked a lot. We were like most teenage couples during this time. We all stayed up chatting, on our house phones, for nearly three hours at a time. Hard to imagine today, what was actually said in order to stay interested in a conversation for so long. At 14 or 15 years of age, how much could there be to talk about? For us, it was never about the content, I guess. Maybe knowing someone you really care for would sit on the phone as long as you would, was the true message in it all. Life was moving on and I was growing up, or down, depending on how one saw it. Things felt better for the first time since Shawn's death. I had wished I could feel the same about my aunt Marie. She fell into a deep depression and began to use drugs and alcohol even more to cope with the loss. No one really noticed how bad things were except for grandma. They all were too confused and dealing with their own troubles to support my troubled aunt. Things felt ok, but the truth be told; my family was falling apart, and I was more confused than I led on. To make matters even more complicated, I received a familiar surprise visit.

During the Spring Break of 1988, my dad showed up from out of nowhere on a nice sunny weekend. It was good to see my dad. He had not been around for a while and I sorely needed his presence. When he came to the house, we talked a little on the porch. He assured me he would be around more often, just as before. He did not stay very long, but he did give me $250 for Easter. I never shared the concert misfortune with my dad; I knew as I gracefully accepted the money, I would not be purchasing any more high-end sneakers. My dad left after placing the entire household in silence. My dad usually placed a bristling effect on my household. In the eyes of my family, my dad was never to be forgiven for the death of my mom. The remaining pain of Shawn's death killed any possibilities of the family reconnecting with my dad any time soon. My dad was very sad about Shawn's passing. It was tough for me to share the news with him. Still, he was headlining this visit and his presence simply brought back all of the sad emotions of 1977.

At 14, I was not interested in any type of negativity, including participating in any energies between my family and my dad. I loved my dad, and I was a firm believer in second chances from the very beginning. My family had made my dad so uncomfortable; he elected not to converse or offer any words to my family on Shawn's behalf. Shawn and my dad were always very fond of each other. Shawn liked how my dad was with me. Shawn's dad never came around, but still sparingly sent support payments. I only saw him twice during Shawn's life. The third time was when he learned of his son's death. The family was shocked he even showed up at the house soon afterwards, but not as surprised as they were about Shawn's resemblance to his father. It was a scary thing to witness. My dad and I also share a striking resemblance. My dad coming around made me feel special. He somehow stayed as a frontrunner or favorite to me, in reference to all of my family members and friends, besides Mama. He loved me. I knew it, no matter what anyone thought of him.

The feelings about life and my union with Tracey encouraged me to write more often. I would spend hours at a time expressing myself to Tracey on paper. It was nothing for me to write a six- or seven-page letter to her, just after leaving her house. I simply enjoyed writing. As always, many of these letters never made it to her hands, but I had fun putting them together. I would take the best lines I created from the writings and use them later during conversations. Tracey was awesome, but as a whole, my compassion for females was growing to newer heights. I view females at a very high regard. I believe all women deserve to be treated like queens. I feel the majority of women simply want to be loved. I've always detested the feeling of guilt I received whenever I mistreated a female in any way. I have always had a soft spot in my heart for women, but as a teen, I believe this often got pushed to the side for personal feelings of lust.

Tracey being a vital part of my sanity was a blessing I was totally unprepared for. My relationship and the ability to express myself gracefully gave me a ton of confidence to socialize with anyone; male or female, at any place. I was eager to put my social skills through the test with finally setting my buddy Evan up with the most popular girl at Northern High. I figured the test would be a simple one, considering the two were already fond of one another. Vikki was in the 10thgrade as I, but Evan failed the 9thgrade. My friend had already failed three times, but no one spoke to him about his failures. He had the most structure at home, but something went very wrong. I never asked and he never told. Evan was a private guy and I could relate. This was what made his infatuation with Vikki so interesting. I believed I was already in love, so it was nice to focus on a possible relationship of a friend.

After getting through the holiday injury-free from hoops, and being able to add a new pair of Nike Air Force One sneakers to my collection of thirty, I returned to school feeling pretty good. My grades were decent. I had an overall average of 88%. Not too shabby for a confused teen with an unstable home environment! I was eager to increase my GPA by the end of the semester. I was also looking forward to continuing my great relationship with Tracey. Elroy and I still shared lots of laughs, and I was thrilled Evan gave me the nod to put a good word in for him with Vikki. Again, Evan hardly found an interest in girls. When we were younger, he would even throw rocks at them, just for liking or trying to talk to him.

Vikki presented something different for Evan's approach. She was so beautiful; it was nearly impossible not to see yourself with her; if only for a second. She was simply hot. I encountered the bombshell in the cafeteria sitting with a table full of other very pretty girls. Evan and I sat to the far left of the young ladies. We all were eating mediocre school pizza and drinking chocolate milk. Several of the school's high rollers; Javon, Doc, Donny, and Pat, were engulfed in a dice game, undetected in the corner of the cafe. I was cordial with these guys, but they were all better affiliated with Hubert, and the guys from Old York Road. The Old York Road students at Northern High were the guys who made Elroy a bit nervous, and his hustle look a lot smaller. A few of these 10thgraders would hop into their brand-new Toyotas after school. Vikki turned their heads as well, but showed little interest in them because of her boyfriend Frankie, who they all knew quite well. Frankie was also a known dealer from Old York Road.

After purchasing a three-pack of chocolate chip cookies, I decided to drop in on the beauties. The slower I walked, the faster my heart rate became. I was only able to relax because I was not the one displaying the crush. Did I have one? Yes, but I could not admit it back then. "Hello ladies," I stated gently. An array of, "Hey O," returned. "I don't mean to interrupt y'all, I just wanted to tell you, my buddy Evan wants to meet with you," I said with a slight smile in Vikki's direction. "Oh yeah," she said calmly. "That's cool, I wanted to ask him if he had a girlfriend," she indicated. "He doesn't," I replied quickly. "I don't know about him though, you know how those light-skin dudes are," she said while looking at her nodding friends. "Nah, he's not like that at all," I said passionately. "He's cool; that's my boy," I followed confidently. "I'll let you know something during Gym class O," she stated. "Cool," I replied. "Yeah, I may leave early tomorrow," she said. "Ok then, see you in class," I said smoothly. I got up from the table, feeling the eyes of the entire café beaming at me as I waved goodbye. I was on the radar; under surveillance for possibly cheating.

The entire student-body was watching closely to see if they could gain any information on me to tell Tracey. I turned to read the fright on my buddy's face, only to hear, "O, O, O," Vikki yelled. I jogged back a few paces with eyebrows raised. "We all wanted you to know how sorry we are for your loss with your cousin," she said while the others innocently smiled. "Thanks ladies," I uttered passed the lump in my throat. I got away from the ladies before my tear ducks fully opened. It was good to know people still thought about what I'd been through. I went over to the girls to play matchmaker, but I achieved so much more. I realized at this moment; I had more friends than I thought.

I sat back down at the table after preventing myself from crying. "I got good news buddy," I said to Evan. "What did you do O?" he replied smiling. "What do you think I did?" I asked. "It's cool, I think she likes you too," I said with confidence. "She thought you were the funny-acting type, but I fixed all of that," I added. "Oh yeah," was all I could get from my friend at this point. He was nervous as hell. "I want in on this shit," I stated excitingly. "Hey, y'all can use my room," I added while smiling. Evan's intimidation in reference to Vikki would swell by the second. My friend had gone from having virtually no experience at all with females, to the most wanted girl in the entire school. Evan handled pressure on the basketball court just fine, but this literally was an entirely different animal. "Are you alright buddy?" I said as I watched my friend's complexion change from white to hot pink. "Don't worry, you're about to make history," I said enthusiastically.

I decided to let up on my friend about Vikki. He clearly needed time to take it all in. We finished out the lunch period simply finding amusement from the social diversity in the cafe. We were forced to stop chatting by a loud outburst from Evan's younger cousin and funny-man, Ross. He studied on the lower-level with Elroy. Whenever Ross and Elroy shared a stage, someone would come close to dying from laughter. "Dirty Reese," he yelled. Ross was yelling at one of the star football players as they all exited the lunch line. Most students at Northern High didn't look up to their student-athletes. Instead, they would taunt them with hygiene jokes. "Dirty Reese," he yelled again. Reese was one of the school's finest football players, but to the students his reputation was based on his occasional dingy appearance. "I'm going to fuck somebody up when I find out who sayin' that shit," Reese yelled out. Evan and I, along with the rest of the cafe, were in stitches. Ross was one of my childhood drawing partners. He's an unbelievable artist. He's so good; he actually gets bored with his own gift. He continued to taunt the running back as he tried to eat his lunch, then the big one came. "Dirty Reese, you dirty bitch!" Ross yelled still hiding in the sea of students. The roar of laughter startled the staff, causing security to enter the area, but it all quickly settled down. This was Northern High alright! A place where, in the drop of a hat, you may forget you're even in a school.

After assuring Tracey the small talk I had with Vikki during lunch time was innocent, I hurried off to the gymnasium. I had no intentions on messing up my good relationship with Tracey. I was simply having a lot of fun. Ok, perhaps I was living a bit of a fantasy through my buddy. There, are you all satisfied now? I got dressed in the green and white uniform we all were instructed to wear during Gym class. I took to the court and played with a controlled grace, and powerful speed. Donny joined me as we conquered the court on 6th period. Vikki and others cheered from the top of the bleachers, as I demonstrated my 36 inch vertical leap to create an array or assortment of dunks. I still was not a very good player, but I could often portray one. I could dunk a basketball with ease at 13 and a half, and run with the best of them. With Donny running point guard, I was able to run freely in transition and create; portraying greats like Larry Nance, and one of my all-time favorites, Dominique Wilkins.

"Looking good son," Mr. Kemps stated as he smiled. "Thanks sir," I replied as I headed to the bleachers after my first loss in four games. Mr. Kemps was everyone's favorite teacher. He was like the great uncle or father figure so many inner-city kids never had. My uncle BoBo was sort of like

Mr. Kemps, minus the spiritual knowledge and the consumption of vodka, on my uncle's end. Mr. Kemps would often play ball with us. At 6'3 he presented a problem for us kids. Lots of students would seek advice from Mr. Kemps. I probably would have, if I truly realized I ever had a problem. As I watched the late 30s teacher school all of his students on the court, I heard the question, "Where are we going?" It was Vikki looking down from above. I looked upwards to catch the smile of the angelic beauty, and a little more from her legs being partially open. "We're going to my house," I stated with confidence, knowing it would be very tough to go to my house during school hours. Grandma did not monitor me tightly, but she would never let me inside of the house during school hours unless I was sick, very sick or almost dead.

I somehow managed to put this problem on the back burner. The focus was on hooking up with Vikki outside of school property. The way I saw it, an opportunity like this only presents itself once in a blue moon. I was so excited about the 12 noon meeting scheduled for the next day; I went to sleep the night before actually preparing my whereabouts lies. I hardly ever lied to my grandmother in the past. I convinced myself, I was due one. I was still excited, even with knowing Vikki was not interested in me. I hardly cared. I was content with possibly being the guy who once had a naked, Vikki inside of his bedroom. When I shared the news about the location with Evan, he did not seem too receptive. To be honest, I could still read the fear on his face from earlier. He understood he was about to spend time alone with a young lady who was not at all shy. This scared the mess out of my good friend.

Time flew by, and it was time for a meeting for the ages. The entire school wanted to get close to Vikki, and she was leaving school early alone with Evan and I. She decided not to drive her boyfriend's car to school on this day, just to play it safe. I was so excited, I found myself cutting class for the first time in nearly two years. I was actually surprised Evan met me in the hallway before Art class. He did not appear to be very enthused but he was there. He made the walk toward the exit feel as if I was escorting him to the gas chamber. I saw something totally different. When we exited the school on this beautiful day, I could see her from a mile away. She wore a Guess Jeans outfit; dark blue to be specific. She always wore the latest fashions most of us could not afford regularly. As we approached the smiling diva, I said gently, "This is going to be fun." Vikki was all about fun. This situation was nothing like what I received from Tracey. Although Tracey was tremendously sexy, our relationship was based on loving and positive emotions. Excursions such as this were based purely on the physical. We all greeted and headed for a nearby bus stop. During the walk, Vikki and I were laughing and joking, while Evan spent most of the ride to the city with his head down. "What's wrong man?" I asked in concern. "Nothing, I'm cool," he replied. After transferring from the # 44 bus, near the school, to the # 8 and exiting on York Road, we headed towards my house on McCabe. Moods drastically changed. All the poor lies I conjured up the night before, all seemed stupid as we drew closer to my home. Evan seemingly perked up, knowing how my grandma could be. I believed he was hoping she'd turn us away. Even Vikki was afraid. She heard how impulsively violent the guys on McCabe could be. She also knew it was not an issue for them to disrespect a female, especially one from Old York.

The closer we got to my front door, the more nervous I became. It was only 1 p.m. therefore many of the street soldiers were still asleep. There were a few guys who noticed the beauty walking in between Evan and I. We heard lines like, "Got damn O," "Who the fuck is that?" "Hook me up?" "Is that that girl Vikki?" "That bitch is bad!" one guy yelled to another. None of these lines drew a response. We had reached my porch, and I just knew my grandma was sitting in her favorite chair. I was unsuccessful with coming up with a good lie, therefore I decided to just pretend as if we got out of school early. I then took a deep breath and opened the front door. We all walked in and I believed my no-confidence expression gave us away early. "Hey Ma," I said hesitantly. "Why in the hell are you back here for? It's not three o'clock yet?" Mama stated. At this very moment, I knew we were finished. The lie I came up with could have been the truth, but it still would not have mattered. "Y'all must be crazy," she yelled. "You better get the fuck out of here and come back at four," she stated with certainty. Before I could even start to lie, a resounding "BYE!" exited Mama's mouth. We lasted about 8.7 seconds inside of the house, before we could have been seen walking back in the opposite direction.

After the embarrassing encounter with my grandma, we were in desperate need of a second plan. I was beginning to feel like my hopes of maybe seeing Vikki naked, or hearing her make sexy sounds from having intercourse with my friend were slipping away. I learned early through observing my sister, most popular females are typically impatient. I believed she would eventually decide to just head home. Old York Road was out of the question. Vikki's boyfriend Frankie was probably already waiting for school to end to pick up his sneaky little girlfriend. Who am I to be calling someone sneaky? Soon, we would be headed back in the direction of York Road with no true destination, when Evan finally opened his mouth. "Let's just go to my house," he said. "Are you sure?" I asked. "Yeah, my mom is at work until five," he offered. "Man, why didn't you say that at first?" I shouted with laughter. "You had us go through that ordeal with my grandma, knowing all along we were riding right by your apartment?" I shouted. "You're a funny guy E," I added while shaking my head. We redirected ourselves and ended up walking back north in the direction of the apartment where my friend had been living since his family's move from McCabe Avenue.

On the way, we walked pass the historic Senator Theater, located on York Road. "Hey y'all, I'm going to write movies one day," I said with eagerness. "Can I be in it?" Vikki asked as she smiled. "Hell yeah, you can be in it," I replied happily. The Senator Theater has welcomed many artists from around the world to showcase their talents in acting and in film making. I was simply passing by having one of my three second dreams. Little did I know, ten minutes later, inside of Evan's apartment, scenes would begin to unfold just like a major fictionalized comedy, and we were the stars, especially my pal. When we first entered Evan's apartment, I became really giggly. What made this all so interesting was, we knew what Vikki wanted. She was not joining us to just hang out, talk or act shy. She had no desire to go steady with Evan. He was too broke. We all were. She knew it, but she was physically attracted to him, and not even being spoiled rotten by her hustling boyfriend was going to stop her. Vikki honestly believed Evan was a virgin. This was the major reasoning behind her hot pursuit. She wanted to be someone's first. I was never sure if my buddy was a virgin. He may have been. I never saw him with a female before this point. All I knew was now was the time. "Hey, where's the Kool-Aid?" I asked while chuckling. "It's in the fridge O," Evan replied in a lower tone. The time had come and I had a front row seat. We all sat at the end of Evan's twin-size bed, watching his 19 inch television. Evan sat in between Vikki and I. He was still looking pretty darn nervous. About five minutes passed when suddenly, I looked to my right and Vikki was instantly sucking on Evan's neck. "OKaaay, there's my sign," I said with a huge grin. I got up, closed the door on the two, and entered Evan's mom's room. I fell backwards into laughter on his mom's bed, excited for my friend. I was kicking upwards in the air while trying hard to hear sounds and make sure not to make any. "Yes!" I whispered with excitement. My boy Evan was making out with the girl of everyone's dreams, so I thought. I sat in Evan's mom's room with a smile cemented on my face. I was relaxing and really looking forward to hearing the details. I turned on the tube after sitting in silence, trying to hear sultry sounds coming from my buddy's room. My eyes danced back and forth from Evan's bedroom door, to the hit soap, General Hospital. I was hoping my friend and Vikki were into one another as "Luke" and "Laura" were on television. During a commercial break, I heard a little movement in the other room so I turned the television off. Seconds later, I heard a furious Vikki exiting Evan's room, exploding into the room where I sat. "OH MY GOD!" She yelled in frustration. "What?" I replied while trying to hold a diminishing smile. "That muthafucka is scared as shit!" she stated with embarrassment. "Hah?" I replied with a confused expression. Vikki violently slammed Evan's mom's room door and stated in a lower tone, "He's in there acting like he is fuckin sleep and shit." "For real?" I stated while giggling. "Yes O, that shit ain't funny," she replied with a slight frown. "That shit ain't funny O," she followed. "I've never seen no shit like this in my whole fuckin' life," she said confidently. "I'm sorry!" I stated while trying to control my laughter. "Hold up… are you saying to me right now, my boy is in his room pretending to be asleep?" I asked with a smile. "Yes, I don't fuck with him no more, at all," she stated seriously. "He's weak as shit O." "Wait a second, hold your horses," I suggested in a calm tone. "Let me go and talk to him. Let me see what's going on." I followed. "Go ahead, but you're wasting your time," she insisted with disappointment. "Sleep," I said in a low tone. I wanted to know what had happened to my boy, and why would he totally ignore a horny, Vikki to get some shut-eye. I had to go see what was going through Evan's mind, but more importantly, I needed to see this fake sleep act.

On my way across the hallway, I could not help reflecting on my own sexual meltdown from years prior. I opened Evan's bedroom door only to witness exactly what the bombshell had explained. My buddy was laid across his bed, with a passion mark on his neck, fully dressed, pretending to be asleep. I realized the performance could have finally given Evan his very first "E", or even a daytime Emmy Award, consistent with the show this silliness pulled me from. Vikki was steaming and totally turned off at this point, but perhaps still moist; maybe slightly still interested. I felt it was safe for Evan to let the act go, but he didn't. I gently shook Evan by touching his shoulder. "Yo, what are you doing? Are you crazy?" I asked in a low tone while moving Evan back and forth. "Man, you're blowing this big time," I followed while looking back to see if Vikki was watching us. "Man, she's mad as hell," I offered with hopes of receiving a response. My friend had made his mind up. It was as if he slipped into a coma as he made out with Vikki. Yes, I was thinking of a few other places he could have slipped into. Vikki had pulled off the impossible; knocking a dude out without punching or having sex with him! "Man, you're crazy," I stated while losing patience. Still, there was no reply, therefore I made one last attempt to end this pathetic stunt Evan was sponsoring. In a last-ditch effort to hold on to this historic teen moment, I grabbed both of Evan's arms, raised his entire upper torso from the bed and held him up. "Wake up man. Don't do this to yourself," I desperately stated. Vikki was now watching us both look like clowns while shaking her head. I really did not expect my boy to alienate me because of his lack of confidence with females, but he did. Evan fell backwards from my grasp, finding his previous position, and once again held it. He stayed in this position for at least fifteen minutes. I truly believe he literally fell asleep after a while. I gave up. I chuckled a bit and stated, "Ok buddy, I'll call you later," as I headed out of the room to offer Vikki a walk closer to her home. "I told you O," she said while still shaking her head. "Get me the hell out of here," she insisted eagerly. "I never had this happen to me before," she added. My buddy had emotionally shut down and locked Vikki and I out in every way. I peaked in on my buddy one last time to see any signs of movement, but he still was dormant. Vikki snickered as we passed by, but was visibly disturbed by this bizarre incident.

This plan definitely did not go as structured. I didn't really know what to think, yet I was still thrilled to get a chance to hang out with the most popular girl in our school. While my buddy continued sleeping, we exited his apartment without even saying goodbye. I decided to walk Vikki all the way home. We were approximately 45 minutes to an hour away, on foot, from Frisby Street where she lived. Frisby happened to be around the corner from Old York Road, and like McCabe Avenue, which was not just the name of the street, but also the name used for the entire community.

So, there we were, walking as if we really knew each other. We spent a few moments giggling and trying to understand all that happened at Evan's place. The rest of the walk was spent on socializing about school and our significant others. After talking to Vikki awhile, I realized she was quite different than what people thought. She was smart, and not stuck up or rude as people assumed. She had a great sense of humor and she didn't appear to be a greedy person either. She usually wore the hottest fashions, but during our conversation materialistic ideas were never mentioned.

Despite my deep feelings for Tracey, I took a liking to Vikki. She had all I mentioned going for her and she was simply stunning. Physically, Vikki was a cross between the very pretty T-Boz, from the trio TLC, and the always wonderful, Jennifer Lopez, but she was only 16 years old. Our conversation went great, but there were periods where I didn't hear a thing she was saying. I was too busy making sure our elbows periodically rubbed. The 45 minute stroll in the sun passed by in what seemed like 15. I had made it down to Old York and back to McCabe in one piece, but not without getting a first look at Vikki's boyfriend, Frankie. He was about 22 years old, and oddly, he actually resembled my dad, of all people. He was driving the brown and gold Toyota Cressida Vikki often brought to school. He saw me but thought nothing of it. I left the two behind and headed north. "Tell your boy he's cut off," she whispered as her man parked his car. "Alright, I'll tell him," I stated while wiping the sweat from my forehead. "See you in school tomorrow," I suggested. "Cool," she replied. I walked through Old York Road alone with my head on a swivel, just observing guys. I passed through, camouflaged just enough by all of the other returning school kids. As I got passed the crowds of people, that's when I heard someone yell out, "Hey Limon," from behind. I turned quickly, and made brief eye contact with Jody's boyfriend, and the guy McCabe recognized as one of Old York's main leaders.

I enjoyed the lengthy walk home from Old York. Walking always gave me a chance to reflect on everything. I was able to really see just how bad things were turning. Much younger people were beginning to get involved with drug dealing, and plenty of young girls were ending up pregnant. There were no more kids racing up and down the blocks, or vibrant young girls jumping rope. The music even changed. I truly love hip-hop music, but I occasionally require a substantial dosage of the R&B of the past. As a 15 year old, I loved songs like, Al Green's, "Love and Happiness," and Stephanie Mills' hit song, "Never Knew Love Like This Before." Sadly, the good days were few and far between; fading away quickly.

I entered the house wondering how my grandma would react to my attempt to hook school in her presence. Surprisingly, she never said a word about it. However, she did instruct me to clean ALL of the windows in the house, and sweep or rake the backyard. Perhaps this was my punishment without the title, but it was all good. I loved helping out grandma. The tiny bit of structure and responsibility qualities I had, stemmed from chores like cleaning the yard and running errands. The funny thing with teens; you actually know you need to do these things to grow, yet, you just never feel like doing them when it's time. Days later, I would run into my friend Evan. I believe he had been avoiding me due to his embarrassment with the Vikki disaster. I took the bus home with him after school one afternoon, and we discussed the matter, only to let it go for good afterwards. He said he was too nervous and that his penis would not get erect. He couldn't explain it, and I did not see a reason to carry on about it. "Don't worry about it, it's done, and so is she with you, but that's cool," I said while hunching my shoulders. "There will be others buddy." "I know she is," he replied. "She stopped speaking to me."

After all of the excitement with Evan and Vikki, I would drift back into my comfort zone. I made sure I spent more quality time with Tracey. My feelings were still evident in our relationship. Thankfully, she and her mom had recently moved to the eastside, making it easier for us to hang out. I would usually borrow Etton's mountain bike he once used to ride around the neighborhood, before climbing the success ladder in the drug game. He now possessed a brand-new Isuzu Trooper SUV in addition to his Audi. Several guys from McCabe were raking in big bucks. The cocaine business was controlling the northeast side of Charm City, recruiting youths by the hundreds. On McCabe, this, along with the friction between the two hoods, left all moving with a sense of style yet paranoia.

My relationship, grades in school, my prowess on the court, and the writing all elevated to new heights. I enjoyed these things very much, but I still was not structured enough to work towards perfecting any one of them. I used my relationship to get away from the inconsistencies within my heart. Tracey and I were doing fine except for when Vikki was around. Now, it was I who was helplessly falling for her. Tracey and her friends were not friendly with Vikki and her crew. Tracey's approach was one reason I admired her so much. She reminded me of a place and time where life as a whole was better. Vikki, however, represented where life was going. She was a nice girl like Tracey, but with a new school approach that comes with less compassion, but perhaps more improvisation and fun. Over time the females would become more aggressive and unpredictable. Although they were not as pure or wholesome as those with traditional morals and values, they made the male/female experience much more exciting. Being a confused 15 year old, I gradually developed a desire to sample both energies.

I knew of the tension between the two female groups. Tracey hated the attention she received from gossip-based issues, yet, Vikki ate it all up. By the time the 1988 school-year drew to a close, Vikki had made a point to consistently make passes at me, showing a tremendous amount of interest.

I figured this to be a ploy to upset Tracey or Evan, therefore I would just grin and keep on moving. I hated to see Tracey upset, but I liked the attention I received from the "dime-pieces" or beautiful young ladies. To be honest, a small part of me was glad school was nearly over, although I felt safest there. I was afraid I would allow trouble to come simply because I was too weak. I was sadly beginning to get more involved with matters of the flesh. I took my 95% average to the11thgrade, knowing my time to elevate financially was coming. Unlike so many kids, in a year, I was going to have my high school diploma and over $40,000 big ones.

I made a mistake with sharing the details about the resource I had coming with Tracey. I felt very comfortable talking to her about everything, but I was not comfortable with myself enough to speak as if I was sure we would be an item by the time I received this money. Now, not only was I confused about life, I had a relationship I was not prepared for; compromising an innocent sister's emotions. I made tons of poor decisions during my final years of high school. All I would ever do to counter my problems was play basketball with Evan or write. Basketball was one reason we clicked so well, the other; I felt comfortable hanging around someone else who didn't know what to do with himself. At 18, Evan still didn't deal with females much. He was flunking in school, and he never had a summer job. Being around my buddy actually gave me more hope and energy. Lost or not, we were really good friends; we remain as such.

Summer 1988 would get off to a good start. It seemed as if a decade had passed since good music, and the aroma of barbeque or steamed seafood consumed the air. For a brief period, all of the negativity appeared to be a horrible nightmare. Everyone seemed to be getting along again, the cops were almost nonexistent, and the gunshots momentarily seized. The neighborhood was actually normal again, as it was eight years prior. Happy moods were evident alongside the anticipation of disaster. All one would have to do, observe the gutters or drains. There you would find various types of paraphernalia; used syringes, small baggies or capsules used for packaging, along with discharged shell casings. These findings were the norm on McCabe Avenue and the majority of the inner-city of B'MORE.

At home, the mood would also lighten for a minute. However, my granddad's declining health slightly raised eyebrows. My grandmother also slowed considerably, yet flashes of normalcy somehow returned. The family felt no need for panic about our most beloved grandparents. With the exceptions of a few coughs from granddad and a little more of a struggle for Mama to climb the stairs, everything seemed to be as before. The beat was going on as Etton's progression in the streets was elevating, and more youths in the neighborhood would try their hands at following in his footsteps. There were a very few number of arrests, creating an overcrowded environment in the streets. Younger guys were growing up, and older hustlers were breeding them to follow suit. This meant the older guys could now pull themselves out of the danger zone, while the younger kids risk it all for a smaller fee. Still, everyone seemed to be doing well with the dealing. No one had been captured, and guys from years before were returning home from their lengthy jail sentences. Business during the summer was viewed as a success by McCabe Avenue standards, but a new sheriff was back in town, anxious to make his mark once again.

Enter "Genius;" Grant Banks, a pudgy, 250 pound convicted felon in his late 20s. Genius was returning home from a nine-year prison term for his role during an armed bank robbery in 1980. He was captured and sentenced just after we moved onto the block. He too lived on McCabe, directly across from our home, with his grandmother and several other relatives. The others gave him a resounding welcome home celebration. Genius being an old childhood friend of Benny's, immediately drew him to Etton. The two quickly became close friends. The foundation of a new drug cartel was set in place. While home life improved and my grades progressed in school, my block's mood, once again, darkened. Tracey and I usually hovered above my block from inside of my bedroom. Directly outside of my front window the cocaine epidemic was spreading out of control and into the palms of nearly every teen and adult in the area. I continued to try to live the life of a normal honor roll student while continuing to be a blessing to everyone I came in contact with. During these times, I was doing a fairly decent job at simply ignoring the ways of the streets. I stuck to my own guns. I struggled with my identity, but drugs, weapons, violence, and dropping out of school, just did not apply to me.

The basketball court was the only stage I would allow myself to associate with the guys in the streets for longer than 30 minutes. In the city, dealing drugs and knowing how to play basketball is commonplace. Basketball happens to be the sport of choice in the hood. Several dealers in the hood play the sport pretty well. Evan and I would usually play in my neighborhood at an outdoor court. This court was located at a group home we once called, "Child Study." The Woodbourne Center; a small facility for troubled teens who committed various offenses. We often used the facility's outdoor court for pick-up games amongst friends. Several of the dealers would also play there. Ironically, the dealers loved picking with the inmates while they observed from their barred room windows. However, "Child Study," was not the court recognized in the area as the place to play in the area. East Baltimore had a famous facility called, "The Dome," but here in northeast B'MORE, we had Dewees Recreational Center or playfield. This was where the neighborhood's best talent would come together. Before playing a pick-up game at the group home, we all would stand at one end of the court and watch from afar, the more seasoned guys play a little further north at Dewees. There, the guys were much taller and much more gifted. We simply were not good enough to compete there. Even if we were, they still would not let us play. Dewees was their ball court, and "Child Study" was ours.

Freddy, his buddy "Black," Elroy's older brother Steve, and several others all played at Dewees. Here, the guys often held local tournaments during the summer months. Some of the city's best were there. I was only familiar with a few. As Evan and I got set to play ball at "Child Study," we observed David Wingate a second time. Here, he was not dressed for play. He just came through to socialize with the others he had known for years. David, along with Randolph, another hustler in the area, and Freddy, all attended Northern High School. He was their childhood pal well before they decided to break the law. He no longer affiliated with the guys, but he passed through on this day, just to say hello. Northern High was not the primary school to attend if one had aspirations to become a highly recognized student-athlete. After two years at Northern High School, David Wingate transferred and joined the basketball program at the prestigious, Dunbar High School. My pal Tee was now a starter for the school's football program. From my point of view, the move appeared to be paying off dividends for both. Evan and I waved at the local great from a short distance. He waved back with a smile, while leaning on his brand new Mercedes Benz 500. "Hey brothers, how are things going?" he asked. "We're cool," I stated with a grin. "We're good," Evan followed. "Come on niggas, fuck that sucka man," Etton interrupted us both. "Check the ball up man," he added. "That nigga is in the NBA, and I bet he don't do shit for nobody around here." Evan and I looked in David's direction to see if he heard Etton's comments, then we looked at each other. David didn't hear the comments, or he did and ignored them with continuing conversations with those closer. I curiously asked the question to Etton, "What does any of this have to do with us speaking to the guy?" "And we have to do something for ourselves!" I said frankly. "Fuck him, don't jock that sucka man," he replied while catching the ball to begin the game. "Whatever buddy!" I replied just before burying the very first shot of the game. Etton, who I actually liked, was bothered; he understood, no matter how much cocaine he moved, it was all peanuts compared to what David made playing pro hoops.

Appearances by professional athletes were not everyday occurrences in our hood. Most times, it was strictly hard-nosed, trash talking, pick-up basketball games amongst peers. Fights nearly broke out every time we played, especially when the inmates were allowed to come outside for recreation. I would get into a shoving match or two, but nothing too serious. The inmates actually displayed more discipline than the guys from McCabe. Tensions would often rise so high, I honestly believed most of the guys forgot they were supposed to be having fun. Etton and the others played so violently, at times the inmates hardly ever came out to play. I guess they really were not in a rush to get into more trouble. One inmate there, I was familiar with. He called himself "Shadow." His real name was Whittmore Jackson. He was from Old York Road, but no one besides Evan and I knew. I remembered seeing him from the past while walking Vikki home. We both would nod at each other whenever in sight of one another. Shadow's presence was an easy excuse for a riot to break out at Child Study, but Evan and I kept his identity under wraps.

The competitive nature of an athlete is just as addictive as the drugs my peers were selling on the street corners. We would play ball until the sunset, only to talk trash about it until the sun peaked again. School was out for us and no one believed in working a legal job, therefore there was plenty of time to hang out and do nothing good or productive. The only time guys were not yelling at one another on the courts was when they all were screaming harmless threats at my buddy Elroy. Elroy sensed how popular I was becoming with the older hustlers and now wanted to hang out more at the courts. However, because of his inability to play, he had to stay off of the court itself. He would find his comfort zone on the sideline, constantly making jokes out of everything. The guys often preferred Elroy to simply stay away from the courts all together. Whenever he decided to join me at the court the games never seemed to be as rewarding or as exciting for the others. It's a bit more difficult to concentrate on your game when there's a heckler on the sidelines. Most NBA All-Stars can handle this successfully, but not your average, hostile, troublemaking, b-baller. Elroy often used the basketball courts as center stage to his very own stand-up routine for his latest antics and obscene gestures.

Whenever my buddy Elroy came up to the court, you would hear phrases like, "Here come this bitch ass nigga with his jokes n' shit again," or "Why the fuck he keep coming up here crackin jokes n' shit?" or "Man, somebody please tell Elroy to chill with that goofy ass shit today, please," they would plead. I would usually be grinning while everyone else would quickly grow in irritation. Even Evan, a long-time neighbor of Elroy's, would show frustration. My buddy was strictly there to distract and upset everyone besides me, especially an already struggling player. Everyone would be forced to play through all of Elroy's silly and vulgar pranks. If anyone challenged or threatened Elroy, he had older brothers who regularly welcomed drama and trouble. As I said, guys were FORCED to endure my friend's unbelievable but hilarious comedic routines.

Guys tried really hard to ignore Elroy and his devilish grin on the sidelines, but he would not allow it. He was too good at being ignorant. If a foul was called during the game, Elroy would quickly interrupt and yell out, "Oh… y'all think that was a foul?" "I'll show you fools a foul," he'd say. A three to four second-long fart would follow, and that was just the beginning. He would sometimes sit and wait for the ball to roll over out of bounds by his feet. He would trap it with his foot, wait, and fart near someone's head, very loudly, as they would bend over to retrieve it. "Yo, you need to stop that nasty ass shit, for real," Etton would state in discuss. "Excuse me," Elroy would state through his giggle. There were guys on the court who wanted to seriously hurt Elroy, but they knew retaliation would swiftly follow. So they all settled and let Elroy joke around until his beeper sounded. Everyone understood there was a possibility of being seriously hurt or even killed, for something that began as harmless horseplay. So the pranks continued. Elroy would even pull out his penis in silence, stand, and wait for guys to look his way. A person's first reaction when observing anything is to decipher what's odd or peculiar. The first thing someone would see odd on Elroy would be his penis, resting outside of his pants in broad daylight. "Yo, what the fuck is wrong with you man?" "Bam-Bam," another hustler would ask. "Well, I think you got a problem," Elroy would say while laughing. Elroy called this sick game, "The Eye Problem." This was one of his most disrespectful pranks. Nothing on earth could stop Elroy from joking, but one afternoon, he would be forced to take a break.

Elroy's ignorant but harmless humor continued throughout most of the summer. One afternoon at the court would prove to be one of Elroy's best but worst routines. He had made everyone incredibly mad or upset. A few of the guys wanted to physically go after Elroy, despite the counter he possessed of going to his older brothers. On this 95 degree afternoon, he somehow continued to produce the loudest farts ever. I'd never met a person who can control all of his farts and burps at will. Elroy could easily produce both on demand. Elroy passed gas at least 40 times; loudly enough to pierce through the hard-fought noise of tough street hoops competition. "Hey guys, can y'all fools smell that?" he would ask. "Well how about that? Or that?" he repeated while continuously farting. "Come on fellas, I know y'all can smell that one," Elroy stated with his patented grin. Guys got so upset with Elroy they even blamed him for the losses and missed shots.

A few guys left the court stating, "I'll just go elsewhere to play" or "This court is a joke, along with that silly ass nigga over there." Just as guys were deciding to finally pack up and leave the unthinkable happened. While guys were replenishing with Gatorade, Elroy insisted they all take something more. "Hey before y'all leave, take this," he yelled out while smiling. Suddenly, Elroy's smile immediately turned into a look of desperation and embarrassment. His legs quickly gapped open and he turned and ran towards McCabe Avenue. In an attempt to produce one last fart, my buddy Elroy had just crapped in his pants.

The court had gone from several tired players, to a collection of reenergized dudes, all jumping up and down, celebrating Elroy's misfortune. It only took seconds for the guys to explode into laughter while yelling at Elroy as he quickly trotted away with his legs wide open. "That's what you get bitch," Bam- Bam yelled. "Ha, ha, that nigga shit himself, that's just what he gets," Etton yelled as others fell over into the grass in laughter. Even the group home inmates were laughing from their windows. I laughed too, but hurried to go make sure my friend's pride was not too bruised. Evan was in stitches with the others. Soon after, I made it to Elroy's house; there he stood, on his porch, smiling but meshed with a look of embarrassment.

Elroy and I began to converse about the crazy farting incident. "What did those niggas say O?" he asked. "Nothing really, except they were glad they stopped when they did," I offered. "They thought they would have missed it if they were in the middle of a game." "Fuck them," he added with a smile. "They didn't say much buddy, but they're all up the court on the ground laughing," I stated. "Did you really shit on yourself son?" I asked with interest. "A little bit," he replied with embarrassment. "Was Evan laughing too?" Elroy asked. "Yes, even Evan," I replied. "Nah, he can't laugh, he's scared of girls n' shit," he jokingly replied. Elroy's embarrassing situation hardly dampened his sense of humor. After taking shots like, "That nigga shit himself" or "I bet you stop fooling around now," all night long, he picked right back up where he had left off. "That's not going to stop me O. I just have to make sure I drop a load before I play The Fart Game the next time, that's all," he explained.

Elroy's antics, Tracey's beautiful presence, and periodic visits from my dad, made the summer quite enjoyable. My dad had only come to see me a handful of times throughout my sophomore and freshman years of high school. My dad was not involved with my progress in school. He did well for me financially, yet he never made a single visit to any of my schools throughout my entire life. He also did not even know the names of any of my teachers throughout my entire time in school. The reoccurring visits still made me feel good. I was thrilled about having a father in my life. The tension between my dad and my grandparents was still present. My grandma believed the $40,000 plus I had coming was the sole reason behind my dad resurfacing. "You better not give him any of that money, you hear me?" she demanded. I was confused about several things in my life at this time, yet I was clear on how my sister and I obtained these resources. I understood my dad had absolutely nothing to do with me and my sister's finances, besides being responsible for us receiving this money without our mom being present. For as much as I loved my dad, I knew he would not get any of the money I was due to receive.

As the considerably more peaceful days of summer would end, disturbing news would re-enter the fold. As I headed into the 11th grade, carrying along with me good grades and a positive attitude, I learned my buddy Evan would not be rejoining. Evan mentioned receiving a letter from the school informing him not to return. His lack of focus and determination to perform above satisfactory in the classroom had finally caught up with him. "Hold up," I said in amazement. "You're telling me the school told you not to come back ever again?" I asked. "That's what the letter says O," he answered. "My mom is pissed," he added. "Why would a school do something like that without doing more to help first?" I asked in confusion. "I don't know O, fuck it! I guess they felt like I failed too many times," Evan stated in disappointment. Evan is a good natured, kindhearted type of person. He's smart! However, he simply could never seem to take academics seriously. He would hardly miss a day in an entire school year, but somehow he would hardly ever pass a class for the semester. My buddy was simply one of those kids who really disliked the idea of school work, a lot. I asked Evan, "So what are you going to do now?" His answer was simple, but at the time I didn't realize this was the worst possible answer he could have ever given me. He said with disappointment, "I don't know."

With my cousin gone forever and Evan kicked out of school for good, I only had Elroy to travel back and forth to school with. Elroy made it to the 11th as well. He was held back a few times just as Evan, but the Special Education Department was much more lenient towards its students. I knew I would hardly ever get to see Elroy inside of the school, but it still was cool to have someone from McCabe there with me. All of our other childhood pals were enrolled and doing well at other schools. Well, except Troy. He was now dealing drugs in Dundalk, close where my dad still lived. During this period, I was often alone. It seemed as if everyone was a part of a group except me. Most guys were either drug dealers, jocks or scholars. I fell somewhere in the middle of them all. The writer and sketcher side of me was fine with this reality, but there was a weird social void at times. Tracey usually took my mind off of things, but she was not a replacement for them. In the beginning of our relationship, I thought I truly loved Tracey. I always cared for her tremendously, yet being in love was impossible for me during this time. I had no clue who I was or where I was going. I hoped for the best, but inside I knew I would try to escape the pressure of being the perfect boyfriend sooner or later.

I made it halfway through the school-year before things would really began to fall apart in my life. My grades were the only true positives during this time. My desire to escape commitment was fueled by Vikki and other flirtatious females. Since Shawn's death my popularity elevated significantly. All of the females he was familiar with became associates of mine. Vikki stated how she loved our talks and how I carried myself. She said I had an innocent flare that was really attractive. Although I was not innocent, I told the bombshell, "I like that a lot." I guess my interest in wearing nice attire without making a scene got the ladies attention. Wearing a sports blazer, a button-up dress shirt, pricey jeans, and a pair of Nike Air Force One sneakers in 1988 was a normal practice for me. This was me. I really just liked to throw on the nice rags from time to time.

Dressing up periodically gave me confidence. My life was as shaky as it had been in years just as high school was drawing to its end. The older I became, the more confused I was. I didn't know if I should hang out with Elroy and others, or stay away from the dealers all together. I was unsure whether or not I wanted one girlfriend, or three. I couldn't decide if I should write more or play more basketball. I even became confused on wearing shoes or sneakers. I could not make up my mind on anything. To make matters much worst, my grandfather became very ill. The persistent cough he once had intensified. My grandfather was the financial foundation of the household; now this too was in jeopardy.

As my granddad's health worsened, grandma became worried sick. The rest of the family was too unstable to comfort their mom properly. Drama continued to unfold in the area. Coming home from school one afternoon, I walked right into a sea of onlookers, laughing about an altercation involving Craig, a friend of Todd's, and younger cousin of Rock. He happened to live two doors up from my house. He assaulted a guy named Tyran. Craig had just broken Tyran's jaw over an apparent argument over money. I entered the house after momentarily observing the mayhem and took a seat on the end of my bed. I rolled around and slithered downwards, like a snake, to my knees and began to pray for strength, and for my granddad. In the blink of an eye, life was miserable once again.

By the start of the new year, my relationship with Tracey had deteriorated significantly amongst other things. Only my bond with my grandma, the writing, and my grades in school showed signs of hope. I knew 1989 meant I was a year closer to having some money to possibly open new doors with, but I felt horrible. I was a little excited to know having my very own car was not going to be a problem. Still, everything around me was unstable;

my household, my relationship, and my neighborhood. It gets worst. In the midst of all the uncertainties and hardships, we all were pushed up against another thick wall. We would drift into 1989 suffering another tragic loss. My grandfather was hospitalized for a serious case of pneumonia. After putting up a struggle; ironically allowed to briefly return home as my mom had, our 77 year old granddad passed away. The devastation of 1977 and 1987 had suddenly returned in a devastating manner.

The death of my granddad came as a complete shock. The family spoke on the horrible cough he had, yet no one believed he was seriously ill. They all attributed his coughing to the many Winston cigarettes he inhaled daily. His death placed a discouraging stronghold on the family. My granddad was the breadwinner for the household. My grandma quickly slipped into a depressed state from the loss of her life long companion of forty-plus years. She now had to take over all of the financial responsibilities of a crumbling home, inside and out. I watched my grandma's zest for life gradually fade. I observed her gazing at the antique chair once occupied by her hubby. I witnessed the concerned expressions on her face as she periodically would thrust forward to see what was taking place outside of her front door. She was growing uncomfortable within her own home. She was lonely.

Our family was in trouble in more than one way. We were lost and struggling; all of us. We all needed something more, something stable, something real, but could not find it collectively, or as individuals. I knew I would soon have to step up. Graduating high school usually symbolizes growth. It says to the world, one is ready to enter society and become a functional responsible and positive citizen. As senior year approached, I needed to be ready to assist my family, but I was not. I was everything but ready. Although my grades were nearly excellent, I felt totally unprepared. So much so, I actually wished I had two more years of high school left at Northern. My mind was fixed on the deaths of my loved ones, and I still had no idea who I was or what I wanted to become. The closer I drew to 12th grade, the more confused I would become. All I was left to do was continue aimlessly, searching for any kind of solid pathway to a better life.

# Chapter 10

# THE FAILING GRADUATE

The year 1990 would slowly drift into senior year of high school. I was still struggling to choose a good path, yet I understood my current position could have been worse. Understanding I would not be financially struggling after high school promoted more confidence and peace. Also, I somehow managed to hold on to my relationship with Tracey, but only by a hair. Vikki continued with the seductive flirting and I enjoyed every second of it. She knew I was interested, but she was not sure about trying to get involved with me. We both sort of knew it was all wrong for us to hook up, but the mutual crush felt pretty good. She was not thrilled with being viewed as the potential "home wrecker," by the other students, and I did not care to be viewed as the guy who "traded his soul for riches." No doubt about it, Tracey was my true heart, but Vikki was always on my mind. I knew the entire school of females would take me off of the "cool dudes' list," and the guys would add me to theirs just for connecting with two bombshells of two different mindsets. I had always approached most things in life with compassion, but my heart had taken a beating from the many tragic circumstances I had endured. I believe I was growing a little tired of leading with it. For the first time ever, I felt myself not really caring much about anything.

Impulse began to push aside my compassionate and empathetic character traits. Tracey deserved more than a screwed up guy who simply was not sure which way was up. I was so confused at times, it seemed to be a struggle to locate my own shadow or reflection. I cared enough to hold on, but not enough to make things much better by ending the flirting. As a result, by spring break Tracey and I would break up for the first time.

She had seen and felt enough emotionless energy from me. She was simply tired of my instabilities. Oddly enough, I felt alright with the split; I was numb to it. I expected to feel a lot worse, but my heart was now temporarily out of service.

I spent spring break playing basketball and writing more than in recent years. I decided to try something new. I wrote a few short, non-fiction stories and several comic book themes. I still scribbled an occasional romance letter to Tracey, Vikki, and Melody, a knockout ninth grader I met in French class, but they all were used as a means to help me cope with my failing emotions. Melody, the 9th grader, was a sweet and innocent 14 year old. I was now 17. We met in French class because I was instructed to take the course; I was never assigned a foreign language class throughout high school. I really had no business making advances towards the younger beauty. With her, my heart actually managed to ignite again, and ignore my new selfish way of living. In the midst of these great emotions, I feared this too would not last. Melody was the type of sister every level-headed guy craved to be with. She had morals, the perfect smile, the right attitude, both of her parents living under the same roof, a beautiful face, long silky hair, and yes, a tremendous body. She had it all. The connection made here caused me to lose interest with the more lustful attraction I felt with Vikki. Melody represented what was right in the world with females. I immediately pictured myself with her, but only after I somehow straightened up and found my way. Unfortunately, I just could not envision this happening any time soon.

My undying interest in the young ladies not only gave me more confidence, it also elevated my popularity out in the streets. Females and the writing also kept me out of harm's way. McCabe Avenue was now at its lowest point. Several scuffles and a few shoot outs ensued just outside of the block. The increasing crime promoted me to have several daydreams and nightmares about being shot, or even receiving another beat down from a large group of guys. Although I speak on nightmares, and I thought of death a bit, I still never felt frightened. I still desired to be around the others here and there. The way I saw it; if I was murdered, I would gain an opportunity to reunite with my mom, Shawn, and granddad.

We all must go someday! That was the phase I embraced to cope with the concept of my own demise. The approach allowed me to try harder to deal with the pain I still felt from the passing of my immediate family. With the many loose thoughts roaming inside of my head, I reluctantly decided to spend more time with my new friend, Melody. I was at peace with her. Things seemed a lot better whenever I was around her. I felt like I could be myself to the fullest with Melody. I had spoken too openly about the money I had coming, but Melody could care less. She probably had more coming from her parents down the road. She seemed to have life figured out. This made her even more attractive to me. Folks at school learned of my financial situation, and this added to the Vikki and Tracey dynamic. Melody was my "beautiful release," an escape from the foolishness I created. That's a confused individual alright; make a mess than leave it or run. Whether folks knew or not, it was good to know money was on the way. On the flipside, no one knew a lot of this money was already spent. With Shawn no longer alive to share with, I had already planned to help out my grandmother even more, and I was already set on spending five figures on a brand new car.

Resources were in need for the upkeep of the house. 731 needed a makeover in a major way. My uncles started the restoration process with the house, but it all stalled. The dedication to manual labor projects were compromised by the increased abuse of drugs and alcohol. At this point, my uncles were extremely lazy and late for pretty much everything. My family always had good intentions. They all were simply going through the familiar pattern of never being able to admit when there's a serious problem. I told grandma, who was feeling better, I would help out with bills and repairs to the house. The memory of the happiness on grandma's face is cemented, as I assured her that I would help make things a little better. Make no mistake, there was still lots of love in my household. It just could never manifest into positive forms of progression for the future. The negativity would swallow the love up before it could grow. Therefore, I tried to progress the best way I could on my own. I continued to thrive as a student, despite distractions that stemmed from the romantic concoction I had created with Vikki, Tracey, and Melody; Melody, overall, I felt I truly loved.

Before I reached my senior year in high school, English was my favorite course, but soon after meeting Melody, French was the course I was most excited about. Unlike my initial high school crush with Jody, I could usually count on seeing Melody in class. For the few times she was not present, I would spend much of the period gazing at her empty chair. I would likely be picturing the perfect smile she often gave me from over her left shoulder. If only for this one class, I felt happy. School allowed me to feel more in control of my life, but college never became a topic of discussion in the household for my future. I briefly tried to entertain the thought, but with the new commitment already made to financially help out at home, I would quickly discard the notion. Nevertheless, I still would work very hard to achieve the best grades possible. By the halfway mark of senior year, I pushed my overall average up to 97%, which included a perfect score of 100% in English class. I made honor roll both semesters, and once again, I became a member of the basketball team. This time as a starter on the varsity squad. In school, life felt great overall. On McCabe Avenue, things were the exact opposite.

Coming home from school opened the door to the grim reality of a sad change in modern times. My neighborhood was steadily sinking to a point of no return. I still got along well with all of the guys there, specifically those who liked to play basketball. The others were mostly underage drug dealers, doing whatever it took to enter into the world of the pretty young ladies, cars, jewelry, and fresh gear. Education was never really an option for them. Every so often, I would ask a 13 or 14 year old dealer about attending school. "Hey LiL Bug, why aren't you in school?" "O man, fuck school, I don't have time for dat punk shit! I'm getting this money," he said forcefully. LiL Bug's slightly older brother, Herald once said to me, "O, what's the use of goin' to school?" "Yo, I'm making more money than all of the teachers, the, the principal, and that, that superintendent lady; is that how you say that shit?" he added smiling as I nodded with confirmation. "I hear your point, but everything is not about money buddy," I replied with a slight grin. His reply was simple, "Yes it is," he said with rippled eyebrows and twisted lips.

I thought about the comment Herald had made about money, and it actually made sense. Everything did seem to be about money. On the block, no one went out of their way to help out a neighbor unless some change was involved. Spirituality was kept from classrooms, but the idea of working a job was being preached inside of schools, in the streets and within the household. In one way or another, I was being shown how money influences us all. My dad was popping up unannounced every other day, due to the money I had coming. My sister and Freddy never changed as the resource drew nearer. My sister was awesome always, just distant. Older females could not wait to sink their claws into me, and Elroy thought I was his ticket to him becoming an overnight kingpin. Elroy consistently asked me to buy a kilogram or two of cocaine; he wanted me to buy the drugs and he sell it all for us both to make a great profit. This was the period when I really began to understand the hunger for, and the power of money, and due to the folks I was learning from, I hated it.

Possessing a five-figure income at just 17 or 18 years of age was rare for most inner-city kids, yet this is what my life was aligned to soon experience. As prom night and graduation grew closer, so did Melody and I. Vikki turned up the heat as well. Her boyfriend Frankie was serving time for drug possession. Then, of course, there was still Tracey. She was very emotional. We both were; the two and a half years of caring for her was harder to walk away from than I anticipated. So there I was, holding hands out in public with Melody, riding a bike to Tracey's house in any kind of weather, while sneaking Vikki up my back alleyway, trying to keep her out of the view of the guys on the block. I was not hiding her for flirtatious reasons as before. I was protecting her from possible physical harm or disrespect.

Just weeks before, Vikki carelessly drove through McCabe Avenue to drop in on me in Frankie's Toyota Cressida and was nearly killed by Lil Bug. He unloaded a 9mm handgun in her direction. She was not hit, but the car was struck twice. The situation was scary, but this was when I realized Vikki really cared for me; even after being shot at, she returned to McCabe. Vikki and the two other young ladies were familiar with one another, but there were other females outside of this entanglement. There were also a few other females I showed small interests in. Tina was one of these young ladies. She lived only five doors down from me. I called myself liking her as well until I got myself caught on the night Vikki and I were creeping up the back alleyway. Well, I said I was very confused, but I was never bored.

My difficulties with picking and choosing women were not all one-sided. These wonderful personalities I shared time with were all in search of something as well. Tina was three years older than I, therefore I knew she was out and about. Like with other older females, I was looked at as a rookie. Vikki may have had honest feelings for me, but she was notorious for engaging in relations with local kingpins. Melody, for as sweet as she was had a boyfriend just prior to our union. He just so happened to be from, where else? That's right, Old York Road.

Nysheme, Melody's ex, held a position consistent with my own in my neighborhood. He was there, but not really in. Meaning, like I, he had no personal problems with any individual from McCabe. My comrades on the block likely forgot; as they sold drugs and stay confined to the streets, I was attending school with many of the guys from Old York Road. The tension between myself and those guys was not very high. We all knew of the escalating issues surrounding our neighborhoods, but we all remained cool. Guys like Nysheme, myself, and a few others tried to do the best we could to stand clear of the stupidity. We were just young confused teens, trying to feel our way through life. Unfortunately, I was making more mistakes than necessary throughout my journey. I should not have been as close to the trouble or as many young ladies. I unconsciously used the females to cover up the extreme emotional pains I felt within. People all around the world often use drugs, alcohol, violence, money or gambling to blanket their shortcomings. I regretfully used beautiful young females in an attempt to hide from my internal demons.

I would hate myself for the times when I took advantage of the compassion of these beauties, despite their issues. Still, the regret did not surface often enough. Just like any addiction, I struggled to shake myself free from the attention, intimacy, and the beauty of these young ladies. This allowed me to become a promoter of heartbreak throughout my journey, only to catch myself after it was far too late. From my upstairs window I observed the block from above with Vikki peacefully seated behind me. She was wearing a colorful summer dress; pricey sunshades rested just above her hairline as she replenished her lips with gloss through a travel-size mirror. Sex with Vikki was not the focus, but the opportunity was certainly there. I was too busy lying to myself about how cool I thought I was. A part of me feared true adulthood; the other side wanted to believe I had arrived. It was overwhelming to know over $40,000 was on the way in just a couple of months. The game was changing. I was gradually being chosen; one of the most popular and most attractive females in Baltimore City, was catching a vibe, inside my bedroom.

Instead of having sex with Vikki on this late-afternoon, we talked about life after school, and the Old York /McCabe rivalry. We agreed things would probably fall completely apart before they would get better. Although sex would wait for us, the temptation was still active. We kissed and would feel on each other a little, but pulled back every time the juices began to boil over. The sling Vikki wore helped this delay. Vikki's shoulder was partially separated from an altercation with one of the school's most popular guys. "Squirt," an early classmate of my cousin Shawn, and a close friend of Donny, who I played ball with during Gym class. Squirt was a very cool dude; a very young drug dealer, but extremely charming, stylish and personable. He and Vikki were an item, on and off, in the past despite her union with Frankie. I felt like he was too cool of a guy to conflict with, and decided not to seriously interfere with their union.

Everyone liked "Squirt." Our palms met several times for sure. Nothing more would materialize on my end. Unfortunately, Squirt suffered a similar fate as my cousin a few weeks prior to Vikki's arrival to my house. In an unrelated incident from the rivalry, "Squirt" was murdered near his home. Some believe the tragedy was drug related while others made mention of a domestic situation with an older woman. Baltimore City as a whole was taking on a new identity in terms of murders. Drugs were consuming the neighborhoods and the schools. The dropout rate had also increased. I sensed it all; with the money I had coming, I often thought of just relocating, far away from B'MORE. On the other hand, there was Mama, and I simply felt I had to be there for her.

Aside from the ladies, attending college periodically dripped into my head, similar to the water that leaked from my ceiling during heavy storms. Periodically, I thought about higher learning therefore I decided to take a shot at the P.S.A.T exam. This was a pre-test, usually offered to students in 11th grade, to gage a collegiate prospect's IQ heading into senior year. With a 97% average overall, I felt I had nothing to lose. My family's unwillingness to talk about college much made the idea seem odd or weird. Looking back, I was never sure why no one cared to mention it. Maybe it was simply because none of them attended college except my sister Gina and my uncle BoBo, and they never finished. Then again, perhaps many felt they would receive some easy money if I remained home. Nevertheless, I went at this test with confidence and inner-peace, knowing I was fortunate to have the grades to even take a chance. Not many of the senior males or females had good enough grades to receive the offer. They still had access to take the test, it just was not presented to them without asking. I was offered the opportunity because I was elevating academically, but in all other areas I stalled; I lost ground.

A week later, great news returned from the test I had taken. I passed. Long ago, it was required to get a score somewhere around 700 to pass. I earned a score close to 820. Scoring 1000 on the SAT is pretty good for any era; 1300 is outstanding. Today, 1600 is great. The confirmation of having above-average book knowledge of the requirements felt great. More good news followed when I was not inside of the classroom during a special announcement. I was told in April, I had a month to prepare for an interview. "An interview!" "For what?" I said to my classmate Ronnie when I was being filled in. "What?" "Are they giving out jobs before the students graduate now?" I asked jokingly. "That's not a bad idea," he replied. Ronnie was a very nice guy; he was funny. We met in English class and hit it off immediately. He was clean-cut, quiet, but funny. He dressed nice and loved the ladies. These things we shared, but there were differences. Ronnie had more of an exclusive approach to a union than I. Ronnie, not a huge fan of school, was also working. He also would cheat off of my paper assignments regularly during class. I saw him, but I liked him so much I pretended not to.

The news my new pal shared with me was for The National Honor Society. TNHS is the prestigious academic organization recognizing the country's brightest students. When I learned what the organization stood for my heart dropped. I received a standing ovation in the classroom when I returned. This attention was so powerful I could feel my temples beating. "Wow," I thought. The stacks of text books and hours of studying actually paid off. I could not get home fast enough to share this great news with my grandma and the others.

I hurried home and shared the news of my accomplishments with Mama, and she was thrilled. However, I don't believe I received the proper attention for my accomplishments but I never blamed grandma. She showed as much enthusiasm as she could, but it was clear, she was clueless as to what all these tests and organizations entailed. I explained it all to her, but all this did was take the beauty away from it all. No one else really paid much attention. My sister's pregnancy stole headlines in our home. I was never very big on lots of attention, but this did not ease the pain. I did want to be celebrated, just this one time.

After coming to grips with my uphill climb, I gradually lost interest in education. I was going to go on the interview, but the entire situation I now saw as an afterthought. Therefore, I reconnected with entertainment; basketball, music, money, and females. The disappointments I felt about school even began to affect my desire to write. Playing basketball was becoming my favorite hobby. On the court, I rarely thought about home, school, or females. I loved the ability to eliminate stress simply by lacing up my new Jordan sneakers. So there I was, back outside, hanging with the guys my heart told me to keep at a distance, but my mind said, "What the hell!" All I had at this time was a little faith. This was seemingly not enough for me, therefore I proceeded to do things I probably should not have. Eventually, I stopped trying so hard to separate myself from the others. I still had no desire to sell drugs, drink alcohol, or gamble, but I would draw closer to the guys in the streets, who I felt listened more than my immediate family, outside of Mama. I understood, no matter how troubled or menacing they all were; we still are brothers.

By May, The Northern Vikings would get ousted in the playoffs by Patterson Park High, in a double-overtime thriller, at Patterson Park High School in the southern region of the city. I finished with 13 points. Making the transition from the playground to organized play was still challenging. I tried to enjoy the sport, but to never have an adult visit a game bothered me. This, and circumstances alike, allowed me to begin to experience reversed fortunes. Gradually, I became much more comfortable in the streets with Elroy and the others. I still religiously declined Elroy's offer to sell drugs for me. "O, you change your mind yet?" he would often ask. "I'm telling you man, you'll never have to touch a thing, I promise," he insisted. Before allowing dealing to compromise our friendship, I decided to assure Elroy would never ask this again. "Man, I'm going to say this one last time buddy. I'm never going to use the money I gained from my mom's death to buy drugs with. I don't care if I can make five-hundred million dollars off of it, it's NEVER going to happen," I said strongly. I could tell

I pierced Elroy's soul with my determined expression. His face cracked as he realized his "masterful idea" had been put to rest, permanently.

As my celebrity grew out in the streets, my interest in school dwindled. Luckily for me, I only had a little more than a month left. The interview I was so anxious about weeks earlier had ended in disaster. I was not accepted into TNHS. I did not prepare for this interview, therefore I did not perform well. I was unprepared from the start, but I did try. I left home for the interview with an unsecured necktie. A white woman I frantically approached at a nearby gas station quickly secured it for me. I was extremely nervous in the huge boardroom full of unfamiliar faces. There were a few black students, but the others were white or foreigners; all were unfamiliar to me. Two of the students were from India, another was from China, and the other two were white. The students were not an issue; I was simply out of sorts due to the fear of the unknown. The majority of the questions are blurry to me today, but I can recall one vividly. One of the officials asked, "Mr. Richardson, how would your parents or your mother feel if you became a member of The National Honor Society?" My mind went blank, and I became lightheaded and emotional. This was the one question I hoped would never be asked; a mother question. This sealed my fate, yet I recall still thanking the board for granting me the opportunity.

I must admit, I was disappointed about coming up short at the interview. I really wanted to be celebrated or recognized for my academic efforts. I was anticipating wearing the additional gold rope that specify "Society" members. I knew this drapery represented far more than the heavier, more expensive jewelry my peers proudly celebrated in the hood. Still, I did not beat myself up about it too much. I was upset enough to throw my tie inside of a dumpster outside of the school. Back at home, hardly anyone cared about my missed opportunity. They were all too busy eating crabs and drinking brews. I continued to hang out with Evan on the ball court and with Elroy in the hood. I would also begin hanging out with a friend of a friend.

Bennett Lawson was a cool younger guy from the neighborhood. Elroy and I used to hang out a bit with his older cousin, Big Nate. Nate was a three-hundred-fifty-pound, lovable dude from the neighborhood. I once sold dozens of G.I Joe action figures to Bennett for a small fee. Now in 10th grade, he was able to venture out more with the older guys. He had both of his parents living in the same household throughout his childhood. Both parents worked as well. Regardless of struggles, this helps in some way, rather than to never have had this structure. Bennett attended Carver High/Technical School in west Baltimore. Carver like Dunbar, in a few ways, demanded more than average from its students.

The three of us, myself, Bennett, and Elroy soon became quite the trio. We were a click of three who shared common ground to live a fun and trouble-free existence. We didn't care much for lots of trouble. We all enjoyed the company of females, loved good hip-hop music, and enjoyed sporting nice apparel. This was my weekend crew. We all would marinate in the hip-hop music. We could not get enough of, A Tribe Called Quest, Public Enemy, Special Ed, Poor Righteous Teachers, Brand Nubian, Gang Starr, De Le Soul, and quite a few others. Hip-hop had grown to newer heights, and I was blown away by a lot of it. We really could identify with the lyrics, and it was being delivered with perfection. It was always exciting for me to witness artists come from the streets and grow into stardom. I've always had much respect for literature, film production, music or entertainment as a whole. They're all great! They're all relentless go-getters! Unfortunately for me, I could not seem to make up my mind about what positive idea I wanted to go after. All I was sure to chase were the fine young ladies; last I checked, there's no real future practicing that.

The distant future was too scary for me to concentrate on in 1990. I felt more comfortable staying in a range of a month or two at a time. I focused on my upcoming senior prom and graduation. Confusion even stifled my ability to choose a mate for the prom. It should not have been too difficult. Vikki took herself out of the drawing. Frankie returned from prison just in time to take Vikki to her prom. Vikki would be returning to school after Senior Prom to complete a few more credits. Elroy was previously held back, but was eager to reach his upcoming final year. He hardly cared as long as he continued to make money dealing on McCabe.

Tracey and I continued to keep in touch throughout the split, and somehow rekindled a slight spark from the past, but had not fully reconciled. Melody was my very first option. She was the only female I was intimate with during this time, and the person I knew I belonged with. My grandma loved her. Even my uncle Frank asked, "Odell, is that your girlfriend?" in a distorted tone compliments of Thunderbird liquor. "Yes, she is Frank," I replied while smiling at Melody. "Hello," Melody stated pleasantly. "She's pretty," Frank uttered as he walked away with a slight yet unstable giggle. I immediately asked Melody to join me for the prom, and she accepted before I even finished the question. I thought I was sure she was the one for me in every way. She was the only female I had no drama or arguments with at the time. The only problem was me. I still was not sure who I was or who or what I wanted.

As prom approached, the more confused I would become. Tracey made her presence felt; throwing hints which stemmed from a growing interest in the already filled prom seat. I never felt as weird in school around everyone as I did at this time. I would have to pass Vikki flirting with me in one hallway, only to read the worry on Tracey's face in another, then go and observe the beautiful, carefree spirit of Melody during French class. All of this, yet I still found my eyes glued to another perfect score on my final report card; 100% for English class. I could dunk a basketball with the best of them, I've always had a great sense of humor and the ability to express myself well, both, in person and on paper. I also tried hard to keep myself up and dress nicely. I received good grades in school, and I also had a five-figure income knocking at the door in a matter of weeks. Oh, did I mention I also could do push-ups from a handstand position. Still, my entire world felt empty. I was lost! I did not have a clue about how to find a good path to travel on. At a time when I should have been excited to soon become a high school graduate, I felt like a complete loser; a failure to the fifth power. At this time I just wanted out. I felt as if I could go far away to another country, another planet even, and never return.

Two weeks before the senior prom, I caved in to the pressure I felt coming from everyone who believed I should definitely take Tracey to the dance. That was not all. I still felt something for her. She gave me more than two wonderful years of connecting or trying to love me. I felt obligated to allow her to join me, but I really cared for Melody, who I already verbally offered the seat to. What a mess I was forming! She was excited and already making preparations with the help of her wonderful family. I knew she would simply fall apart if I were to take away an offer not many freshmen get to experience. I truly felt I was in a bad way, an impossible fix. I had committed to two beauties, neither of which I deserved to be close to. Time was running out and I could not convince myself to tell Melody, "I changed my mind." I didn't really! I felt her more than any other female in my life at this point, but the pressure distorted my thinking. I was an asshole, period! Unfortunately prom night would come, and I found myself walking up to knock on the door of the wrong female.

While Melody waited for me to arrive at her home for the biggest date of her early high school life, I was at Tracey's house, putting on a fake smile. I really cared for Tracey, and periodically entertained reuniting with her, but I was in what I thought was love, with Melody. I was wrong! Very wrong, but too unstable and unable to handle this situation properly. I convinced myself with difficulty, Melody would be alright. I told myself, "She's a freshman, I'm a senior. She'll get over me faster than I know." I also said quietly, "She has at least two more proms to attend." I knew I did not want to be without Melody, but I also felt she deserved much better, so I was willing to see her apart from me. Still, I would shed a frustrated tear for the pain I know I caused her and her family. More tears followed long afterwards. Not solely for the situation at hand, but for the unstable life I lived. I was afraid; afraid of life, love, and myself. The scary place where I lived which housed many lost souls is where I became fearless. The fear of living a good life actually gave me a shot at practicing fearlessness; the setting was the real issue.

The prom was interesting from a classy standpoint, but I hardly enjoyed it. Tracey had no idea how close I came to actually leaving her sitting at the prom alone, just so I could go to Melody and leave the city for a night or two. Only my inability to drive and the lack of funds held me back. Freddy escorted us to this event in my sister's silver, Volvo 740. My family did not have the funds to rent a limo for us. He was due back after the festivities.

I had broken the heart and spirit of an innocent and beautiful freshman. I hurt a person I truly cared for because I felt obligated to another. Tracey was awesome, but Melody was the most positive, beautiful, honest, real, pleasant, complete, and humble young woman I've ever met. I was so worried about hurting one young lady's feelings; I managed to hurt both, simultaneously. I was an unstable young man with no direction, trying hard to care for two good females. At 17 years old, my life was quite confusing, and I was getting ready to receive at least $48,000 on my 18th birthday in June.

The prom was a memorable evening, if nothing else. Most of the night was spent on making sure Tracey never saw Vikki flirting with me every chance she got. No matter where we were, Vikki would wink an eye, show more cleavage, or simply get close enough to pinch my rear end. She was relentless. At least she was honest with herself. That's more than I could say for myself. She displayed more courage than I was able to. She was blowing me kisses while slow dancing, even from over Frankie's shoulder. This was easily one of the most stressful, awkward, and uncomfortable nights of my young life. I was actually thrilled when it ended. I was very glad this was my first and last prom.

Surprisingly, by the grace of God, Melody still wanted to see me alive afterwards. She was hurt, but felt my sincere apologies. Vikki continued, despite Frankie's resurgence, to make her presence felt once again. She periodically drove through McCabe in different vehicles, asking of my whereabouts. Elroy informed me how several of the guys were mesmerized by Vikki's sexiness. Elroy stated Etton went out of his way to offer information to Vikki and her friend, Amanda. I knew they all liked Vikki, but I really didn't care. These guys were as reckless as ever, especially Genius, who was now the new man in charge on the block. Elroy had introduced him to Hubert, his old connection, and the rest was infamous history. After just a few months, Genius had nearly every young guy on McCabe Avenue selling cocaine for him. The guys that did not work for him, bought from him. His come-up was faster than Benny's and Etton's combined. Benny introduced the area to heroin, Etton personified the cocaine business along with others, but Genius was "bringing a lion to a dog fight." Genius introduced McCabe Avenue to the "new jack," crack cocaine.

My adolescent life as a high school student ended on June 10th 1990. At the same time the crack cocaine epidemic was growing stronger by the day. I was a 17 year old student with an overall average of 97.5%. Surprisingly, Tracey and I would briefly reconcile. She even attended my graduation ceremony. A week or two later, I got weird again, and we sadly called it quits for good. In a matter of weeks, I would be receiving almost $50,000. I celebrated the time I was still able to spend with Melody. I was trying to mend her crushed heart, but the pure but broken pieces were far too small and scattered to gather. We also struggled. I fought harder as we continued seeing each other but her pain added to my fear of soon losing her. Eventually, I became exhausted with emotional failures and turned to a focus with less substance. I guess I felt financial gain would counter the emotional drain. I figured materialism and more interactions with beautiful women would help me cope with my emotional failures.

As Summer of 1990 approached, I slowly began converting my mindset from R&B to hip-hop. This was not really deliberate. As humans we find ways to cope with pains or loses, and even poor decisions. I knew I would always present myself as a nice guy; a gentleman, but in my head, I replaced love with lust, humility with ego, quietness with swagger, and calmness with uncertainty. To boot, there would be no more walking, riding skateboards or mountain bikes, or even stealing my sister's or Freddy's vehicles. I was going to buy my own brand new car, right off of the showroom floor; all cash. It caught my eye from the television set during a commercial as I sat in our infamous living room. A silver Toyota Celica GT. slid across the screen and my eyes hypnotically followed. "I'm getting that one," I uttered to myself from the couch. It was not a wish, a hope or a dream. This was the truth!

I may have been set on driving, but I still had no clue what direction my life was headed in. Throughout the tragedies, the horrible decisions, and the bad endings to good relationships, I still became a high school graduate. On McCabe Avenue, I was the only recent male graduate to casually stand on the corner in the midst of all of the hustlers. I had reached a milestone many inner city blacks don't get to experience. I had successfully completed high school, but make no mistake, inside I really felt like a complete failure.

# Chapter 11

# "BIG BOY"

After graduation, I had about two weeks to relax and attempt to devise some sort of plan for my future. I struggled to find ideas for myself that made real sense. No one else offered any suggestions even if they had, no one would mention until after I shared the money. I was forced to make all of my own choices and decisions, and I hated it. I simply was not ready. I needed a little more time and a lot more attention in some areas. I was growing up way too fast, and I would soon become the person within the household with the most money in the bank. I was never very big on the concept of money. I always felt this since I was a younger teen. It hardly mattered whether I had five bucks or two-hundred; I still felt and treated everyone exactly the same. Everyone around seemed to be more excited about the upcoming resource than myself. The last good feeling I received was when I strolled across the stage to accept my high school diploma. Before my name was called, I sat and listened to the cheers coming from the audience for the other graduates. Some received moderate cheers, while others received emotionless or routine applauses. I was very surprised by the explosion of cheers and the applause I received. There were even a few whistlers out in the crowd. This was truly unexpected, especially considering the way I handled things with Tracey and Melody. I guess I did not see what some of the students may have; I graduated high school in the midst of losing my mom, Shawn, and my grandfather. I guess that does take some focus. It's fair to say, receiving my high school diploma gave me my first real sense of accomplishment.

A week later, images of far more than receiving the first important document of adulthood was clearer. I had a scheduled appointment at

The Post Office and Courthouse in downtown Baltimore. I was set to discuss the particulars of the estimated $48,000 I had coming. Uncle Bobo would accompany me. I had to be escorted by an adult. My grandma was not able to make this trip. Mama's legs were giving her a bit of discomfort. She was fine. She blamed the slight irritation on constantly being on her feet cooking, hanging up clothes, and cleaning. I was not sure how the money ordeal would turn out in regards to expectations of family. I never considered how much to give a specific member. I was sure of three things; helping out grandma, purchasing the Toyota Celica GT, and taking a small trip. I figured King's Dominion again, Hershey Park, or perhaps, Disneyland.

Before looking too far ahead, I would have to attain a driver's license. Freddy and my sister were instructing me regularly in their new 1989 Nissan Maxima. The transmission was a five-speed, but I still handled it pretty well. He and my sister also possessed a Nissan Sentra, which I used for most of my practicing. The permit test was the easier part, especially since I still had academics fresh on the brain. Thankfully, I was quite familiar with the Sentra. This came from the past where Shawn and I stole the car keys while the two were asleep. Sneaky moves such as these now served as nothing more than humorous flashbacks. I would soon be able to buy my own brand new car. Not the "Hot Wheels" toy cars I bought for two bucks a piece from Two Guys department store. The cash purchase would apparently be the same, but for much more; five figures to be exact. The closer I drew to receiving this cash, the more I had my sights set on the Toyota. Still, in the midst of my emotional struggles and my zest for hot wheels, at night, alone in bed, I thought of my mom. Life goes on; nothing stays the same, and things got wild at times, but I was sure to never forget about my beloved mother Denise.

I always remembered that my mom was the sole reason I would be in a position to purchase a nice new vehicle. Regardless of the circumstance, buying a car at 17 or 18 years of age can be exciting. Not being an experienced driver was not. I believe I just wanted a car to be different but in a popular way. I never really pictured myself constantly driving it. Days passed by and the anxiousness of all this intensified. So did the amounts of company I kept. Normally, I would spend my time with Evan, Elroy or Bennett. Now, just days away from receiving this money, I found myself surrounded by people I hardly conversed with before. Family members were more delicate towards me than normal. Folks were a lot friendlier. I noticed it all, but said absolutely nothing. I knew money was very important to people, but I refused to let this pressure me. No matter what others were up to, I knew I would try to practice common sense, compassion, and class when dealing with people and money.

June 29, 1990 appeared with the sun brightening my bedroom, forcing me to retreat beneath the thin sheets. I awakened just enough to realize the day had arrived. My heart fluttered and my mind said, "Hurry up run!" Yet, I still took my time. Everyone was still sleeping except for grandma. She always would get up no later than 6:00 a.m. I watched my uncle squirming about in his bed with a sock missing from his right foot, but I left him be. I immediately thought of Shawn, and how we may have celebrated together at this very moment. I'm certain he would have awakened me sooner. I washed my face and brushed my teeth as always. A moment of disappointment hit as I noticed my gold tooth was damaged. I guess I bit down awkwardly, allowing the tooth to frequently crash into one of the others. I immediately tried to pull it out, but it was still well cemented. Getting a gold tooth was one of my poorest decisions at the time as well. I hesitated the day Shawn and I went. That's why I had one on the side tooth, not in front. Shawn had similar feelings about the decision. That's why he decided to get a crown, not the gold over his full tooth. I could live with that option. This was trendy years ago; overall, I think it's silly, but it appears to have resurfaced. Today, I'm thankful the gold mess became loose years ago and fell out.

After shaking my head in disappointment, I headed downstairs only to learn from Mama, "The Egg Lady," would no longer be visiting us for the first time since I was seven or eight years old. She was our family's supplier of fresh fruits and vegetables, straight from the source; a small farm far out in the county. Her health was deteriorating therefore she could no longer make the trips from her farm to the city. Morning visits from the aging small woman and her two grandchildren were fond memories leftover from better days in B'MORE. The squeaky voice of the very nice, older white woman served as an alarm clock to us all. This news was enough for me to sit down and momentarily join grandma in silence. The newer era was evolving into the opposite of its predecessor. Grandma was not a huge fan of change. Despite the dramatic rise in income I was due to receive, I felt exactly the same.

My uncle overpowered his slight hangover and we made it to the courthouse in one piece to discuss the terms of my account. This was my very first court appearance, and it felt weird, but I was pretty sure I could get used to this type. I witnessed several guys in the area going to the Clarence M. Mitchell, Jr. Courthouse. Courthouse, directly across the street. They were going to criminal court for murder, selling drugs, armed robbery, and other crimes in an attempt to get a hold of some cash. A few gave me weird stares. They wondered why was I at a courthouse smiling. It only took a minute for me to realize, they may have been thinking I was there to snitch on someone. For those not in the streets, it's unsettling to be in court and see another kid from the hood smiling, while walking along with a white man in a power suit. On the inside looking outward, this could look very peculiar. I sat and listened to a lawyer explain how much money I was entitled to and what my options were. I could have taken half of this money, placed the rest in a separate account, and allowed more growth to take place. I also could have left the money in the account and withdraw only from its interest. My choice was the original, but not very wise. Give me access to ALL of the money, NOW. Well, I did immediately withdraw the interest; all of it. In all, I had $47,457. It was actually more than I originally thought. Due to a four year age gap, my resource was significantly larger than my sister's lump sum. Having money does feel good! Very! Money is NOT bad. Stupidity with money is bad, even deadly. The joy I felt as I left the courthouse could never be classified as bad or negative. I was good; I left the courthouse, smiling, with an interest check for $6000.

After cashing the large check at Provident Bank, I quickly hopped into my uncle's Ford Thunderbird. Giggly, nervous, and excited, gazing forward yet not seeing a thing, I realized I was holding more money than I'd ever physically observed. Both hands were fully extended while holding a total of $6000. I tried to find a place to hide the cash, but to no avail. I guess the excitement my uncle felt altered his thinking as well. With no place to conceal the cash, I was headed home with the sole focus of being a positive force for my family. The closer we would come to McCabe, the more nervous I became. There were so many people outside on this beautiful sunny day, I felt weird about having to get out of the car with the stacks of money. I thought to put my hands underneath my shirt. Then I searched for a bag, but had no luck locating one. Next, I tried to put it all in my pockets. That didn't work; my jeans were too tight. Don't laugh! We all wore the tighter fitting pants back then as well. All I could do at this point was to instruct my uncle to let me out of the car directly in front of the house. Everything was official. At 18 years of age, I likely possessed more money in the bank than any of the hustlers on my block. In street terms, I was now a winner, a "Big Boy."

One of the most notable traits of my personality has always been my compassion. I've always had a kindhearted vibe with my approach to all others, even when I screwed up. The females I dated over the years would likely vouch for my character and huge heart. I genuinely love all people and love to see people happy or doing well, even when I'm not. I've been teased in the past for being "too nice," if there's really such a thing. I'm no fool. I just simply follow my heart. I'm not perfect, but if a person deserves it, and I feel their spirit, in me they will have a good friend for life. Whenever I chose to do what I thought when I was young, I usually messed up, but leading with my heart will typically showcase the real me. Despite my failures, I am internal; love will always be my main thing.

Before exiting my uncle's vehicle, I looked over to him and smiled. "Here you go Bo," I said vibrantly. "This is for you," I followed as I handed him one of six, $1,000 stacks I possessed. Looking surprised, he replied, "Are you serious?" "Are you sure?" he asked with a reluctant reach. "Yeah, definitely, absolutely," I replied with a smile. "Thanks Odell, I truly appreciate this, really, thank you very much," Bo stated while looking into my eyes. Throughout my life, it always made me feel much better to give rather than receive. I know today this is a key approach to a good life. Making someone else happy has always made me feel better about myself and about life overall.

After dashing up the steps and into the house, I immediately entered the living room to drop off more money. "Hey ma, I got something for you," I insisted. "Oh yeah?" she replied with a smile. "Yes ma'am, here you go," I replied. I handed my grandma the $3000 I had in my left hand and gave her a tight hug. "Thank you son, I love you boy," she stated emotionally. "You've been one of the few bright spots around here lately," she offered. "You're a good person," grandma added. "Thanks grandma," I replied emotionally. After swallowing nothing but dry air, I hurried upstairs to stash the remaining $2000. I closed the door to my bedroom and sat on the edge of my bed, full of excitement. I received such a positive rush for being responsible for making the day of other people. My next move was to catch up with my peers. I was not about to allow any amount of money change the pure friendships I had developed over the years.

I returned outside with my peers. I noticed quite a few weird stares from the guys and the females, but I stayed poised. I wanted everything to be as normal as before, but I lived in a neighborhood where everyone based their existence on how much money they could make, or take. To stand in the midst of at least a dozen street hustlers, with over $40,000 of legal cash within reach, I must admit, made me feel a little weird. My mild manners and respect for others helped keep the negativity away. If I were a "hard case" or a guy no one cared for on the block, I would have certainly run into trouble. All of the guys seemingly liked me. The guys understood I was from the same environment, but they knew I was different; this was accepted and respected. At some point in their lives, people, no matter who they are or what they do, will never truly be able to resist being human.

After treating Elroy and Bennett to meals at the Sizzlers restaurant, I returned home and began to piece together plans for the upcoming weeks. The summer had just began and fun was the primary theme. I still had my sights set on the Toyota GT. Soon, my uncle BoBo and Montell would accompany me to the dealership. Until then, I would spend my time pondering on which female I should spend the most time with. Melody was growing tired with me for not being the boyfriend she deserved. Understandably, she was still dealing with the pains from the prom ordeal. I remained very upset with myself behind that incident, but I was too caught up with freedom and resources to be sad. I knew we would always have chemistry, but we were not nearly as close as we could have been. Tracey was a bit distant due to my cemented physical attraction to Vikki. Tracey still would be sure to visit me here and there. There was a huge part of me that really wanted her to be as close to me as possible. With her, I struggled with the fast pace world and the running in the streets. Tracey was good for me if I were mentally and emotionally on a better path. She simply deserved more than I was willing to give, and I hated myself for failing her.

The weekend of July 4th displayed fireworks in more than one way. I made the decision most guys would have likely made at the time. I hooked up with Vikki for an explosive evening at the Days Inn Hotel in Towson, Maryland; Baltimore County. With this new income, I was able to join the world of guys who she would give her maximum attention. In the beginning, I knew Vikki was not the best option for me, but she was always exciting to hang out with. Although the premise of our bond was mostly physical, I liked Vikki's attitude; despite her expensive taste, she was peaceful and compassionate. I could go on and on. To give more context of this sister; Vikki, physically, was viewed at that time in B'MORE, as a sister like Lori Harvey is acknowledged for her flawless beauty throughout the world today. Comparisons to celebrities are never fair, but Vikki's ability to physically attract dudes, on first site, was undeniably rare. She was extremely sexy, friendly; many guys wanted to get closer to her, yet it was I who she wanted to stay, lay, and play with.

Vikki and I shopped a bit, tried a few nice eateries, and talked about life; our conversations had a fair amount of substance. Despite this choice, I continued closer relationships with Melody and Tracey. These unions were quieter, mainly due to my environment and affiliation with the streets. The money spent to this point had hardly put a dent in the remaining $40,000 plus. Out of this, I gave my grandma another $2500, my sister and Freddy $2000, and I treated myself, Evan, Bennett, and Elroy to Air Force One, Nike sneakers and Russell sweatsuits. I tried to spread the wealth with those I spent time with, and my core family members.

My aunt Marie and my dad were the only members of my family I withheld money from. My aunt's addiction to drugs was still evident, and my grandma and I believed a lump sum of cash was the last thing Marie needed. Also, I made a promise to God during prayer to never spend any of the money on anything drug related. The idea of giving my dad money simply felt wrong. It was a given his visits would increase, but I was rarely home to meet with him. For the times I was there, I simply would duck him out or avoid him. There were a few instances where he actually saw me running away from him. I knew what he wanted, but I could not bring myself to reject him while looking in his eyes. Still, the way I saw it, if it was not for my dad's negligence, I could possibly still have a mom, and that would be priceless. I handled all of this the best way I knew how as a teen, and for the time being, I simply enjoyed the opportunity to live present life with no concerns about finances. I could feel early on, money was a good thing, but I also understood, more importantly, it cannot assure true happiness.

While the guys in my neighborhood struggled to outdo one another for illegal cash profits, I was getting set to pay legal funds for my choice of vehicle. The Toyota Celica GT still hovered above the rest in my mind. I remained excited every time I viewed the same television commercial. Soon, my two uncles and I would head to Russell Toyota, an automotive dealership in Ellicott City, Maryland; about forty minutes west of McCabe Avenue. Despite watching the commercial countless times, I still overlooked how much the car was actually being sold for. Therefore, I brought along my Provident Bank checkbook not sure about the most important part of the desire; the price tag. I felt strongly about having enough cash to cover the price and finally bringing home my very first personal vehicle.

With $40,000 left in my account, my uncles felt my best move would be to purchase a car for no more than $18,000. This would leave me with some money, but maybe this still was not the best advice. We arrived to the dealership relatively late. While my uncles entered the office to the dealership, I spent some time strolling and browsing throughout the lot of vehicles. I observed many different colors of the Celica I wanted. I also took a very long look at the Toyota Supra. This vehicle was more powerful and larger, but lacked the new sleek look I really liked. It was also more expensive. The Celica I craved sold for around $18,800. The Supra was at least $25,000, or a little more. Wanting to stretch the money as far as I could, I focused on the original vehicle. Next, I had to decide on a color. First, I thought silver, then it was black, then I felt maybe I'd like red. This part was actually a bit frustrating. I suddenly realized I spent an hour looking around and I still was not completely set on a color. As my uncles dealt with the salesman, I ultimately drew to the conclusion, purchasing a car was really no fun at all.

By the time we were finished with all of the paper work, I was set to pay $16,600 cash for a brand new, fully loaded, 1990 Toyota Celica GT. I decided on a light-blue vehicle, only because there were no silver or white, fully-loaded models in stock. For as long as we sat at the dealership, I really wanted to take a car home the same evening. The car I signed the check for was fully-loaded,; this included a sunroof. It actually looked better on the lot than it had on the television screen. The car was so clean I refused to drive it during the test drive. I still only had a Learner's Permit as well, and was not about to crash my first car before getting it back home. I allowed the salesman to drive it as I sat in as a passenger. The portly salesman was professional throughout the entire process. He displayed the car's quickness and assisted me with the operation of the power mirrors, doors, and sunroof. Making large purchases is an exhilarating experience, especially when you are able to do so legally, and you have more than enough to do so. This was me, at 18 years old.

The excitement increased during the drive back home. I now owned my very first car. However, I was clueless to the responsibilities of having your own vehicle. Hell, during this time, I struggled mightily to care for small pets I had on three separate occasions; a turtle, a frog, and a rabbit. I tried, but would often get distracted with peers; completely forgetting about caring for the pet. Still, as we made our way back east from the dealership, although I was not driving, I was riding high. I possessed a new car with no car payments. Only 15 miles registered on the speedometer, and I still had access to over $20,000. Everything was working out according to plan. The only unbelievable event during this time; Mike Tyson's devastating knockout loss to James "Buster" Douglas. I actually ignored this news when it was first stated. I thought folks were playing a cruel joke. By street standards, I was the new knockout artist, about to "pull up" or surprise intensely, I was just minutes away from delivering a solo shot to the rest of the hood. I was certainly living in a faster lane, but no one including me, knew for how long.

I allowed Montell to drive us back to northeast Baltimore in my new car. I really didn't want to let my excitement get us involved in an accident. First, I needed to make sure I got the vehicle home in one piece. With only a Learner's Permit, I was not very experienced driving on expressways, highways or interstates. At this point, having a car was much more important to me than actually driving one. "This is very nice Odell," Montell said while glancing over to his right. "You think so?" I asked with a slight grin. While my uncle drove, I was also surveying the interior of the vehicle. I was opening and closing the sunroof, fooling with the power windows, and fondling with the stereo system. The Toyota was sporty and quick, but was not a luxury car; one that comes with cherry-oak or wood grain interior furnishing. At the time, my car turned heads because it was rare; a newer model of a familiar vehicle which was already seen as slightly above average. "Hey Montell, I'll take over the wheel when we get closer to McCabe, ok?" I confidently stated. In minutes, I was about to return to the block with a different image than the one I owned hours prior, and I knew it. In the minds of virtually everyone in the streets, due to the added resources and material possessions, I would be seen now as a winner; a "Big Boy."

I swapped seats with Montell in my new car once we were about two minutes away from McCabe Avenue. My adrenaline was pumping as I pulled closer towards home. The year 1990 introduced a fleet of new cars with more of a futuristic or aerodynamic appeal. The Celica I purchased received mixed reviews because of this, but I liked the idea. Consumers thought the appearance of this particular vehicle was too far ahead of its time. I figured it would have a longer life span in terms of style. Meaning, years later folks would think the car was virtually still new. This futuristic look was gradually becoming much more popular with vehicles. My new vehicle would now be the latest of all other models on the block. Genius had a total of seven appealing vehicles, but none of which were produced in 1990. He owned a navy-blue, Mercedes Benz 190 with gold BBS rims, a navy-blue, Volvo 240 sedan, three, Toyota Cressida vehicles, a green, Toyota Camry, and a black, Nissan Maxima. He was quickly succeeding Benny and everyone else in the area in the drug game. He truly loved material possessions, basketball, and pretty women, as we all did. He relished in turning heads, but this time around, I would create a bit of excitement, by turning his.

Everyone on my block understood I was never a show-off or an arrogant individual. I like nice things, but I've always been an "inside/out" type of guy. Meaning, I believe character and attitude are so important, they can actually help your attire look better on you. Meaning, how you carry yourself, or your attitude can actually impact your outer appearance. It was nice knowing so many different people viewed me simply as, "a cool dude." "A good guy driving a nice car," didn't sound too shabby when referring to me either. I turned onto McCabe Avenue around 10:00 p.m. on this evening. I pulled up to park only to see a dice game taking place on the corner. I slowly and nervously parallel parked the car. I could feel everyone pause and look over at me as I tried to focus on completing the perfect maneuver. While doing so, I also heard a few comments like, "Got damn, that car hard as shit," or "It's cool, it's alright," or "Yo, O must got some real fuckin money." After finally completing the skill of parking, I headed towards the house, looking backwards of course. I spoke to all of the guys and followed Montell to the house. My name was called. "Odell!" It was Genius. He was standing on the corner, slightly away from the others, with his arms extended and plenty of cash balled up in both hands. "Yo!" he added with a surprised expression. I turned and replied, "What's up?" He then asked, "What the hell you got there boy, a mini space ship?" "Do you like it? I asked with a smile. "Fuck yeah, I like it," he shouted while smiling. "You a 'Big Boy' now son," he added. Meaning, by the account of Genius and others, I would now be viewed as a real man, with a boy's spirit; a man with money, a guy making big moves. Montell giggled as he went up the steps first. "Hey, that's a slick muthafucka, ain't it man?" he yelled toward the ongoing dice game. We smiled at each other. I watched Genius look back and forth, from my car, then in my direction, smiling. He had his hands on his hips, as to say, "O, you scored big on us with this move, and I respect you for that." Genius based a lot on money and possessions. Just by purchasing a new car, I now had a kingpin, drug dealer as a pal.

The conversation about the car was the most Genius and I had ever spoken. Before entering the house, I looked backwards at the crowd of guys gambling on the corner. Staring, I realized every one of these guys were out on the corners trying to make the necessary money to do exactly what I just did quite easily; buy a car. I wondered if these particular guys really had to sell drugs, hurt people, or have a loved one pass away to gain riches or wealth? I entered my house slightly shaking my head in confusion, wanting to be completely wrong about these thoughts. I went straight up to my room after kissing my grandmother on the cheek. I sat on my favorite corner of the bed realizing all of the excitement over the $40,000 was suddenly diminishing quickly. The money still could not eliminate the negativity all around me. My life was one huge oxy-moron. I was content, confused, and sad all at once. I smiled while counting the money I had in my Nike shoe box, yet, still aware of the true reason I continuously checked on it. I feared a few members of my family would attempt to steal from me, if the opportunity presented itself. I would also look out of my bedroom window to see how nice my new car looked from above, wondering the entire time, if it would even be there the very next morning.

That night I laid motionless and silent, staring at the ceiling illuminated by the glare from unending bypassing traffic. Everything painful in my heart would return. I was still reliving how Shawn bled profusely on the floor just below me. I was also considering how I obtained the cash I had tucked away in my closet. Mentally, I traced the funds backward; imagining my mom depositing smaller amounts of cash into a (CD) for my sister and I. I even recalled the once or twice granddad actually smiled at me. These memories, along with the energies inside and outside of 731 began to promote a defeated outlook for my future and life as a whole. After daydreaming at night for about an hour, I would finally drift off asleep. I was lacking hope for the future, but the present was not all bad for the moment. I guess for now, my existence was the exact opposite of the old popular cliche, "Everything gets worse, before it gets better."

The next morning, I popped up, headed to the bedroom window, and immediately fixed my clouded vision onto my car. I reached for my glasses I'd been wearing for the last few years, making sure the car was in its original position. I honestly believed most guys in the neighborhood liked me. I did not think they would actually try to steal my car, but there were a few young knuckleheads who I know would have loved to go joy riding with or without my permission. These kids were already outside selling drugs at twelve and thirteen years of age. I understood nothing was off limits to how they thought.

After coming to grips, again, with the knowledge of having a brand new car, I quickly entered the bathroom for a hot bath. At this point, I had only experienced taking a shower once or twice, and this would be inside of a hotel with Vikki. We never had a shower in the homes we lived in over the years. The idea of going for seconds with the beauty had me washing up before the tub filled with water. After drying off and throwing on my brand new Adidas Forum sneakers, and a royal-blue, silver and white, Adidas sweatsuit, I gave the young lady a call. To my surprise, I learned Frankie was incarcerated again, yet on another drug possession charge. This time his prison stay would be a bit longer.

Frankie already knew of me, but was beginning to find out more about Vikki and I through folks who love to gossip. I believe the pressure of knowing I had a little money caused him to try a lot harder out in the streets, likely causing more slip-ups than usual. However, Vikki said the two were all but finished a little before his sudden arrest. I never asked her too many questions; I never had any intentions on becoming exclusive with Vikki. She represented infatuation at its finest. I liked Vikki a lot, and I simply loved her company and her sex appeal, but that's really as far as I allowed my emotions to go with her.

After splashing on Cool Water cologne and retrieving my Provident Bank card from the pocket of the previous day's pants, I headed to Guilford Avenue where Vikki lived with her grandma. Vikki lived only a few miles from both Kennedy Avenue and Asquith Street. I drove with a double dose of nervousness. Vikki's presence normally gave me butterflies, and I was still driving with just a Learner's Permit. Knowing my driving skills were mediocre at best, I was in no hurry to go to the MVA. Besides, I knew Vikki had her license for awhile from seeing her drive to and from school. I had two choices: drive on city streets and risk being pulled over, which was pretty frequent for young blacks, or let one of the finest girls in the city drive me around all day. This decision was easy. Vikki was going to do the driving. "Hey O," Vikki said while smiling as she opened her front door. "What's up?" I asked while embracing the beauty. "I'm almost ready, I just have to grab my shades," she insisted. "Where are we headed?" she asked with a surprisingly nervous grin. "I don't know," I answered. "Anywhere, nowhere, somewhere, everywhere, I don't know, I don't care," I followed while giggling. Neither of us really knew what to do or where to go. We understood we were living in the moment, excited, but still clueless about how long these times would last.

Vikki and I went to IHOP (International House of Pancakes) for breakfast. I got an opportunity to get to know her better. Because of Vikki's physical attributes, it was not hard for her to obtain labels like "gold digger," "freak," "whore," or "bitch." I was never big on name calling of any kind; male, and especially female. On McCabe and abroad, I've encountered the types who frequently and willingly wear these titles, but Vikki was not one of them. I was surprised by her humility and mild nature. She really is a nice person. It was clear she was a bit tainted by the elements around her, but we all were; especially myself. I did not sell drugs, but my best buddy Elroy did. I had a problem with dating too many young ladies. Vikki unjustly received these degrading stamps. She may have loved the material gifts a bit much, but I was learning she actually had a heart of gold. So, I decided to change my approach after a while. I wanted to continue with having a good time with Vikki, but I began to think about drawing even closer to the bombshell.

By the end of July 1990, Vikki and I were unexpectedly rather exclusive. We were not an item or labeled as such, but we were very fond of one another. We were not destined for marriage or greatness, but we were a good uncommitted couple for the rest of the city to chat about. The hotel stays, the shopping getaways, and the nice restaurants were common practices for the two of us. I even attended her family outings; theme parks and bingo nights. We were just two very young teens having fun at any cost. Vikki rarely asked me for anything; I gave her plenty, but not what people believe. What did I care? To me it was only money. Perhaps I was a little green or inexperienced, but it all felt good. I've always loved the company of women. In the midst of the perfect fun Vikki and I shared, I still found a little time to chase behind Melody. Tracey still wanted to spend a little time with me as well, despite having a new friend. That was a huge surprise after having to literally run away from her to avoid Vikki interrogation questions. Vikki indeed, had my nose wide open, but not enough for me to get upset about another guy she knew, or for me to stop seeing another female. Our relationship was not built on complete openness, honesty nor commitment, but man was she beautiful, fun, and very good in bed.

Whenever I was not with Vikki or Melody, I was on McCabe Avenue, or on one of the many basketball courts. I could hardly sit still long enough to write at this point. If I found time to write, of course, it would strictly be love notes to one or all of the three beauties I shared time with. Each letter would be, at least, four pages long. I still enjoyed the time I spent with my two closest pals, Bennett and Elroy. Together we represented what was cool about inner city young teens; fresh gear, good attitudes, and street credibility. My closeness with Bennett branched from our ability not to take part in the drug game, while my closeness with Elroy stemmed from our sense of street, humor, and our ability to do whatever we wanted because of the money we both had. I may have had five figures in the bank, but I made nothing. I had no income! Elroy didn't have a bank account, but he was making at least $1000 to $1500 a day. He did not possess the lump sum I had, but I was sure Elroy was able to spend just as much as I could, if not more.

While Elroy hustled the street corners for profits, Bennett and I used our weekends for fun. We would hang out at the amusement parks or at the movies. We liked being different from the others, yet we wanted everyone to know we too had backbone. We frequently drove up and down Greenmount Avenue in east Baltimore, a notoriously poor environment, making sure we were seen by all of the hustlers on the eastside. We wanted to make the statement, "Look at us, we're doing fine, and we don't sell drugs, act like idiots, or senselessly hurt innocent people." There was always a love/hate vibe with Bennett and I verses the others on McCabe, and other dealers, with the exception of Elroy. Everyone loved Elroy and his undying sense of humor. The periodic bitterness was not fully to be blamed on the guys' decision to sell drugs. We didn't accept the fact guys felt they had to; we hated the excuse. At the time, we didn't understand the depression and the addiction that comes with the dealing. We were still agitated for losing the positive way of life we once had in our neighborhood.

While I was flexing around in my new car with my peers, jobless, I hardly paid any attention to the money being spent which was not seen. With no money coming in from anywhere, I was steadily dialing the installed expensive car phone's key pad, just to hear the pretty voices on the speaker system. I also never kept an eye on the $400 a month, full-coverage payment I had to pay to Nationwide Insurance. With nearly $20,000 still left in my account, I would only take short glances at the receipts after several trips to the ATM. Money was depleting quickly, but I hardly noticed. I was spending too freely while doing exactly what Jim Kelly's character confessed to do in the Bruce Lee film, "Enter the Dragon;" 'too busy looking good.'

I was looking pretty good with my new wheels and apparel, along with a fresh haircut. Still, I was not very sure of myself. I still used all of the running around and the money to hide from my insecurities. I was lost, yet not truly hopeless. I believed I actually made not knowing what to do with myself look ok. Despite my issues, females were still in heavy rotation. As you may have noticed, I was certainly down with O.P.P. (an abbreviation which stands for: Other People's Property. Hip hop terminology created by rap trio, Naughty By Nature in 1991). So there I was, on the cell phone talking to Melody, but thinking about Tracey and Vikki, while trying to count in my head how much money I had in my pockets. I was a mess, but remember, I was looking good though, right? Yeah, whatever.

Without a true destination, I found myself hanging out a lot with Elroy and Bennett; spending money and running behind the females who loved to be chased. I was sure to continue with the sport of basketball to help stay away from the negativity as much as I could. This hardly worked. As I stated earlier, basketball is the #1 sport in the hood. Because of my ability to play a little, I was unintentionally becoming one of the boys, even without selling drugs. Most of the older guys were impressed by my ability to interact with the beautiful females, and the slightly above-average talent I displayed on the court. Having a little money also helped develop these, so-called friendships as well.

By August, I managed to make several new pals on McCabe Avenue. I began to get several offers from the older guys to join them at Dewees playground for hoops. Freddy and many of the others were not into the sport as they were years ago. David Wingate was now a seasoned pro in the N.B.A. He was making his money, while Michael Jordan, who usually embarrassed him on the court, made sure he saved some. When it came to basketball, I really did not mind being a part of a group. In sports, it's cool to be recognized by your peers for good play. Only difference here, these peers of mine may have committed a murder or a robbery the night before a pick-up game. As my game elevated, little by little, my circle of suspect hoop buddies grew larger. All I saw was an opportunity to show up some tough guys on the court, but again, grandma began to feel the presence of something far more sinister.

One warm Saturday morning, I awakened to Mama's loud yell, "ODELL, ODELL! SOME GUYS ARE ON MY PORCH LOOKING FOR YOU. COME AND SEE WHAT THE HELL THEY WANT!" "Wow," I said in a sleepy whisper. "OKaayy!" I struggled to shout. After quickly rolling over and touching the floor with my right hand, to keep from falling completely out of the bed, I threw on my shorts and crept down the stairs. Halfway down the stairs, I observed an old pair of beat up

Forum Adidas. I bent downwards and made eye contact with a hardened expression made by Genius; just one guy, the guy. "What's up buddy?" I said to the kingpin. "What's up man?" "Come on and hoop with us," he insisted. "We all about to go up the court, come run with us," he said enthusiastically. Genius often struggled to withdraw his dominant personality. No matter who he spoke to, he always seemed to tell folks what to do; he never asked. I gave him this one for free, because I really wanted to play with them all anyway. "OK," I replied excitedly until I looked over towards my grandma.

The look Mama had on her face said, "Don't do it!" Then the words, "Don't do it!" actually came from her mouth while also shaking her head. "What in the hell does he want with you?" she asked in anger. "Ma, everything's cool. They just want me to play basketball with them, that's all," I said confidently. Mama gave me a devilish smirk with her head downward and her eyes looking upwards. "I don't want you messing with that man, he's crazy," she assured. "He sells those drugs and shit." "Ma, I assure you, it's just basketball," I said confidently. "Alright!" she replied. "Don't be hangin' around those guys like Shawn was doing," she added with eyebrows raised that read, "You may be next to go!" "They all ain't nothing but fuckin trouble," I could hear as I headed upstairs to get dressed.

After struggling to convince grandma all was good in the hood on the ball courts, I headed to Dewees with my duffle bag in hand. Inside, I usually would carry a few extra tee-shirts, an extra pair of socks, a knee brace or two, and drinks. Lets just say I came well prepared. I even had prescription goggles to play in, so my glasses would not get damaged, as they had in previous years. Back then, glasses were not too cool, but I pulled it all off smoothly. Others brought along their bags as well, but the contents were notoriously different. During a break on the court, in some of the guys' bags, I'd see drugs, a gun or two, lots of money or all three. Nine times out of ten, I would be the only guy from McCabe on the court who was not affiliated with drugs. Bennett and Evan were the only others when they were present. Knowing this did not make me feel differently. We all shared one idea. We all needed something and none of us could find exactly what we were looking for. Surprisingly, somehow, I never felt weird or uncomfortable. I felt good. I still often felt at "home."

The games played at Dewees were pretty intense. These games were much better than the games we played at Child Study. Here, there were guys who played in, or nearly made the cut to play in the N.B.A. Guys like Steve Smith from Southern Cal. Look him up! Not the great guard from the N.B.A. who many are familiar with, or the great football player, but a great guard nevertheless. He usually schooled us all pretty well. Some players you come across have a certain feel for the game and you know they've been around the greats. Steve was one of those players. Steve has been on the same court as Joe Pace from the Bullets, Ken "Foots" Bannister, from the New York Knicks, Quintin Daily, Michael Cooper, and a player and person we all know of and love from the Los Angeles Lakers; Earvin "Magic" Johnson. All of these great players and many more were said to be teammates or opponents of Steve's or "Milk's" at one time or another in his illustrious, but shortened career. Steve was drafted by the Atlanta Hawks, but suffered a career altering knee injury, forcing him to leave the center stage of the game very early.

Playing with Steve, three of his younger brothers, and others allowed me to gain more toughness and determination while enhancing my skills. Steve noticed a little talent in me. He actually recommended I tie my right arm behind my back and dribble all day and night, for months, with my left hand only. He felt if I could dribble better lefthanded, I could make some real noise in the city. I was out of school, but I had just turned 18, therefore I still had a little time, or a small window before my chances to develop into an elite player would pass me by. I followed Steve's instructions for a week or two. I practiced in seclusion, due to the embarrassing look of it all. The regimen actually worked. I noticed results and began to feel much more comfortable dribbling the ball lefthanded. I loved playing basketball, but I never felt I loved it as much as guys like Steve or David. I felt good whenever I would play pick-up ball, but the thoughts never would progress much further. Although I still had enough money to go to school, it never really registered. I never planned to stop playing the sport, but it was more of an afterthought than a dream for me. It was not my calling. I was sure of that! In the midst of all the interesting events surrounding my life, I was still clueless to what I was placed on earth to become, but it was not to pursue a career in basketball.

Even with this realization, basketball consumed plenty of my time during the Summer of 1990. I also began to try my hand at hanging out at the local nightclubs. The club scene was a big deal for our neighborhood. It was really the only time the guys would give themselves a chance to mingle with females outside the area. None of the guys attended school much, compromising their own social growth to go along with their academic deficiencies. If there was one thing I knew: I understood education and success is forever connected. That is what's so scary about the drop-out, drug dealer. What about later on, if you do manage to survive or stay free? School is important, and it really helps us all socially. Money without social skills will only carry a person so far. Social skills build character, and character builds important relationships. I've been comfortable with people from all walks for most of my life. I love people, and the idea or fact that no two are exactly alike interests me tremendously. Trying the club scene proved to be a nice experience, but I've always preferred a more intimate or private setting. The nicest idea about attending a club was everyone would get their opportunity to act out in their very own music video. There, you have your loud music of course; plenty of females and you must wear your finest apparel. The club scene allowed everyone to be a performer; representing his neighborhood, starring in his own short film or movie.

I had a little fun at the nightclub ironically named, Odell's. The club's slogan was, "You'll know if you belong." For me, I was never really sure. Again, I enjoyed more private moments with the females. Keeping Vikki's company or pulling up to Melody's rear parking pad served as better settings for my romantic imaginary production. I'd be listening to old school classics like, The Stylistics,' "I'm Still in Love with You" or Alicia Myer's "You Get the Best of Me (Say, say, say)." I always enjoyed the music from the earlier years. As a teen, this music gave me a small connection to the happier days of the past. Although I endured many devastating circumstances surrounding my family, I believe the people as a whole still treated each other better in previous years. I've always noticed the difference, and I've always despised it.

The desire to be romantic would soon permit Vikki and I to take a nice summer drive to Kings Dominion. I visited the amusement park twice, but never exclusively with a female. This excursion was also going to be the first long ride I would experience in my new car. However, during the drive I grew irritated. I did not care to practice on my driving skills. I really just wanted to stare at Vikki's glossy, crossed legs draped in a frock. I got over it. A man can't be afraid to drive his own damn car! Halfway to the park, I began to get very comfortable with my driving. The nervousness of beauty still existed, but that too became a good thing. My car was new, but the excuses not to have a Driver's License were getting old. I still only possessed a Learner's Permit. Procrastination was a regular practice whenever a subject or situation arose I was not very comfortable with. Luckily for me, Freddy was growing tired of teaching and driving me around the city everyday. Plans were finally set in place for me to visit Mondawmin Mall, in west Baltimore to take my driver's test for the first time. But for now, I studied Vikki closely. The type of "ride" she would provide was still undetermined. Therefore, I continued to practice being charming by impressing Vikki with my sense of patience, romance, style, generosity, respect, and humor.

The Holiday Inn Hotel in Virginia, near the fun park, was the destination where I realized the true meaning of a roller coaster. Sexually, Vikki was more mature than any female I had been sexually active with, although no one compared to my experiences with Tracey. Melody and I felt the best; we always made love, never having just sex. But here, Vikki and I felt like celebrities as we dipped in the hotel's large outdoor swimming pool in the hot sun. I felt I did a fairly good job maintaining my cool by holding on to the borders of the pool while Vikki played in the deeper portion. Throughout my entire life, I was never taught how to swim. Vikki was a very good swimmer, dressed in a very nice Victoria Secret swimsuit. I was feeling pretty good, despite my struggles to stay afloat without assistance. Still, on this trip, I did not need much help; I had all the "riding" and "swimming" I could handle. We stayed at the park for the entire weekend, living out all of our desires and sexual fantasies. I had no idea when I walked across the stage to receive my high school diploma, a little more than a month later, I would be receiving favors while driving a new car on 95 North, from the young lady of everyone's desires.

Miraculously, I managed to somehow practice good lane control on the highway well enough to make it back to Baltimore safely. I figured since I was able to pass this "driving test," I must be ready to go to the M.V.A. The very next morning, Freddy and I headed west for me to take my law test. I was more nervous than I anticipated during the testing. In less than twenty-four hours, I had gone from one of the hottest females ever, to one of the coldest. My test instructor was pretty, yet very focused and intense. Somehow, I managed to muster up enough poise to get through the testing. I passed.

It was a liberating feeling to finally have my driver's license. I also gave Freddy his life back. He no longer had to listen to me beg him to join me for long boring days of driving. Freddy showed great support and patience while helping me learn to drive. Still, I could not get him back home fast enough. "You should have been taken that test," he stated while smiling. "You're right man. It was pretty easy, but I was just nervous for some reason," I replied after sighing in relief. "You're alright now boy," he added. "Come and pick me up tomorrow at three and drop me off around the way please. I'm going to give your sister the car so she can go to the mall early. My cousin has my other car," Freddy stated. "I'll be here," I assured Freddy as I pulled into his apartment complex. I left the parking lot glad to now be a licensed driver. I actually took the long way home to simply enjoy a lengthy ride alone. I still periodically loved to spend time by myself. I was constantly trying to figure myself out. I was sure I was growing physically, but not so sure if I was advancing in the right direction in some of the vital areas of life; spirituality, love of self, and drive.

The first day of officially being able to drive unattended left me with a cramped buttocks. I spent the rest of the evening writing more love letters to both, Vikki and Tracey, who I was scheduled to meet with on the following day. I'd heard through a friend Tracey was exclusively dating another guy from the school. I had mixed emotions, but I was not surprised. Tracey, as I had stated, was a good girlfriend and an even better person. It was clearer than ever, I was not ready to be in a steady relationship with her. Although I was really looking forward to seeing her, I knew the meeting would be the beginning of the end for our nearly three years of connecting.

I awakened quite early on a hot, August morning looking forward to hanging out with Tracey later during the evening. I took a hot bath and got dressed in the third new outfit in as many days. I stopped in the living room to chat with the only person in my life I felt I could truly trust; my grandma. My grandma was a person of substance despite her lack of education and her foul mouth. She still made sure I understood character, compassion, and humility were far more important than material wealth or individual successes. As long as I remained respectful and peaceful, she would never relinquish confidence in me to make it in life, no matter what I chose to do. My biggest problem was the choices themselves. Somehow, the positive ones I had at my disposal never really crossed my mind for the future.

Conversations with my grandmother gave me an optimistic view of the possibility of living a happy life. However, our talks only covered matters of the heart in which she would state, "Your heart is your pathway to the Spirit of God." I did not fully understand exactly what she meant, but I felt it was a good idea to care about people in order to get God's attention; to love giving better than receiving. My grandma was easily my best friend and the main reason why I made everyone smile whenever I found the opportunity to. For as much negativity as I found myself around daily, grandma had enough of my attention to know I would never intentionally let her down.

After our talk, I had a brief chat outside with Genius and a few others about basketball. I then headed to pick up Freddy to give him a lift back to the neighborhood. I quickly drove up McCabe, turning heads in every passing block leading up to York Road. Twenty minutes later, I retrieved Freddy from his apartment and headed back towards McCabe. "O, is this the only tape you have man?" Freddy asked while shaking his head. "Nah, I have two cases full of music under your seat." "Why?" I replied. "Every time I see you, you're playing the same song," he emphasized. "Man, I'm telling you, "Looking Out The Front Door," is the shit," I stated in reference to hip hop group, Main Source's hit single about a hard-to-please girlfriend. Although it was I who appeared to be hard to please, I loved the song and the melody it carried; perfect. I drove Freddy crazy with the Main Source hit for weeks. Not long afterwards, he would do the same to me with DJ Quik's hit song, "Tonight." He loved the song mainly because it briefly mentioned gambling. Freddy liked rappers who spoke truths about hustling, gambling or making money more than he preferred the artists who preached about the mistreatment of blacks or racial and social issues, like KRS-One. On the day I picked Freedy up from his home, we had no clue we would soon be experiencing the negativity preached about so passionately in the "teacher's" rhymes.

After making a quick stop in the house to grab a few hundred bucks to shop with, Freddy and I got back into my car. He briefly conversed with Chuck, his close friend and the boyfriend of my sister's closest friend, Retta. Retta is the aunt of Todd, the guy who accidentally killed my cousin Shawn. The two were great friends long before my cousin was killed. That incident severed the relationship between my sister and Retta. Freddy agreed to join me for a trip over to the Shoe City sneaker outlet where he worked. I wanted to check out the latest Michael Jordan basketball sneakers. Every time a pair released in the early 90s, I had them. Here, we could use his employee's discount. Freddy preferred Adidas Top Ten sneakers. We drove up McCabe Avenue and around the block onto a street named, Glenwood Avenue. As we approached The Alameda, the main road the #36 bus travels on, I took a brief look into my rearview mirror. Freddy was asking me to allow him to take the Celica for a quick spin later on in the day. Seconds later, I noticed a dark blue car advancing abruptly. "What the hell?" I stated in a low tone. "Shit, it's the cops," Freddy said nervously while observing in the opposite mirror. Seconds later, the unmarked patrol car lights flashed with only a small chirp of its siren released. We were being pulled over for some unknown reason. This was my very first time experiencing a traffic situation with the police. The police needed some answers, but I was still clueless about what the questions were.

Seconds after pulling over for the unmarked Crow Victoria, several blue and white patrol cars would swarm in from all directions. The ambush happened so quickly, I could not even think straight. The phrases, "Get out of the car!" "Let me see your hands!" "Get on the ground now!" all pierced through my vehicle as officers on each side of the car snatched Freddy and I out and onto the blacktop. Without any explanation, we were thrown onto our chests and held under our own will. We both were pretty silent, but I was extremely nervous. Freddy's demeanor allowed me to control myself enough not to overreact. I could tell he knew something. Moments later, he spoke. "What the hell are y'all doing?" he asked the officers. "Shut the fuck up!" one officer replied while assisting the others. The police were rummaging through my new vehicle. "Hey! Do y'all have a warrant?" Freddy yelled out from the ground. I looked back at the officer with his knee in my back and noticed he would not make eye contact with me. The situation had similarities to the George Floyd incident. "Why y'all fuckin with us?" Freddy yelled. At this moment, I felt Freddy was really onto something. Here we were surrounded by cops and onlookers, and he was cursing at them all. It took me five minutes to understand we were totally innocent, and the cops were using their authority without any merit whatsoever.

Another five minutes passed with me watching the Carpenter ants from up close before the ten to twelve officers realized they were wasting their time. We soon would be allowed to stand as the police closed the doors to my car. Still without a reason for the raid, Freddy again would shout, "Why the fuck did y'all pull us over?" The officers never replied. They only offered up expressions of embarrassment, similar to my own. Whispers from the small crowd about a possible lawsuit for an illegal search slipped into my ears. I was not getting arrested, but my nerves had been. Freddy had gone from being frustrated to extremely confident. He had gone from asking questions to shouting threats at the officers. "Man y'all muthafuckas thought somebody was selling drugs or had guns, but y'all fucked up!" "I should sue you bitches for not having a warrant," Freddy said with a devilish but distorted grin. The truth was being spoken before dozens, but not by police. Freddy suddenly found himself performing his best Kris Parker impression.

It was now clear, the police believed me to be a drug dealer because of the new car and nice clothing I possessed. Freddy was actually a dealer, but managed to stay trouble-free throughout his dealings at the time. They were there for me, not him. The more Freddy yelled, the faster the officers would return to their vehicles. "Stay out of trouble," one officer said to me while hurrying away. Moments later, the officers were speeding away, all in opposite directions. "Bitches!" Freddy screamed from the top of his lungs. I stood in silence for a few minutes while Freddy would tend to the onlookers. I realized in the hood it can be quite easy to get in trouble, yet very difficult to keep your nose clean. It may not matter whether or not you're a troublemaker or a lawbreaker here. To so many of the police officers, top officials, and upper-class citizens out in society, us inner city blacks, we're all garbage; "throwaways."

Freddy and I would lose our appetite to shop for sneakers after the traffic incident. Instead, I ended up dropping him off back at home. I then headed to meet up with Tracey. Before picking up my ex, I took a break to reflect on the situation that had just taken place with the police.

I was wondering how long were police watching me, and did Freddy's affiliation with the streets play a role with this mishap. I also wondered if my relationship with Elroy had anything to do with this tremendously embarrassing act. I reached Dolfield Avenue, located in west Baltimore, where Tracey had recently moved, knowing how important it was to stay close to grandma and keep away from trouble. My visit with Tracey was supposed to be a counter act on what had just taken place, but this visit was an indication trouble would come in many forms or variations.

As I sat and waited in the car for Tracey to come outside, a weird feeling came over me. My excitement to see her was quickly replaced by nervousness and uncertainty. I'd almost forgotten how badly I had hurt the high school senior's feelings. I assumed she was now regretting having to share a few classes with me in high school. It was no longer a good feeling to be around her family. Her mom and her close cousins were all disappointed in how things turned out between the two of us. For a brief moment, as I waited patiently, I daydreamed about another run-down, but not by authorities. I pictured being set up and maybe robbed for mistreating Tracey. All kinds of silly thoughts entered my head. It was my guilt! My life was getting messier with each passing day, and I had no answers and not many people to go to for help.

By the time Tracey entered the car and we made our way towards Towson Mall to shop a little, my paranoia had left completely. Tracey and I were thrilled to be together again, but her mood still showed signs of the pain I created with my poor decisions. The cute, small-framed sister periodically smiled, but was rarely able to make eye contact with me for more than a second. We had a decent time hanging out, eating, and riding on the open roads. We shopped a little. I purchased a Reebox sweatsuit, and female Reebox "Pump" sneakers to match for Tracey, but the deflation had already taken place, and would be too tough to restore. The few hundred dollars I spent on this evening meant absolutely nothing. That money spent was nothing more than a poor afterthought.

Spending money on Tracey too late made things feel a little phony. She was the first female to know about the cash, and the one who may have loved me the most. Deep down inside I knew I had screwed up, but I felt I had no need to push backwards. The damage was done. I knew the time we shared together would possibly be our last. During this final ride home we both became very emotional. Tracey knew I still loved her. She was also aware I was too weak to stop myself from destroying our union. In all of this I've never been or felt like a victim of any sort; I was just troubled emotionally, very.

As tears slowly rolled from all four eyes in the car, Tracey stated, "I'm pregnant." I was shocked by this news, but more so saddened by our situation. I tried to become a little excited, but with us, nothing was for sure. "Yeah, how far are you?" I asked nicely. "Almost two months," she answered with very little passion. Having a child when you still are one within is never a good idea, but this may have been the only miracle to help save our relationship.

About two months had passed since Tracey and I were intimate, and she had been seeing another guy for this same period of time. Tracey's new boyfriend's name was Phil. He once asked me if it was cool for him to deal with Tracey immediately after our breakup. Phil and I were not friends, but we were cordial due to pick-up basketball, which we played together with others on a few occasions. I think he asked simply because I was a very popular graduate, and the bond Tracey and I shared was even more so. It was a great gesture of respect on his part.

In reference to Phil's gesture, I pretended to think nothing of it at the time. Still, I figured: if she was fine with I, why would I squabble? I told Phil not to hesitate, but I was really hurting inside. Part of it was love, the other half was selfishness, on my behalf. All along my heart was sinking as I was forced to let go. In the car Tracey said to me, "The baby might be yours. I hope it is," she added. I dropped Tracey off that night wondering if I would soon be a father. A few days later, I learned the baby living inside of Tracey was not my own. It was Phil's. This was the last meeting and conversation Tracey and I ever had. I had let a very trustworthy and beautiful sister slip away. In the midst of all the shopping, partying, and the other females, I was never too busy to remember to feel stupid. On the outside I may have been a "big boy," but internally I was a little idiot.

# Chapter 12

# LEAVING

Losing Tracey truly hurt my heart. Looking back on things, I believe I left good unions or ran away from good situations as a way to cope with the losses I endured with family members. My resolution was a counter action to how I dealt with family members prematurely leaving me; in return I began leaving others. Here, I would convince myself spending time with the other young women and blowing money was a more suitable way to live for an 18 year old. Tracey was gone forever, but I continued to spend quality time with Melody. With her, I would get over the loss relatively quickly, but she refused to fully give in to my persistent charm. Hurting her once was more than enough. The trust was bruised. I still would date Vikki every chance I could, but the flame here was burning out as well. I still liked her a lot, but she was living far too fast of a pace for me to keep up for much longer. I knew most girls just wanted to have fun, but I was growing a little tired of running or chasing. This uncomfortable pace was quite visible on my bank statements as well. I had a little more than $10,000 left in my account. My car insurance was steadily chewing away at this figure while I ran the streets like a struggling or out-of-work celebrity. As the year 1990 drew to a close, so did all the fun and anticipation of the previous year. My buddy Elroy, in a surprising last effort attempt, again, pleaded with me to take him up on his offer to buy a kilo of cocaine. Now, I didn't even have enough to pull off a purchase of two or three. I still refused without hesitation. Elroy felt I would get a little desperate because of my decreasing wealth. In 1990, a dealer in our neck of the woods needed around $22,000-$24,000 to purchase a kilo of good cocaine. After the rush the cops put on me earlier, there was no way

I was going to be that ignorant, or even bold enough to make a move like this. Besides, Mama would have killed me for dealing any type of drug, after nearly disowning me first.

Drug dealing was never a part of the plan I didn't have. I felt I needed a job, but I really hated the idea of working at places which had little to do with what I really felt passionate about. The problem was: to me, my passions seemed unrealistic as a means to a comfortable lifestyle. This mentality forced me to consider the average job. By the time the year 1991 rolled in, I swallowed my pride and found myself downtown, ironically, selling shoes at a Shoe City Sports sneaker outlet. Freddy helped get me the job through his manager at this different location. Now, instead of purchasing from the store every week, I sold shoes to those who could. I really had no choice. I needed the money. By the time I started the job, I only had $6000 left in my bank account.

By the start of the 1991-92 school year, I was an employee for Shoe City Sports, located on Lexington Street in downtown Baltimore (no longer at this location). I'm a huge sneaker head, therefore this helped me cope with the transition of taking things one day at a time. I was confused, but I still wanted a more normal existence. Despite my initial lack of interest with jobs, having one actually made me feel more at peace with myself; more mature. My life began to have more structure and discipline, yet I struggled with the idea this was all that life could offer. Watching my co-workers, who were much older, confused me. I could not understand why folks appeared to hate their jobs yet stayed. I was amazed to see most folks seemed content with living a lifestyle where 85% of the time, they're working for smaller amounts of money, yet doing things they really don't want or desire to do. They would often say, "I hate this fuckin job, but I have no choice. I need the money." I would be thinking to myself, "Well, go and do what it takes to find a better job!" I truly understood life can often deal a nasty hand, but this did not seem to be the issue in every case. Here, I began to understand the concept of settling for less. This is when I really learned about self-inflicted pain. In our culture folks are exposed to negativity so much, they actually convince themselves that things should be negative. In turn, when something positive does come their way, they freak out, get weird, and reject good. For many in the inner city, bad is good, and good is bad. This goes for brothers and sisters. I now understood clearly what it meant to screw yourself, but I still was not strong enough to be different. So after a few weeks on the job, I decided to join in on this mediocre mental approach as well.

The idea of working for a living, of course, came with less money than breaking the law, but stressing about being arrested or shot was still not a major concern for me as it was for my peers. However, the possibility of being harmed was always available on McCabe Avenue. It hardly mattered if you were a dealer, man, woman, or child. You never knew when a car would come through shooting, or when someone on the block would fire at someone else. Therefore, working everyday did have its advantages; like school, it kept you safe, AWAY from home, if that makes any sense. Although I knew I was doing the right thing by working, it still felt, not wrong, but weak, wack or lame. Waking up to go to work every day, coming home tired, going back to sleep early in order to do it all over again seemed stupid, especially for a measly $450 every two weeks.. At the time, I did not realize this was alright for a teen.

The older I became, the more ignorant I was. My bi-weekly checks did allow me to stay away from the local bank machines. I even managed to make a deposit; my first ever. I felt good about being able to continue to pay for my full-coverage insurance without getting upset about my remaining balance. My car was very dear to me. Not because of the year, make or model. I viewed my car as the only physical symbol I had to remember my mom. Pictures and other personal effects managed to elude the family over the years. During my prayers at night, I would talk to my mom repeatedly, promising her I would hold on to the car, at least, until I made something out of myself; until I made myself whole as a man. I still was at a loss for a direction to take, but I was confident something would come to me sooner or later.

Meanwhile, I continued to conserve the little money I had and lived life with a more peaceful mindset. I had blown all of my attempts at dealing with one female exclusively. I was struggling to forgive myself for how poorly I conducted myself during those relationships, specifically with Melody and Tracey. I let Vikki get in the way of a good thing, more than once, only to watch her drift away into the fast lane I no longer could afford to cruise in. On the contrary, many people believed I had spent tremendous amounts of money on Vikki, but that simply was not so. We had fun, but the money I had simply allowed me to be around her and her ways. There were plenty of times where I didn't spend much of anything. By the time I gave money to my sister, my grandma, my uncle; along with the purchasing of a new car, I did not have too much to give anyone else. I also treated my buddies and myself regularly. I was content with what I spent on the females, specifically Vikki. It truly was not very much at all.

I soon would have a little more than $5000 left in the bank, but I lived life as if there was significantly less. However, this amount was still more than any of my friends had in the bank. None of my pals even had accounts. However, I can't vouch for what they possessed in shoe boxes or sock drawers. Genius, Etton, and especially Hubert, certainly possessed more than $5000 cash. Elroy was horrible at saving lots of money, but he was sure to constantly remind me by bragging; he was now profiting over $800 a day. It was taking me at least four weeks to produce that kind of cash profit, but I was still feeling alright. I was growing up, but feeling down, yet I held on to my peace. I took my little bit of money, deposited some, treated Melody when she allowed me to, and often used the rest on tunes for my car. In retrospect, I didn't really have anything to complain about.

Luck would strike for what felt like the tenth time, as I began dating Melody exclusively again for a while. Vikki would call, but I usually told my aunt to say I was not home. I still liked Vikki, but I knew hanging around her could result with me spending too much money. I was not mad at her at all. Again, she did not ask for much. She liked to have fun, and fun cost money. Obviously, I no longer craved this type of lifestyle. With Melody, you never had to worry about money, possessions, or anything superficial. Although she was young, she lived by old school rules. With her, you either liked someone or you didn't. It hardly mattered what they had. We loved each other and I was sure to keep her aware of this. I even began picking her up from the school while Vikki was still attending. Melody did prefer to be picked up from the side of the school, away from the crowds. She didn't care for too much attention or local publicity. Still, several people still observed us leaving the school together regularly.

The eyewitness accounts of students from Northern High School led to Vikki approaching me inside of the mall one weekend evening. I was there window shopping, for the first time ever. "Are you with Melody now?" she asked with a disappointed expression after appearing out of nowhere. "Why?" I replied with a smirk. "I didn't even see you!" I stated with a surprised expression. "I don't like it, that's why," she stated with raised eyebrows. I stared at Vikki's pretty face and shook my head. I realized at this moment, Vikki was just as confused as I. She used several guys to cover up all of her insecurities, just as I did with the females. "Call me O," she offered as she quickly walked away. "Alright," I replied softly as I gazed at the bombshell. I didn't call Vikki after our mall encounter. I knew placing a call to her would allow things to go too far. I was tired of the entire vibe. I was doing an alright job with managing my time and my money. I was also only seeing one female. Melody was not as receptive to me as she was once before, but I understood a halfhearted Melody was still better to be with exclusively, than any other girl I knew.

Exactly six months had passed and I was still employed at the sneaker store. I was even given a small raise. I had become a friend of my coworkers, including the managing staff. They all would frequently tell me how nice of a person they believed me to be. I never like to see any person hurt or angry, and I love to hear people compliment me on my attitude. I never had to try hard to be nice or respectful. For me, it's simply a good thing to have character and a positive attitude to match. Thanks to grandma, this practice came naturally. However, working everyday and not enjoying life much was becoming irritating. My bi-weekly checks were looking a little better. I loved customer service, but I still felt myself growing a little tired of the environment. Quitting however, was not an option at this time. I refused to let my grandmother down. I was still unaware who I was, or what I was to become, but I did not want to give up for no apparent reason. Instead of leaving my job, I decided to make sure I still had a life, even if I was going to be extra-tired the next morning. I figured if I can play basketball all day and hang out with my buddies, I should be able to make it to work on time with no complaints.

Feeling pretty secure with my decision to continue working at the shoe store, I began hanging out with Elroy and Bennett even more. These guys were still my two closest pals who both had experience working and playing at the same time. Elroy and Bennett each worked at local supermarkets. Bennett was now a junior at Carver High and was getting set to be a senior or a "free man," we all called it. In the hood, we all believed high school graduation meant we no longer had to listen to strict adult rules. Most of us felt the time for structure and discipline was over. We believe we are ready to be completely on our own. We were dead wrong! The years after high school graduation are not the running wild years of life; they should be the years we began to work harder to place ourselves on a specific chosen road of our interests. Whether attending a university, a trade school, or whatever it takes to pursue a dream, these are the years of focus. It's NOT time to lose yourself and run crazy with no direction; not at all. I've always tried to be a realist. I was fully aware of how unprepared I was to be out in the world on my own. I still needed my grandma badly. At home, things were still very unsettled. To complicate matters more, the McCabe Avenue and Old York Road feud had just taken another fatal turn, and I somehow ended up right there to experience it.

One day after Evan and I finished playing ball, we ran across an old friend from Winston Apartments. Berry was an old school mate from Winston Middle who I once had a small altercation with on school property. Winston Apartments was where a couple of Evan's aunts and uncles lived. Berry, also from Winston, waved us down on the road as we passed him by on Greenmount Avenue, the southern portion of the road that becomes York Road slightly further north. Berry was familiar with the guys from Old York Road, but I still decided to give him a ride. Moves like these helped to solidify my stance as a neutral party within the rivalry. I was still accepting confirmation calls from Benny McGirt, who reminded me not to join in on the rising nonsense. "What's up fellas?" Berry asked while out of breath from running the car down. "What's up B?" Evan stated as I simultaneously reached for a pound or handshake. I immediately received satisfaction from this handshake until Berry quickly shouted, "O, run me through Old York real fast please, so I can holla at my man real quick?" The hairs quickly stood up on the back of my neck, but I really did not know the reason why. "Cool," I replied. I was never involved in a dispute of any kind with anyone from Old York Road. Still, for some strange reason, I felt weird about going through what McCabe Avenue called, "enemy territory."

I made a right onto 39th Street, a cross street off of York Road, then turned left onto Old York Road. Before I got passed a block on my right, we could see several police cars ahead. I gazed forward with mixed emotions, wondering what was happening and asking myself, "Are these the same cops from the illegal search episode I recently experienced with Freddy?" "Make this left," Berry instructed. "Make this right," he instructed twice. Now we were in front of the action, on Old York, looking backwards. We were parked near the 1921 established church where we once held the dance competition during renovations. I watched the activity from my rearview mirror while Evan and Berry watched directly through the back windshield. The scene was intense and people were reacting very strangely from my vantage point. My head moved up and down a little, then also side to side a bit, trying to see all from afar without exiting the car. Suddenly, Berry yelled out, "Let me out O, I know that's not my boy Jimmy," he shouted. Suddenly, I could see a guy stretched out in the middle of the block, motionless. Berry dashed from our presence and into the crowd. Evan stated, "Let's roll out O" while tapping my arm. Moments later, I pulled off quickly. I found out Berry's pal, Jimmy had been murdered just minutes before we entered onto the block. Later, we were not surprised to learn who was to blame for the homicide; someone from McCabe Avenue.

After Jimmy's death, it took police only a few weeks to place "Black" under arrest for first-degree murder. "Black" was one of Freddy's best friends and a known dealer in the area as well. Many speculated "Black" was falsely accused, but the evidence held enough to give the young male in his early 20s a life sentence for murder. While a frustrated "Black" sat in jail awaiting his shot at an appeal, the rivalry began to elevate to a new brand of negativity. This rivalry began well before my family moved onto McCabe Avenue in 1979-80. It was now 1991, and negative situations were escalating more frequently. A feud once controlled by the older guys in the streets was violently being taken over by much younger kids. Most were simply looking for a reputation to live by. This feud, for many, was an opportunity for new hustlers to make names for themselves. On both sides, younger guys were getting exposed to the negativity they once watched on television or on the movie screen. Many of the older hustlers were now down on their luck. Many would fall victim to the seduction of addictive drugs, while others, like Black, were placed in prison for lengthy sentences. This opened up the door for their younger brothers and nephews to attempt to carry on a family name. The rivalry, along with the love of money, sucked all of the air out of any positive life force left on my block. The downhill spiral was enacted. Although I continuously discarded the idea of selling drugs, and continued to work everyday, I still found myself in the middle of it all more times than not.

By the Fall of 1991, everything pure or positive in my life began fade. Melody, again, slowly pulled away from my grasp for unknown reasons besides my actions on prom night. I knew she was still struggling with this incident, because I was, and she was quite uncomfortable with the neighborhood feud situation. Our relationship finally ended as if we had moved away to separate cities. Melody and her parents moved away from their home on Kingsway, which was just 15 minutes away, but it felt as if she simply vanished. I truly wanted to be Melody's king, but with her I could not have things my way. I tried to catch her before she left, but I was unsuccessful. I even tried to ask the mailman in her area where her mail was being forwarded to, but of course I was denied this information. I realized shortly afterwards, I had struck out for a second time. Melody, like Tracey, was "wifey" material. To me, these were the females a guy should want to stay with from high school until death. I just could not locate the consistency required to perform as a young man should for a good young lady.

Devastated and frustrated with my inconsistencies with good, smart young ladies, I decided to take a break from having girlfriends all together. Although I struggled to perform up to task in the infidelity department, I had used a great deal of emotional energy trying to prove my love to Melody. I continued to work, write a little again, and play lots of basketball. I also began to connect closer with my pal Elroy. Elroy still attended Northern High, but he quit his part-time job to sell drugs everyday. Ironically, he no longer appeared eager to influence me to do the same. I had a steady source of income, but no more than $5000 left in my account. I felt compelled to hang with Elroy because of his sense of humor. Despite all of the negativity surrounding the area, Elroy always seemed to find humor in something, or everything. With a little money, a job, a car, and a funny friend, life somehow began to feel a little more enjoyable. Soon Elroy and I would be considered the best of friends. Only work and basketball separated us. It meant a lot to me for us to draw closer after my money was nearly gone. I viewed this as his way of apologizing. He tried so hard to get me to go against my will to never affiliate with drugs. In Elroy, I felt I had a friend I could count on. He kept the both of us smiling. The "beef" between McCabe and Old York Road was the only situation Elroy found no humor in. The feud bothered Elroy more than he led on. He always felt there was a chance he may be shot or killed. I thought something like this was off limits to us early on despite what was taking place nearby. We had no ill will towards no one, but in this rivalry that hardly ever mattered.

By the Winter of 1991, the feud between the two neighborhoods was a heavy topic of conversation throughout the entire city. Various shootings and club brawls exposed the already declining city to more bad news further north. This was once a place where homicides and arrests were once held at a minimum. Simple ideas like peace were really becoming very complicated. It was not a guarantee for a person to return home from the store if he ventured out alone at night. Young knuckleheads from the Old York Road region constantly drove through McCabe Avenue, strapped with semi-automatic pistols. Sometimes shots would be fired, while other times guys would simply ride by just to be ignorant and show bravery. I left the neighborhood a lot more than the others, therefore I often knew what vehicles the troublemakers were driving before they came through. I saw them even when they didn't see me. I warned the guys more than once, to watch out for these "bad asses." Unfortunately, for Elroy and a few others, I would not always be there to share this information.

Elroy's senior year in high school may have been a breeze to many, because of the curriculum he was placed in, but graduation was further away than he may have thought. Not only did the feud hit closer to home with repeated shootings, troubles were also being brought into the school. Some of the younger guys from Old York Road were informed of students from McCabe Avenue still attending Northern High School. Elroy and a few others soon received the news; Old York guys were seen trespassing on school grounds. The previous year, when I attended the school, no such news was heard of. However, there were times when I witnessed Elroy's older brother Nardo, and Tray, involved in disputes with Old York Road affiliates nearby. However, this recent news gossiped about proved to be true, bringing Elroy's fears to reality.

I met up with Elroy after work one day and witnessed a look of concern on his face. Earlier during this same day, Elroy, along with two other dealers from the neighborhood named Pierce and Rick, were attending class. Suddenly, after class they were chased throughout the hallways by a few guys from Old York. These guys were carrying guns with intentions on killing the guys inside of the school. Elroy and I discussed the situation on my front porch. We stood on my porch and watched the other two guys share the intense details with the rest of the guys in the neighborhood. "Yo, I told you O," Elroy stated adamantly. "You hear that shit?" he added with anger. "You lucky as hell you graduated last year O," he added intensely. "Those suckers came up the school n' shit," he shouted forcefully. "They had guns n' shit! Those bastards were strapped son," he added. "Damn, for real?" I asked surprisingly while shaking my head. "Hell yeah," Elroy replied. "I was with Pierce and Rick in the hallway, and dat little nigga they call 'Nut,' the other kid they call 'Casper,' and that dude name Miran, started chasing the shit out of us," he explained. "Three little dudes hah?" I added. "Yeah, that's why they all had guns O. If not, we would not have ran, and we would have beat all the shit out of dem little niggas," Elroy said confidently. "I had a gun O but the shit jams." Elroy had a small handgun but it only fired every other shot. "That's some crazy shit there buddy," I stated. "Fuck yeah, those muthafukas are not playing at all, you hear me?" Elroy stated seriously. "Fuck those little assholes, fuck Old York Road, and fuck school too," were Elroy's next three phrases. Things were officially out of hand, and Elroy's next plan solidified just how wrong things were.

Our conversation lasted for at least an hour. I spent the last half of that hour trying to help Elroy reach a positive alternative other than discontinuing his senior year in high school. "Elroy, no one drops out of high school in the 12th grade buddy," I stated frankly. "Oh yeah? No one gets chased with guns in the hallways of a school either," he replied with certainty. "You have to transfer or something son," I offered. "I'm not going through all dat shit man," he replied frankly. "They'll just turn up there too O," he stated disappointingly. "Besides, I don't need the school shit anyway," he shouted while drawing a large ball of money from his left pocket. "That's beside the point, you may need it later," I suggested. "For what? Tell me please!" he asked with irritation. "Like I said man, no one drops out in the 12th Elroy," I repeated. "Didn't you see the movie, 'An Officer and a Gentleman'?" I asked while smiling.

"What?" he replied with a confused grin. "Here O go wit the movie shit again," he followed. "Yeah, I saw it," he insisted with interest. It's a natural reaction for me to reference good films during real life, no matter how intense a situation has become. My pal was nearly killed in school, and I was referencing "An Officer and a Gentleman." "Ok O, what the fuck does this have to do with anything?" he jokingly asked. The guy in the movie dropped out (DOR) of the academy right near the end," I explained. "Yeah, that fool white boy nearly died when he was there too," Elroy replied. "Yeah, true, but you heard what the blond girl said right?" I asked with a smile before illustrating. "Got damn you, no one drops out after eleven weeks, got damn you," I tried to quote jokingly. "Yo, you say I'm funny, you funny as shit," Elroy stated while giggling. "All jokes aside, you need to finish school buddy, for real," I suggested. "O, I hear what you're sayin', but as far as I'm concerned, I'm finished, and my diploma is the ten ounces of 'girl' I'm about to get later," Elroy stated while slowly walking down the steps from the porch. "I'll catch you later O. Fuck this shit! I got money to make," he added before sprinting across the street.

Elroy kept his word and never returned to high school. I guess no one would attend school if they believed they would be shot or killed. Today, the media thoroughly cover these unfortunate, senseless and sad mass school shootings, but no one from my era is surprised by them. This sad reality is not new at all to us blacks. Guns were in schools during the 80's! Elroy finally decided money is far more important than school. The way they all saw it, they may as well make a few thousand a week if they're going to risk it all anyway. For as bad as I felt for Elroy, I felt twice as confused for myself. I still held on to my job, but the frustrations would mount up once again. My life felt stale, but I could not make the correct decision to promote more progress. The constant routine of waking up early six days a week, going to work, struggling to find a parking spot, only to go stand all day was growing old. I was wondering why I had to be the person selling sneakers to all the addicts the city had to offer on welfare check day, while my buddies stayed in bed all day with thousands of dollars in their sock drawers. At Shoe City Sports, I was exposed to some of the most swollen feet on earth. Several of the people I had sold shoes to were heroin addicts. Some addicts even came in to purchase sneakers with a blood/pus mixture saturated in their socks from missed vein attempts. Others had open wounds or sores on their legs, feet, and ankles; yuck!

I increasingly grew frustrated with the job. Honestly, I believed I just had an issue with working altogether. Looking back, these were excuses! I truly liked my coworkers, but I just could not grasp the concept of working everyday for a little bit of money. By the time 1992 approached, I had spent as much time as I could, pretending to be in the bathroom taking a crap. The "#2" was my best excuse I had to get off the floor and into isolation for peace and quietness for a few minutes. I began hiding in the stock room, extremely bored while counting Nike boxes. I was trying to figure out how much money Michael Jordan raked in from the sales of his shoes in my city alone. The idea of making more money was forming in my psyche.

A war between good and evil was brewing inside of my mind and spirit. My heart and my mind were at battle with one another. They were beginning to play a game of "Tug of War" within me. The stage was being set; the battlefield of the mind. My position in life frustrated me, and I still felt I had no direction or stable person to turn to besides my aging grandma. There were times when I would feel as if I was yelling at the top of my lungs, but I would be in complete silence. Life as a whole was starting to get the better of me. The need to be something was there, but I still had no idea what to go after. I was afraid to dream; everyone here was. Everything felt wrong or useless. The only way I could grow in optimism would be to retool or refocus by trying to talk about life with my grandma.

Whenever I felt too frustrated or wore out from everyday life, I would simply go into the kitchen, grab a chair, and sit next to Mama in the living room. I would never have to say much and she would already know something was wrong. Mama understood how drastically things changed on McCabe, therefore seeing me reach out allowed her to understand. She knew I really wanted to live life honorably. She knew I truly needed help with my new adult journey. I used my grandmother's words to re-energize my positive thinking. Mama made me feel like there was a better world out there somewhere, and it was all within my reach. I never located a plan during these talks, but I would grow in optimism. Grandma was never completely sure where my journey should start herself. How could she be sure? Although she experienced a lot throughout life, this road was one even she had never traveled on. For the most part, the road to high-level success out in society had eluded my entire immediate family.

Grandma often preached patience and made sure God was mentioned, although she never went deeply into detail. Her personal accomplishments in life were few, but her heart was more pure than gold. She knew these internal ideals could eventually help create a good plan. She would say, "God don't like ugly," or "Just pray to God and you'll be fine" or simply, "God knows best." This was as much church as I received throughout my entire life. I prayed a lot on my own, but I was always cloudy on too many spiritual issues. The most important ones were: "Who Is God?" followed by "Who Am I?" and "Why am I even in this world?" Still, I believed a little and continued to pray, and with this 20 minute conversation with grandma, my zest for life returned. I regularly tried to be conscious enough to give thanks and to remain humble. I soon returned to the job with a positive or more enthused spirit. My heart and soul was still planted, and I was being watched over by a very special lady.

Grandma's talks helped blindfold me from the increasing size of Elroy's pockets. He and the others were making so much money, so quickly, at this point, it was as if it was raining cash on McCabe Avenue. Elroy and the others were easily making four figure incomes every day. Just being around the guys usually would get me free food, free haircuts, and periodically, free outfits and sneakers. I was working to build my bank account back to respectability and pay my car insurance on time, but the fellows often supported all of my other cravings. I never asked, but I hardly ever said, "No thanks." With periods of bad spending habits, like purchasing sneakers the minute they came out, my account was now down to only $3000. While the others were swimming in money, I was struggling severely to hold on to a few thousand. Everyone around me had plenty of money, yet hustling never crossed my mind. I know today, there was a slight need to fit in; therefore, I continued to hang out around Elroy and a couple of others. I still was unable to come up with a good plan to make money without breaking the law, but I knew as long as I continued to kick it with the guys, I would at least be able to stay away from the A.T.M. machines.

Without really noticing it, my pockets would slowly begin to swell without me having to do much of anything. After work, I would be around the guys just conversing about females in the area, or sports. A guy might ask me for a ride home, or even for a lift to a certain female's house, and I would agree. Despite the money made by these dealers, several of these guys still did not have their own cars. Elroy and many of the others could hardly read. They could not pass any of the required tests to obtain driving privileges. They knew driving without licenses opened the door for more troubles with the police. I took them places whenever I could or whenever I felt like it. I figured, "It's just a ride, I'm not going to do anything illegal, and I have virtually no miles on my car." For a small fee, and a promise from the guys to leave the drugs and guns behind, we usually had a deal. Most of the guys liked me, and I felt the same about them as human beings. I was just from a different genre than most of them. One I felt was filled with a better mental state and a more compassionate approach toward others. Respect would still dominate any personal feelings I had towards anyone, therefore meshing was not necessarily a bad idea. Although I was a working young man with a positive spirit and a little hope for some kind of decent future, I was gradually becoming one of the boys in a very bad place to live.

Hanging around the younger guys and Elroy gave me a deeper look into the world of the millennials in the ghetto. My peers and I considered ourselves from the 80s; most of us were born in the 70s. These kids had a different thought process. School, work, a positive attitude, fun, and a genuine respect for elders were not a given for these younger individuals but certainties for us. Money, sex, war, street credibility, and material gain were the main ideas of these young guys on McCabe Avenue. Cash ruled everything around these young guys. As youths, we too demanded a certain level of respect as teens, but we were not willing to go to prison or take a life behind it. These young guys were. There's no question about it. My respect came from my ability to be genuine, "real" or straightforward with all of the guys. I'd tell them all, "I'm no tough guy," "I don't want to sell drugs," "I'm not with all this shit!" "I care about all people," "I love all y'all brothers man," and even, "Fuck you," if necessary, but I tried hard to stay away from the foolish talk. They respected me for this, and many of them told me things they would not dare say around their closer street peers. I'd heard the phrase, "Please don't tell nobody O," a thousand times.

Again, no matter who we think we are, what we choose to do, or where we are in our lives, we will never be able to resist being human.

These young soldiers treated me fairly and respectably. Just hanging around the area with the guys would allow me to go to sleep with an extra $200 dollars a day. I guess some of the ignorant dudes in the streets would say I was a "hack," or a hood only taxi with benefits, but I beg to differ tremendously. That's funny! One reason: with some of the conversations which took place in the car, I know I was giving more than receiving. I was giving what my grandmother was passing onto me, compassion. I fit in well all the same. I listened to rap music with these guys and we shared a similar taste in a few things. In fact, I helped the guys understand the messages in the artform of music better; a message which is often overlooked. Another reason I was not a sucker: I was one of the few guys who could leave McCabe Avenue without always looking over my shoulder every other second. It was usually stated all around town, "The McCabe Boys all travel together or don't travel at all." This simply was not the case for me. I got around town, "beef" or not. One minute, I would be on McCabe, the next I would be at a basketball court 50 miles away. The next morning, if you were to look hard enough, you may have seen me sitting in The Yellow Bowl Cafe (now closed) in east Baltimore, eating alone. I may not have known who I was, but I was still living life. We had plenty of hacks around, but I was far from one of them. Besides, the guys gave me $20 more for every one of those sort trips. Hacks never made twenty dollars an hour where I'm from, even during the 90's when cash was more plentiful in the streets.

On my real job I was making $7.50 per hour; more than the average minimum wage during that time. That would total a paycheck of $300.00 per week, before taxes. On my block, I usually would profit a minimum of $100 a day, just hanging out, shopping, or flirting with the young ladies. This total in a week would roughly be around $500-$600; broke by hustling standards, but good by society's outlook, especially for a teen. These proceeds came from just how much drug money circulated throughout the area. Something was certainly wrong with this financial picture I painted, but I stayed with my heart and continued to work at Shoe City Sports. I was never a huge fan of quitting anything. If I started something, I normally would see it through, or until something in me finally says, "That's enough!" Keeping a job and hanging out in the neighborhood allowed me to feel a sense of balance and significance. I was able to impact people in both settings in a positive manner. This was a good feeling to have while trying to figure out life. I never questioned what kind of person I was, just what kind of life I should have? The big question always remained: "Who or what will I become?"

The American crack epidemic was becoming quite a disturbing force in our neighborhoods by the early 90's. Genius was on top of his game, raking in massive amounts of cash daily. He elevated his business by continuing to connect with Hubert, who he had met through Elroy. Genius had things totally his way. Etton was right there as well, but was involved with a legal matter. He was facing a few years in prison if found guilty on a felony distribution charge. This meant Genius would pretty much have McCabe Avenue solely in the palm of his hand. He knew he had something major materializing, and he was not shy at all in displaying his dominance to the public.

Besides the seven cars Genius had, all usually parked one behind the other, he also loved to dress in apparel others found to be a little too expensive. It's easy to speculate, at the time, a man in his 30s would be more interested in casual apparel such as linen suits, or maybe pricey sports jackets, but not Genius. He only preferred to wear expensive athletic gear. Whenever he wore an outfit he knew no one else had or thought of, he would simply stand and profile on the corner, like a model. He would actually say, "Look at me niggas," while smiling. "Y'all can't fuck with this," usually followed. "This shit is slick, ain't it man?" He would ask this question, already expecting everyone to say the answer he preferred. Guys would say, "Hell yeah!" just as he expected them all to. One outfit brought to the "runway" or street corner, would be an all leather NFL, New York Giants sweatsuit he found somewhere, or a leather jacket or a mink coat everyone else felt was ridiculously expensive. He was a showman, and his own best friend. Genius happily symbolized the word "GREED," and the new jack B'MORE hustler. He simply wanted all of the money to himself, or, to at least have something to do with the success of all the others in the streets. McCabe Avenue, unlike other neighborhoods, was small and only had room for one personality like Genius. He made sure everyone knew who was in charge. It's almost like the others were waiting for a guy like him to show up and control things on the block. It was clear many of the guys needed a father-like presence. Most were searching for this figure; a leader, and Genius arrived to take care of them.

In the 80s before Genius returned home from his lengthy prison stint, there were other older guys capable for heading an organization of this magnitude. Freddy was a perfect example. He or anyone he associated with would have never taken orders from another. Benny may have been the most successful guy on McCabe Avenue before his run-ins with police, but he did not solely control the destiny of all of the older hustlers. They all controlled their own destinies. However, I learned in the drug game everyone is connected to someone larger. Most of the "hoppers" or young men on my block were connected to Genius. In the 80s, many did view Benny as the head or the ringleader, whether they all dealt with him or not, but even he had a leader to follow.

Watching Genius exploit the younger guys gave me one reason to stay firm with my decision not to get involved with dealing drugs. The other reason would usually be piercing through the front window of 731, looking directly at me in concern. Mama periodically would sit up in her chair just to observe our every move. Every time I would notice her looking, a feeling of nervousness and embarrassment would pass through me. Although I knew I was not breaking any laws, a small part of me knew I should have been elsewhere; somewhere more positive. Before, the only time I would be seen interacting with the others would be on a basketball court. I was too blind to see how just being around guys with a different set of objectives could affect the way I was being viewed. I thought I knew better, but I really did not. I was not aware the company I was keeping was, in fact, distorting my quality of life.

Instead of recognizing these very important realizations, I continued to co-exist with the guys on the block while casually taking things one day at a time. At this time, I honestly felt I was not involved with any negativity. I actually found a bit of humor in these hustlers. Watching Genius steal customers from guys who worked for him was a funny sight. Although he had kilos of cocaine at his disposal, he still felt obligated to make gigantic "dime"($10) or "twenty"($20) sacks to distribute himself on the block. He was something. If everyone was surrounding a customer during a drug deal, Genius often would burst through the crowd shouting, "Look at these main man. I got the big ones." Genius made rude and impulsive moves regularly. Although he would "step on the toes" or interfere with his peers, did not mean he was not going to pressure them for his money. He didn't care how you handled a package as long as you would "Hurry the fuck up," I'd hear him say. Completing a package quickly would be the best way to keep the peace with Genius.

The more I hung out with Elroy and the others, the more I began to feel the guys were not as ignorant as they originally appeared. There was never really a threatening feeling while in the company of these guys. It appeared as if they all just craved money to purchase cars and gear, or to sleep with the hottest young ladies. A few of the guys would always seek me out with intentions of getting close to any of Vikki's female friends. "O, hook me up with one of those 'dimes' your girl Vikki hangs out with," Tareek, a close friend of Elroy's, would state often. Tareek was one of the many new guys on the block, but not as new as the others. He periodically had been seen with Elroy over the years. He was one of Randolph's, Freddy's pal, many nephews, and one of the many new representatives of "Generation X" on McCabe Avenue. This "Generation X" share one similarity to the original reference, Generation X, years of description (born 1966-1976). This "Generation X" was said to refer to a generation of young black males that could not get any worse, and should be totally eliminated from society. Most of the newer guys on McCabe Avenue were at least four years younger than I. They all could care less about peace and order. Again, money, girls, gangster rap music, cars, drugs, and violence were their primary concerns.

Although these guys were very direct, trying to figure many of them out was no easy task. Most of these newer teens on McCabe Avenue had actually come from somewhat decent families or neighborhoods. Most of their mothers were drug-free and employed, yet a choice to "go far left" or a turn completely for the worse, still was made. As for most of these guys' dads; like so many guys from the hood, they were all either non-existent, dead, or incarcerated. Only Bennett and I had our fathers in our lives, but even he claimed he didn't like his dad much, due to a drinking problem. My dad was periodically around, yet he actually served as the lone reason I was the only guy around without a mom. Unstable households connected us all in a way. The younger black males coming to McCabe Avenue to fit in or mesh with the original guys was a recipe for destruction. Tray, LiL Bug, Harold, and Big Bug, who were understudies of Etton and the nephews of Bam-Bam, another older dealer, were already creating an unsavory atmosphere within a very small space. I was there most of the time, watching a group of young radicals come together without a cause, breaking any law, without hesitation.

In the midst of gradually drawing closer to the fellows in the neighborhood, I managed to find a way from the grasp of the streets. I used working and playing basketball to shift gears away from the darker side of reality. The guys and I were very comfortable around one another initially. Before long, they were hinting around the idea of me possibly dealing drugs alongside them. "O, why don't you just take $200-$300 and cop a quarter?" Harold would ask. Harold was the brother of LiL Bug. Harold always stayed around me whenever he could. He claimed to like my style or my ability to stay calm most of the time, in spite of circumstances. "O, all I have to do is hang around you, get this money, and I may not get myself killed or locked up out this bitch," he said more than once.

Selling drugs was still not a factor in my life. I was content with the money or "little change," they all called it. At 18 or 19 years old, I already knew how it felt to purchase a car with cash, dress in the nicest garments, and sleep with the prettiest females on the northeast side. It was no big deal to "fall back" or step away from having the most or the best. The money I earned from Shoe City Sports and from hanging out with the fellows was enough for me at the time. The money was not enough to splurge and treat different women to Reebox sneakers, but I was fine. I still hung out with other females in the area who were more into me and less into things. There was one in particular. Her name was Penny. She was a cute young lady, also with a history from Old York. She was 18 and already with two small kids by two different guys. Her oldest child's dad was Craig, a close friend of Todd's, and the guy who broke the guy Tyran's jaw awhile back. Her youngest child was the son of a guy called, "Scrapple." He was an understudy of Limon's. I felt something when I laid eyes on Penny. I was too confused to really know what the feeling was, but I knew it was a good thing.

Dealing with a female with two kids was no different from dealing with a female with none, for me. Like I said, I love people, I'm a people person. Kids, I love even more, due to their innocence. I understood early, we all were in a struggle living this inner city life, and we all seemed to lack proper guidance, which will usually lead to folks making mistakes. I try very hard to never judge anyone! I never truly understood how a drug dealer believed HE or SHE could be too picky or judgmental? The crush I had on Penny and my ability to gel with the guys without selling a single drug allowed me to spend more time in my neighborhood. I continued to play basketball with Genius, Etton and the others. I was keeping my word to never sell drugs, but perhaps I was making the mistake of being around and enjoying nearly everything else.

With summer approaching, I found myself in my bedroom, staring up at the water-stained ceiling, congratulating Vikki on her high school graduation. As we talked on the phone, she shocked me by stating the words, "I miss you," but I didn't overreact. I was content with knowing Vikki and I were more than just sex-buddies or two people who mainly shopped and partied too much. I felt good about our chances of hanging out in the future. For the time being, we kept a short distance and only talked on the phone or brushed shoulders at the local hangout spots. My financial situation slowed my desire to party or hangout. Financial related issues were not the only concerns. Later on during this same day, I would have another heart to heart with Mama. She seemed to still be a bit troubled with the company I was keeping. The increased sound of shots fired caused my 66 year old grandmother to become even more paranoid. "I don't want you around those damn drug dealers, you hear me?" she stated emotionally. "Ma, those guys don't mean any harm, really. They all just want a little money for cars and gear, and to mess with girls," I explained. Again, this new breed of guys was far different from the dudes of the era I had come from. Here, it was normal to believe you could only get a fine girlfriend or hang out with popular females if you had a nice car, a lot of money or both. I enjoyed putting smiles on the faces of others, but I never felt obligated to pay for sex or the company of females. If this is the new way of life, what does this say about the ideas of love, personality, charm, character, and confidence?

I talked passionately to my grandma until she settled back into her old tan chair. I was far from being sure of anything at this point, but I was able to truthfully tell Mama I was not breaking any laws with guns or drugs. However, my affiliation in the streets was not the only topic discussed. Mama shared information about my sister and her relationship with Freddy. I was surprised when I got the news of my sister and Freddy possibly being headed towards a breakup; five years, and a one-year old daughter later. I recently became a new uncle to my first niece, Lia. Apparently, making erratic relationship moves was hereditary. My sister Gina inexplicably decided she needed to make sure she did not miss out on life as a young lady. At 23, Gina was searching for more self-awareness. She and Freddy had been exclusive throughout her teenage years, creating a void within her heart which possibly needed filling. "She'll be alright," I stated to grandma. "Yeah, maybe you two can move in together," she offered with a smile. "Me and Gina, I don't know about that ma," I replied with eyebrows raised. "What if the three of us moved in together?" I presented excitingly. "I'm not going anywhere, thanks to your grandfather," Mama stated sadly. Mama felt our grandfather had taken far too long to attempt to purchase a home. 731 McCabe Avenue was not even close to being paid for. This, along with the unfinished repairs to the house and the piles of bills which again would accumulate after granddad's death, caused my grandma to feel stuck on McCabe Avenue.

I continued to pitch in, helping Mama, my uncle BoBo, and my sister Gina with the finances. My aunt Marie was still struggling to place her feet on solid ground. She was still drinking heavily and abusing drugs. My aunt Marie is a very strong woman, but the loss of her son, my cousin Shawn, was understandably too much to endure still.

Todd, the guy who mistakably killed my cousin Shawn, surprisingly returned to the block. Any healing my aunt managed to gain was snatched away by this news. All of our partially closed wounds were reopened. Not only was my aunt struggling with addiction, she had to watch Todd return to the neighborhood practicing his old ways; bullying. Todd's charge was reduced from First-Degree Murder to Manslaughter. He received a four-year sentence for the death of my cousin. Since Todd's original sentencing, every year on Shawn's birthday, I would console my aunt through an emotional meltdown. It was disheartening to watch my aunt slip into her depressed state, not knowing what I could do to really help her. She was hurting too badly to help grandma out financially. This instability in my aunty placed an early strain on Shawn's younger brother Jayson. Money became scarce, forcing my family to use Uncle Frank's disability check to supplement the income. Mama no longer would allow my uncle to spend his money on $800 worth of booze and cigarettes. My grandma now monitored Frank's finances very closely. From this point on, Frank's check was used mainly for bills and for food around the house.

Despite our desperate need for more money and a better house, we clung together and somehow made ends meet on McCabe Avenue. I still worked as a shoe salesman while holding onto a few thousand bucks. I was kicking myself for not handling most of the money I came into, the same as I was handling the last of it. The year 1992 was drawing nearer and so was a zero balance in a bank account once holding over $48,000. However, I did manage to make a handful of small deposits. I still stayed clear of the out-of-control spending and much of the partying. Staying put in the neighborhood actually allowed me to save even more money. I only left the hood to take occasional long drives to nowhere, just to get away from the city all together. No one ever knew where I went during these escapes, and they never asked. Back home, I was hanging with the dealers, and flirting with every cute face in the area. Still, there were times when I just wanted my peace of mind and my Anita Baker cassette.

Mama held our small family together, but physically there were more signs of her slowing down. A moderate smoker, and over-weight, Mama stayed busy trying to cook, clean, and oversee everyone's well-being. I constantly monitored her physical condition as much as a young man could. A "hater" of all hospitals, Mama always said, "When it's my time to go, God will come for me." She never fully admitted to discomfort, but I could see the decline in her strength or the lack of stamina she would have when climbing the stairs. I always made sure I was available to help out. I often scrubbed Mama's back as she sat in the tub securing a towel over her frontal. Her width made it complicated to reach certain areas alone. Still, grandma put everyone at ease no matter how she felt or how strange things were. Although I paid close attention to Mama's health, something inside always told us she would likely outlast us all. In our household, Mama was always the last person anyone would be concerned with.

As grandma slowed down, showing more signs of physical struggles at home, the neighborhood detritus sped up. The ridiculous shooting of guns without targets spiraled out of control. Guys were shooting guns up in the air for fun or just for kicks. Street lights were shot out to make it more difficult for dealers to be spotted by police. Guys could be seen running up to vehicles as addicts came through to buy drugs. Every time a potential customer would enter onto the block, a foot race towards the car would ensue. Order and discretion was out the window. Guys were snatching customer's money and literally throwing the drugs at them as they sat in their vehicles. Genius continued to bully his way through to remain in first place, while others would jockey for secondary positions. McCabe Avenue was in a free fall. The erratic actions coming from the guys from Old York illustrated much of the same. Elroy, Bennett and I fell somewhere in the middle, despite being original residents of our block.

Surprisingly, here, I felt right at home on the block in the midst of all the turmoil. Internally, I told myself, "I was here first." I liked the guys, but I refused to allow a group of young outsiders make me feel uncomfortable on the same corners where I once danced and played "Hide N' Seek" as a child. I tried to hold onto what was right and good, but I was weaker than I believed. I could not see my own decline. I was slowly getting away from my inner being. I was sort of "looking at my own front door," gradually leaving the "Heaven" from within.

By October 1991, Gina returned to McCabe with her now, two year old daughter, Lia. Mama was elated to have my sister back at home, but unenthused it all had come at the expense of Freddy's heart. He was devastated over the breakup. Gina admitted Freddy was a good man, and an excellent boyfriend and father, with very supportive parents, but she needed to find herself as an individual. I needed to do the same with myself, therefore I understood. No one else truly understood her move, but there were few questions asked, as usual. Soon talks of my sister and I moving in together really did materialize. It was clear grandma's celebration about Gina's return would be short-lived. Gina was disappointed with the way the family had let the house fall apart, and how all of the bills were overdue. My sister, a former resident of Towson, Maryland in Baltimore County for the past few years, took cleanliness very seriously. She hated dirty dishes, full trash cans, dust, stains, piles of dirty laundry and nasty smells. 731, as Mama slowed, grew to consistently have all of the above, and then some. My room stayed spotless until it rained. The massive hole I had in the ceiling was growing wider every month. A large section of the ceiling and its soaking insulation abruptly awakened me one morning, falling directly onto my backside as a slept. It was clear right away, 731 was nothing more than a pit stop for my sister, just until she could locate another place to live. Being responsible was not my finest quality as a 19 year old, but I was trying. I was about to endure many new tests, as living with my big sister became a decision confirmed. Washing dishes, doing laundry, cleaning up on a regular basis, taking out the trash, and dusting regularly were going to be frequent practices for me, and I was not looking forward to none of them, at all.

Two months later, my sister had finally found a place for us to move into. My sister and I, along with her beautiful little girl, would soon be a family of our own on Homestead Street, located in east Baltimore. Homestead is about 15 minutes south of McCabe Avenue. I actually liked knowing I no longer lived on McCabe, but I still didn't mind being there. In fact, there was apart of me that relished in doing so. However, my new place was not exactly foreign territory. Several guys from Northern High were from the area. Ironically, Homestead Street is a lot closer to Old York Road than McCabe. I had mixed emotions about this realization. One side of me viewed this move as a way to show the guys from the other side I stood alone. The other side of me said, "Oh shit!" I was not alone with this situation. Bennett's family moved much closer to Old York as well, to his dismay. He once spoke of a night when he took a look out of his back window, only to see Nut staring up at him while holding a gun. Nut would also do this during the daytime while guys were at red lights, malls, or just sitting on a stoop.

The move to Homestead was as confusing as everything else taking place around me. At this point, I was filled with many contradictory emotions. One minute, I wanted one girlfriend; the next, I wanted four. One week, I would wear sneakers; the following week, I'd rather walk around in Bass, Kenneth Cole, Rockport or Cole Haan footwear. The music presented much of the same. I would listen to greats like Stephanie Mills, Anita Baker, Sade, Whitney Houston or Mikki Howard throughout the week. Then, on weekends I would feel compelled to blast music from

Public Enemy, KRS-1, A Tribe Called Quest, Nas, N.W.A, E.P.M.D, Main Source or Big Daddy Kane. To break it down, I was confused, scared and lost, but I still managed to hide it all very well.

Speaking of rap music; N.W.A had completely taken over the minds of males all over Baltimore City. The harsh lyrics gave the troubled youths on McCabe Avenue and abroad something to study and live by. I enjoyed the music as well, a lot, but it hardly motivated my decisions. The melody of it felt as good to my ears as my favorite dish would to my belly, but it did not taint my brain. I would usually concentrate more on how these artists made it out of compromising situations and neighborhoods; I watched their personal journeys.

Taking rap music far too seriously, the drug money, and the lack of positive role models gave most of these guys a feeling of invincibility. The guys from McCabe were arming themselves with guns and negative ideas to place their stamp in the city as one of the tougher blocks in east Baltimore. I stood in this circle, but never had plans to follow suit. I was too busy romancing the young ladies to hide from my own shortcomings. I felt no desire to hurt anyone. While the dealers made their paper on the block, I was receiving winks, pinches on the buttocks, and seductive gestures from most of their young women. I was never the suave type, nor did I carry a "ladies man" or flirtatious mentality, but females seemed to stick close by. I hardly ever needed lots of money or to say things I didn't mean to impress a female. Again, I honestly believe some guys just understand women or care about how they think and feel better than others. As time went on, I realized I was effortlessly getting better at being one of these rare individuals.

I continued to draw nearer to Penny on McCabe by showing her the side of a male she had only witnessed in the movies. Most of the guys the females showed interest in were beating up junkies for having "shorts" or too little money for the product they desired. I respected the fellows, but I had enough trouble trying to find myself. Creating more confusion in my life and someone else's was not an option of mine. I was too busy wondering where I would be in a year? I pondered on why I was now having trouble writing? Trouble in the streets I tried very hard to disregard.

I placed strife as the furthest idea from my mind. Hell, I spent more time pondering on why Ralph Tresvant (New Edition) still was not as huge as Michael Jackson. No one knew what I felt or what I was thinking. To all of the outsiders I was a "McCabe Boy." To myself, I was really just one of "The Lost Boys."

Being an original resident of McCabe Avenue allowed me to do a lot of observing and very little acting. I could watch stupidity or violence all day long and never be tempted to join in. Money making presented a different scenario. I slowly began to grow tired of watching the younger guys make these tremendous amounts of money, everyday, seemingly trouble free. Meanwhile, I was adding more miles onto the Celica, just to keep pocket change and my nose clean at the same time. Elroy was still making thousands of dollars every week. However, he was arrested and released a couple of times on minor possession charges. He was also chased by the undercover police countless times, but he escaped and continued dealing. He believe his brother's infamous history brought forth the heat. "Man, my brothers be making me 'hot' as shit at times," he would say in frustration. "Hot, just at times?" I sarcastically asked in suspicion. "I thought if you're hot once, you're always hot," I stated. "Hell no O," he yelled. "Oh, ok, well, maybe that only applies to LL Cool J or someone like that?" I replied while smiling. "Yo, you're nuts!" Elroy replied while laughing. Elroy and I kept one another in stitches, but the fading morale of the block shortened the humor. Now, there was a deadly war materializing outside, and in any hood, that's no laughing matter.

Hanging out in the streets and going to work at the shoe store for over a year was taking its toll on me mentally. The little purity I had left in me to do the right thing was gradually depleting. Unconsciously, I was trying hard to live two separate lives. I was attempting to live life as a law-abiding citizen, but I actually enjoyed the company of the criminal minded. It seemed as if all the fun took place around the way, but more peace was evident whenever I decided to stay away. I was simply too confused to establish which idea was more important for my life. McCabe Avenue was a place where, at times, it felt like we all were filming an intense movie. As a writer, and a huge fan of film and television, I've always seen life as art; as a movie. Even when someone got hurt really badly, it just did not appear to be real. Well, not until an old pal was involved.

On a warm, late Indian-Summer night, I returned to the block from work. I hardly ever went to my new home afterwards, despite the job being significantly closer than McCabe Avenue. Looking back, I can relate to how important it was for my uncle Frank to take those long walks down to Kennedy Avenue where we once lived. Within my confusion came an attachment to the place I knew best. I walked the block, chatting with street soldiers in every section. McCabe Avenue's infamy was dominated by the guys in the 700 block, but there were also other dealers in the 800 and 600 blocks. Before going into the house, I stood in front of my former stoop observing a dice game from across the street. Elroy was there "side betting" or staying off of the dice, frustrating Randolph and a few of the other older guys, including Genius. Genius usually got a kick out of Elroy as well. Besides, Elroy introduced him to Hubert, supposedly now one of the richest guys in the city. Genius was also sleeping with Elroy's only sister Rebbie. This helped keep the love in the air between the two. Genius lived about ten houses north of Elroy on McCabe. He had two women in separate homes on the same block. There was also a third; Kerry, Penny's cousin from east Baltimore. Elroy's sister I liked a lot although she was my sister's age. She had plenty of style and a nice frame. She and her jeans turned my head daily.

As I sat and watched the different emotions circulate through the ten man game, Tray emerged from the circle in frustration. "O, tonight just ain't my fuckin night man," he said while wiping sweat from his forehead. "Try again later," I offered with a pat on his shoulder. "Nah, fuck all that, I have to 're-up' first. To "re-up" or "cop" in the streets, is when a dealer, or an addict, goes to purchase more drugs to sell or use. In Tray's case, he needed to buy more cocaine. "I just lost five hundred over there n' shit O," he stated in frustration. "That's crazy son!" I shouted in disbelief. I had major trouble understanding how the hustlers could risk it all for the money, only to be so casual or cavalier with their cash in an hour long game of craps. "I hope Genius' shit is better this time. I had a time selling that garbage last time," Tray shared. Genius often found ways to stretch his money and his product. He was a hustler. Mixing an ounce of baking soda with an ounce of cocaine was a normal practice for Genius. He hardly cared how good the product was, as long as it sold on the block. It didn't matter to him; everyone had his product anyway. Getting your hands on good product to sell was tough at times on the block, but this would soon prove to be the least of Tray's worries.

I learned of some disturbing news while talking to Tray on the block that evening. Tray looked up at me while lacing his Nike Air Max sneakers and said, "O, did you hear about that Old York Road bullshit?" "No, what happened now?" I wondered shaking my head. "Some nigga supposedly smacked LiL Bug's cousin Tiny or something," he explained a little. "Oh yeah?" I asked. "For what?" I added inquisitively "I don't know man!" he stated while hunching his shoulders. "Now what?" I asked calmly. "They want you to 'beef' with them now, right?" I added with a sour expression. "You know it," he replied. "Man, fuck that shit," I stated in anger. "Don't get mixed up in that madness Tray," I insisted. "Benny told me back in eighty-six, not to mess with that man," I continued. "You right man, I ain't fuckin wit that shit O," he assured with a slight grin. "Cool buddy, just do what you feel is necessary out here to get your cash, that's it! No need to get involved with that silly shit! All that mess ain't even needed," I explained. "O, I'm being like you man, cool as a muthafucka," he said with a huge grin as our palms met forcefully.

As I pulled Tray closer to embrace in agreement, I could see a couple of guys from the hood advancing towards us from over his shoulder. "Here they come now," I whispered. "Yo, you coming with us?" LiL Bug stated in anger. "One of those bitches slapped my little cousin Yo!" "Hold up son, I'm 'rappin' with O. Imma 'holla' at y'all in a second," Tray answered. "We going to go get "Diamond" too," he replied. "We be back in a minute," LiL Bug added. "We have to get these dudes now man. They disrespected my fuckin' cousin yo," he added while walking down the block. Diamond is the younger bother of Etton. He was not a mainstay on McCabe when we were younger. He would be seen more often just as others began to migrate to McCabe. Previously, most of his time was spent in west Baltimore. He, LiL Bug, his brother Harold, Antmo, a former member of our dance group, and a few others gathered to pay the guys from Old York a visit. It was clear they all wanted Tray's leadership for the matter. Tray had been so experienced in all kinds of mischief over the years; the younger guys would often hunt for him during very testy situations. He was their best option since Nardo was incarcerated in a parole violation. "O, I'm not going down there, I promise!" Tray stated while watching the guys gather up. I'm not sure if I was surprised more by Tray's apparent decision, or the fact he felt compelled to make a promise to me, of all people.

Tray and I watched the others down the block stir up and promote hostility within themselves and anyone who was bold enough to get involved. "Yeah, fuck that shit," Tray whispered periodically while looking back and forth between myself and the commotion taken place several yards ahead. Suddenly, "Odell, Odell!" yelled my aunt Marie from the porch front. "Yes, here I go," I replied loudly. "The phone!" she yelled again but much louder. "Who is it?" I asked. "I don't have the slightest idea. It's some girl," she added casually. "Do you want me to tell her you're gone?" Marie asked. "Nah, I'm coming now," I replied calmly. "Don't move Tray, we not finished buddy," I insisted. "I'm right here O," Tray replied while still focusing on the commotion down the street. I leaped the first five steps and dashed up the second set. "Hello," I answered slightly out of breath into the phone. "Oh, hey, how are you doing?" I said cheerfully. It was Penny on the other end. She was asking me to come down the street to see her. She was inside of her friend's house; the house where the commotion was taking place directly out front. Penny once dated LiL Bug, who was a major rival of Old York Road's LiL Scrapple. Both guys were very dark-skinned and very short. I'm six feet and brown-skinned. I guess Penny wanted to try out something new.

The conversation with Penny lasted only five minutes. "I can't talk long," I stated quickly. "Tray is out front waiting for me. We were having a serious talk," I explained to Penny. "I'll be down there in a few minutes, ok, bye!" I said before hanging the phone onto the wall. I hurried outside, only to notice Tray was gone. I first looked over towards the dice game. It has swelled to around 15 players. Tray was not one of them. Elroy was still there, and he was winning. "You fools can't do nothing with 'Obi-Wan Kenobi,'" he yelled while laughing. After bursting into laughter, I yelled over to my buddy. "Elroy, did you see where Tray went? "Nope, but I think he went somewhere with LiL Bug and em," he added pausing briefly. "Stupid bastard," Genius added without ever rising up in reference to Tray. I stood in disbelief, realizing Tray had just lied to me. He could not follow through on his promise immediately after making it. Tray and several others were headed down to Old York Road to violently prove some kind of negative mute point.

About 40 minutes after my conversation with Tray was interrupted, I was standing in the same spot witnessing my worst fear coming true. I was standing a few yards away from Antmo and LiL Bug, watching them sweat in a panic. Diamond was also rattled as his older brother and others momentarily delayed their gambling. There must have been a dozen of us surrounding the guys, when the yell, "They got Tray!" pierced the souls of us all. Tray had been shot multiple times. He would never return home to McCabe Avenue alive. His decision to go down to Old York Road proved to be a fatal one. The scene erupted with yells and screams followed by Etton's explosion. He wanted to know details of what took place and which of the guys had a firearm. I stood in silence, shocked. I could almost still feel Tray's presence still standing beside me. He was there no more than 45 minutes prior. While angry members of the neighborhood listened to the details, Tray laid down Old York Road mortally wounded. Just like that, in the blink of my eye, Tray's life was in the balance.

Tray died in the hospital later that evening. Attending Tray's funeral refreshed my memory and took me back to the previous two sessions I experienced with my granddad and Shawn. I made sure I gave Tray's mom, older brother, and younger sister a hug. Standing over Tray's body gave me the chills. I'd seen my relatives' bodies just the same, yet their deaths were not as coldhearted. I could not help but think about the times when Shawn and Tray danced side by side, or shared a laugh and a firm handshake with one another. I remembered the days Tray stole items for us all to have a picnic. My cousin Shawn and Tray were quite fond of each other. Both would no longer be with us.

I sat alone at the funeral, just as I had come. Many of the guys from McCabe bunched together in a separate section of the funeral home. From most of their expressions, retaliation seemed to be a certainty. I sat and listened to the pastor preach a powerful message at this funeral. Being a confused individual, I know I missed some important details of the sermon. I listened as if the message only applied to violent, drug dealers. I watched several guys from the neighborhood get out of their seats, very irritated by these passages. I wish I would have paid more attention to the message. Instead, I sat there lying to myself, nodding, as if I had it all together. I was slipping into the crowd to my left faster than I was willing to admit. Although the message was intense, many topics preached on confused me. I used guys leaving their seats to conclude that the harsh truth was being delivered to us all, and it hurt.

After the funeral everyone in the neighborhood spent the entire day mumbling and planning ways to get back at Old York. Meanwhile, I went home to spend time on Homestead Street with my sister and my niece. My sister had found the house-apartment we shared through a friend for $600 a month. We were to split the bills evenly. This was going to be my very first experience with paying bills of my own. I still helped my grandma, but not the same time every month. At this point, I only had my car insurance and the car mounted cellular phone to pay for. The cell phone bill was already past due. Downgrading my car's insurance to liability was inevitable at this point. I only had $2500 in my account, and this bill was also at "Due Now" status. The money I made on the job and from my peers allowed me to continue to dress nicely, but everything still seemed to be unraveling. Still, moving to Homestead came at a good time. This presented me with an opportunity to reconnect with my sister, get to know my niece, grow up a little more, and spend a little more time alone. I still loved the moments when I felt it was just myself and the Holy Spirit.

Like our mom, my sister was quite a young lady. At 23 years of age, she decided to step away from the father of her only child, for no apparent reason, to pursue fulfillment and unknown goals all alone. As we all know, it's usually the other way around. Freddy had made several attempts to reconcile, but my sister's mind was apparently made up. I struggled observing Freddy, who I looked up to, confused and depressed from decisions made by my sister. Freddy was certainly faithful. He also made plenty of money hustling and working full-time. He treated my sister like a queen, but as I said, with her, something was missing. When my sister began going steady with Freddy, she was only 15 years old. He was 19. Eight years later, my sister realized she was simply missing out on being young and single. She felt she needed to see life as an individual first, even if this meant falling flat on her face later. Even with this emotional decision, it appeared my sister's feet were firmly planted on the ground. Here, I was anxious to see what lied ahead at Homestead Street, living as an adult with my big sister.

I immediately learned living with my sister was going to be quite different. As I previously mentioned, my sister is only comfortable in a very clean setting. Meaning, she does not want to see a single dish in the sink or on the table. She also has a huge problem with leftover water droplets around the sink or faucets in the kitchen and especially the bathroom. She even gets irritated by clean dishes being on the dish rack for too long. The laundry hamper should not have any more than a few items inside, and the trash goes out everyday, even when it's not trash day. Stoves, floors, windows, or anything with glass, must be spotless. My sister's most important things to continuously clean were the refrigerator and the bathtub. Spilled Kool-Aid on floors and bacteria in a tub drives her nuts. I honestly believed I was a very neat person, but my sister's practices caused me to second guess myself. I've always been a pretty neat young man, but my sister Gina redefines cleanliness. On Homestead Street, it appeared as if I was going to need my very own cleaning supplies. However, this was not the end of the world at all. I simply would accept this challenge to be cleaner. It was all good!

I was learning, growing up consisted of more than simply hanging out with the older guys and doing whatever fell into our minds. On Homestead Street, my sister Gina was laying down all of the new rules on order. My sister worked at the Diplomat shop, a casual clothing outlet at the Old Town Mall, in east Baltimore. Gina always maintained a steady job. I continued to work at Shoe City Sports. I was growing so tired of selling sneakers; I actually offered to watch my niece regularly for a small fee. I've always loved kids. Being an uncle for the first time was a good feeling. I enjoyed the sense of maturity that comes with being an uncle. I learned how to change Lia's diaper. I also fed and bathed her. Watching over a small child is a rewarding experience to me. A child has so much love, trust, honesty and innocence. You can see it all in their eyes. It's a magnificent feeling when a child smiles while reaching upwards for you to pick them up. I loved spending time with my niece, but Gina was not feeling my proposal. I was not going to get off that easy. I had to get up, get out, and get something. Like every normal person, I had to go to work and get the job done.

My grandma periodically would say to me, "Son, you're young; if something positive bothers you, it's probably the best thing for you."

This phrase allowed me to be somewhat optimistic about living with my sister. I'd been working at Shoe City Sports much longer than I had anticipated due to this idea as well. Although I would be exposed to new rules, ideas or concepts, I realized I brought more peace and fulfilment to both Penny and my sister. My sister had my help with Lia and the bills, while Penny reaped the benefits of having an unselfish young man in her life; one who was not a drug dealer. We had the components of a decent inner city lifestyle, but I still did not have my mind completely made up about my future.

Thinking about the future was still a thought I would discard quickly. I did what felt good to me, while being conscious of how I treated others. I continued to concentrate on the people around me, just so I could ignore suspect parts of my own life. Penny and her two children kept me busy as well. The kids needed more attention from a male. Both of their fathers were drug dealers. Penny, a strong personality, decided to disconnect totally from these guys. My neighborhood and Old York Road was a place full of confusion, and Penny was a casualty of both sides. Penny had children by a guy from McCabe, Craig, and another by a guy from Old York, Scrapple. Women were getting prematurely pregnant, people were dying, cocaine was destroying households, and I was blindly meshed within it all in one way or another.

My sister Gina originally disapproved of my relationship with Penny. "Why would you mess with a girl with two kids by two different guys?" she asked me during a conversation in her room. "It's no big deal, the kids are fine," was the best response I had at the time. I believe Penny's position as a single mother of two took away the unwanted pressure I had placed on myself to become something grand in life. My sister would also ask, "Why didn't you just stay with Tracey or that pretty girl, Melody?" "They were good for you," she added. Those questions were only answered by two words; "I know." Penny having kids had nothing to do with how I felt about her. She was a tough person emotionally, but she was honest, passionate and cute. She was not physically put together as well as Vikki, Tracey or Melody, but she was much more mature. She was encouraging, and that's a big deal to all men, especially the young black male. When I was around Penny, no matter what happened, she really made me feel like everything would be fine.

Penny's "Ride or Die" approach to men was attractive, but the setting of our introduction was unraveling. The steady decline was obvious to most, but I still housed a desire to marinate there. I guess this was the same feeling inner-city guys all over the world feel. In many hoods throughout the country, there's a need to be noticed or relevant in society. It does not really matter if the situation is negative or positive. People from the streets simply want to be heard. Many kids feel trapped or they unknowingly place themselves in a box. This is when folks feel there is nowhere else to turn, therefore they decide to love the position or place that they're in. I never got to the point of needing to "represent" or announce where I came from or where I lived. If someone asked, I let them know. Still, there was apart of me that felt right at home on McCabe, whether things were horrible or not.

After settling in at home for awhile on Homestead Street, I later returned to McCabe simply to hang out or play basketball. Elroy informed me things were getting way out of hand. He said guys from Old York Road had been coming through the block regularly, shooting. It would only be a few days later before I witnessed this with my own eyes. It soon became clear, these kids who drove through the block shooting were not the same individuals I was familiar with from Old York Road. LiL Bug's brother Harold mentioned the names of three younger guys from the other side. "Nut", the younger brother of Romeo, my sister's ex, seemed to be the boldest of the three. His two closest buddies were Miran and Casper, my pal Donny's little cousin. These guys were getting involved with the rivalry simply for the pleasure of using guns. They were the same dudes who participated in the infamous school hallway chase. These younger guys were quicker to take a life; they had no clue what life was all about. My friends and I struggled mightily with our identities, but we practiced a little more common sense. Once these younger guys began to factor into the equation, I could just feel the tension mounting. Everyone knew things were getting testy. We knew all hell would eventually break loose.

Watching Nut race up and down McCabe Avenue made everyone extremely nervous. He did this nearly everyday for weeks at a time. He usually could be seen in a gray Acura Legend. Most claimed it was stolen. A lot of the younger guys were below average hustlers. They stole vehicles to give the appearance of doing well in the streets. I stood and watched, more than once from an elevated position, the 19 year old smiling while pointing his gun out the window at guys. Sometimes he would shoot up in the air a time or two, and other times he would simply point his gun at guys just to watch people scatter and take cover or dive onto the concrete. I picked up a scrape or two. "Let him keep that bullshit up and I promise y'all niggas I'm going kill his little ass," Tareek stated as we all watched Nut peel away. Things were deteriorating at such a steady pace, it was no longer about if an attack would come, but when.

Nut's decision to strike continued. One sunny day, he was observed creeping alongside parked cars about a block away from 731's front door. Undetected, he was able to get off a few shots, hitting a guy named Tockey in the lower leg as he stood on the corner. Tockey, another new street hustler, survived and fully recovered from his injuries. However, this shooting set off the rivalry even more. Now, there were dozens of young guys, separated by only a couple a miles, willing to kill one another for blocks they were not from originally. Several non-fatal shootings would take place creating a warzone-type of atmosphere on McCabe. During these times, many of the guys began inviting or recruiting dealers from other areas of the city to join in on the feuding. Simultaneously, McCabe Avenue was turning into a "gold mine" and a "battlefield." In the midst of the increased violence, Genius was thrilled new hustlers were coming in. All he saw was more workers to put on his payroll. He and several other older guys hardly cared about affiliating with the rivalry. They gave the impression of joining the violence, but when shots actually rang out, the "OG's" were missing in action.

Elroy and I shared the misfortune of experiencing a few of these senseless shootings. Elroy was growing totally frustrated with the feud. He and I agreed the feud was stupid and likely would not end well. "How in the hell can I keep making money if these dudes keep on shootin n' shit everyday?" Elroy explained. "It's bad enough those 'knockers' fuckin harassing me n' shit," he followed. 'Knockers" was the nickname given in the area to narcotics agents. Elroy was getting the attention of the police as they began passing through more frequently. Authorities were growing irritated with seeing Elroy continuously on the street corners. He was hot and I was getting tired. I continued to force myself to go to a job I was sick of in order to pay my bills. My bank account now had just $2000 in it. Frustration allowed me to prohibit guys to get inside of my car as much as before. The beef was spiraling out of control and I did not want to get caught in the crossfire despite my confused state. My life was confusing as ever inside and all around me. I had no direction or plans for my future at 19 years old. My mentality towards life became more compromised. I was falling into a comfort zone in a poor environment, full of people whom lived life on the edge. I was not aware it was really my life with the most trouble. The others had their minds already made up. I was lost, getting further away from the purest form of myself. I had no idea the world of peace I once knew and loved was about to end, all at once.

I would proceed with my normal routine of hanging on McCabe Avenue, working, and playing basketball as much as possible. Basketball, and the moments spent with my grandma, allowed me to get through most days optimistically. I enjoyed basketball the most when Evan and I would venture outside of the neighborhood to play against the better talent in the city. We played in the city at Cecil Recreation Center a few times. This brought back memories of when Shawn and I lived in the area. We also made it to play at Barclay Recreation Center, which happened to be just a few blocks away from Homestead Street. There, I actually played with, and against, a few guys from Old York Road. Tracey's new boyfriend Phil played there. Whitmore or "Shadow" was often there as well. He was the kid from Old York incarcerated at Child Study (The Woodbourne Center) years ago, and the brother of the guy responsible for killing Tray. Whitmore and my first girlfriend Christina share two sons. I've always been curious about how those two met. It appeared as if he was able to do a much better job than I did with her back in the 80s. Today he is cool with me as well. Whenever we encounter one another, usually there are not many words, just smiles.

The many games of hoops played at Barclay always turned out to be clean, competitive and without hardly any altercations. Evan knew I was all for peace, therefore we made sure we continued to hang out almost as much as we did on McCabe. My game was a lot better, but he still showed me a lot of the "ins and outs" about the sport. Over the years, I got a lot better and this allowed me to play above-average at times. I had my moments outplaying a few local hoop stars. I was gradually noticed by some of the "playground heroes" or exceptional street-ballers throughout Baltimore City. They all saw me as a guy who could hold his own out there. Not bad for a "late-bloomer," or player who started to play a sport far later than most. I was never a great street-ball player, but a respected one for sure, and that was good enough for me.

Meeting popular, local basketball players outside of the neighborhood and hustlers from other hoods in clubs was great during this time. It gave me a glance at a life outside of the constant negativity which consumed McCabe Avenue. I liked being viewed as an individual by everyone. Throughout my entire time on McCabe, even before the foolishness, I was recognized as a person, not a person from a specific hood. In the midst of the troubles I faced internally, it was clear grandma's instructions on character and attitude still glimmered within. Treating people in a decent manner and impressing people with inner qualities has always been a normal practice. This took place with me regularly although the actions of others would usually distort the process. No matter how my life was turning out, I could at least feel good knowing I did not deliberately mistreat anyone. I lacked direction, but I still learned a lot from my grandma. On a very warm summer evening, 1992, I realized whatever lessons I still had to learn, I would be traveling that journey alone.

Standing in front of 731, occupied with grandma, Uncle BoBo, and Uncle Frank, I watched dozens of hustlers, frantically making drug transactions. My old neighborhood had become a place consumed by drugs, gambling, and violence. One night, Bennett, Elroy and I watched as Genius entertained the others on the corner. "Yeah, I lost big tonight," he claimed while smiling. "How much did you lose?" Harold asked in amazement. "Just twenty thousand, not too much; ain't nothing," he said with a broken mug or fake frown. "Got Damn!" LiL Bug yelled out. "What the fuck?" Tareek stated with a giggle. "That shit don't mean nothing to me niggas," Genius preached while slowly browsing at all of the guys. "I just gave the dude the keys to the new Amigo," he added. "I got seven more cars, and I'll get another one next week," he reminded everyone. Genius lost five figures to a hustler in east Baltimore during a dice game. He simply handed over the keys to his new, candy apple red, Isuzu Amigo. The guy was another connection he conducted business with. His new red Amigo was gone, but his pride and ego stayed firmly planted.

Genius was always a major show-off, but there was something about him I actually liked. He was very generous. Maybe he was stern with his workers, but he often showed sensitivity for the neighbors and the smaller children. He always showed me respect. We only really spoke to one another on the ball courts, but I still was able to see a side to Genius others overlooked. Mentally, I believe we shared similar ideas about how to be towards good people, and we both hated to see women walking barefoot outside. Genius understood I was different, and I could not be easily impressed by riches or material gain. I think we were a little intrigued by each other, but felt no need to display this to the public.

I continued to relax outside with Elroy and Bennett, trying to enjoy the very warm weather. Bennett was flirting with every female who passed by. I simply would smile while keeping quiet. I didn't want any rumors to get back to Penny. I was trying hard to be faithful, but it was not easy. My roaming eyes were still getting the better of me. "Yo, she's phat as a muthafucka," Bennett yelled out. "Phat," to those who don't understand this term: It is a reference used in the hood when acknowledging the sex appeal of a young lady's physical frame; mainly referring to a female's rear-end or buttocks. "Phat" simply stands for Pretty, Hot, and Tempting. Bennett was referring to Summer, a cute girl from around the way, and the ex-girlfriend of a young hustler named Keffy. Summer was one of the few sisters in the area no one spoke negatively about. She was only 15, but she was easily built like a 25 year old. "Man, y'all out here trippin, I'll be back. I'm going in the house for a minute," I stated. I ran up the steps in a good mood, enjoying the interesting conversations we all were engulfed in. I entered the very warm house and walked towards the secondary kitchen we had and gave my grandma a tight hug. I was totally unaware at the moment, the importance of this hug.

"Man ma, it's burning up in here," I stated while wiping my forehead. "I know it son, but I need to get this food finished," she replied while dabbing her mouth with a handkerchief. "Let me help you," I offered with a smile. "Ok, get that pot of water and sit it over there near the sink. It's very heavy. It's for the greens," she added with exhaustion. I moved the hot pot of water out of the way and immediately grabbed the pitcher of red Kool-Aid from the fridge. I poured a cup. It was so hot in the kitchen, my clothes dampened almost immediately. "Ma, do you want some?" I asked. "No boy! You know I don't drink that mess," she emphasized. "You need to drink some water," she stated in a low tone. "Eat and drink healthy son," she added with a slight smile. "That's why I'm cooking. I know you've probably been eating that fast food mess." She was right as usual. I had been to McDonalds three out of the last five days. "What are we having ma?" I asked. "I made a meatloaf, cabbage, potato salad, and pie," Mama promoted slowly. Soon after going over the menu, her smile would gradually be interrupted by a shortage in her breathing. "Are you alright ma?" I asked in concern. "Maybe I should go get the fan." I stated. "I'm alright!" she whispered. Concerned, I turned only for a second to place my cup on the table, and when I turned back around, suddenly Mama's eyes were locked in on me as if I were a ghost. "Maaaaaa!" I yelled.

Seconds later, Mama fell hard to the floor. "I can't breathe," struggled to escape grandma's mouth. "Help, help!" I yelled in a panic. I dropped to the floor on my knees and grabbed her right hand. "It's going to be alright ma," I stated while stroking her right hand. "Mama, Mama!" "Oh God!" Marie yelled as she quickly appeared from outside. My uncle BoBo also emerged, quickly contacting the paramedics. "They're on the way," he shared in a panic. Once again, bedlam suddenly broke out within the confines of 731. Sadness shifted from the living room years ago, into the kitchen. "Ma, can you hear me?" BoBo stated in a broken tone. My grandmother was still alert, but now unable to speak. She was looking upwards at everyone with a frightening expression of uncertainty on her face. I backed out of the confusion surrounding Mama. In total disbelief, the tears silently began to roll from my eyes as my spirit would slowly crumble.

The sound of the approaching ambulance could be heard in the distance as I watched my grandma's eyes fall weaker. Paramedics quickly entered and supplied her with oxygen. Mama's 275 pound frame was raised and placed on a gurney by three male medics. In the midst of her struggles, grandma had the presence to turn her head my way; making eye contact as she passed by. More tears fell. "It's going to be alright," BoBo turned to us all and stated. Seeing my uncle worried and confused made the situation tougher to endure. He was a stern individual who hardly ever showed compassionate emotions in the past, but this was his mother. He quickly elected to go along for the ride in the ambulance. I watched the vehicle as it sped away with emergency and caution lights flashing. Onlookers fixed their eyes on me from below. "Man, that's messed up," Genius stated. "What? Was that O's grandmother?" Tareek asked. "Damn," he added. My sister arrived shortly afterwards, devastated from the phone call she received a few minutes prior. All we were left to do at this point was await a report from my uncle. Everyone sat in the living room, in tears, holding their collective breaths. Once again, I was falling apart and the little ray of life I held onto was steadily leaving my spirit.

A cold silence dominated a room where we had already lost two members of our immediate family over the last five years. My family all piled on the couch holding hands with our heads bowed. I was daydreaming, replaying Shawn's tragic accident in my mind, only to look over to my right at our granddad's remaining empty chair. We all remained stationary for more than an hour. My uncle had not called and my aunt was once again growing impatient with a lack of communication from the hospital. "Fuck this shit," she stated while hopping up quickly. Just as Marie began to dial the phone, the front door crackled. It was BoBo. With his head bent downward and his shoulders slumped, our heads raised further. "What happened?" Marie cried outwardly. BoBo slowly emerged and walked into the living room. He looked us all in the eyes, began to cry, and stated pass his trembling lips, "She's gone!"

My uncle's words created a total emotional avalanche inside of the house. Everyone collapsed except me. In shock, I sprung up and exploded out of the front door and down the steps. I took off running up McCabe Avenue as fast as I could. I accelerated faster than I had ever been able to on any ball court. "O, you alright?" someone yelled as I passed by quickly. I was running so fast, everything was a blur, similar to the Easter incident. Only this time no one was chasing me; I was not running away from a pack of fools, I was trying to run away from life. I accelerated so quickly, my tears quickly traveled backwards, towards my ears. By the time I tired myself out and stopped, I was at Dewee's field a couple of miles away. My meltdown took place alone in this dark park. I stayed in the grassy park on my knees for an hour crying and praying in the moonlight. I needed answers, but I simply couldn't ask the correct questions. I was very confused about my life and life in general. My closest relative and my best friend was now gone forever, leaving me with an emptiness I'd never felt before. I picked my head up and looked all around and up into the sky. This was the day I realized I was all alone in this uncertain world.

My frantic ten minute run became a slow, 30 minute walk back to McCabe Avenue. The tears poured as I tried to pull myself together before I returned to the block. I reentered the dwelling to a more controlled atmosphere. The screams there had been reduced to constant sniffles. I sat in the same seat I had ejected from and immediately began observing one empty seat across from the other. I listened to the conversation between my sister, aunt and uncles. BoBo informed everyone Mama suffered a massive heart attack. He stated she may have not gone through this ordeal if she would have been willing to go for regular checkups. Mama hated hospitals. As I said, she would always say, "When it's time for me to go, I'll go." We had no idea the reality of this phrase would hurt us as much as it did on this night. Perhaps there was a part of my grandma that knew this time was approaching. However, the surprised expression she displayed on her face during the time of the incident illustrated something far different. If she was ready in some way, we sure were not, especially me.

I returned to my bedroom during the evening, realizing at 19, I was without a mother, my closest cousin, my grandfather and my beloved grandmother. My father was nowhere to be found ever since I declined to give him a portion of my inheritance. I truly felt I was on my own at this point. The purpose of life I searched for no longer mattered to me. A part of me figured I would be next on the family's list of tragedies. Life really felt meaningless. I attended my grandma's funeral and burial, which was finalized at the Woodlawn Cemetery in Randallstown, Maryland exactly where Shawn and our granddad rested as well. The saddened emotions returned as I watched Mama's body get lowered into the rich soil. Only this time I hardly cried at all along with everyone else. I was frustrated, sad, and angry all at once. My grandmother was not the only person gone. Dressed in fine casual garments, my body still stood, but my spirit withered and died away with my most important loved one. I was officially gone as well; from within. My spirit had completely left "Home."

# Chapter 13

# FALLING HORIZON

Grandma's repass was held back at the house on McCabe Avenue. The aroma of a great meal scented the home as it had in the past. Distant relatives surfaced once again. The three deaths of the last five years actually made our distant relatives appear as regulars. Funerals were really the only times we all would come together for dinner. After burying Mama, eating was the last thing I had on the mind. I spent most of the night sitting on the bottom three stairs, dabbing my reddish eyes with a wet paper towel. This death really came as a shock. My grandmother was only 66 years old. This reality had me spacey or detached as I sat inside of the infamous 731 with distant relatives. I stayed as long as I could before I would return to Homestead Street to seclude myself inside of my room. I fell deeper and deeper into a low. I had given up on any thoughts of a solid future. I no longer cared to think about anything ahead. I figured to just live day by day until it was time to endure another tragedy; possibly my own. Just days after my grandma's funeral, I would suddenly quit my job at Shoe City Sports. I was so depressed, I felt I really had nothing to live for. I did not want to commit suicide. I simply did not want to do anything. This mindset placed me back on McCabe Avenue with Elroy and the others. Only this time, it was not a matter of if I would be "in," but when?

After a few months of hanging out with the guys in the streets, I would hardly ever set foot in the house I grew up in. 731 was now occupied by my uncles, BoBo and Frank, my aunt Marie, Montell, and their two kids, Monnie and Jayson. Jayson was Shawn's little brother he never really got a chance to know. Marie and Montell were recently forced to move back into 731. Their afflictions compromised their ability to maintain their bills on time. However, the home they once loved on McCabe had become a decaying shell with restless souls inside. Alcohol was continuously eating away at my uncle BoBo's pancreas. Marie and Montell were abusing crack cocaine. Frank was an alcoholic as well, but he somehow stayed the same regardless. These factors would help shift my approach to life. Whenever I was on the block with my peers, I would hardly ever pay any attention to the members of my family or the home I grew up in. The dwelling was nothing more than the platform for my brokenness. I was suddenly starting to become a lot more comfortable with the dealers in the neighborhood who shared similar feelings about their home lives, and life in general. We all shared in some form of extreme pain we struggled to deal with.

I received lots of emotional support from the brothers on the corners following my grandmother's passing. They all experienced various forms of upbringing trauma. With this, we would form a bond and somehow found a little solace with the help of rap music. Ironically, at the time two of my favorite songs were, "Me, Myself and I" by De La Soul, and "Reminisce" by Pete Rock and CL Smooth. Folks on the outside often view rap music as garbage or unnecessary language, but we in the streets read the artform much differently. Hip hop is simply stories told about everyday life from an urban prospective. This story is Hip Hop, but it considers those who don't get it nor want to. The Long Way "Home": The Testimony is hip hop for the masses.

Genius would also show much compassion towards me with the loss of my grandmother. He truly understood the power of "big mama." Fortunately, he was blessed to still have a grandma around. Miss Martha was over 70 years old and still very alert and mobile. He kept a close eye on his grandma whose home happened to rest in between two of his female companions. The new relationship I was developing with the guys on the block allowed my time in the streets to increase significantly. Penny was often in the neighborhood, therefore we grew closer as well. Her presence made it pretty easy to be around her and kick it with Elroy and Bennett. No matter how much I was paid, the steady income at the shoe store was no longer. I didn't really regret quitting the job at the time, but I did feel bad about suddenly leaving behind the friends I had made there. I left without giving a solid explanation.

Giving up on working may have been indirectly linked to my grandmother's death, but I was sure to try and hold onto all of the internal teachings she instilled. Despite my shattered heart, I continued with trying to be a kind and compassionate person. I would discard any ideas concerning success for my future. I still received great satisfaction from being the guy who made others smile or feel better. I guess it was fair to say, I was headed down the wrong path, lost, but with a smile.

Standing on the outside looking in was no longer working for me. I slowed tremendously with giving my pals short rides for sums of cash. I was turning down hundreds of dollars a day, and yet, I was nearly broke. I only had $1100 in my bank account. This, and no longer having a steady income, finally forced me to switch my car insurance from full-coverage to liability. The Toyota Celica GT was still in good condition so I held to the full-coverage policy. I managed to stay away from receiving any speeding tickets, but Elroy and I were involved in an accident once. Elroy and I were hit pretty hard by a woman driving an Oldsmobile with an infant inside. She ran a red light at 33rd Street and Guilford Avenue, ironically, right in front of the hospital my mom had passed away in years ago. The crash resulted with significant damage to the driver side of my car. The full-coverage policy was a last-minute blessing for this situation. Miraculously, no one sustained any serious injuries, and I decided not to sue the 55 year old new grandmother. She indicated the sunlight blinded her as she crossed into the intersection.

Despite not filing a claim against the older woman for damages, and quitting my job at the shoe retailer, money was still a need. My monthly bills were still due, and I had always declined handouts from the brothers in the streets. This was evidence of an early poor decision; leaving a job without a backup plan. I was actually leaving behind everything without a next course of action. This lack of planning was a component of a growing ego.

At times, when I was on the street corners, I felt the guys out there could have gone about their business a lot better. I felt guys were too reckless. I believed I could also produce a significant income. I knew with the feud worsening, McCabe Avenue would soon be seriously targeted by all branches of law enforcement. This would not deter my interest with learning more about the details of hustling while studying how not to get arrested or killed in the process. My mentality became tainted before I did anything wrong. I continued to casually hang out with Elroy on the block, now with more motivation. For the first time ever, I flirted with the possibility of selling drugs. I soon began doing my homework again, but now I was possibly entering a totally different and more costly classroom.

Suddenly, my academically challenged pal Elroy became my favorite teacher. I was pondering becoming a drug dealer. "Cocaine 101" began with the understanding of profits and "re-up," or the continuous buying and stocking of product. During this time, crack cocaine was already steam-rolling through every inner-city neighborhood in America, but pure powder cocaine was still attractive as well. I was familiar with most of the terminology used to reference drugs by word of mouth, from watching movies and television, and from hanging around the actual dealers. Elroy was ready to show me several true realities of the drug game. "Remember in school O, at lunch before, when I said, 'Never say never,' when you said you would never hustle?" he asked with the same devilish grin. "I told you," he added. I just emotionlessly stared at my pal.

Elroy began the lessons of hustling by showing just how cocaine was cooked. He also explained how often a person used the substance on average, and how to create a clientele of my own. One evening, as I watched Elroy during a transaction, he stated, "Watch this shit O. He'll be back in less than an hour." The middle-aged male returned in no more than 20 minutes. "See what I'm saying?" he'd ask while smiling and repeating the sale. Another key I witnessed immediately; detach from the sick. In the street hustle game, the addicts are not really seen as normal people. They're figures who need what you have and have what you want. They're objects for money. That's it! It's all business, never personal. Outwardly, I became very intrigued by how easy it appeared to be able to make money selling cocaine on McCabe. At home or with Penny, I would struggle a bit emotionally, but on McCabe Avenue, I began to feel more in control of myself. I really had no idea I was falling so quickly. At this point, I was too weak and confused about life to try and catch myself. Even had I known my issues, I likely would not have done anything about it. I was far too weak mentally.

In the midst of the growing neighborhood feud, and on the heels of grandma's death, I made the decision to request a meeting with Genius.

I was 90% sure I was ready to start "a new job." I was going to meet with Genius with the intent on purchasing cocaine to distribute for the first time ever. I was convinced I could sell drugs, but I was not ready to label myself as a drug dealer. However, I was lost. For the first time in my life, I was going to deliberately and feloniously break the law.

The relationship I had developed with Genius on the basketball court was about to strengthen, but in a compelling manner. This was about business, and on McCabe Avenue the ball was always in his court. He always won. The plan was for me to get started by asking Genius to "front" or advance me a "quarter ounce" (7 grams) of powdered cocaine. Elroy and I agreed I should not spend the last of my own money. He feared the product may not be good enough for a newcomer to sell quickly. He also thought it would be much easier to pay Genius with this personal money if things did not run too smoothly. "O, if all goes well, you will knock that shit off hella fast; pay him his two fifty, bag a three hundred dollar profit, without ever touching any of your own money."

Ironically, for the first time ever, I had a plan. If everything were to go as described by my pal, I would make no less than $250 dollars in just a few hours. It took me more than a week to make this at the shoe store. I could do it in a day by taking on a lesser role with just hanging out with the guys. Again, that idea grew old quickly. 1992 was the year, and this was the very first time I found myself walking up McCabe Avenue towards Genius' house. He would often drop by 731 to invite me to virtually harmless hoop sessions, but this was much different. Unfortunately, my mind was made up. I was going to his home to become a drug dealer. Even before I reached the kingpin's home, I was a bit nervous, but in my mind I was already "in."

Following my heart was no longer the approach I took to life. My heart was extremely tired. For the first time, I would allow my thoughts to dominate or control my actions. As I advanced towards the kingpin's front door, there was a lightening-quick feeling in the pit of my belly that whispered, "Keep on walking by O." I quickly ignored my gut trying to convince me to abort, and proceeded to Genius' front porch. Elroy then reluctantly tapped on the screen door. "Who dat?" Genius yelled with his back towards us. Pass the screen door, the front door was wide open. Genius was sitting inside on a leather recliner, playing a Sega Genesis basketball video game. "It's us man. O wants you," Elroy stated. "I'm staying out here O," Elroy stated nervously. Elroy always seemed to be a bit intimidated by Genius, although they were pretty close. He was likely worried Genius would chew him out for playing a role in something as serious as me becoming a drug dealer. "Come in man," Genius ordered calmly. The game paused and I stood and watched the recliner slowly spin to face my direction. So there I was, face-to-face with a ruthless, convicted-felon drug kingpin, about to talk business.

Genius and I stared at one another for a few seconds, and this weird feeling came over me. Surprisingly, I could notice a disappointing expression on his face. It was like he already knew. The vibe was synonymous with the feeling I received as a child when my uncle BoBo learned of a wrongdoing. "Look man, I need some help. I'm damn near broke," I stated bluntly. Money was an issue, but my reasoning for being in the kingpin's home was far deeper than that. This was an excuse! I was traumatized and depressed. I knew Genius hated being broke more than anything, so I said I was, knowing it would certainly get his attention. Genius remained quiet and shook his head before slightly grinning. "Are you sure man?" he stated in a relaxed tone. "Yeah, I'm fine," I replied with a single nod. "I don't think this shit is for you tho O," Genius expressed with disappointment. "What do you mean?" I replied confused. "I mean, there's probably something better out there for you man," he said confidently. "Like what?" I asked sarcastically. "I couldn't tell you all that. I don't know," he answered a bit irritated. Immediately afterwards, he stated, "Alright then, I ain't going go through all that righteous shit with you man." "What's up?" he added impatiently. "I need a 'quarter.'" "I need a quarter ounce," I indicated for a second time. "I didn't think you were talking about a 'quarter brick' O," he replied with a smile while reaching underneath his seat. He then pulled out a freezer bag full of "quarters" and "halves." He tossed me a "quarter" and stated, "That's two-fifty alright?" "Cool, I'll get it to you by tomorrow," I assured reluctantly. I turned to walk away and Genius asked again, "O, are you sure man?" "I'm cool man, for real," I replied with a slight grin. "Got damn," slowly exiting from Genius as the squealing screen door swung open. A gasping sigh followed as the door slammed shut.

Elroy and I walked away from the house quickly. A minute later, something simply forced me to turn around. I turned back and Genius had made it out to the porch. He was staring at me, shaking his head as he leaned over the banister. It was clear Genius was disappointed, but in my mind the damage was already done. In 1992, I certainly was not "Cool like Dat." I was lost, and stupid. For the first time ever I had illegal drugs in my possession. I had yet to make a sale, but I was officially a drug dealer.

As a dealer, I realized quickly, I did not like the idea of owing anyone. I knew this was no act. I also understood, there were no true success stories coming from those who dared to enter this game. Still, none of this was carefully calculated. The circumstances within my life were too much for me to bare, opening the door to very poor decisions. That's how I became a drug dealer, and although I struggled with the title, I still wanted to succeed. I was determined from the start to be great at this deadly game, therefore my approach here in the streets was to bring the same focus I had brought into the classroom at Northern High. There, I graduated an honor's student. Now it was time to embark on a lesser but tougher course; becoming a graduate from The School of Hard Knocks, where the percentages of those who make it through are extremely lower.

I was not feeling the idea of owing Genius, although many of the other hustlers possessed that debt. I understood he was the last person anyone wanted to deal with over blown funds. I wanted Genius to not factor into much as I began this process. Holding these drugs for the first time gave me an intense but nervous feeling. Elroy agreed to stretch the use of the drug as far as possible by simply adding a little more baking soda to it than normal. He decided to package the drug for me in small plastic baggies. The guys on McCabe Avenue mainly sold $20 bags of cocaine or "girl" it's called. Heroin's nickname is "Boy." I still don't have a clue where these names originated from.

Again, crack cocaine was taking over in the streets, but we all still gained large profits from distributing powder cocaine. After scoring from Genius, Elroy and I headed to my house apartment on Homestead Street to package the drugs for distribution. Watching Elroy use precision to insert the product into the baggies with a single, folded playing card was quite interesting. Precision and patience is not expected for a former high school student who dropped out of school in the 12th Grade, but Elroy was sharp. So was Evan, who also just entered the game. Elroy found something he was pretty good at, but was not necessarily too good for him, or anyone else. This held true for me as well, but we both were too blind to focus on the downside to hustling. We were living for the moment and there was no telling how long the moment would last. Elroy eventually packaged up $550 worth of cocaine for me to sell. It would soon be time for me to take to the streets; a street where death resided in more than one form. Turning back was not an option for me at this point. I was sure I was going to get this money.

Again, looking back, I don't believe the tragedies I suffered in my life as a teen were the sole or primary reasons behind my decision to sell drugs. However, I do believe I was quite depressed, and this helped to promote or allowed such a horrible decision to come about. Although I had just about given up on any positive outcome for myself, I still understood selling drugs was very wrong. I understood this from the start, and still ended up getting involved. In the beginning, the plan was not to deal drugs forever. Like Elroy stated previously; that's hardly ever the plan. I didn't know what would happen in a few weeks, or in a couple of months, or throughout many years. A small part of me wanted something good to come from somewhere else, but the focus was certainly now with the hustle. I convinced myself money was most important, so I simply wanted to make lots of it. Many of those guys who vowed to only hustle for short periods were no longer living; everything was cut short. There were guys who saw drug dealing as the only option. I always thought this was crazy. I never believed this, but I felt I had nothing left or no one to truly believe in anymore, not even myself.

I struggled to get myself to think rationally, but I would manage to periodically take a little pressure away. Before heading to McCabe to sell the $550 worth of "girl" or cocaine, I would head to the ATM to withdraw $300 from the $1100 I had left. I took the $250 directly to Genius and thanked him for trusting me enough to give me something "on the arm" or up front. "Damn son! That's how you do it?" he asked with raised eyelids. "Nah, I'm not done, I just decided to give you the money from my account first. I wanted to get it over with," I stated while shaking Genius' hand. Although I promised to never spend a dime of this money on anything drug related, I did not really see this as such at the time. And, I really felt getting Genius out of the way first made more sense. "O, I'm sorry about your grandmother. I know you really loved your grandma," he added.

"You still don't have to go here though man," he followed. "Thanks, I appreciate that buddy, but I'm good," I replied. I left Genius' porch with a lump in my throat and a thumping in my chest. Out of all the people I surrounded myself with daily, my emotions nearly resurfaced around the one guy everyone viewed as arrogant and inconsiderate. What part of the game was this?

I would sell the cocaine alongside Elroy for a little over an hour. Later on, I quickly purchased a half ounce or 14 grams for $500. Elroy then showed me how to package up my own product. I managed to get $1200 worth from the "half." The very next morning, I returned to McCabe alone. By the afternoon, I was calling Elroy to grab another "half" from Genius. "Damn son, you rollin' ain't you?" Elroy stated over the phone. "Something like that," I replied with a grin. It's crazy how selling drugs can cause you to become emotionless. During these actual transactions, nine out of ten times, I felt absolutely no compassion for those I dealt to. "Alright, I'll have it for you later O," Elroy replied. After hanging up with Elroy on the phone, I sat on a corner of my bed and pulled out the ball of money from my pockets. I was amazed, but confused about how fast I had made $1060. It took me less than two days to produce this kind of money. This money I could spend on anything I chose. This money was real. It certainly did not give me the same feeling as the legal funds I once had, but it could produce the exact same results. Still, it was different. This money even looked different. It came in various denominations. Some of the bills were filthy and a few others were slightly torn or ripped, yet it served the same purpose as any. The income was coming in and growing quickly, for the first time in my young life.

I covered my bills for the month and proceeded to buy more "quarters" and "halves." In just a couple of months, $1000 a week was the least amount I was able to profit. I was selling drugs relentlessly, but I really did not feel like a "drug dealer" or what folks believe most drug dealers are; violent and ignorant. The act is indeed ignorant, but not always done with malice or poor attitude. This does not excuse anything, but it gave me a certain level of calmness as I dealt the drugs. I really presented myself well to society whenever our worlds would meet. Making money in this manner was really all I would allow to be different about me, although I was sure to bury any compassionate emotions during the actual act.

I impressed Elroy so much with my ability to get money, we quickly decided to form a partnership. We were already hanging out plenty, so looking out for one another on the block made sense. The police were not too much of a factor when I first began hustling. Besides, I was in such great shape from playing basketball, I never thought about the cops. In the beginning, I was so silly I actually wanted to see if I could out run the authorities. This was how far my mentality had dropped off. Elroy also needed the help. He needed to get away from McCabe Avenue more and spend time with his one year old daughter, Yasmen. Before I entered the drug game, I felt money was great as long as you earned it through working hard, or by dreaming or participating in something positive. Now I thought: it hardly mattered as long as you don't physically or violently hurt someone and just stay low. Life in the game moves at a very fast pace, often creating a lack of focus on the flipside to dealing. It was very odd to start thinking more positive after I started dealing cocaine. Still, I never considered the addicts or the sick people out there, or their families I was contributing to hurting. This ignorance was very strange considering my own family was falling apart from drug and alcohol abuse. Soon, nothing really mattered. All Elroy and I saw were dollar signs stamped in front of at least $1300-$1500 a day.

Morals, integrity or principles no longer mattered to any of us on McCabe Avenue. Here, and all over the city and country, poverty stricken neighborhoods and projects were all living by a "fuck the world" code. The #1 question from these people remains: "Who cares about the lost souls?" The money we were producing in the hood would now seduce Bennett as well. The nice sneakers and fine apparel we frequently modeled often eluded him throughout his childhood. He continued to work part-time at the local Giant Food supermarket, but he still struggled to get the things he desired. Bennett was one of the few kids on the block who still lived with both parents. Although he was not in the streets as much as Elroy and I, he joined. The three of us were not interested in the violence at all really, nor did we make it our duty to be disrespectful and ignorant towards others. We simply were chasing money in the same area where we once ran after the ice cream truck and searched for pretty girls while playing "Freeze Tag." Fast cash was flowing throughout our neighborhood, therefore we felt we were certainly entitled to plenty of it.

Elroy, Bennett and I understood we were not cut from the same cloth as the others. Back when Benny was on McCabe, guys were simply making money and keeping quiet, unless things had to be addressed. The Wilbert incident was an isolated event during the time in reference to homicides and gun violence. Although Benny's actions may have opened the door to the ongoing tragic situations, they were few and far between back then. As rough as that era could be, we were now hustling in an era 20 times worse. The mentality of most of the younger guys on McCabe was of total ignorance, coming completely with a strong disregard for human life. As the money possibilities increased, so did the number of carefree youngsters with no direction onto the block. Myself, and my two buddies understood we could suffer harmful acts, both, from Old York Road and from where we grew up. These younger guys would simply hurt anyone, for no reason at all, at any given time. There was a #1 rap song in 1992. It's a track produced by a rap group called, "Black Sheep." The song was ironically titled, "The Choice Is Yours." My friends and I were these black sheep, in a pit full of savage wolves on the block. The choice to do what was right was ours, and we all got with the wrong idea, screwing up our lives in a major way.

By the time winter rolled around, there were too many young, wild, drug dealers on McCabe Avenue to count. The neighborhood was pretty small, and every young kid with the heart or courage to commit senseless acts, would cram into this deteriorating environment to prove worthy. On McCabe there were original younger guys like, "Spoon" and "Shorty." These were Retta's nephews, and the younger cousins of Todd. Although younger, they were there with Shawn and I on McCabe. Like Bennett, they too were older; they would join Todd, harassing anyone they felt posed a threat or challenge. "Shorty" was a compact, five feet six inch kid. His cousin "Spoon," the opposite at six feet-plus and weighed over 250 pounds.. Shorty was an above-average wrestler, but quick to tote a handgun. Spoon much rather beat a person to death; literally. Elroy's pal Tareek decided to affiliate more with these younger guys instead of falling back or staying out of trouble as much as possible. Tareek, about the same age as Bennett, was from one of the largest family of males in the area.

As I stated before, he was one of the younger nephews of Randolph and local basketball legend Steve "Pearl" Smith or "Milk." Tareek was the most unpredictable of them all. His relationship with Elroy meant very little to Bennett and I. Tareek had an often calm, but very volatile nature. He also had a tremendous fetish for automatic handguns and assault weapons. Tareek always would show trigger-happy tendencies. He loved playing with guns. He was one of the hardest guys on the block to figure out. One day you could laugh and joke with him on any topic. The very next day, you could be lacing your shoe, look up, and be staring directly into the barrel of a 9MM handgun. He'd simply smirk at you and yell, "Fuck You!" I asked Tareek, only once, never to play that game with me again. He was aware of my cousin's tragedy. Fortunately, from then on, this made me exempt from this demented style of horse playing.

Spoon, Tareek, Shorty, and others would often mesh together with LiL Bug, his brother Harold, Antmo, and Big Bug, who nearly possessed the same physical and mental attributes as Spoon. These younger brothers only made up a third of the "soldiers" on McCabe Avenue. The rest were fairly new to the block. Two others, Nick and Killer Kev were originally from Old York Road. Nick's mom lived off of Old York Road. Kev fell out with the guys from Old York. He came around McCabe on the strength of Marcus, a former member of our old dance group. Genius met Nick in prison and brought him around to get a piece of the pie after his later release. Genius marveled about Nick's skills on the basketball court. Genius immediately made sure we both were on the same court. We had a chance to test one another to the limit. Much respect was due and given. He would always rack up all of the inside baskets, while I knocked down the jump shots in bunches. Nick was a cool older guy, but no nonsense on and off the court. Like I, Nick was a quiet guy with uncharacteristic manners for a hustler. It's not typical for a hardened dealer to ask, "How are you doing today?" "How are you feeling?" Kev was the opposite. He was loud and very vocal, a younger version of Nardo. Kev was simply "America's Nightmare." He was the type of guy who would murder, rob, steal, and deal drugs, all in the same day. Like Tareek, Kev also loved dealing with automatic firearms.

There were other new and suspicious characters in the area like Tareek's little brother Lamar, and their cousins Rob, Mel, and Dro. The list goes on in an upwards of 25-35 guys. This number does not include Etton, who was serving a brief stint in prison for a parole violation stemming from a second drug felony charge. McCabe Avenue was still a block where an outsider from an unfamiliar neighborhood should elect not to casually stroll through. In the early to mid-1990s, taking a shortcut home through McCabe Avenue may have very well cost you your life. I was engulfed in this lifestyle of violence, drugs, and total disrespect of humanity and self. The few remaining homeowners from the past were frustrated with the state of the area; praying some godly miracle would just sweep through and rid the block of all negativity. I would casually witness the frustration in them, and the hardly noticeable conferences they held amongst each other on their porches. Although I was a part of the negative activities these neighbors despised, I was thankful they would still smile and speak to me in passing. This told me, I was troubled, but not completely hopeless as I may have originally believed. I heard quite a few adults refer to the others as such.

Whenever I'd be outside hustling, I've always took the time to observe my surroundings. I was trying to be very careful of police, who began to periodically swoop down from all angles. I watched all corners and people carefully. I was thorough. The money was coming in too fast to think for very long, but I still noticed the recklessness most of the guys displayed regularly. I refused to get myself into trouble for lacking in concentration and common sense. I understood these guys were not raised the same as my peers and I. Aside from all of the many tragedies I endured, I experienced a decent childhood. Unlike many of these guys, I attended school activities, summer camps, picnics, and fun parks. Most of these guys on the block had never made it to high school and endured unloving upbringings. Now hostile and confused, guys were trying to collect or hold anyone accountable for their shortcomings, even if it meant taking a life. I honestly believed Elroy, myself and Bennett were the only guys on the block who would never take a human life. At this point, I never thought of killing another human being. Indeed, I may have been a little stupid, but I knew I was not crazy.

McCabe Avenue became a revolving door for lawbreakers. There were so many dealers there at once; you would actually forget a guy just received a lengthy prison sentence, because two others would be released during this same time. "Chip," another loose cannon, made his presence felt by perpetuating fights throughout our hood and in other neighborhoods as well. My two pals and I would co-exist in the midst of this mass of lost souls daily. We were blinded by the thousands of dollars we profited weekly. Penny and her two kids were the only reasons I decided to stop sleeping on 731's porch awaiting for addicts to come spend money from all angles. If it were not for her, I would have never gone home at night. I was becoming as addicted to the money as the users were to the product. More than once, a "sale" or an addict would tap me on my leg as I slept on my old front porch at 5:00 a.m. During this time, I was very comfortable with selling drugs on McCabe. We all were, and the guys dared anyone to try and move in on our territory. McCabe Avenue was almost like a refugee camp. However, we only held ourselves captive. We did not have to live this way, but at this time it somehow felt as if this life was all we had.

In the midst of the negativity, Penny and I drew closer. She began staying over my place more and more. I loved having a female to go home to. This gave me a sense of accomplishment; a feeling of maturity. The money was continuously coming in, leaving me with only a little time to flirt with other females. I still managed to slip by Tina's house, down the block, on occasion. I also met a real cutie up the street on Homestead. Her name was "Pumpkin." Despite my feelings for Penny, I really liked her, but she hardly ever noticed. Luckily, I was too busy in my mess to focus much on this new bombshell. She was heartbreak material indeed. I periodically would stop by her house, but things always fell into a stalemate. I still enjoyed talking to "Pumpkin." Like with Melody, the talks we had reminded me of a better time in my life. With her, I would once again be in a better place, simply enjoying the company of a very pretty girl. This was always a good experience for me, with or without the romance.

Penny and I would become exclusive as a new year approached. I realized she cared about me tremendously. It felt like decades had passed since I had a person love me wholeheartedly. After awhile, the basement area I occupied on Homestead Street would become far too small for me, Penny, and her two kids. This led to discussions about moving in together to a much larger place. My sister hated the idea of me moving in with a girl with two kids. She also was a bit concerned about having to solely fill the void for the rest of the bills. I was paying $450 a month in bills. My sister was also my friend, and she showed me positive things I could apply to my future, once I thought of one. However, she certainly could not advise me on any relationship issues. She messed up the best relationship she ever had, and I'd ever seen, only to get the tides reversed. Gina finally woke up and tried to rekindle the flame she had intentionally put out with Freddy, but it was too late. He cried his last tear, and eventually moved on with another young lady. Freddy left my sister hanging in the same terrible emotional state he had already passed through. Freddy also managed to stop selling drugs after serving a prison sentence. Freddy's decision to stop hustling, and my decision to start was the reason our communication was jeopardized; not my sister. After recovering a bit from that meltdown, my sister Gina began dating an ex-con from west Baltimore named, "Blue."

My first impression of "Blue" was not a very good one. He was very quiet; almost too quiet, giving off the same sinister aroma of armed robbers or "stick-up artists." From the start, whenever we'd cross paths, I would briefly speak to him and simply move on. I usually could feel a person out quickly, but not here. Therefore, I decided to stay out of my sister's romantic situations and concentrate primarily on making money.

As profits grew for us all, an increased presence from narcotics agents was evident throughout the area. The occasional drive-by shootings from Nut and Miran continued, and produced a few more non-fatal injuries on McCabe really forcing authorities to grow in their concern. One day, I decided to ask Elroy if he thought we should relocate our efforts elsewhere, and he lost his mind. "What?" "With all the fuckin' money we're making?" "Are you fuckin' crazy O?" "Fuck them niggas O," he added. "We'll work around that bullshit," he promised. Elroy, Bennett and I were still getting it done despite the foolish violence. We were now making over $10,000 a week on McCabe. No one was really aware of how well we were doing financially. They were all too busy chasing their own profits, getting involved with violence, and spending money on the same outfits I once wore while attending middle school.

The three of us continued to profit significantly on McCabe Avenue, but we also were able to spend a reasonable amount of downtime at home with loved ones. We made several attempts to stay clear of the violence, but for me, it was complicated due to where I now lived. I was hoping the other side would view my decision to live closer as a subliminal peace offering, but conditions continued to deteriorate. This was a direct result of Nut's desire to pull triggers at random. I soon became quite paranoid knowing I was an easy target to acquire on Homestead Street. Penny's desire to relocate to the county suddenly made a lot of sense. I knew the history; I was not interested in taking part in senseless shootings with younger guys who did not know much about the rivalry. Our profits increased weekly, but so would everything else. Again, the shootings, the fights, and the arrests were all growing in numbers. This was my life; a full-time drug dealer in Baltimore City, living recklessly in the midst of extreme violence. By this time street soldiers all over had even changed Baltimore's nickname from "Charm City" to "Harm City."

As mentioned previously, during the early-1980s and 90s, crack cocaine significantly altered the illegal drug trade in Baltimore City. However, I was still a new dealer, therefore like with other aspects of hustling, a hesitancy to switch products was evident. The raw "powder" cocaine was quickly losing its popularity on the block, but I really did not care to change over. Economically, all was still fine, but crack cocaine was overpowering the powder cocaine market at record pace. Elroy observed it all closely and suggested we too make the switch. He promised we would double or triple our profits with this decision. Therefore, after nearly six months of selling "powder," the move was made to join the others and manufacture and distribute crack cocaine on McCabe Avenue.

I believe my hesitant mannerisms involving the transition came from me knowing crack to be a much deadlier and more addictive substance than raw cocaine. I felt nothing when dealing, but I was aware of the more potent substance and the horrific tales attached to it. The exploding homicide rate, the decreased black marriage rate, and images of folks who had fallen from grace were all attributed to the crack epidemic. Thoughts were there when I was alone in bed, but there was no fear. By this time, I found a way to disconnect my heart to fully process emotions. I understood cocaine in any form was no good, and I knew crack was known to take over an entire life and turn it inside/out. I was always reluctant to change because I was never sure of where I was going or who I was. Change was always tough for me early on, whether I was going from good to bad, or from bad to terrible. I just wanted to stay put as long as I was comfortable. This was my dormant internal make-up as I began a career as a drug dealer. "O, don't worry, we'll make out much better with the 'ready' n' shit," Elroy stated. On McCabe everyone considered "crack" and "ready rock" as two in the same. "Crack" or Crack cocaine was said in the hood to have a combination of substances other than raw cocaine and baking soda. My experience is crack and ready or "Ready Rock" are one in the same. "Ready Rock" is cocaine brought into hard form with solely the assistance of the baking soda. I never saw anything added to the cocaine during preparation of the substance. I often tried not to think about all the chemicals and substances involved. I may have felt nothing 90% of the time, yet I still housed a bit of guilt for ever allowing myself to get caught up in the streets to begin with. Still, I wore my title as a crack dealer with confidence, swagger, and focus despite the internal battles. No time for sensitive and righteous thoughts here; that could cost you your life. From the very beginning, death I was close to; I was falling deeper into the web of destruction this life brings to a large number of inner-city young black males.

During this fatal version of a crossover, Elroy assured, "O, the powder shit is over, it's dead." "We don't have a choice. This crack shit is serious, and we have to get with it to stay ahead," he added eagerly. Elroy usually called things right when it came to drugs. The pushing of a newer product on the block brought along more consumers which made McCabe Avenue appear as a busy downtown intersection; talk about "rush hour traffic." I could see a difference in the significant damage this particular drug was causing. However, the love I developed from making large sums of money discarded the method used to do so. I was clear on what I was doing, but I still could not see how I was headed toward my own demise; to a point of no return.

Early on, Elroy and I would usually possess 2 to 4 ounces each. Does not sound like much, I know, but when you're moving product at a rapid pace, especially in the early 90s, profits would be decent. We were now in search of a good cook. This was the guy everyone knew who could not only stretch the product, but could also make sure it maintained its potency. There were a few "chefs" in the area, and Elroy saw to it we kept one on the payroll. His name was "Old Man." Old Man was an addict in his mid to late-30s, but appeared to be a lot older. He simply had the vision and feel for cooking cocaine. Whenever a person used Old Man to manufacture for them, they always received good feedback. Old Man knew right away, whether or not you were sold garbage or bad product. If we had a bad batch, he'd say, "Sorry fellas, but this shit is garbage." If the package was a hit, he would not say a word; he couldn't.

Some addicts would actually lose their ability to speak after inhaling very good crack. Still, Old Man was so good at cooking crack, he knew how to make bad product respectable. Of course, you always had to take a loss when dealing with poor product. Bad product certainly owned its share in the city's violence and homicide rate during this time. With our new "cook" only living two blocks east of McCabe on Chateau Avenue, near Winston, Elroy and I easily had things set in place. We were ready to open up shop on the corner directly across the street from the house I grew up in.

Selling drugs in front of the home you grew up in during better days felt weird at times. Before, I managed to ignore the decaying home, but there were a few times I actually pierced in its direction. Whenever this took place, I actually felt like my grandma was still inside, staring at me in disgust. Again, for the most part I hardly ever considered the home. Everyone inside of the house at this time took part in it all anyway. Montell and Marie were smoking crack, while BoBo and Frank still abused alcohol to no end. Surprisingly, my aunt and uncle did not appear to have much of a problem, like so many of the other addicts in the area. They still managed to take care of my two little cousins the best they knew how. They did not appear as the addicts we all observe in the movies or on television. You only noticed their struggles through their accomplishments as adults; there were not many. Neither one of them worked. Marie and Montell were not alone here, but could not gain the normal adult things; they never could keep a place, and they never possessed their own vehicle. They both usually received some type of government assistance. Still, they appeared to be much better off. I guess it is a little harder to succumb to any drug addiction quickly when you're always flat broke. The short daydreams were powerful, but realizing my grandma was not really leaning forward in her window, allowed me to proceed with minimal to no guilt while dealing. I've always found tremendous rest in knowing grandma never saw me as a drug dealer.

Profits improved drastically. Elroy and I would usually share $10,000-$15,000 worth of crack cocaine for our profit per week. With the "powder" this is what we made, not profited. We made an effort to never stash or store the drugs near where we slept. We found ourselves a place to keep the drugs. A female from the neighborhood agreed on a weekly payment of $250 to hold the drugs for us and to respond quickly whenever we needed a package. We normally would try to clear at least $500 each, everyday. Tisha, a single mother, was usually on time when we needed her. She lived directly up from "Child Study," the group home with the ball court that we no longer frequented. The only time Elroy and I handled all of the drugs was during packaging on Homestead Street. Elroy and I, along with Bennett, who mainly sold drugs on the weekends due to work and school, were moving up quickly on McCabe Avenue. We were raking in large profits, while the others were more into forming plots for the rivalry. We felt we were going along beautifully, undetected by virtually everyone, until reality drove by one day on Homestead Street.

On a late fall afternoon, Elroy and I were in my room in the basement of the two level, house apartment on Homestead Street. We were breaking down 6 ounces of crack cocaine while ironically watching the television show, "Cops." For some strange reason, Elroy loved singing the show's "Bad Boys" theme song. Because of what I was doing, I hated the song, and the program. During packaging, we feared it would be a little difficult to get rid of the product in a timely manner. Police were once again combing the area searching for handgun violators. There were two drive-by shootings on two separate days during the previous week. No one was struck or injured during these incidents. Ironically, halfway through the tedious routine of packaging, we both heard a loud blast from outside. It only took seconds for me to catch on to the sound. My head slowly dropped towards the floor as the razor blade in my right hand suddenly paused. The first word to come from my mouth was, "Shit." "What?" Elroy asked calmly. "Didn't you hear that shot?" I asked. "Yeah why?" he replied clueless. "Those bastards just shot my fuckin car," I whispered in frustration as I hopped up. "Get the hell out of here?" Elroy shockingly asked. "Yep, watch," I followed as we both quickly raced up the staircase. A few minutes later, Elroy and I were standing on the corner of Independence and Homestead Streets staring at a single, quarter sized bullet hole in the driver's side door of my car.

Elroy and I spent a few moments observing our surroundings and focusing on the sizable hole in the door of my car. "This shit is getting out of hand," Elroy stated while shaking his head. Elroy headed back towards the house, but I stood and locked in on the hole in my car door for a few more seconds. An instant daydream surfaced; the shot hitting the car a short while prior, when I was still sitting inside. Frustrated by the negligent act, I desperately wanted to know who was responsible. I was not concerned with the hole, just the principle of others thinking I was involved. I was also disturbed to entertain how someone may have wanted me dead. Although we physically did not witness anything during this shooting, I was 99.9% sure the shot came from a guy from Old York Road. I was pissed off. I figured the shooter to be one of the younger guys. I believed older guys from Old York would not take part in such a silly stunt; they had nice vehicles as well. I truly did not want to give any energy to this very intense situation, but I had to do something. I re-entered my home knowing I would likely be responding to what had just taken place.

I thought about a probable conversation with the guys on Old York before the incident, and figured I was probably viewed as a gang member in the eyes of the Old York crew. I considered going to talk to a few of the familiar faces I knew from the block. This incident had Nut written all over it. I usually didn't entertain hurting someone, but I felt this action warranted retaliation. I wanted to simply knock his teeth out. I'm an old school cat. I certainly didn't want to shoot or kill him. My spirit was dormant, not dead! Somewhere deeply rooted within, I knew the gunman was a lost soul, just like the others; just like me. Therefore, although he shot my car, I still just wanted to beat him up, but not too badly. You know, push him around a little, or make him cry or something. It really did not have to be Nut. Casper or Miran would have done just fine as well. Momentarily, I was so upset I would have liked to fight all three of them, at once. I actually really liked my chances.

Time passed by, and every time I observed the hole in my door, I felt weird. I shared the news about the incident with Bennett. Bennett was closer to the ages of these knuckleheads I wanted to beat up. He, like Tareek, possessed more of a volatile personality at times. Bennett was sort of like my cousin Shawn, but much more controlled. Ironically, he actually shared a bit of comical information with me about my cousin. In the past,

Bennett said Shawn, who was a very close friend of his cousin Nate, would often chase him home from Winston Middle School for no reason at all. He claimed Shawn did this several times. I found this to be hilarious. Bennett and I were growing closer as the negative situations began to spiral out of whack. Together, we began to make sure we were not considered to be a part of this silly but hostile group of guys.

Bennett occasionally displayed his feelings towards both, the guys from around the way, and the younger guys from Old York. We would often sit on 731's bottom three steps and specify things. "Man, all these dudes around here are chumps for real O," he said with a devilish grin. I giggled. "First of all, these dudes don't even belong here," Bennett stated with a look of certainty. "The only reason they're here is because no one gives a shit about anything anymore," he added seriously. "You know as much as I do O, Benny and the older guys from the past would not tolerate the stupid shit these punks be doing," he continued. Most of the guys on McCabe, at this point, had never met Benny, Freddy, Black, or any of their affiliates personally. A few chatted with Benny over the phone after his reign had ended, through Etton, but they had never formally met him. Benny knew nothing of these guys when he was home. However, Benny also knew he could not oversee McCabe Avenue from prison. Therefore, he connected with newer guys or whoever was there to listen via telephone. In our hood, it really did not matter who stepped up or put money in your prison account. Benny was heading into his eighth year in prison on a 50 year sentence. Understandably, if this was the exact truth, it hardly matters who a man incarcerated receives favor from.

Bennett and I conversed for an hour about the personalities of the guys on both sides. "I just want to beat one of those little niggas up from Old York," he said. "Those dudes are scared to fight head-up down there. I'll beat all of them up. They too little," he continued with a sinister smile. "I'll mess around and kill one of those dudes with one punch," he added while nodding. "BOW!" he added while demonstrating his knockout or killer punch. Listening to Bennett talk like this usually had me in stitches. I laughed so, because I knew he meant every word of what he said. Elroy often had an opposite reaction to Bennett's threatening words. His face would simply crack from the honesty in which Bennett spoke. Bennett and I connected from this standpoint. I respected his honest and stern approach, and he commended me on my ability to stay cool in very stressful situations. Bennett liked Elroy, but only to a degree. He'd often say to me, "O, Elroy play too fuckin much. I'm not with that playing around shit all the time." "All that farting and joking all the time, I can do without," Bennett stated. "I'm going to fuck around and slap the shit out of that nigga, watch." Most of these words stemmed from Elroy's latest prank, "The Hand Problem." This perverse game was similar to the original, "The Eye Problem" game, but instead of simply showing guys his penis, he would slowly walk up on the back of them, and as their arms naturally swung, he would make sure their hands came into contact with his penis. Thankfully, he never got me or Bennett with this one. Elroy played so much, guys actually took it easy on him. My pal Bennett still liked Elroy despite his pranks, but he was a rare breed for the hood; a tough guy who truly disliked thugs. He never looked for trouble like many of the others, but like my cousin Shawn, he often welcomed it with a smile whenever it presented itself.

For weeks to come, my peers and I continued to make good money hustling on the block while constantly looking over our shoulders. To make matters even more complicated, we were not exactly on the same page as the guys we hustled alongside. We were making money so fast, Bennett was now making $1000 a week. Bennett was only dealing two or three days a week, and had no intentions of hustling fulltime, but he still decided to quit his job at the Giant Food supermarket. While Elroy spent more time indoors preparing for the birth of his second born child, Bennett and I grew closer and would tackle life in the streets together. We hung out at the local clubs regularly. We also played a lot of basketball, and mingled with the pretty young ladies often. Penny even introduced Bennett to one of her close friends. Bennett and Tira hit it off pretty well, and the four of us would hang out here and there. Bennett and I would sometimes take rides to different high schools in the area, just to checkout other fine young ladies. One cool and sunny afternoon in December, we decided to venture up to my old alma mater.

Northern High School in 1993, was a far cry from the establishment I attended in the late-80s. To date, 1993 is Baltimore City's worst year in homicides, 353! Nut was trying to become the award winner for adding to these statistics. Whenever he and the other teens were not driving through

McCabe shooting either at someone or up into the sky, they were at certain local schools causing trouble. Bennett and I were in the area and decided to cruise through the circular drive/street Pinewood Drive, which curved directly in the front of the school. Northern High School (later named the Reginald F. Lewis High School of Business and Law and the W.E.B Du Bois High School of Environmental Science) was a public zone school located near the city/county line. We were also in the area because I had managed to give a couple of upper-middle class whites my pager number for the first time. On McCabe Avenue, I had secretly told a few white couples I could deliver the drugs from this point forward. I cut a few customers off at a distant corner before they made the turn onto McCabe where the other dealers awaited. I gave these folks an option so they would not have to come into such a crazy environment. They agreed. I now had these profitable couples all to myself. They would never return to the inner city to buy drugs. This new side venture was a good move considering these three couples spent about $800 each, every week on crack.

We slowly drove through Pinewood Drive observing the dozens of cuties advancing towards and by the car to get to their designated buses. I was desperately looking for Melody, who was now a senior. Bennett, he was looking for Nut. "I swear O, I hope I see that sucka." "I'm going to jump out the car right here and beat all the living shit out of him, right in front of the entire school," he said in one breath. I never saw Melody, but Bennett soon found a possible "catch." It was Casper, one of Nut's sidekicks. "There go one of those fools O," he said while pointing. "He's getting on the thirty six," he added softly. "Follow that fucka O," Bennett instructed. I didn't really care to bother Casper. He was the younger cousin of Donny. I liked Donny. However, the adrenaline and the slight possibility Casper may have been responsible for the hole my pinky finger was fondling, allowed me to pull quickly behind the bus. It was on. No matter where Casper would exit the bus, we were going to be right there waiting for him with very bad intentions.

Before Casper got on the bus he observed my car nearby. He was all alone, and cell phones were not as popular for teens during this time. Casper quickly became aware of the tail we had on the bus he was riding. He was in a tricky position because of the long distance between Northern High and Old York Road. I was sure to stay in a position to run him down quickly if he was to try and bail out at any bus stop. "O, stay behind the bus. I'm going to get this dude good son," Bennett said while anxiously rubbing his hands together. "His little ass ran out of luck today," Bennett would add with certainty while smiling. "This for all the people him and his little nappy-head ass buddies fucked with for no reason," he added while nodding. I remained relatively silent, making sure not to turn my head for a second and possibly lose Casper running away. Bennett and I unbuckled our seat belts, one behind the other, as the #36 bus finally turned right onto Argonne Drive. Despite the lengthy ride, a stroke of luck presented itself to Casper. Argonne Drive is a street opposite of Old York Road. Casper was, surprisingly, just minutes away from the corners where all his friends usually were. However, it was impossible for them to see the bus from where they were. His friends had no idea Bennett and I were so close. I pulled over on a side street near Old York, about two car lengths behind the bus, and waited. Bennett jumped out of the car and waited. Suddenly, Casper dashed from the bus!

The chase was on immediately as Casper launched himself from the bus, clearing all steps. He was instantly in a full stride. I quickly pursued Casper, quickly catching up to Bennett. "Come here you little bastard," Bennett grumbled. The three of us were running as fast as possible towards Old York Road. We both clearly underestimated Casper's foot speed. With only yards to go before Casper would reach Old York Road, Bennett and I reluctantly pulled up, and immediately began to retreat. If we would have continued this pursuit, the tides would have turned instantly. We possibly would not have made it back to my car alive. We would have possibly run directly into an ambush. "That little bastard is fast," Bennett stated while gasping for air. We both chuckled and quickly ran back to my car and quickly sped off. All the basketball and exercise I took part in meant nothing. Casper was simply too fast or too scared for us to catch. In the car we laughed about it, but this really was not very funny. Retaliation was inevitable. Casper was not timid; he was someone who would certainly strike back. We knew this before and during the attempt to capture the teen. It's a great thing we were unable to catch up to Casper. Bennett and I both knew there was a good chance Casper may have been killed if either one of us would have been a little faster.

Make no mistake, Bennett and I did not set out to kill Casper, and neither of us would intentionally kill any human being, now, or years ago.

However, we would have likely been foolish enough to beat on Casper so intensely, he may have suffered life threatening injuries. After the missed beat-down opportunity, Bennett and I parted ways. I had been involved with enough excitement for one day. I returned to Homestead where Penny was waiting patiently in my room. I shared the details with her about our chase with Casper. "Boy, you better leave that shit alone," she stated with concern. I'm leaving it alone, but those chumps should not have put a fuckin' hole in my damn car," I replied adamantly. After spending quality time with Penny, I took her to a friend's house on Greenmount Avenue, only to return home. I sat alone in my room and counted $6600 worth of $20 and $100 bills. I was building my bank account back to respectability. The $7000 I had saved came with a shady price tag. I was now viewed as a member of a reckless bunch of radicals. I was a full-time drug dealer, and I had a bullet hole in my vehicle to confirm the seriousness of the trade I practiced. I was never a violent individual, but in the streets your hand gets forced quite often. You're constantly tested, especially on a block like McCabe Avenue during the 1990s. I knew taking a life was not in the cards for me, but the violence was very real. Soon, I truly felt I needed some protection. Violent or not, I felt I needed a gun.

I was often a witness to gunfire on McCabe Avenue over the years. Still, it was hard to believe how difficult it was to get a decent gun. Outsiders believe it's easy for convicted felons to gain access to guns. They have a subtle point based on violent crime statistics, but it's far more difficult for many criminals to get a new or a clean firearm. At this time, everyone possessed a firearm. Obtaining a clean gun from one of the guys on the block was the equivalent to confessing to a murder you didn't commit; it was not happening. Most of the guns the guys had was said to be used in murders, robberies, and even sexual assaults. Others were considered to be trash or junk; meaning they were repaired by an unskilled hustler, or they would jam up easily. The guys were honest in reference to these issues.

On the block, in most cases, guys wanted everyone to know about their capers, so they were usually honest when given the status on a weapon. They were quick to say, "Man, this gun is 'dirty,' you don't want this one." There were many guns in the hood, but very few to choose from. Devon and Skippy had sold all of their weapons to guys in other neighborhoods before moving further east. I still saw all types of guns in the neighborhood.

Killer Kev possessed a 9mm he claimed once belonged to a Baltimore City police officer. I was never told how he ended up with it. It was clear asking the fellows on the block for a gun was a horrible idea. I could not help but notice how supportive these guys were with attempting to provide me with a firearm. I needed a new gun, but I was unfamiliar with who was running the gun trade in the city. Throughout, I didn't really consider guns, violence, or jail time when I entered Genius' home to begin a life of crime. At that time, all I knew; I was lost, broke, and felt I had nowhere or no one to turn to. My choice to sell drugs was opening a lot of doors I really did not want or need opened. There are so many components with the poor decision to deal drugs, and I was gradually experiencing them all.

After another financially successful week on the block, Elroy and I found ourselves back on Homestead Street, in my room chopping up nice size rocks of crack into small chucks. We both were slightly irritated with the rise in the prices for an ounce of crack. The price had soared from $900 to $1100 an ounce. On top of this, the quality of the product was not as up to par as it had been in weeks prior. In the hood, depending on what moves the federal government decides to make, or who they decided to "wash up" or arrest for good, situations like this periodically presented itself. It's very frustrating to the dealer. One time you could purchase a few ounces and the customers would rob a bank to deal with you. The very next time, you could deal with the exact same guy, and the product would have you actually owing the junkies. We endured this problem, on and off, along with the struggle to obtain a good piece of artillery or weaponry. However, I tried not to lose any sleep over either of these situations. I was more interested in where Penny was considering moving. There used to be a saying when we were young; my grandma often said, "When you want something, don't press the issue, and it will come to you when you're least expecting it to." I was learning this rule or folk tale still may have applied. It didn't really matter if I was on the good or evil side of life.

After we finished packaging up another $8000 worth of crack cocaine, we had the chance to formally meet my sister's new boyfriend, Blue. My sister was in better spirits after the emotional roller coaster she and Freddy endured had ended. The three of us, Blue, Elroy and I, shared street tales about our respective sides of B'MORE. We also learned how small Baltimore City actually is. Blue was an old acquaintance of Elroy's older uncle, Pearl. Pearl was incarcerated for a bank robbery a few years back. We soon learned Blue and the other guys from Franklintown Road were really fond of Elroy's uncle. This surprising news created a more relaxed conversation. Now, with no need to beat around the bush, we decided to ask Blue an important question. "Blue, I know we all just met and all, right, but we're dealing with some assholes on this side of town," Elroy stated calmly. Blue nodded while slowly rubbing his chin. "Do you know anyone who can get us a good 'banger'?" Elroy asked. "You need a gun?" Blue asked quietly. We nodded. "For real?" he asked. "Yes," I answered quickly. "Here's the situation. Our neighborhood is bringing us a bit of unwanted attention from outsiders," I offered. "This is for insurance purposes only," I added. We anticipated Blue would come up with a lame excuse like everyone else. It's not very often someone asks another for a gun during a first meeting or encounter.

The raspy words, "Meet me here tomorrow," whispered by Blue, really surprised Elroy and I. "Bring $250 with you," Blue instructed. "That's it? Do you have two?" Elroy asked with a smile. "Nah," Blue said with a low giggle. In just minutes, we had put in an order for a brand new, Tech 9mm, with three extra clips. "I like this guy," I said while observing Blue pull away in his black, Volvo 240. "Me too," Elroy agreed while chuckling. I was not sure if Blue was the second right guy for my older sister. He was an ex-con, once in for murder, and he had a totally different personality than Freddy. However, he appeared to be a man of his word. Although Elroy and I were successful financially on McCabe Avenue, it appeared to us both, most of the heavy hitters or most successful and focused dealers were from the westside. "I wonder if Blue knows of anybody with some good shit too," Elroy stated. "I don't know, lets find out," I replied. "Maybe he knows someone with better prices," I added. Elroy and I were probably the only two guys from McCabe least likely to shoot at another human being. The desire to carry a firearm came strictly from not knowing when someone from Old York would strike. I did not wish to hurt anyone, ever really. I was already hoping one of the guys from the other neighborhood would not make another move. I truly did not care to hurt or kill a human being, but if I were to be placed in an awkward position, I was sure I would not hesitate.

Blue kept his word and showed up at the house-apartment on Homestead Street with my sister around 8:20 p.m. on the very next day.

Elroy and I were on the porch eating submarines from a popular carry-out named Venus,' ironically on Old York's territory. Oh yeah, we called in this pick-up order! We hurried and chased our food down with Kool-Aid, directly after receiving a slight nod from Blue as he and my sister passed by going inside. After a five-minute wait in my bedroom, Blue came down the basement with a black duffle bag. The sound of a second pair of foot steps followed. "What are y'all doing?" Gina suspiciously asked. "Chill out!" I replied loudly. "It's cool," Blue said in a lower tone. "Go back upstairs please," Blue insisted. "Everything is cool Gina," Elroy stated while giggling. "It better be," Gina said while retreating. Inside of the bag was a silver box. Blue opened the case and there it was, a brand new, Tech 9mm, semi-automatic weapon. "It's nice ain't it?" Blue stated with a grin. "Hell yeah," Elroy answered in excitement. "Well, it's yours. Do you have the money on you?" Blue asked. I silently handed him the $250. "Cool, let me know if y'all need anything else," Blue offered. "Oh yeah, do you know of anyone with some 'girl'? I asked. "'Hard' or 'soft'?" Blue replied. This meeting inside of my bedroom was not exactly "boardroom material." This was big time "Hood Business 101,' and we were in the midst of handling it.

In drug terminology, "hard"= crack, "soft"= powder or raw cocaine. "Don't matter," Elroy and I said together in reference to Blue's question on preference. "I can get y'all some real good powder for $900 an ounce," Blue offered. "Oh shit! When?" Elroy shouted. "Whenever," Blue answered. "Cool, we'll call you later on tonight," Elroy stated. "Alright, let me know," Blue said before hurrying up the steps. "I like this guy," I stated. "I love that guy," Elroy followed. In less than two days we were connected to a guy who had better prices on cocaine, and he provided us with a serious piece of artillery. Elroy and I were likely two of the cooler hustlers in Baltimore City during its worst period, but make no mistake, we were getting things done; we were still ready for whatever. We had to be!

Holding the silver, semi-automatic in my hands for the first time gave me a weird adrenaline rush. The assault weapon reminded me of something I'd seen on The Terminator movie. For $250, Blue also threw in a few extra clips and plenty of rounds. Smiling with eyes opened wide, Elroy quickly reached for the gun. "Let me hold that sucka O?" he asked in excitement. As Elroy pretended to be Scarface in my bedroom mirror, I heard a slight rumble above. It was my little niece Lia running in the living room above. "Yo, you keep the gun," I insisted. "I don't want it here," I added with certainty. "We'll determine who will carry the gun later," I insisted. "Alright, I got it," Elroy replied. No matter how engulfed I was in this lifestyle, I would continuously have these quick flashes of decency. These weird feelings would normally only last for a few seconds. In spurts, In spurts, I would simply do what's best, but still proceed with the opposing matter at hand. My conscious periodically would tell me I may have been in over my head, but everything else simply allowed me to ignore all of the warning signs.

Another meeting was set for us to begin dealing exclusively with my sister's new boyfriend, Blue. I had a plan to expand our enterprise on McCabe. Blue promised us the product he possessed was by far, much more superior than any on the eastside. Elroy and I knew Genius' product was not the best. All the other connections we were affiliated with were not always easy to contact. A few of them were afraid to deal with any guys from McCabe Avenue. McCabe Avenue's reputation compromised many business opportunities in the streets. Major distributors did not want to deal with guys from McCabe, because of the fear of unwanted heat while others feared being set-up or robbed, or even killed. With plans to elevate in the hood, Elroy and I would make strides to be atop the best distributors of crack on McCabe Avenue. Everyone was looking for something better for their money. Tainted and confused, I stepped my game up above most on McCabe Avenue, in less than a year of dealing drugs.

After making a transaction with Blue for seven ounces of cocaine, Elroy and I spent most of the day with Old Man. By the time the product had air-dried, everyone was out on the block. Elroy and I agreed not to share our new connection with anyone. We wanted the product to speak for itself. We knew the crack on the block was shaky or not very good. Genius continued to stretch his product to its limits. Guys on the block were hoping Etton's upcoming release would, again, open things up or produce better results on the block. Etton was one of the few popular guys from the block. He knew a few other connections throughout the city. He would be back on the block in less than a month. For now, it was our turn to shake things up a bit. With the new product we brought to the corner, making $1000 a day became average. The product we scored from Blue would prove to be a huge success. Heads quickly began to turn our way.

The others were amazed how fast things were elevating for Bennett, Elroy and I. As they all began to focus on us, we were turning towards each other in amazement. It took us three days to sell five of the seven ounces of crack; all packaged in all $20 sacks. That's about $12,000 cash!

By the time Etton returned home, Elroy and I were enjoying the profits of a $10,000-$15,000 a week income. It seemed as if we were making the most money strictly because we lived on the block the longest. With the rivalry gradually rising, our own climb remained virtually undetected by authorities as they appeared to have shifted focus more on violent perpetrators. By the end of the summer, Elroy and I were on top. In the midst of the growth, we never lost sight of the possibility of jealousy from others on the block. All we had was each other. Bennett was down as well. Two of Elroy's most controversial brothers were incarcerated. Another entered the armed services, and his oldest brother Ty became a victim of the substance we were dealing. The security blanket we had enjoyed for most of our teen years was torn. Luckily, the beef had consumed most of the personalities on the block, therefore everyone seemed fine with our progress. Soon, they all came running to Elroy and myself to enhance their own incomes. It had only been a short time since I had received that "quarter" from Genius. Now we were being approached with orders for crack by virtually everyone. Whoever wanted the best product on the northeast side of B'MORE, came to see us first.

# *Chapter 14*

# FULL ECLIPSE

lroy and I were producing five figure incomes while dealing exclusively with my sister's relatively new boyfriend, Blue; an ex-con from the Franklintown Community in west Baltimore. Blue was surprised by how quickly we moved the product. He was clueless to where McCabe Avenue was located. A lot of folks heard of McCabe, but few knew about its actual location. Meanwhile, the senseless drive-by shootings and club brawls continued. We tried to stay exclusively concentrated on the finances, but the violent element began to seriously interfere with our routine. On McCabe, the violence was evident beyond the feud. Unbelievable incidents also began to sprout up internally within the neighborhood. Younger guys were beating up the addicts for owing them no more than $10. On one occasion, Elroy and I observed Killer Kev running top speed, shooting at Nut as he drove through the block; it was broad daylight. Dozens of small children were outside screaming and scattering about. At night, dealers still used the street lights for target practice; creating more darkness to evade police easier. Things were getting out of hand, and it would only be a matter of time before Elroy and I would truly feel the impact of the negativity we were a large part of.

Due to the increased violence on the block, we decided to work in much smaller increments. Normally, I would try to handle a stash or sandwich bag filled with no more than $500 worth of crack to get rid of. With increased police activity due to the violence, I only felt comfortable with $300-$400 worth of product with me at a time. I figured this would allow me to get done sooner and evaluate whether or not to return to the block later. I was fortunate to have three prominent couples in the county contacting me regularly for crack. The $800-$2400 a week I received from an income-tax business owner, his brother-in-law, and his best friend were considered extras. This was my own personal endeavor. This move initially came about because I had an inclination that the end was drawing nearer in the neighborhood. I knew trouble loomed ahead, but the money was coming so steadily, I hardly thought of this probable end, or any of the negativity. I believed I was at such a low; no matter how testy things were becoming, I still had no plans to pull myself out.

After making thousands of dollars throughout the year, I received confirmation from an unwanted source how well I was doing at remaining under the law's radar. My run as a dealer had been trouble free from the start. I had not experienced any run-ins with police. Practicing how to conduct most of my transactions in the alleyways helped. Most of the guys were much bolder with their approach. They did everything out in the open. I always tried to be cautious of authorities. I had respect for the authorities, always. Although my life was a mess, I managed to use a few ideas or character traits I practiced from better days, to conceal things more and create a better flow with my hustle.

Drug dealing is based mostly on greed; my hustle was based on a depressed state of being. Still, I was able to offset the greed by implementing decent qualities to an unpleasant lifestyle. Although I was a drug dealer, core values grandma instilled were still embedded just not practiced very well. I applied these to drug dealing. This is how the prominent clientele manifested. Yes, I also felt a bit ashamed periodically. There were times I did not want any of the few decent citizens left on McCabe to observe me dealing drugs. Again, no matter how much money I made hustling, selling drugs was always a bit embarrassing for me whenever I took a second to think about it; not very often.

The confirmation of the success of this new unique brand of hustling came one afternoon on the block. I was approached by a car full of undercover officers on McCabe Avenue. I was calm when the officers pulled up to me, because I had finished my stash an hour prior. I felt pretty good about my ability to remain discrete. However, this sudden meeting had little to do with me. The police stopped to briefly chat with me about my buddy, Elroy. As soon as the officer known as "Serge" said, "Where's Elroy?" while smiling, I said to myself, "Damn, Elroy's hot."

Serge was a white male; a "go for broke" or relentless narcotics agent who made every dealer in northeast Baltimore nervous whenever his name surfaced. Every inner city has one or two officers who know how to play the drug game very well; they have the know-how to gain victories over the dealers more times than not. Serge was not onto me just yet, and he knew all who were involved with drugs on McCabe. Over the years, I've been amazed how drug dealers actually believe the cops are clueless about their identification. Crazy! Sorry brothers, but they likely know who you are. In most cases, they know exactly who you are, and they know all of your brothers and cousins who also sold drugs. When in need of an answer to a question always place yourself in the opposition's shoes. If I were an officer, I would know to do my job well enough to locate the identity of every guy who hung out in a drug infested neighborhood. It's not very hard to determine what an unemployed, homeless, high school drop-out with an attitude may be up to, really.

The conversation or encounter I had with Serge only lasted for a few minutes with me only hunching my shoulders to answer Serge's question in reference to Elroy's whereabouts. The other officers were trying to get a good look at me as he spoke. I was unfamiliar to them all. Two of the officers inside the car were looking at me strangely, already figuring I may be involved as well. I could read their minds through their expressions. It did not help my cause to be dressed in all new clothing, and the latest Michael Jordan sneakers. "We're gonna get your friend Elroy, and when we do, he's going away for a long, long time," Serge promised with a satanic grin. "You may not want to be around him as much. He's trouble. He's a drug dealer, and thinks he's bigger than the law. He believes we'll never get him," he insisted while smiling. "Don't hang around that guy! He's been selling drugs for a long time, and I would hate to see you get in trouble with him," he said smiling. The unmarked, blue Chevy Cavalier pulled off slowly with the other two officers in the rear seat. They were oddly piercing backwards at me as they drove towards York Road. I stood in the middle of the street in silence; in shock. I was wondering how could a younger white police officer sound strikingly similar to a deceased older black woman, my grandma, as he spoke to me. "What a difference a day makes," I said in a low tone while shaking my head. "O, What them bitches say to you man?" Genius asked from his porch. "They were talking about Elroy. They're onto him," I stated with disappointment. "Man, yeah they're watching his silly ass." They always have been. He's 'hot' O! Shit, we all are!" Genius confirmed. Not only was the block hot, so was my partner.

Later, I caught up with Elroy at his home and we discussed the run-in I had with the cops. "Man, you 'on fire,' I stated in concern. "Fuck those cops O man. I'm not worried about them. They don't have shit on me O," he replied emphatically. "That guy Serge has it out for you buddy," I offered. "I know," he replied as he laughed. "He's mad he can never catch me doing anything. A bitch! It's killing him," Elroy explained. Elroy was hardly concerned about the police. It had always been my understanding; if you're selling drugs, you should really try hard to remain anonymous. I realize this is very hard to do, but there seems to be a lack of effort in this department for dealers. I also believed if you're "hot" or being looked at, naturally you should soon leave that particular neighborhood. None of these rules applied on McCabe Avenue. Elroy may not have been a violent lawbreaker, but at times, he could be just as reckless as all the others. "O, I'm going to keep doing what I been doing, making this dough. They can't stop me pal," he stated boldly. "I'm like that new producer; that cool new dude from New York, Puff Daddy!" "I'm never goin' to stop!" "My sister read about him in a magazine; she told me about him." I had to laugh at the timing of that joke, but seriously, nothing was funny. The money was coming to us in droves, the violence was escalating, and police were getting annoyed. I was in deep, and on one damp night, I would literally fall in even deeper.

I left home one evening after conversing with Penny about moving. She planned to begin searching for our new place after the Christmas holiday. On most rainy days I would stay indoors, but I became addicted to making money in any form of weather. I had close to $9000 saved and thousands of dollars worth of product at Tisha's. We increased her pay to $350 a week for her efforts in helping us keep home clean. I got to the block just as the daylight would dissipate. I only withdrew $200 worth of crack from our safe at Tisha's home. After arriving on the block, I quickly made $100 in less than thirty minutes. I thought of going back to Tisha's after making another $50 just five minutes later. I walked towards 731 with intentions on first using the bathroom, when suddenly I observed a patrol car approaching slowly without headlights. Unlike the encounter I had with the undercover officers days prior; this time, I was "dirty." I had five, $20 baggies in my "dip" or down the front of my sweatpants. I was four houses from 731's front steps when the police car stopped at my side. I walked slowly, but my heart rate sped up. For the first time ever, I was confronted by police while holding drugs. For years trouble had been all around me on McCabe, but the time had come for it to finally land right at my door step.

My face was mostly covered by a hooded sweatshirt I wore only for protection from the misty precipitation. I took a glance at the patrol car while continuing to walk towards my old home. "Hey son, come here for a minute," one of the two officers insisted. I stopped walking, but did not advance towards the patrol vehicle. "Do you have a gun on you son?" the officer asked while exiting the car. His hand was on his gun. As the officer approached, I panicked and took off running in the opposite direction. "Hey, freeze! Don't move!" the officer yelled. I continued to run only to suddenly notice four other uniformed officers were coming from all angles. I was cornered. Only one or two others were outside, but no one was close to the incident. I continued to run, but soon ran out of real estate. I had drugs in my possession, and was running directly towards one of the officers. With officers closing in on me, I only knew of one thing to do.

When Shawn and I were small kids we would wish we could fly by pretending bath towels were our capes. As the police surrounded me as I tried to run away, it was clear only high elevation could have given me a way out of this situation. Nervous and confused, the only thing I could do was pretend to be Pittsburgh Steelers' running back, Franco Harris, as I often did as a young kid. I ran with all the force I had in me, head on, directly into one of the officers. I dislodged his glasses and violently knocked him onto the wet blacktop.

After this very hard collision, a brief opening presented itself, but I was not able to take advantage of it as the Hall of Fame running back once could. The hole closed very quickly. While on his backside, the officer reached up and grabbed my left foot, causing me to stumble onto the damp street. Before I could look up, there were at least five officers all over me. One immediately placed his knee in my back, while the others held my arms. Everything was happening so fast, but I'll never forget turning and observing a huge white fist, wearing an unfamiliar school ring, approaching the right side of my face with much force. I was punched hard in the face, but still conscious; I was stood upright and searched thoroughly. I stood, wet and battered as policed retrieved the stash of five bags from my sweats. Montell suddenly made his way out onto the front porch just in time to see this embarrassing situation unfold. "Odell, are you alright?" Montell asked just as the police wagon approached. "Yeah, I'll be alright. I'm going to jail though," I replied in distress. "For what?" he asked. "Drugs!" I replied while stepping into the wagon. "Damn O," Montell stated. I was on my way to jail for a first time, for my very first drug charge, and this was just the very beginning.

I had settled down by the time I reached the Baltimore City Jail. I was booked and charged with possession of crack cocaine. I was not charged with dealing or distribution, due to the quantity, and the fact I was not caught in the act of selling. The surprise came when I realized I was also being charged with a felony for assaulting one of the male officers. I did not intentionally mean to hurt the officer, although it appeared as such. I was just very nervous. I ran into the officer out of fear. I sat in jail for two days before going before a court commissioner. Having a completely clean criminal background at 19 or 20 years of age was rare on my block; a reality that obviously had its advantages. The surprisingly nice commissioner listened to my side of the story and decided to release me on my own recognizance. Unfortunately, I still was faced with having a criminal adult record for the first time ever. I brought the year 1993 in with a misdemeanor conviction for drug possession. Thankfully, the officer involved during the arrest elected to drop the assault charge. I received six months of probation for possessing a little more than $100 worth of crack cocaine. I also had to perform 80 hours of community service. I apologized to the officer, before thanking him for not pursuing the more serious violent felony charge originally set against me. I could not offer an act of sympathy for the drug charge. I was still guilty. Even worse, I knew immediately after I left the courtroom, I would pick right back up where I had left off.

Whether good or bad, I've always been pretty good at disclosing a situation I did not care to let out. My arrest had come and gone so quickly, it was as if it were a short nightmare. Only the frustrations of cleaning up old syringes and dirty diapers at Perkins Projects downtown, for community service, would bring my situation to real life. Cleaning at the projects for my probation hardly made me regret selling drugs. At this time, I struggled to realize I may have actually been disturbed mentally and emotionally. All I could think of was how much I did not care to work, and how much money I was missing out on while servicing the community for my crime. I tried to act as if I was never arrested. Police were called in on the night of my arrest solely because someone claimed a guy in a dark, hooded sweatshirt was toting a firearm. The police were not even there on a drug sting. As far as I was concerned, I received this charge because I was new to the game. "I slipped up!" was my rational approach to my only charge. "I panicked!" I told myself. "Now, I know what to do," is what I forcefully said to myself. Just like with the initial ideal of dealing itself, I somehow had relocated the word "never." I said to myself: "This will never happen again!"

I continued to sell drugs on McCabe with Elroy and the money was coming in faster than ever. We still were responsible for assisting Genius and the others with getting the best possible product. I could now do things my way. The pressure to stay grounded or straight had been sadly eliminated with poor decisions and the death of my grandmother. I felt I really did not have anyone, except myself, yet I hardly knew who I was during this time. Every other person in my life, I felt were only characters that didn't care or existed on the extended path of wrongdoings in my life. To me, everyone were figures involved with my lifestyle, a way of life I should have never been a part of. There were no people to look up to. There were no role models. I was surrounded by dozens of confused people who had no idea what life was all about. During this time, I constantly found time to share laughs with several beautiful young ladies, but I was lonely as ever. I was in a relationship, but I was lost, lonely, and miserable, all while making several thousands of dollars a week.

Spring of 1993 drew nearer, and Elroy and I were supplying most of the block with crack cocaine purchased from my sister's boyfriend, Blue. The quality of the product scored from Blue made everyone content. There was more than enough money to be made on McCabe for everyone. Still, along with this money came more police patrols and more violence. Etton returned to McCabe, and so did Elroy's older brother, Nardo; both released from prison. Their older brother Steve was in on weapons charges, and set to make his return in a couple of years. The feud between Old York Road and McCabe Avenue was ever present. No one had been hurt or killed recently, but there were a few very close calls. I still found myself diving on the concrete more times than I can recall, avoiding stray bullets. However, the violence I noticed more still came from within the confines of the neighborhood.

Sitting on 731's steps taking small breaks allowed me and my two buddies to witness quite a few disturbing instances on the block. We would witness one of the guys slap a female who was short on funds for drugs. One guy even jumped up and kicked a woman in her head while wearing swim shoes, for owing him a few dollars. "Aqua-Man bitch!" Tavon, another young dealer, yelled as he violently kicked the woman. Guys were laughing, but the humor in the matter actually came with the female addict's response. "Hey, are you fuckin' crazy man?" she yelled while holding her head in pain. "You need to be in "Preppard Shack" or something." Although I felt for the woman, I burst into laughter at her response. The young woman meant to say, "Sheppard Pratt," which happens to be a facility for disturbed or mentally and physically challenged individuals. Genius even got into the act of violence. He struck a heavy-set woman in the back with a two-by-four for cursing him out one afternoon. I also watched him knock a guy out with a short thick pipe, by creeping up on him from a hidden entrance to an alleyway. Genius was simply taking up for one of the others.

Old York Road was viewed as McCabe's biggest adversary, but there was always an internal war brewing on McCabe Avenue within itself. Unlike those from Old York, guys from McCabe were not all familiar with one another as kids, as Elroy, Bennett and I were. Everyone appeared to be on the same page, but I observed many instances indicating the exact opposite. We all had a common goal to make lots of money, but it was very clear to me, these guys were far from being true friends.

One spring afternoon, I sat on the porch on McCabe talking to Elroy and Bennett. We were growing quite disturbed by the unnecessary violence taking place on the block. It was slightly stifling business while creating a gap between the three of us and the others. "Man these dudes round here make me sick," Bennett calmly stated. "I know," I replied. Elroy simply shook his head. "The dumb shit messing with our money," Elroy offered.

"This shit can't last for too long, I hope," I pleaded. "I don't know O, it's not getting any better," Bennett stated. Just as he finished his statement, we all observed Rick approaching. Rick, Bennett's next door neighbor, was another one of the many young hustlers on the block. He was smiling as he drew closer. "Yo, Yo, ya'll wanna see a dead body?" he asked with certainty and a grin. "Man, you sound like the little kid from the movie, Boyz n the Hood," I replied with a slight grin. Even in my mess, I religiously referenced my interests in films. "I'm for real man, there's a man in the alley, dead," he assured us all. "Get the fuck outta here man!" Elroy shouted. "I'm serious. Come and see, watch!" Rick instructed.

We all quickly got up to see exactly what Rick saw around the backside of the block. Rick was Bennett's next door neighbor, but the two never hung out. He was not one of the bigger troublemakers as the others were. He was mostly interested in fighting pit bull terriers, smoking Cannabis, and occasionally robbing guys in the surrounding neighborhoods for their riches. We once observed Rick kill a pit bull for losing a fight with another dog. He shot the large white dog with a.45 automatic handgun, killing it instantly. We followed Rick through an alley we all used as a shortcut to get to the local McDonald's. As we walked quickly, I could hear a chopper off in the distance. About 20 yards ahead, we all could see a body lying in the tall grass. We all began to jog towards the body, anxious to see if we recognized the person. An addict we all called "Peanut" suddenly appeared from the other end of the alleyway as we drew closer. We reached the body of a man and realized he was still alive. "It's Mr. Darwin," I uttered as I stared. "Shit, 'Painter Man,'" Elroy stated as Bennett froze in silence. This was the nickname Elroy humorously gave the addict, but this visit was no laughing matter. He had been shot once, directly in the head.

Throughout all of the close calls and violent fights I witnessed, I never expected to see up close, in my lifetime, a man on his back with a bullet enlarged in his forehead. "I told y'all," Rick stated. "Y'all thought I was lyin'," he stated. "Nah, I was just hoping you were," I stated while gazing down at the body. "Did anyone call for help?" I stated. "Yeah, they're on the way," Peanut assured. We could soon hear police sirens in the area. "Here they come now," Bennett stated. "I'm leaving. I hate cops," he added. Mr. Greg Darwin was a professional painter, and substitute teacher who periodically came through McCabe to score a 20 sack or two of crack.

The drug does not discriminate. The same guy who acknowledged my academic wit in high school was also a crack addict, now on his backside in the brush clinging to life. "Greg, Greg, Greg!" Peanut yelled while bending over. I stared attentively as the body slightly quivered. His eyes were rolled back into his head. "He can hear you," I said to Peanut. "Greg!" "Can you hear me?" Peanut yelled out emotionally. Elroy left shortly afterwards. I glanced back and forth between the emotional but high addict Peanut, and his convulsing friend in his mid-40s. The bullet was still visible in Mr. Greg's forehead. Blood trickled from the wound as he continuously shook in the lengthy grass. I looked into the sky and observed what appeared to be a Shock Trauma chopper, trying to locate the scene of the incident. I slowly backed away in amazement before heading back out to the front. Police and paramedics soon followed, but it was all for nothing. Mr. Darwin or "Painter Man" we all often called him, died at the hospital shortly after arriving.

There were some speculations about how "Painter Man" ended up in the brush with a hole in his head. Talks of a missing stash of heroin surfaced. Everyone immediately assumed who may have been responsible for the hit. "Drez" was one of two heroin dealers on McCabe. He never conducted business in the same block we all were in. He usually stayed to himself. I knew him pretty well. He had been a resident of McCabe even before my family moved there. My sister Gina would hang out with his sister during the early 1980s. Drez, like Bennett, was not very fond of the way the block had turned out. He did not care for any of the newer guys on the block. It was rare to see Drez converse with anyone. Even when he would speak to me on the block, not many words would follow. "What's up O?" Drez would say. "What's up buddy?" I would reply. "Are you alright out here?" he would usually ask. "I'm cool," I would reply. Drez always spoke in a soft tone and could never look me directly in the eyes. Everyone knew Drez and his two younger brothers were not to be taken lightly with anything. Speaking with him a few days after the murder made me feel he may have had knowledge of the incident, but I really didn't know. I personally liked Drez, but I strongly felt, if he did pull the trigger or know something, he may have punished the wrong guy. Who steals $2000 worth of heroin and return to the same area, short on cash, to buy a $20 bag of crack? I believed Mr. Darwin's death was a direct result of ignorance and rumors.

Experiencing shootings and witnessing deaths were becoming normal occurrences for me during the early 1990s. I observed so much negativity I actually became a bit numb to it. I sort of expected it. It concerned me a bit, but I never felt much of a need to panic. I was more focused on making money and spending as much time with Penny as possible. I really enjoyed the peaceful moments I shared with her and her two children. This was the only time I felt like a normal person. The rest of the time I simply feltlike an unfortunate, fill-in in a disturbing and very sad hood movie. This was truly bad news, because at times, I felt the life I lived was the best there was.

Despite more arrest attempts made by police, and a few more random shootings, the money situation remained stable for us all. Thousands still poured in each week. The one noticeable problem we faced came from the undercover agents. They were really displaying their ill feelings towards my partner, Elroy. I sat and repeatedly watch Serge threaten Elroy from the porch. "Elroy, we're going to get you," he'd say while smiling. "You're going away for along time pal," he stated while driving by. "Leave me alone man. I'm not doing anything," Elroy stated once. "You're a drug dealer, and we're going to lock you up and throw away the key buddy," Serge insisted. Elroy was so hot, Serge never even bothered to jump out on him as he would with the others. They knew Elroy was too sharp to be caught easily. They knew in order to catch Elroy they would have to put a plan into place. Elroy truly believed he could not be caught selling any amount of drugs of significance, no matter what tactics were used by the authorities.

Summer 1993 exploded full throttle with drug dealing and violence throughout the Govan's Community and Baltimore City. Elroy and I were still responsible for the majority of the crack in the neighborhood. Everyone was making substantial amounts of money; courtesy of Blue's product. There only seemed to be one major issue with this operation. After months of scoring kilos of cocaine from Blue, most of the guys began to complain. Not with the quality; they were all curious as to when they would receive deals or discounts. I spoke to both Genius and Etton one night after a few games of basketball at Dewee's Playfield, on this issue. "O, let us talk to you man," Genius stated with a slight grin. "Yeah man," Etton followed. I sat between the two on a bench at the court. "What's up guys?" I replied while slightly out of breath. "What's going on with your boy son?" Etton asked. "I know we're all making money, but this shit is crazy," Genius offered. "We're spending a hell of a lot of cash with dude, and there's never a break in the price," Genius stated in disappointment. "Is the nigga greedy or something O?" Etton asked."We all are fellas." I offered calmly. "For real O man, take care of that!" Genius added. "I'll check into it fellas. I don't know why he wouldn't offer any deals by now," I stated calmly. "Yeah, get on top of that please. That nigga's going to make us take all his shit O," Etton stated in frustration. "Yo, take care of that for us man," Genius stated as we parted ways. "Alright, I will holla at him later," I replied. "Alright O!" "Nice game," Genius stated with a nod. The two then hopped in a car and pulled off quickly. Blue had been charging the guys the same price for months, and their patience with getting a better deal with the prices was wearing thin. They needed answers, and since it was my connection, I was sent to ask the questions. By the mid-90s I was entrenched in the drug game. I never believed I could be as comfortable as I was with selling crack. It seemed like just days earlier, B-Mack was telling me and my friends to get off of the corner so we could stay out of harms way. Now, I was far down the wrong road, and going nowhere good. To a certain degree, I was B-Mack.

Before going directly to Blue for information, Elroy and I decided to check things out for ourselves first. Elroy had once made a comment about how Blue handled his business. "O, I don't think the shit is his man. He's way too long-winded," Elroy stated. Elroy believed a third party was involved. This would explain the slow pace Blue operated in, and the fixed prices he never altered. Later, these assumptions were confirmed through a five-minute chat I shared with my sister Gina, as she prepared to go to work one morning. My sister knew I was a drug dealer, but hardly ever cared to talk about it. She would make small comments about me getting a job, but never pressed the issue. My sister loved me regardless. I guess she never tried to talk to me about drug dealing much because all of the guys she dated, at one time or another, all dealt drugs.

Despite preparing to move, I was still helping Gina out with my niece and paying all of my bills early. Although my sister knew where I stood, I was still embarrassed to converse with her about any details surrounding my drug dealing. Again, these conversations were virtually non-existent, but for the few moments the topic arrived, I would usually shift the conversation on her relationship with Blue. Only this time, I kept it short and simple. "Blue's doing pretty good in the streets hah?" I asked. "I guess so," she replied sarcastically. "He's alright. It's not like that though," Gina stated. "What do you mean?" I asked. "Blue is not the one with all the drugs and the money," she insisted. "No?" I replied. "No, it's some dude named Scott," she offered with certainty. "That's not Blue's stuff," she stated. "It all belongs to a guy named Scott," my sister informed casually. "Scott?" I asked for clarity. "Yep!" Gina replied while folding clothes. This was all I needed to know. I called Elroy later that day stating, "Yo, we need to head west." The dude we need to see name is Scott."

As we got set to take the trip to west Baltimore, more drama was unfolding on McCabe. Elroy's out of control brother Nardo, had clashed heads with Drez over his heroin profits on the block. Nardo, along with a guy we called "Baby Chris," grew jealous of the success Drez was experiencing dealing heroin in the 600 block of McCabe Avenue. The two instructed Drez to leave the neighborhood or close down his operations on the corner. Drez was born and raised on McCabe. He lived on the block before many there ever heard of the street. Understanding the number of guy she would be up against, he supposedly obliged. A few hours later, a black, pickup truck sped down McCabe with four masked occupants. Two guys sat in front seats while two others rested backwards, in the bed of the truck, strapped with semi-automatic weapons. Shots were fired in broad daylight, striking Baby Chris several times, including once in the neck area. The incident took place directly in front of 731's doorstep. By the time Elroy and I returned from Franklintown Road, Baby Chris was dead.

We all knew Baby Chris well. He and Tray were really close. He too hustled in the area, and was also a very close friend of Elroy and Bennett's cousin, Nate. As I walked towards my old home, I observed the aftermath of the shooting. The gutter in front of the house appeared as if someone poured a few gallons of transmission fluid down into it. Most of the neighborhood observed Chris as he bled to death in a matter of minutes. The information we had obtained was placed on hold as we were brought back to reality. Tray, Baby Chris, and my cousin Shawn were all very friendly with each other. They all were young, Black, and now dead from gunshot wounds.

Many speculated Drez orchestrated the hit. Old York Road guys never wore masks. They wanted the guys from McCabe Avenue to know who was trying to kill them. People also believed Penny's ex, Craig accompanied Drez, along with two other guys from the area. No one knows for sure! Elroy's brother Nardo was said to be the attended target, but he somehow slipped away just minutes before the hit. The shooters settled for Chris. He was the only person shot or shot at during the incident. Again, this is pure speculation. Drez took the high road and left the neighborhood he grew up in all together.

After attending Chris' funeral, my sixth in as many years, we got back to business. Elroy and I made the profitable decision to cut out the middle man. Blue had turned us all on to the best product, but we saw an opportunity for promotion. When we landed west, we were directed by a guy who stood post near the alleyway he forwarded us to. We learned of Scott's whereabouts and found ourselves in an alleyway, full of westside hustlers gambling. One head after another popped up as each guy observed my unfamiliar Toyota coming to a stop. Elroy grew very nervous, but I was calm. I knew we had some exciting news to share with this guy Scott. We assumed through Blue that Scott already knew where we were from, although he had never paid a visit to McCabe. Hustlers always know where their money comes from, especially when it's in the high five/six figures.

As soon as I drove to a stop in the alleyway, Elroy stated nervously, "Yo, let's get the hell outta here man, they don't know us," "Not yet they don't, but they will in a minute," I replied while stepping out of the car. "Man, you're crazy," I heard from Elroy just as I closed the car door on his words. I believed my short sleeved Polo shirt, white shorts, and new, Nike Air Max sneakers spoke volumes to all of the players at the dice game. "Excuse me guys!" "Has anyone seen Scott?" I asked calmly. "Yeah," a guy replied. "Hold up," he added with a quick glance upwards. There I stood on the west side of B'MORE, watching the amplified version of a dice game. The amounts of money differed from the cash the guys in my hood played with. So was the mood. Everyone here was much more controlled, quiet or laid back. They all seemed to be more focused and very observant. Out of respect, I walked several paces backwards and leaned up against my vehicle. Elroy was still too nervous and not ready to exit my car, but I signaled a "thumbs up" to ease him a bit. Several minutes later, I watched a clean-cut guy pull away from the game. It was Scott. This guy had McCabe Avenue in his palms without ever stepping foot at its location. Scott was the person who controlled McCabe's crack business. To make everything even more interesting, he was only 19 or 20 years old.

Scott represented a different type of 19 or 20 year old in B'more; one we were not very accustomed to. He was cool, calm, quiet, and very successful at dealing drugs and keeping his nose clean. We talked with Scott for an hour, sharing information while feeling each other out. Scott was not too familiar with McCabe, but mentioned he once heard of a neighborhood in an area that was "crazy!" he put it. "That's where y'all be at?" he asked. "I heard those guys are wild, he stated. "People say they be ova there killin each other n shit for nothin," he added smiling. "Is it like that?" he asked. "Is that where y'all are?" "It's something like that, but we don't take part in the foolishness," I replied embarrassingly. "I see there's a lot of money there though," he stated. "Blue can't keep up with y'all, can he?" Scott asked. "That's one of the reasons we're here," I stated calmly. "Guys are getting mad with how slow he moves, and with the prices," Elroy stated. "He claims it's his product," Elroy added. "What?" Scott yelled while smiling with frustration. All of the other participants of the dice game reacted when Scott raised his voice. They soon realized we were just talking; not arguing, but Scott's facial expressions and body language told us that Blue was bluffing us all along.

After hearing details about our affiliation with Blue, Scott replied, "That's crazy." "I'm going to pull him up on that one," he added. "Blue just came home a while ago. I was just helping the nigga get on his feet," Scott emphasized. "He don't have shit," he implied. "It's all me," Scott assured us. "What was he chargin' y'all an ounce?" Scott wondered. "$900!" I replied. More sarcastic laughter followed. "This nigga is crazy," Scott said calmly. "$900 an ounce?" he asked. "Well, this day ends his little game," Scott stated. "I'll holla at the dude, but we'll deal face to face from now on," he insisted. "Excuse me," followed. Scott walked over to a new Lexus with a very cute female inside. He spoke briefly with the beauty and returned. "Go back to your hood and do what you need to do, and call me tomorrow," Scott stated. "I'll tighten y'all up," he said. As we pulled away from the dozen west side hustlers, our connection with Blue had ended. Our operation had immediately been upgraded. We were officially connected to the source. This meant more profits, better prices, and much more product. We had merely scratched the surface on McCabe Avenue.

It was time to make a larger statement in the game as front runners in northeast Baltimore.

We shared the good news with Genius and the others. They all wanted to literally kill Blue, but they all stayed focused on the upcoming opportunities to make even more money. After taking large orders from nearly the entire block, I paged Scott; only punching in "O," just as instructed. He replied by putting in the number 650. This was the amount he was charging for an ounce of cocaine. This also meant Blue was profiting $250 off of each ounce he had sold to us all. I sort of understood. Just as I did with my new clientele in the county, I too, saw another opportunity for advancement. The lying was interesting with Blue, not his hustle, as far as I was concerned. Everyone is his own businessman in the game of hustling. There are rules, and we often make up ones suitable for ourselves, but there are no true laws here. Any and everything is subject to change. Will you survive the decisions made and the changes? That's the #1 question!

Not only did I decide to not share the information about the price of $650 an ounce with the others, I also declined to tell Elroy. I gave all the guys a price of $800- $825 an ounce; less than the $1000 they all were paying. I was also willing to take $750. The only way anyone would get anything was through me. While everyone was getting upset with Blue, I was actually following suit, but this was a practice every hustler took part in at one time or another. For every ounce I would grab for someone, I was setting myself up to profit a quick $175. I had Genius, Tareek, Etton, Craig, Randolph, and at least three others, all waiting to score big. If each guy was only purchasing just one ounce, I was sure to profit $1400, without spending a dime or selling any of my own product. Fortunately for me, there was no way on earth Genius would ever only buy one ounce. He normally would never purchase below nine ounces (a quarter of a kilo) at once. Genius' purchase alone would make me a profit of $1575. I was disappointed Blue felt he needed to lie about his position, but I agreed with his tactics to earn more. I was not about to make deals for these guys without earning some sort of profit. As I said earlier, I was no "hack" dude before hustling, and I was not about to be a "runner" in the game, for anyone.

Besides the orders I was set to take for Genius and the others, Elroy and I decided to spend $7000 on the purchase of 11 ounces of cocaine. If Elroy and I were to play our cards right, or sell this product with no distractions, we could split nearly $20,000 cash. We were easily packaging $2000 worth of product off of each ounce. This meant we would make around $1800 cash an ounce, after "shorts." Last I checked; $1800 multiplied by 11 comes out to be $19,800. Give or take a thousand or two. It did not matter. $9900 a piece was a great figure as well, especially when we knew it would only take us a week or so to completely finish the entire package. With this money coming in, along with the extras from satisfying the others, I had found my niche in the streets. NO, I was not a kingpin, or one of the richest, young drug dealers in Baltimore City; that was NOT me! In the area, Hubert usually wore this crown, but he was recently picked up by the feds. Still, I was nothing of this sort, nor did I desire to be. I was clueless about my future, but I was certain not to be struggling as I navigate my soul search.

Concentrating on making money shadowed my thoughts. I hardly took the time to consider how messed up I was. I understood something was wrong with me, but I'd just ignore it. Still, a feeling of embarrassment would periodically come over me at times. I still did not want to be known as a dealer by anyone. Selling drugs was something I tried to keep secluded to the block. Staying out of sight during normal business hours was huge for me. I was lost, but I still realized selling drugs was just another way to say, "I give up" or "The world is just too much for me to handle without breaking the law." I felt this because I never felt like I was a drug dealer. I simply felt like I was a guy who would sell drugs until something better came along. Not "if" but "when." Without question, when I was not on McCabe selling drugs or creeping around in the county doing the same, I did not want to be known or seen as a drug dealer. I simply wanted to be known as, "O, from school" or "O, from the basketball court." I never wanted to be known as "O, the big shot I scored a brick or kilo from." That was NEVER going to be a good look for me.

The next day came, and it was time for me to round up the figures from all of the guys on the block. I picked Elroy up from home and headed to McCabe to see just how much money everyone was spending. I soon found it hard to gather up the funds from all of these guys. Therefore, we headed west to handle our own personal business. I was more comfortable conducting business with the others on my own time. We soon reached the rear of Scott's grandma's house. We were instructed to pull to the back to remain undetected. Scott himself lived at an undisclosed location in one of Maryland's surrounding counties. In west Baltimore, I was observing an older lady hanging garments on a line. I watched the old lady wearing her one piece summer dress, as she secured the bed sheets to the line with clothes pins. I stared a moment asking myself, "Where did those days go?"

"Excuse me ma'am. Is Scott here?" "Yeah, I believe he's in there," the woman answered. "You wait right here. I'll go get him. He was in there a minute ago," she uttered as she walked away. I looked over at Elroy and he was already as surprised as I. We both understood; Scott's grandma likely knew he was interacting in illegal activities, and apparently was surprisingly assisting him. Ironically, I noticed Scott's nana had on Nike sneakers. My grandma would often have on sneakers you would not think she would wear. Mama would say, "Don't you throw those good shoes away, shit, give them to me, I'll wear them." Still, it was funny. "He's in there. Go on down the basement stairs," she instructed. Elroy was in a good mood and was finding time to make jokes as we were about to do business. The goofy expressions he was making made it hard for me to regain a more business-like posture. We entered the poorly lit basement of the house and observed Scott sitting in a recliner. He was inside with three others, scattered about in the basement. "What's so funny?" Scott asked comfortably. "Nothing, my boy here is a fool," I answered. "Oh well! Let's get down to business," Scott stated with a slight smile.

We briefly met Scott's younger brother Joel. Joel did not seem to be a huge part of Scott's operation. It was hard to determine whether Joel was a screw up, or if he simply was not too interested in dealing drugs. Scott instructed him around a bit, but it was clear they were not cut from the same cloth. Scott was thin and clean-cut, while Joel presented himself as most of the inner city youths of today. He was a lot heavier than his older brother. His hair was all over his head and his pants were falling off constantly. He walked a hole in the bottoms of his jeans, and his shoes were unlaced and dirty. "What's up guys? What y'all need?" Scott asked consecutively. My eyes squinted before becoming enlarged. In one massive green lawn bag, Scott patted his hand on the top of dozens of ounces of raw cocaine. There must have been over a couple of hundred ounces in the bag. "What y'all do over there 'hard' or 'soft'?" he asked with a grin.

"Hard!" I spoke outwardly. "But, we already have someone to cook it up for us," Elroy stated. "I'm sick of that shit though," I added. "It's too much running around." "Why didn't you say so?" Scott asked while still grinning. He then pulled a similar bag out, with an equal amount, and said, "Here's the 'hard' shit." Scott possessed at least 275 ounces of cocaine in that basement. That's at least 5 kilos of cocaine.

"Oh, you got crack?" Elroy stated surprised. "Yeah, I got dope too. Can y'all move blow?" he asked. "Blow," "dope," in B'MORE, these are words used for heroin. "I can move anything," Elroy replied with a smile. "I don't mess with dope," I added. "The crack is cheaper than the soft coke around here fellas," Scott informed us. "Crack does not move as fast here," he explained. The 11 ounces we scored from Scott hardly put a dent in the large trash bag he pulled them from. "What about those dudes you were grabbing for?" "Where are they?" he asked. Those dudes were hard to track down, so we left," I explained. "I'll be back later," I added. "No, fuck that. Take twelve more," he insisted. "Call me when the twelve are gone," he instructed. "That's $7800," he informed. For me, it was an easy $2100 profit on the side as well. We left Scott's grandmother's basement with 23 ounces of crack cocaine. The dent I had predicted putting in McCabe's illegal identity, just became a pothole.

Unbelievably, six days after we left Scott's grandma's house, all 23 ounces were gone. Genius purchased nine all by himself. The other three went to Tareek and Etton. The neighborhood desperately needed more. Elroy and I were really cleaning up. We had the best product, while everyone else continued to run out. I made sure we sold a massive amount before committing to score for the others. I returned to the westside alone to see Scott. I pulled into the same alleyway and met a smiling Scott. I was also smiling as I parked. "Where exactly is this fuckin' place y'all get down at again?" he asked chuckling. "Northeast Baltimore, on a street named McCabe Avenue," I stated with a grin. "It's some serious money around that muthafucka, ain't it?" he asked with a scowl. "It could be more, but those dudes be trippin'," I offered. "Yeah, that's never good; never," Scott replied.

I scored another ten ounces from Scott, along with three more, strictly for myself. I was running out of hours in a day. I also grew a lot more paranoid. It was uncommon for a young person to drive across town in a shiny, light-blue newer sports car, with 13 ounces of crack cocaine stuffed inside the armrest. Suddenly, I found myself participating in a role I did not care to play. I felt myself losing more control. I always knew I was not living how I should have been. I still was far too weak-minded to change. I struggled mightily to keep what little sanity I had left. I was now being asked to control how much crack came into the neighborhood. I was hardly ever able to sleep. Guys were in need. Sometimes, they would be out dealing at all hours of the night. My lack of sleep even placed our stash holder, Tisha, in a compromising position. She held our drugs, but still lived at home with her mom. Sometimes she would be forced to throw ounces of crack from out of her bedroom window, just so her mom would not hear the front door crackle too many times in one night. I felt bad for messing with Tisha's sleep. We gave her another raise in pay at $400 a week for her extra troubles. Still things were getting out of control. I was responsible for too many hustlers whom I did not trust as human beings, and I didn't like it. There was no turning back at this point. The "full eclipse" was on; the darkness fully replaced any sunlight of my internal being. However, this experience gave me a chance to briefly experience life as a kingpin drug dealer, and I really hated it.

# Chapter 15

# THIN ON LUCK

Elroy and I continued to produce huge waves of cash in the midst of a sea full of lost souls. Scott was so intrigued by what we were accomplishing, he felt obligated see McCabe Avenue himself for a first time. When he arrived and pulled up in front of 731, he never exited nor rolled down his window. He was driving a nice, forest green, 525 BMW with the same color tinted windows and gold BBS custom wheels. I entered the car to chat with one of B'MORE's most successful hustlers. Scott and I talked numbers. He also wanted to let Elroy and I know about a trip out of town he was soon to take. He encouraged us to purchase half of a kilogram of crack beforehand. I agreed. "So this is it?" Scott asked as he observed my neighborhood from inside of the car. "Yeah, this is it!" I replied before following with a huge sigh.

We took a short ride around the block, before I would exit near Tisha's house. The look Scott and I gave one another before parting ways confirmed we were on the same page; a page indicating the financial victories we both were experiencing on McCabe would likely be no more in the very near-future due to the increased violence. The money continued to pour as tensions mounted, including more drive by shootings. In the midst of it all, I still made time for Penny and the kids. I needed a break, although I never really stopped hustling. Whenever I was not on McCabe, I still chased profits through the few reliable customers I had in the county. The three I started with had grown to six. Dealing with these folks who were from Towson, Maryland, made selling drugs very easy. All I had to do was go by a person's very nice $900,000 home, have a glass of tea, comment them on their Picasso painting, and pick up a cool $900- $1000 most times. These transactions normally would take less than ten minutes. A few of those minutes were charged to me taking off my shoes before entering. Two of the original three I visited insisted. I was completely fine with this. I was onto something here. With this new venture, I could relocate from death's door where tightly laced sneakers were mandatory, to an environment where I could literally sell drugs barefoot. The easy and fast money coming in was often laughable; it was certainly now time to celebrate.

On a Saturday evening after arguing with Penny about her considering us relocating to Essex, Maryland, the boys and I headed to Towson Marketplace to purchase new gear. We were getting set to party at Odell's nightclub. Bennett was thrilled to finally be old enough to get into an adult venue. The increased police patrols and the unnecessary corruption on the block gave us time to enjoy the large sums of money we were making. At the mall, I purchased a navy blue Guess jean outfit, and a new pair of white, low-cut, Nike Air Force One sneakers. This was actually the third time I had purchased this same outfit. I guess this was another way for me to unconsciously hold onto a positive piece of the past. Time had moved on, and I was still lying to myself, but I was making lots of money to hide behind. Internally, I hated my life when I briefly thought of it, but on this night I was ready for some fun. I was thinking to myself the tunes of a classic; "I love the night life I got to boogie."

I enjoyed attending the party scene of the early 90s, but I would often lose interest and leave a venue after a little more than an hour. I was never a huge fan of club music, and the hip-hop music I craved was never really played in the clubs or on the radio enough. I loved old school R&B, but this music was considered to be "old folk's music." As for the women in the clubs, they were cool, but with all the loud music blasting, conversations were usually nonexistent or kept at a minimum. It was cool to live in that self-composed music video; the only problem, it never ended. Still, the three of us headed down to North Avenue with hopes of sharing a few laughs and earning a chance to, if nothing else, rub elbows with the finest sisters Baltimore had to offer.

The three of us normally set out to the club early. We intentionally made it our duty to go ahead of the rest of the guys from the neighborhood. We believed this approach would disassociate ourselves from the rivalry;

to us, it was just a senseless excuse to create trouble. I was determined not to get involved with the idiocy with the two neighborhoods, despite a few poor decisions made within the feuding myself. Doing this was not as easy as it would seem. I was sure to not practice violence, but those who did were sort of like kinfolk; distant cousins, but family nevertheless. Most of the time these guys were like the wildest animals, but there were more than a few good moments. The sun actually shines through brightly at times, even within the jungle, I guess!

Me and my two friends entered the club around 10 p.m. Homosexual radio personality and female-impersonator, "Ms. Tony" was already animated and in a full sweat from dancing. He was single-handedly controlling the mood of the club and securing the dance floor. Being a fan of the art of dancing, I stood and watched for a few seconds before my attention would shift to my left. I noticed a guy sitting on a stool with cell phone in hand. I only noticed the guy because of the rare but nice device he held, and he just so happened to have on a similar outfit as I. However, there was something more familiar about this individual. I'd seen him somewhere else before; more than once. Suddenly, as I made my way a few steps closer, I extended my right hand to greet the guy. I spoke. "What up Biz?" I shouted through the music. It was hip-hop legend, Biz Markie, inside of Odell's nightclub relaxing alone. "What's up?" he replied with a nod. We shook hands and parted ways. You never know who you may run into at a club! The brief encounter was cool for me. It allowed me to see for a few seconds, there was still a decent world out there somewhere; sadly, I was just not a part of it.

I dropped Bennett and Elroy off after experiencing a good time at Odell's nightclub. They both asked to be dropped off at different females' houses near McCabe. After these drop-offs, I drove up McCabe Avenue towards York Road. I was on my way to Homestead Street where Penny awaited. As I drove up McCabe, advancing towards where I once lived, I noticed a glare over a slight hill. "What the ?" I uttered. I soon realized a vehicle was slowly headed in my direction. McCabe Avenue had been a one-way street, uphill, from north to south for years. Tipsy from just two mixed drinks, I believed the vehicle to be an addict or junkie, searching for his favorite dealer; me even.

At 3:30 a.m. the neighborhood was surprisingly like a ghost town. On most nights guys would be out dealing until sunrise. Not on this night. I drifted forward as the car approached. I wanted to get a closer look at the only person who did not know the block was a one-way street. Our cars pulled alongside one another due to empty parking spaces near the cross street, Ivanhoe. And in a split second, my small high left me. In the vehicle to my left sat Casper and Nut. We all stood staring for a moment. Nut smiled as I stared from left to right at the two. Suddenly, I observed two large handguns appear from both guys' lap area simultaneously. They both pointed; I ducked quickly, and they fired in my direction. As I got down my foot had smashed the gas pedal a split second before the blasts could come straight toward me. Three to four loud blasts followed me up McCabe Avenue, indicating an exit from their vehicle, but none seemed to make contact with my car. My heart pounded rapidly as I quickly reached York Road. I pulled over onto the busy main road, and put my face into my palms. I struggled with grasping my unsolicited involvement with the foolery. I was learning quickly how the negativity can outweigh the income in the drug game. I was slowly experiencing the harsh realities of drug dealing. I wanted the fast money, but NO amount of money is worth dying for.

A bit shaken, I drove back around to the block. I figured someone would soon be outside curious about the shots fired. I felt more comfortable returning to the block than I did continuing on to Homestead Street. That night, we declined to carry the Tech-9 to the club. It was safe to say, the protection was needed. I figured it would be best if I borrowed a gun from Genius to take home. Although I was never a huge fan of guns, I wanted to give myself a fighter's chance if these two guys were planning to reacquire me at my apartment. By the time I reached 731's front, there were at least five guys outside, all intensely focused with guns drawn. "O, what the hell was that?" Genius asked. "Man, those little bastards just shot at me," I offered loudly. "For real?" Tareek, who suddenly appeared, asked. "Shit, I wish I was a few seconds earlier. I would have killed both of them fools," he added violently. "Which one was it O?" he asked. "It was Nut and Casper," I offered. "They were driving up the wrong way," I added while shaking my head. Giggles followed. "Those the two little niggas I want too," Tareek stated while shaking his head and laughing. "Yo, I swear, I'm going to get that boy Nut," he added. After shaking my head in disgust over what had just happened, "Man, I need a gun to take home. Those dudes may be hiding in the brush near my house," I informed with concern. "What's the brush O?" Harold asked. "The bushes buddy," I replied with a quick grin. "Be careful man," Genius stated in concern while handing me his chrome 357 Magnum just after making sure it was fully loaded. "Yeah, I will. I'll catch y'all later," I stated as I headed towards my car. "Shit!" I yelled out seconds later. "They hit the car?" Tareek asked. "Yeah, a little," I answered. One of the shots fired in my direction managed to produce a three-inch long, glancing mark beneath the right tail light. "Damn O, they always shooting your car up n' shit," Tareek offered sarcastically. "Yeah, I'm not too worried, as long as it's not me getting hit," I stated before quickly pulling off.

Obviously, I was nervous during the ride home. I was never very comfortable when holding a gun. After suffering so many losses within my family, I could never see myself taking a life despite the threats I was encountering. However, there were times when I would envision beating a guy nearly to death or rendering him unconscious. I was growing frustrated with the way things were going in the streets. The money was good, but everyone's focus was shifting to the negativity which was vastly spreading. Making large sums of money through crack sales was beginning to take a back seat to the violence on McCabe. Parking my car with my left hand, while gripping a fully loaded 357 Magnum with my right, was not my initial vision of making a little money and staying low. Aside from Baltimore County, all other areas frequented would come with the possibility of violence, potentially even realizing my own demise.

After walking up the front steps to my home, backwards, I found myself being forced to immediately shift gears. As I reached the porch, I walked directly into a stare down with my sister's boyfriend Blue. We indulged in an intense gaze for at least two minutes. Eye contact has always been important to me. I relish in reading a person's eyes. Eye contact is truthful. It's personal. I don't practice staring at people for no reason; that's creepy, just if there's an important interaction taking place. It does not matter if the situation is negative or positive. Although I was a lost soul, I still searched for the souls of those I hung around. Blue was very unhappy about being derailed or eliminated from the scheme of things with the cocaine business. He was wearing a full cast on his left arm while sipping on a glass of juice with the other. My sister told me later, she believed Blue's broken arm was a tough warning he was given by someone from Scott's crew. Blue's side hustle apparently nearly cost him his life, and he was holding Elroy and I accountable.

More tensions would follow behind closed doors. Penny and I would suddenly split just prior to moving into a place of our own. Arguments about location continued, and my resurfacing flirtatious ways had caught up with me yet again. Penny learned of a few encounters I had shared with Vikki while we were an item. It had been four years since high school and I was still somewhat attracted to Vikki. She was simply a very skilled seducer. The ability to make money and hang out at different venues placed Vikki and I back together periodically. We still shared the chemistry we once had, and we both still ran with it on occasion. Vikki surprisingly expressed her displeasure about my affiliation with the drug game, but she believed I was smart enough not to hit rock bottom, get myself killed, or to go to jail. I believe, at this point, she had more confidence in me than I had in myself. Just as my grandma would say, "I'm not worried about you; I know you will be alright." Vikki felt I had things fully under control. How can this be? When it normally would take just a nice smile from Vikki for me to find a way to jeopardize another promising relationship. Instantly single, confused, and growing frustrated, I would take back to the streets to focus on enhancing my "hood rich" status. However, I soon began to see, McCabe Avenue was no longer just a gold mine for drug dealers. My neighborhood was becoming a degrading and very unfortunate war zone; a last stop, a place where many of us may soon die.

In the midst of it all Elroy and I continued dealing with Scott. Scott still was quite thrilled about achieving such a large income from this virtually unknown or unexpected part of town. McCabe was mostly known to those who understood the rivalry between the block and Old York Road. McCabe was not as large or as well known publicly as many of the other eastside neighborhoods, simply due to the guys not being as outgoing. Not many females nor other dealers in the city knew of most of the individuals from McCabe Avenue. This made me easier to be incorporated within the confusion between the two sides. To many, I was well known. So was Etton and Benny, but they were incarcerated more than they were free; out of sight, out of mind. To some, I was an average, female-friendly, street basketball player. To others, I was a money maker and big spender, but most simply classified me as a cool guy. The latter was most important. No matter what I was involved in, I tried, to the best of my ability, to make sure I held to the idea of being a cool and respectful dude with everyone I came in contact with.

My natural personality was evident throughout, but was often overshadowed by the dealing, senseless acts of violence and pure ignorance. There seemed hardly any room for decency on McCabe during this time. No one really believed in it, and no one cared to practice it. Everyone became fair game. I was susceptible to all types of troubles. So were the other dealers, homeowners, addicts, females, and children. No one was excluded from the possibility of a violent death. This was genocide right before our eyes. Everyone was a target. No one exempt, meant exactly this, no one; not even the white folks.

Many more disturbing and peculiar situations would resurface on McCabe Avenue, having nothing to do with making money, the females, or even the feud with Old York Road. I observed the guys beat an addict up severely, only to leave him in an alleyway unconscious. One of the most unbelievable incidents observed was from Tareek. Tareek once slammed a small, middle-aged woman on her head; she was dissatisfied with the size of her $20 sack, and would not let up with her displeasure. The woman was apparently drunk and upset. She felt she was getting her money's worth, therefore was not willing to leave the area until she was fully compensated. For $20, the decision to act out relentlessly almost caused this woman her life.

On this early evening, I stood on the opposite corner with Elroy and we both watched the entire situation unfold. The woman was no taller than five-feet. Tareek, Keffy, Genius, and a few others were on the corner engulfed in one of the frequent gambling games, which still took place mostly at night. This small woman's powerful voice would soon drown out most of the yelling and screaming coming from the dice game. "Sucka, you better give me my money or Imma fuck you up," she yelled. "I'm not leaving until your bitch ass give me my paper back!" the lady announced.

Keffy had a quiet personality; he offered little rebuttal. He was one of the very few respectful younger guys on the block. "Go ahead lady, I gave you what you paid for," he stated calmly. "This shit ain't worth no twenty dollars nigga," she replied with anger. Elroy and I thought it was funny until the others began to focus in on the argument. "Go head lady, he said he served you already; get the fuck away from here dummy," Tareek yelled as he pointed in the direction of an outlet for the woman to take. Tareek was quick tempered and apparently was not having great success during the dice game. He always hated to be showed up or made fun of. If this woman would have known Tareek a little better, she probably would have just walked away quickly during his original warning, but she didn't.

The woman's response to Tareek's instructions was enough for him to pull away from the action. "Who the fuck you think you talkin' to nigga?" "I'll fuck you up too," she insisted with a frown. This line caused everyone to suddenly fall into laughter. I watched Tareek's expression as the rest of us fell over into laughter. He was embarrassed, but still tried to hold up. "Lady, just get your ole, dumb ass out of here before you get hurt," he offered seriously. "Hurt! Who me? Fuck you," the small, older black female yelled loudly. "Y'all ain't goin' do shit to me, but give me my shit," she instructed. Tareek made a sudden move towards the woman in an attempt to intimidate her. "You can't scare me you little bitch," the woman shouted in response while surprisingly raising her fists. "Well, what's up then lady?" Tareek shouted to the surprise of us all. Surprisingly, now, the two were in a stance, both with guards raised. Suddenly, the woman reached behind her back in an apparent attempt to retrieve a weapon, but she never presented one. She then tried to punch Tareek in his face, but he was able to dodge the punch. Tareek quickly scooped the middle-aged woman up from off of her feet and raised her entire body passed his shoulders. As the woman wiggled about from above, Tareek quickly guided her, violently, face first into the pavement. The woman was knocked out cold instantly. Everyone stopped their laughter and paused in disbelief. After a few seconds of cold silence, the words, "That's a woman man!" came from Genius toward Tareek. All eyes were now firmly planted on him. We all were wondering how he could commit such a brutal act on any woman. He briefly glanced at us all with widened eyes, and suddenly took off running up an alleyway.

Some watched Tareek as he dashed toward the path, while the rest of us focused on the condition of the older woman as she laid face down on the corner. "Y'all better hope that lady is not dead," Elroy yelled in disgust. "She's not dead man," Genius stated angrily but remorseful. "Get her up from there man," he instructed. "Sit her over there on the steps." "Call the ambulance man!" I yelled out to everyone. "I think she's alright O," LiL Bug said. I called the paramedics from my car phone while two others carried the limp woman off to the side. In frustration, I walked over to the front of 731 to sit back down on the steps. I then observed Tareek sitting on his girlfriend's porch up the street a ways. He was shirtless and in a full glaze of sweat from his panic and hasty exit. We made eye contact from nearly a half of block apart. From afar, all I could see was his white teeth. He was smiling.

Although the threat of death still loomed, things quickly returned to normal as if there was not a badly injured woman sprawled off to the side of where we all were. I sat on the stoop with my eyes focused on the woman. Now partially conscious, she slowly squirmed about up against the cement steps as the ambulance surfaced. Just as help arrived, she sat upright and immediately grabbed her forehead. The right side of her forehead was severely swollen. After sighing in relief, I briefly looked above to acknowledge the only reason this woman was still alive. Surprisingly, the woman picked up where she had left off. Still dazed and confused, she refused treatment from the paramedics by cursing them all out as well. She then regained enough balance to leave the area under her own power. She was mumbling profanity as she passed by me. Incidents like these began to occur at least once a week. After every outrageous situation, I thought I had seen it all, but every time, I was wrong, very wrong.

A few days had passed since the incident with the unsatisfied female addict. I was back on the block making money while trying to look passed most of the unnecessary violence. Elroy was still struggling with staying clear from the unwanted heat he had accumulated over the years. Bennett's approach to making money was much safer. He found a trustworthy addict, if there was ever such a thing, and turned him into his personal worker. Surprisingly, it worked out. Every time Bennett left a package with Kam, the money came back straight. Speaking of "comeback," we still had the best quality product in the area. Most of the other hustlers on the eastside of town were still "stepping on" or stretching their product significantly. Greed and fear are the main mentalities behind selling drugs.

Like I stated, drug dealing actually says: "I don't feel I can achieve a good life without cutting a corner or breaking the law." Here, no matter how long we choose to sell drugs, or how much money we manage to make, we never seem to ever get enough. We were all living under the street laws of inertia; making lots of money, playing hard with the cuties, but our lives had stopped, souls tainted. We were all resting in limbo unaware we were preparing ourselves to take a one-way trip to some kind of hell.

Addicts and dealers alike get swallowed up by greed. It's not just the dealers who place themselves in harm's way. On McCabe Avenue, I witnessed addicts use very poor judgment to get high as well. One afternoon, as I sat on the porch, again taking a slight break from dealing, I watched the others jockey for position to achieve the most money for the day. A popular white couple surfaced, and I watched guys from all over the neighborhood swarm to the vehicle. This couple was said to spend an upwards of $400 on every trip made to the hood. The couple often made two or three trips in one night. During this particular visit, I thought it was rather peculiar for the couple to be on the block during the daytime. Normally, the couple driving the nice vintage Jaguar would only be seen during the wee hours of the night. I actually wanted a chance to deal with the couple, with hopes of adding them to my county clientele. I would never get this chance, and the couple would face tragic odds during their last visit to McCabe Avenue.

As the luxury car became consumed by the droves of dealers, the two occupants found themselves nervously trying to select from the many extremities soliciting throughout their vehicle. The guys had no idea, on this day, the couple was not there to spend any money at all. While guys were trying to make their daily quota with just this one sale, the couple was there to score for free. With several arms still inside the vehicle making final pleas, the driver suddenly pulled off. A few shoulders were immediately yanked, likely from the sockets, while others impulsively jumped backwards in disbelief. The couple was speeding up McCabe Avenue seemingly close to pulling off this risky move, but they would forget something; Dro. He was holding onto his stash and the car as it frantically sped up the block. These two whites from the county obviously never factored in the mindsets of some of the guys on my block. Some believed most of these guys were really psychopaths. They craved more than money. Some of them also loved the idea of violence. Chip, although he was not present during this incident, once said, "I was put on earth to kill people!" As the couple tried to make a getaway, Dro, a cousin of Tareek's, was trying desperately to bring the vehicle to a complete stop while keeping his feet from dragging on the blacktop. He was not just trying to save his own life, but we all knew he would also want to take the lives of the occupants of the vehicle.

For more than a half of block, the vehicle swirled from left to right, banging into the left curb, and the parked cars to the right. Little kids and women were running and screaming about on this sunny warm day. A block away from reaching York Road, or freedom for the couple, Dro managed to get the couple to crash into the side of a corner row house. I could not believe what I was witnessing from afar. It was like a scene from an intense action film. Excitement soon returned to all of the shocked and slightly injured guys on the corner. After watching the vehicle crash, they all violently exploded, running towards the crash with malice in mind. I stood and watched as I prepared to witness a very rare occurrence. Several blacks were about to beat up two white people; so I thought.

I was too far away to see very clearly, but Dro seemingly struggled to his feet before apparently reaching into the front of his pants. Stan, another new guy on McCabe, who I did not know well, also ran up to the scene. He quickly pulled out a handgun as well. The entire neighborhood was in a panic, running about trying to find a safe place to take cover. The vehicle had tipped onto its side, but this was the least of the couple's worries. Surprisingly, the two armed guys ran right up on the stalled vehicle and repeatedly fired shots into the damaged vehicle at extremely close range. More folks began to scatter about as multiple blasts cut through all of the shouting. My heart sunk in disbelief, causing me to thrust backwards a few paces. I could not see every detail well, but my imagination meshed what I could see. The shots continued for at least a full minute. As the tragic situation unfolded, I watched in a still panic with my back up against the front door. The other guys immediately dispersed, understanding the difference in this shooting compared to so many others. These victims were white!

By the time the police and the paramedics arrived, the driver of the vehicle, a white male, was dead. His blond girlfriend was still alive, but barely. The two were both traumatized from several bullet wounds from semi-automatic handguns. The entire neighborhood surfaced quietly onto their porches as police searched for clues. I made it back to my original position at the edge of the steps and slowly sat down to observe as well. I was shaking a bit and could actually feel my pulse beating inside of my head. My neighborhood had raised the stakes significantly. I always believed something like this could happen, yet I never really expected it to. The older folks in the neighborhood were in complete shock. This tragedy had shown us all just how close we were to death. The disturbed look on everyone's face asked this question: "If these guys are willing to kill white folks, who they don't know, in broad daylight, how difficult would it be to kill any of us?"

Throughout 1993, I grew more frustrated with all of the negativity. My temper and patience shortened, but my ideas to expand my hustling endeavors grew. I began to feel a need to pull myself away from a place where I was making thousands of dollars per week, because of several unforeseen horrific events. I began to reconnect with Evan just to get away from the drama. We still occasionally played basketball, and surprisingly, his area became another place where I could make substantial amounts of cash and stay virtually undetected. Evan, a dealer as well, lived at home with his mom in the area where he experienced the major meltdown with Vikki. This once calm and quiet area was becoming consumed with crack addicts. Here, along with my growing county business, were near-perfect locations to hustle undetected periodically while still profiting on McCabe Avenue. It was an economically sound change of pace. During this period the money was rolling in, but I was still lost mentally, emotionally, and spiritually. Although I was successful outside of McCabe Avenue, the idea of totally leaving the block still felt very weird. The thousands of dollars factored in a bit, but I know fear was the true reason I felt a need to stay. Even the possibility of death struggled to compete with the idea of change. This fear was compounded by my indecision to discover or choose a positive path to follow. I really felt I had nowhere to turn, therefore I allowed myself to believe I was comfortable in a place where severe violence and death existed regularly.

This defeated mentality plague many people in this country today. Especially the young and those who come from or live in poverty stricken communities. There are several other factors, but I believe we can counter these ways and bring about positive change if we decide to reconsider the basics in life; faith, hard work, and love. The reasoning behind the despair is endless. The excuses are plentiful, yet a complete waste of time and energy. Some of us are initially dealt a pretty ugly hand in life, but it's still time to move on by accepting responsibility for our poor actions. Yes, in many areas, many of us have been taught wrong, but it's still not too late to make much better decisions in our lives. So many blacks, especially males, are being born, raised, and buried in the same neighborhoods, without ever experiencing the beauty the world and life has to offer. Today, I understand this atrocity and want to do my part to help. However, during the mid-90s, I was in desperate need of help myself. I made lots of cash, often smiling while I did it, but I believe I was depressed; I know I was lost, and I did not know myself well enough to make better decisions. Unfortunately, as I struggled internally, things were still getting unbelievably more compromising.

Two weeks after the tragic shooting incident, I learned the deceased man's girlfriend was still alive in the hospital. She had been in a coma since the shooting. There were even talks of someone paying this young white female a visit, and finishing the job. That likely never materialized. Instead, the shooters suddenly disappeared from the area. For weeks, federal agents continued to patrol the area in search of clues or leads. Of course, no one heard or saw a thing. During the 90s, snitching or telling on someone about a crime committed was a sure way to get oneself killed on McCabe Avenue and throughout Baltimore City. With great strides forward made by Dr. King and other great African-Americans, it's sad to say you will lose your life, by the hands of your own race, for trying to create positive change. This is how it is today inside of harsh inner-city living in a lot of instances. Simply put, if someone was trying to die quickly, all they would have to do is pay a visit to McCabe and observe things for a few hours. It would almost be a guarantee they would see some sort of crime being committed. All they would have to do next; call police, and their efforts in getting themselves killed would be granted if someone found out. This was life in many of our city's streets. Whenever you hear of the many dead bodies found throughout the city without clues or motives; snitching, females, and money are likely the factors behind these deaths. Guys were willingly breaking the laws, yet there were also honest, hardworking citizens bold enough to break their code of the streets. In our hearts as drug dealers, life was about survival, therefore I made sure I fell somewhere in the middle; intermediate or in between decent living and death. It was not easy to watch folk die, but I countered my natural character to be selfish; I ignored the failures of others best I could and stayed focused on hefty profits.

While federal agents questioned the entire neighborhood about the tragic shooting, the guys from Old York Road could care less. They still made their presence felt by driving through with threatening intentions. The violent ways usually continued on the block after a tragic event. No one here feared death, so this was not a place where someone would die and others get a "wake-up call." No, not here! Frustrations slowly mounted as the heat from the homicide investigation interfered with our ability to make money on McCabe Avenue. With my other interests, I hardly missed a beat, but I still shared in the concern with Elroy. In Towson, Maryland my illegal efforts were expanding steadily. I now had ten people within a 13 mile radius purchasing crack from me regularly. Coincidentally, all but one of these folks were Caucasian. "Tank," the lone black I dealt with occasionally, was a chemist who handled blood samples for a pharmaceutical company in Easton, Maryland. Race was never an issue for me with anything I took part in. I actually liked knowing these people were responsible or well in control of their lives to an extent; not to mention very well off and friendly. These were folks who became very successful before crack cocaine hit hard in Maryland. Selling drugs to these people felt the same as selling candy bars in rich neighborhoods as kids. I was gradually finding a way to make quiet money, and it all belonged to me.

Selling candy, however, is nothing like selling crack, but even back then greed was a slight issue for my friends and I. On one occasion, we actually kept the customers money we received from orders they placed with us for candy. We never paid the school or took folks their product. We were all punished by our parents or guardians, but this was an indication of the poor decisions beginning early with most of us. Like I said, we were hardly ever monitored, so we got away with plenty of mischief, or tried to.

Baltimore County is no more than a few miles away from the city, but life there is much different. It's completely foolish to believe the crack epidemic decided to just consume lives in the city and never have an impact on white folks who lived some five miles north, in the suburbs. Ok!

I was not the only crack dealer in Towson; I recall at least four others, blacks, but the atmosphere was still very different further north. There were many days I would go from diving on the ground, avoiding stray bullets, to watching a prize fight on a big screen television while sitting in between blond twins from Towson State University. Other times, I would be hanging out with my pal named, Martie, a middle-aged white retiree. There, at his home, I could easily make $1000 or $2000 in a few hours. However, this money only served as interest compared to the money I profited on McCabe. Still, I felt I was onto something huge and different in the suburbs. Therefore, I kept quiet about my increased fortune in the county while continuing to make moves in the hood.

Genius also continued to produce big profits in the city. He and his main female partner moved from McCabe Avenue to a nearby city street, but in a much better home and neighborhood. Genius moved near the prestigious, Morgan State University, in a four bedroom house. Harold, LiL Bug's brother, moved in with the couple. Unfortunately, the home soon became a clubhouse for all of the hustlers in the neighborhood. Genius' desire to be seen often interfered with his business practices. With a safer and more stable operation evolving in the county, I was beginning to see his many mistakes from the outside looking inward. I was able to see how Genius and others on McCabe Avenue could be headed for big trouble. They were self-destructing and couldn't even see it. I was lost, but I was never completely hopeless; this glimmer of hope allowed me to use above-average common sense for a dealer. Still, I did not practice this nearly enough. My peers and I were like so many unstable people out in society; severely blinded by greed, money, possessions, sex, and violence.

I personally spent a little time at Genius' lavishly furnished, semi-detached unit. There were usually pretty young ladies all around. These females were desperate for sponsors, and the boys of McCabe noses were usually wide open, making consideration easy. Whenever these guys were not gambling in the basement at the pool table, or having sex in every room of the house, they all would be sitting at the elongated living room table, packaging several ounces of cocaine. There would be semi-automatic handguns, lit blunts, and slightly filled bottles of liquor on the glass table. I never possessed drugs when visiting Genius' home. This home was an updated version of Skippy's old place around the way; brighter lighting and more contemporary furnishings, but still with a sinister atmosphere. I was usually there only to see the hotties. The house also served as a quick getaway for me, similar to a happy hour. However, I feared with the late hours they all kept and the uncharacteristically loud noise, the guys fun times would be short-lived. Still, I did have several good laughs there. I knew not to spend too much time inside of the home. I would never take a nap or have sex there. There were far too many flashy cars in front of the house, and guys were in and out of the house frequently. This neighborhood was nothing like McCabe Avenue, although it was just a few miles away. The deterioration and rebuilding of a neighborhood often takes years. Unfortunately, negative forces usually win over decency on city blocks, but not in every case; not here.

Genius' new place gave the guys a place to gamble and hang out, but it all felt strange from the start. Whenever the guys were at this new residence, this often left police with a dry neighborhood in Govans. This also allowed Elroy and I the time to continue to dominate the drug market in the hood. We both spent the least amount of time at Genius' place. I would usually give myself no more than an hour at the house at one time. After this hour, a weird feeling would come over me and I would leave quickly. I was not too blind to see; the home was an easy way for police to arrest and convict over ten dealers, all at once. I did not care to be one of these guys. Interacting with packs of people was not one of my favorite things to do. However, I loved hanging out with different types of people on the ball courts, and those from positive social settings. Learning to play basketball well introduced me to several worlds of individuals. Some of the guys were drug dealers, but as time passed, I also made friends with people from many different backgrounds and races. Some of these individuals never dealt, used drugs, or carried a gun in their entire lives.

Statistics show, the highest suicide rates in modern society is located in suburban America. I brought my foolishness to the county, thinking I was escaping death, but I was simply entering another form of it. Hanging out with different people from different social levels in Towson, despite the dealing, actually gave me a better outlook on life. Although I was still engulfed in a world where the endings are never good, I felt more optimistic than I'd been in years. Perhaps it was something as simple as the scenery or the natural quietness that made me feel more relaxed. I still was not able to dream, and the idea of working a real job really irritated me. Working for a living was out of the question. Still, I received a little peace, knowing the decision to affiliate in the suburbs had reduced my chances of being killed or arrested. The more time I spent away from McCabe, the more peaceful I felt. Still, the peace was not enough for me to walk away from the thousands of dollars I profited regularly. I managed to hustle on McCabe for nearly four years with minimal trouble. I had the one arrest I strictly blamed on myself for panicking, but nothing more. Before long, I believed I was too smart for police, and too cool of a guy to fall out with the other dealers. As the neighborhood feud continued to spiral out of control, and the walls began to close in on us all, I learned thinking too much or second guessing can be a very deadly approach while living life as a drug dealer.

Elroy and I made another deal with Scott before he left town. Scott had mentioned having interest in opening his very own music studio in Los Angeles. He felt he could turn a large profit off the hard work and talents of hip hop artists. He informed us; his days as a drug dealer were coming to an end. He was setting up to relocate across the country. At just 20 years old, Scott was certainly at millionaire status. I was thrilled for him when we spoke, but I never considered quitting the game during this time. Oddly, again, money had little to do with this frame of mind I carried. Trying to become rich dealing drugs was never my aim at all. I actually felt guys who thought like this were insane; to think society would actually allow "you," an inner- city, poverty-stricken, black male, high school drop-out, with a criminal past, to become wealthy dealing drugs. If there was ever a time I wanted readers to hear me laugh, it would be now. I realize there are exceptions to every rule. I was trying to become one myself, but to actually believe I could become this guy; I was never that stupid!

In the 90s, my life had absolutely no plans for success in society. I believed the lottery may have been the only plan I had to exit dealing. Hell, the kingpin odds are likely better! Again, I was very stupid, but I figured I would likely somehow stop one day. I spent very little time with this thought but it was there. I also knew once I was able to quit, the amount of money I had saved or made would not factor much into the decisions I made down the road. Unlike so many dealers, the game of selling drugs and whatever life I would have down the line were not at all connected. So with Scott we hurried and purchased 14 ounces of crack with the hope of his return well before it all vanished. We would dread the idea of scoring from others. Most of the quality of the weight or large quantities of drugs sold at this time was mediocre, at best. OK, I'll be blunt. We felt nearly everyone else we knew was selling junk, garbage, trash.

While we were gearing up to sell nearly $28,000 worth of crack, in a little more than a week, the ongoing feud between McCabe and Old York Road was coming closer. Domestic tensions made by the opposite sex on both sides created an explosive situation less than a block from 731's door. Where was I? I was with Vikki, the unshakable bombshell from Old York. While Vikki and I were catching up on lost time, without conversing much, a situation was unfolding between the neighborhoods. The roles had reversed from the fatal night involving Tray. This time around, someone else's sister had been assaulted, supposedly by a guy from McCabe. This someone was Limon, one of the leaders of the crew from Old York. After learning of his relative's troubles, Limon and several others set out to rectify the situation. The situation was strikingly similar to Tray's fatal night. The OYR crew headed to McCabe where LiL Bug, Big Bug, Harold, and several others gathered on Alhambra near Skippy's old home. As they all huddled hustling in the dark they created by destroying many of the street lights, Limon and his crew headed towards the block to seek redemption.

Limon and his counterparts were looking for a guy named Ollan. Ollan was not from McCabe Avenue. His affiliation with McCabe came from Etton, who had recently returned from prison. Etton was dating Ollan's beautiful sister, Jackie, a girl Evan once threw stones at for liking him when we all were kids. Ollan apparently got into an altercation with Limon's sister, Mesha. The two were said to be dating. Ollan was a cool guy I periodically played basketball with. Mesha, beautiful and mild-mannered, was a schoolmate of mine during high school. The reason Limon and the others decided to come to McCabe Avenue instead of Winston Avenue, two blocks over where Ollan lived, is mystifying still. I guess there's a lot of pressure involved when you're responsible for leading a large crew of troubled street guys. Limon and his peers reached my neighborhood before I did, but I was not too late to read between the lines. Limon and his pals surfaced in the neighborhood about 50 yards from where the others stood in the dark. "Hey, has anybody seen Ollan?" came from the crowd. "Nah, Ollan don't live around here," "Go around Winston somewhere!" LiL Bug yelled back at the crowd from his darkened position. Originally, the guys from McCabe had no clue they were conversing with the other side. They simply thought some strangers were looking for Ollan. Once they realized who they were talking with, an argument ensued. I guess it did not have to, but knowing Old York was there was enough to spark a confrontation. Seconds later, a fist fight between several guys would break out. Unfortunately, we were no longer in the days of hard fist fights, followed by handshakes, peroxide, and ice packs. In seconds, gunshots rang out and bodies proceeded to scatter about. While Big Bug and Limon wrestled one another in the middle of the block, his peers chased the surprisingly unarmed guys from McCabe. Harold was shot twice, once in the elbow, and once in the buttocks. He may have been killed if he was not able to somehow dive through the front windshield of his own car. Mayhem was breaking out and I just so happened to be on my way back to McCabe.

As I approached, I thought I heard a few pops from a distance. I believe Gang stars hit single, "Mass Appeal" drowned out all other sounds. It was not until I turned left onto McCabe, I realized something had gone wrong. As I drove down the block, I could see the blue and red reflections glaring from several police units. After turning off my car stereo, I could hear an ambulance drawing nearer. I decided to not park, therefore I pulled directly in front of my former residence. This was when I observed a crying Mesha on the corner, just a few yards away. "What the hell is Mesha doing around here?" I asked myself quietly. I looked pass my old schoolmate, Mesha and noticed a crowd of guys surrounding what appeared to be a wounded person on his backside in the middle of the street.

Despite the authorities in the area, several of the guys still were walking up to the body and quickly retreating. At first sight, I thought people were trying to identify the body. After observing a few violent kicks thrusted towards the body, and some spitting, I quickly remembered Mesha was

Limon's younger sister. As ambulances drew nearer, I walked closer to the injured body. I realized it was Limon. Guys were yelling, "Die bitch die!" and continuing to spit on Limon's body. Harold, and Limon, who was apparently left behind by many of his peers, were both carted off to nearby hospitals. Harold turned out to be alright despite being shot twice. Limon later died at the hospital. Old York had just lost one of its main figures. On top of it all, police later learned it was one of Limon's peers' bullets that actually took his life. Surprisingly, again, no one from McCabe possessed a gun on this night. In an attempt to kill Big Bug during the struggle between the two, Limon was accidentally struck in his upper body and killed. Accidental death or not, the stakes for this feud were now higher than ever.

Limon's tragic death would set off a string of shootings and arrests. Old York retaliated in front of Odell's nightclub one weekend night. Hank, Big Bug's little cousin, was spotted waiting to enter the nightclub. He was shot several times in the back, directly in front of dozens of onlookers. He was trying to run away or escape after realizing he was being acquired. News of the shooting inflamed the guys on McCabe. I observed LiL Bug as he would burst into tears as Hank clung to life by a thread. "If my lil cousin die, I'm going to kill all them bitches," he uttered. Days later, Tareek, Hank's uncle Bam Bam, and Donte, Spoon's uncle, headed down Old York to make a stand for Hank. The three guys, all equipped with semi-automatic handguns, crept down Old York onto Cator Avenue, and waited for any one of their enemies to walk down the street. After nearly an hour-long wait in the brush, Tareek and the others heard a group of guys advancing toward their direction. Ironically, they all heard a disturbing conversation taking place from the approaching group of guys. "We got his ass good at da club son," a guy said with a giggle. "Fuck him, I hope the little nigga die," another stated. This was all Tareek and the others needed to hear.

The three guys from McCabe waited patiently until the bragging voices were almost parallel with the brush where they quietly hid. When this moment arrived, the three exploded from the bushes, unloading rapid gunfire. I was told the guys' screams were synonymous with "young chicks attending a scary movie." Once again, several guys were ambushed with gunfire. All of the individuals were struck by a hail of bullets. A few guys were even shot in the face. Fortunately, this incident produced no fatalities.

Tareek displayed his disappointment after coming up short with adding to the death toll surrounding the feud. "O, I don't understand how we didn't kill all of those punk niggas. They were all standing right there in front of us, frozen stiff, yellin like bitches," Tareek stated. Days later, Old York "clapped back" by killing a hack from around McCabe. There was so much violence and gunfire at this point, it would only be a matter of time before the stupidity would produce yet another "pothole in my lawn."

A few weeks after the last shooting on Cator Avenue, Elroy and I found ourselves back inside of Odell's nightclub. Once again, Elroy and I arrived early. In the midst of violence, we still tried to stay separated from the others. The violence simply had no real merit with us. We truly realized this was beneath senseless. I made sure I still enjoyed myself at the club on this evening. The way I saw things; I was making a lot of money, and I was not going to let a decade-old rivalry rain on my cash parade. As I danced the first half of the night away, Elroy acted as if he were a secret service agent. He was extremely nervous. He felt we would be approached inside of the club, possibly ambushed by dozens of guys from Old York Road. "Chill out buddy, it's cool," I yelled to Elroy passed the music. I was feeling pretty good in the club for some reason. I had already observed a few guys from Old York. Guys Elroy never knew. They also saw me, but did nothing more than nod. I was sure we would be able to have a trouble-free night. Well, until I observed Genius, Tareek, LiL Bug and at least four others entering the club.

The guys from McCabe had come to celebrate Hank's recovery. "Let's go get something to drink," I insisted. "Man, I hope they don't start no shit tonight," Elroy said nervously as he too witnessed the crew enter. "I know," I replied. We knifed our way through the accumulating crowd until we reached the rear of the club. Oddly enough, there were at least five Old York Road guys. Casper was there, along with Ward, a guy I occasionally played basketball with. "C'mon O, lets get the hell out of here," Elroy stated after making eye contact with Casper. I felt it came from the day Bennett and I chased him with harmful intentions. "It's cool. Don't worry. It's fine brother. Just be cool," I said to Elroy.

For ten minutes we stood in the rear of the club surrounded by members of Old York Road. Just as Elroy began to settle down, the others entered the rear where we all were enjoying our drinks. I watched the guys enter the small bar area of the club, one by one. They had formed a "human-train," or a line formed with one guy holding onto the shoulders of the guy out in front. "McCabe! McCabe! McCabe!" loudly came from all of the guys' voices. McCabe Avenue guys and Old York were in a very small area, all together. Tension would mount almost immediately. Seconds later, a riot broke out.

Tareek wasted little time. He threw the first punch, striking Ward in the face, knocking him to the floor. Ward, an exceptional basketball player, never saw it coming. Screams and yells from nearby females dominated the loud music. Drinks were flying everywhere! Guys were being stomped on, kicked, punched, and hit with blunt objects. Elroy and I were mixed in with the negativity. We headed for the front of the club to exit. I observed several of the guys really beating on Casper. Someone grabbed my right leg during the scuffle. I violently kicked backwards, freeing my leg, and I continued towards the front of the club. We quickly made it to my car, escaping any harm. We headed back to McCabe Avenue, frustrated and disappointed about the entire situation. We were having a very good time until the brawl. We reached the block around midnight. The others returned soon afterwards. Cars blasting harsh rap lyrics pulled in, one after the other, and the scene appeared as if the party had simply moved onto the block.

After the commotion at Odell's nightclub, guys were back on the block actually slapping "fives," celebrating the apparent beatdown victory. They were laughing and cheering an apparent score in physically hurting a few of the guys from Old York, specifically Casper. "I really got that guy Ward fellas. I dropped his ass," Tareek yelled. "Oh, we really beat the shit out of Casper too," LiL Bug shouted. Bam Bam and Donte laughed with the others, but displayed their disappointment with them for also ruining their evening. Elroy and I also made the others aware of the unfortunate interruption. "Man, y'all messed our grove all up!" I shouted. I was giggling too. I thought it was a bit funny folks got beat up. I don't want anyone to think I was always thinking positive, spiritual, or that I was always at some crossroads. I WAS NOT! I was laughing too! "I'm thinking about going back down though. It's still early," I said enthused. "What time is it O?" Donte asked. "Twelve-fifteen son," I answered. "Let's go back O," Elroy surprisingly insisted. Bam Bam and Donte also decided to join us. Our night of partying was not done. We knew the others were finished clubbing for the night. I never threw a single punch during the riot, therefore I refused to allow the others to ruin my entire evening. By 12:45 a.m., the four of us were back inside of Odell's partying the night away.

The four of us left Odell's nightclub tickled pink. We were thrilled about the decision we made to return to the club after the brawl. No one from Old York Road was in the facility during our second visit. We left the club eager to share our experiences with the others whom squandered their opportunity. We all crammed into my Celica and drove north on Charles Street. Soon, the low gas indicator light slowly brightened. I had passed on several gas stations on North Avenue, in an effort to hurry back to the block, but was forced to stop. "I need some gas fellas. I'm going to stop at this Crown to fill up," I yelled passed the music. As soon as I pulled up to the pump, Bam and Donte recognized a BMW occupied by two females, and quickly pleaded to exit the vehicle. "O let us out of here!" Donte shouted while pushing into the back of my chair. "We're going to rap to these chicks real quick." Seconds later, all of us exited the vehicle. Bam and Donte quickly approached the two women in the 325i, and offered to pump and pay for their gas. Elroy immediately went to pay for my gas while I unscrewed the gas cap. The party had apparently continued at the Crown gas station as Ice Cube's hit, "Wicked" glared from my sunroof. Elroy was making up his own little dance, and I was nodding my head harder than usual. That song will make you do this. The two others were leaning in on each side of the female's white BMW. Little did we know this party was about to come to an abrupt end, once again.

After I refilled the Celica with gas, I secured the cap to the gas tank and began observing the guys as they continued to converse with the two females. Elroy was still engulfed in a hilarious dance. I rested my chin on my forearm, on top of the car, smiling, and patiently waiting on the others. Before I could completely look downwards into the car from the sunroof to determine the next track to play, I heard a disturbing shout to my right. "YO, IT'S CASPER!" Elroy screamed. I turned around and there he was. Casper was wearing a black, hooded sweatshirt, but I could still see his face clearly. His left eye was nearly closed and his lips were bloody and swollen. He was just a few yards away, close enough for me to hear him sniffling, still in pain from the earlier brawl. We made eye contact, and suddenly he reached in the front of his pants and pulled out a large revolver. He certainly had the drop on me, but he chose to focus on Elroy. I watched him raise the gun then I reacted quickly. I dove over my car and onto the blacktop. As soon as I hit the ground, three large blasts would sound off. Casper was shooting at Elroy, who stood on the exposed side of my vehicle. I could hear the shots piercing through the car's thin metal. From underneath the vehicle, I watched the four feet of Elroy and Casper as the assault took place. The other two guys could be seen partially inside of the BMW, with legs flailing about, as the women sped off up Charles Street. Suddenly the gunfire ended and I heard footsteps scattering away, not sure if my friend had been shot.

I quickly stood up and observed Elroy chasing Casper up Charles Street. "Don't chase him Elroy!" I yelled. I feared Elroy would run into an ambush. I assumed Casper had accomplices somewhere nearby. I was right. I observed a familiar black, Mercury Sable always driven by Ward, parked on a cross street. After quickly glancing at the gas attendant who was also taking cover, I yelled, "No! Come back!" Elroy seemed to gain a little ground on Casper. I already had much respect for Casper's foot-speed. Elroy soon recognized the black vehicle as well and quickly let up on his chase. I got a good look at Ward as Casper quickly jumped inside of the vehicle. They immediately sped off northbound in the same direction as the BMW, on Charles Street. "Elroy, don't ever chase an armed person man," I demanded as he quickly returned. "O, the little bastard ran out of bullets," he replied in a full sweat. "I was going to beat all the shit out of that dude O," Elroy assured. "Man, don't ever follow an armed person son. Don't ever do that," I emphasized. "His boys could have been strapped waiting for you." The others quickly resurfaced, making sure Elroy and I were not injured. No one was shot or harmed in any way, but our pressure was certainly elevated, and I was left with four new holes in my vehicle this time around; a total of five since I purchased the car.

During the time of this shooting my mind state was very erratic and confused. It was like my spirit was a messy construction site, clashing with my being, with no direction, recklessly plowing through and knocking over every cone of righteousness. The next morning, I found myself gazing into the massive holes on the passenger side of my car. One hole was directly below the gas tank. I was upset about my car, but thankful the four holes were not in me, or the end result of four dead people. We all were lucky, but this luck seemed to be wearing thin. On McCabe Avenue, things were not getting any better for sure. This incident frustrated me so, for the first time, I could actually see myself retaliating. I never pointed or discharged a weapon of any sort at anyone, but my patience was wearing thin. I was hardly ever upset enough to want to seriously harm or kill someone, because internally I always knew my decision to sell drugs was wrong. I was addicted to the life, and I would regularly use excuses to hide behind the money, but I knew my life was really garbage at this time. In spite of this reality, I also knew sooner or later, I would have to do something to send a message to the other side.

## Chapter 16

# FEELING THE HEAT

The sunshine appeared the same morning of the shooting, and it's safe to say we were all lucky to still be alive. Instead of becoming another fallen family member, I found myself going over yet another estimate for repairing bullet holes in my Toyota. In all, this was the fifth hole I had to get repaired, I think. In the beginning these repairs were a bit pricey. Somehow, the white manager and I became friendly. I believe he was intrigued by the intense city element I brought into his establishment. It did not take very long for us to began socializing frequently about topics aside from car repairs. Bullet holes were not the only repairs I would get at MAACO. I would occasionally take my car there for any other repairs the body of the vehicle needed. I would often give Josh an extra hundred or two to complete the job faster than normal. Before long, I realized I had stumbled onto a pretty good connection to keep my car looking sharp, but that was not it. Through numerous conversations with Josh, I learned he too liked to "party" or get high. I didn't hesitate to add him and his assistant manager, Andy to my list of private customers. These two raised my side dealings to 13 customers.

The violence continued to escalate and dominate McCabe Avenue clear into 1994. Guns were everywhere and shootouts were frequent as ever. The scary factor for myself; I was becoming comfortable with it. For the first time in my life, I was actually beginning to indulge and take on a more aggressive and negative attitude. I was still truly frustrated with myself for being unable to find the resolve to change. I had recently gotten into a near brawl with Harold over, around-the-way-girl, Tina. I didn't hesitate to go after him after learning he was secretly making unwanted passes at her. I was really getting stupid. I don't fight over flirtatious females, but I will defend the respect of any honest woman I'm exclusive with.

My feelings for Tina were honest, but moderate at best. Aggressively approaching a guy about a female usually indicates insecurities and weaknesses. Guys; let the female make the decision, if she's willing. The attitude and aggression I had during this time strictly stemmed from how low I felt about my life as a young man. I hated my life when I stopped to think about it! I didn't stop with the few senseless scuffles. I even joined in with the guys once, as they chased down a dude for stealing someone's stash. As they all pummeled away on the guy, I helped, focusing in on his rib cage area as his shirt drew upwards during the struggle. Frustrated about virtually everything, I violently punched the guy as hard as I could. "Ahhhhhhhh, my ribs," he screamed. The distressed scream actually surprised me. I immediately felt stupid and regretful, but this was not the time for anyone to display any acts of sympathy. The guy never knew who hit him in his side. His screams were so disturbing, the others quickly let him flee. I learned later, Travis suffered two broken ribs.

I was becoming something I was not; a thug. During this time, I found myself arguing with almost everyone. Etton and I never bumped heads in previous years, but slight tension was there as well. Not only did he like my sister, Gina, he also was making moves on Vikki whenever he could. Even Genius and I had negative words. We briefly argued about Elroy's sister, Rebbie. As my fortune in the streets increased, she began to constantly make passes at me, and yes, I turned them into "touchdowns." Details never surfaced about our fling, but it was an enjoyable experience. "Just stay away from her man," was pretty much all Genius said to me concerning the matter. As I grew older, I revisited all of the women who were once considered to be too old, and with a relaxed approach, I showed them all how much I had grown. I was, once again, out of control when it came to the ladies. When Genius momentarily approached me about Rebbie, my reply was simple. "She's the one coming at me. You should talk to her."

Nothing serious materialized from any of these incidents, but it placed me in another light with the guys on the block. In the past, I would receive assistance from the guys if I had major troubles. Genius and others came to my aid once when I was jumped by a 300 pound, jealous boyfriend of a female. He clocked me pretty good too. He jumped out of a closet as I entered the girl's apartment. I never saw it coming, but I still performed fairly well considering, dazed and all. I guess the place was under this guy's name! The female tried to apologize later. We all ambushed the guy after waiting for 30 minutes or so for him to exit her apartment. He thought everyone left the complex when he exited, and tried to make it to his car, but we caught him. He used sneaky tactics and so did we. "All is fair in love and war," they say. As for the girl, I slept with her a few more times before leaving her alone completely. What can I say? She was still hot.

I was making poor decision after poor decision during this time, but the money was pouring in so rapidly, I hardly noticed. I attempted to use playing basketball as a means to channel negative energy. Even there, Bennett and I got into a scuffle with two guys in their 30s. These guys were winning the game big, and letting the entire court know about it. Trash-talking really irritated Bennett. I usually laughed at trash talkers; it's just funny when a nice guy from great stock does it on the court. The guy Bennett was face to face with on this afternoon appeared to be one of these guys. Someone immediately stepped in to break up the confusion, but the guy quickly punched Bennett in his eye. Bennett lost control and struggled to go after the guy, but too many people held him back. In defense of my pal, I located an opportunity to get closer to the guy who threw the initial punch. As the drama continued to escalate, and my buddy's eye quickly closed, I drew within arms reach. I turned and punched the guy as hard as I could. I maliciously stopped the foul language the victor was spitting out, dead in its tracks. He was out cold before he hit the blacktop. "Somebody call the police!" an onlooker yelled. Bennett took this opportunity to kick his assailant in the head as he lay unconscious. "Bitch!" he yelled while still holding his eye. After hearing the word "police" we both decided to take off running. We ran back around McCabe from Dewees. I wanted to get away so badly, I even left my car. We quickly ran down the grass hill as if we were kids again, but this was not for fun. Thankfully those strangers were not aware of the type of car I drove. They were just two decent ball players, in the wrong area, on the wrong court.

By the mid-90s, Dewees Playfield was a place where you could go to play intense basketball, but you may not make it back home for supper. Nearly every guy on the court would still have a gun in their gym bags, or in their cars. If someone was fouled too hard or created too much controversy on the court, it's possible he could have been shot or badly beaten. More than once, I had to stop Tareek's little cousin, Mell from possibly shooting a guy in broad daylight on the court. He once asked me about a defender who played him too tightly on defense. "O, do yoou know that dude oover there?" Mell stuttered. He and his cousin Dro had this issue. "Yeah, that's Evan's cousin Nep," I replied. "He's a real good dude," I added. "Well, I'm about to kill his ass son," he whispered. "No, No, you can't do that, he's cool," I stated adamantly. "I know him well. He's cool. He grew up around the way when I was younger," I informed the younger teen. "He was born on McCabe Mell," I followed. "Oh, Oh.. Oh, alright then, he is lucky. He keep on fouling me. I I I was just about to kill that nigga O, I swear," he stated seriously. "Nah, he's cool. He's just playing hard ass defense." "Oh, w...well... he's lucky then you came here today. He don't even know h...h...how close he came to death today," he stated while gazing at Nep. I never believed someone could die for playing great defense, but I often would forget where we were. We were far "out of bounds!"

In Baltimore City, guys like Mell and his little cousin Dro came a dime a dozen. Today's reckless younger males are more plentiful, but comparable to those of the past. These young, reckless, trigger-happy kids were everywhere. Watching Mell point a 9mm at a competitive, non-violent, athlete was scary. No one would say much when one of these kids possessed a gun or pointed it at someone. "Please! Please don't kill me!" one kid yelled. This kid talked too much trash to Mell as well. "Now look at you. You a scared little bitch now. I s...sh...should kill you right here," he said as he pointed the gun, smiling, with his finger on the trigger. As we all observed, the guy screamed while balling up and bracing tightly in the corner of the gated court. Randolph often watched his nephews act out, but he too did not trust their judgement. "My...my uncle can try to stop me if he wants. I'll shoot him too," Mell once stated. Randolph would be sitting off to the side on a bench just shaking his head. This was life as we all knew it on McCabe Avenue during the mid-90s. I used my other ventures and different locations to play ball as much as I could to try and keep a balance somewhere between insanity and normalcy. I realized things were way out of hand on the block, but the hefty profits I received from my neighborhood, along with my depressed state of mind, still encouraged me to stay.

During this time, I was aware of my faults, but everything was moving along so quickly you hardly ever had time to regret a poor decision. It would always be time to do something else stupid before a positive thought would kick in. Therefore, I continued having ups and downs on the block. However, this mentality promoted my attention to shift to those who were not in the game at all. I was aware more structure was needed, but I conducted business with the frame of mind not to easily get myself killed or land myself in prison.

By the spring of 1994, I had pals from all walks of life. I had associates in different neighborhoods throughout the city, county, as well as the suburbs. Some of my associates carried guns, while others carried briefcases. Some owned houses, while others broke into them. Some would actually kill, and others would attempt to save lives; some took part in outreach, while others defended folk in courtrooms. By the mid-90s, my county drug operation consisted of a family attorney, a doctor, a nurse, a therapist, an electrician, a longshoreman, a tax agent and his attorney, an ambulance driver, a plumber, a realtor, and a host of others.

This was a lifestyle no one from my hood would ever entertain indulging in. Most guys in the hood believed it was too risky to be around, or hustle near white people. Funny right? Tough guys who only want to harm their own people! How weak is that? I didn't really plan this out, but when the list grew, I actually believed it was much safer. There, in the county, I never witnessed any whites shooting people in the head or pointing guns at people every chance they got. Nevertheless, both ways represented death. I just figured, in order to stay alive and free, I should sway a little, or get out of the city a bit more. It was nothing for me to be in the strained hoods, I just elected to change the approach to dealing drugs there. This double life I was gradually creating gave me an option, although this idea was still nothing more than the lesser of two evils.

In the midst of the violence, business with Scott progressed as myself, Elroy and Bennett hung closely. We all continued to make our presence known at the local nightspots. We spent ridiculous amounts of money on clothing and sneakers. I easily possessed over 200 pairs of tennis shoes, mostly Michael Jordan sneakers or Nike Air Force One sneakers. Spending money was no big deal. I spent so much money on Ralph Lauren apparel, I actually thought he was going to personally call me up one day to thank me. For every colored cotton mesh pullover shirt purchased, I had the same color swoop symbol on my Nike sneakers. I purchased many of the same shirts in long sleeve, or the same shirt made with a different fabric as well. For whatever color Polo attire Macy's did not carry, I would get from Nautica or Tommy Hilfiger. I still really loved wearing nice clothes and shoes. At the rate I was shopping, I was soon going to need an entire apartment for my clothing alone.

Spending time on McCabe, at this stage, did not just expose me to more violence and negativity. It also reintroduced me to Penny. We had split for quite awhile, but our feelings evidently remained. I was still searching for my own place alone, but rarely found time to play those angles. I no longer had a job. Finding a place to put in my name was not a first option for me. I was working on this with one of my white clients. I had to do something. I was in lavish hotel suites far more than I would be on Homestead Street. Was I alone? Never! Still, I was not over Penny. I would still get an intense feeling in my chest as I walked by her on the block. The look she would give me was a dead giveaway. We still cared for one another and we both knew it. Unfortunately, Penny was facing her own demons. We all have experienced pitfalls in our lives and Penny was no exception.

By the time Penny and I shared puppy eyes for the second time around, she had another child. "Shine" was Penny's third child, by the third different guy. In the hood, there are several words for a female who lands in this category. I was one of those few guys who actually understood these passionate young women. Penny continued to make the poor decision of attempting to hold to a man by having his child. She was searching for real love from guys who did not even love themselves much, myself included. Lots of other females were enjoying multiple counts of casual sex with many different guys, but never allowing themselves to get pregnant by these dudes. This made them appear more innocent. Hardly true! Although Penny only dealt with one guy at a time, she was recklessly going through with having their children, a horrible idea.

Penny's new child stemmed from her relationship with Lucky. Lucky was the younger brother of Marcus, a former member of our childhood dance group in the 80s. Everyone in our area had affiliation with each other on one level or another. There were simply too many confused young people, all living in a very tight setting. Our area was filled with lots of ways to make illegal money, no parenting, and plenty of drugs. This is the perfect mixture to produce unwed mothers or broken homes, incarceration, unwanted pregnancies, disease, death or violence and poverty. During this time, I had heard Penny's relationship with Lucky was rocky. Although he too made substantial amounts of money in the streets, it was clear she was unhappy. By her accounts, Marcus and his family were not as clean or neat as my sister and I were on Homestead. Penny was learning that the little things matter; and all men don't pay as much attention to these. When we were an item, I would often converse with her about life.

I may have made money and purchased like I was rich, but I was sure to remind Penny and my peers, throughout, we are from "the bottom." We are from POVERTY! Still, my attitude, despite the silliness, was rich, optimistic, and respectful. I would cook breakfast for her and the kids, every morning. I would usually wash, fold, and put away all of our clothing as well. I may have been lost and confused, but I was still sure of one thing; love. I was stupid, not blind. I understood the sisters we dealt with were entrenched in similar struggles. Some tried to pretend they were not, but they were right there, with us. We try to convince ourselves into believing we are fine, or better off than we really are. People from the ghetto, the hood; we all need to reel it back in and return to the basics. Be proud of your accomplishments, your elevation, your growth, but please understand where you come from and be humbled by it.

Penny soon realized the energy and compassion I presented to her was not a focus of her current mate. It would not be long before she would make a conscious effort to get the message across to me; she believed I was possibly still the man for her. Perhaps there may have been an altercation or problem between Lucky and I, but he ran into two bad situations. His first poor choice was sleeping with Penny's close friend, Melinda. His second mistake was catching a third drug charge. His misfortunes allowed Penny and I to visit the Red Roof Inn hotel, twice. Soon afterwards, Lucky was out of the picture with a five-year jail sentence, and Penny and

I reconnected for another chance to search for some form of love in a zone full of hatred.

Previous plans resumed; with increased violence, a move to Essex, Maryland suddenly seemed like a decent idea. I really cared about Penny, but I still knew I had inconsistencies in my social life despite the choice made to reconcile. Vikki was still very much in the picture. The feelings her and Penny shared towards each other probably helped intensify my relationship with Vikki. They always hated each other from their childhood days on Old York Road. I was not completely sure I would be able to do right by Penny, but I knew I would try much harder this time around. Again, with each passing drive-by, Essex was sounding like the place I needed to be. Besides, I was growing tired of living with my sister although I was hardly ever there. I felt I was too successful in the streets to be living with my sister. A drug dealer, or any grown man living with an adult besides his mate is not the best look, in my opinion.

In the midst of my issues, my sister Gina was experiencing change as well. She was so consumed with keeping tabs on Blue, she was hardly herself most days. The small altercation between Blue and I didn't help the situation. Blue never got passed the way he was eliminated from the fold with Scott. He even tried to steal an ounce of crack from me. I immediately went after him. I wanted to throw him around a little, knowing he no longer had an arm injury, but he quickly grabbed for a hammer, of all things. I had so many ounces when I witnessed him coming from out of my room, I was never sure if he really stole one or not. There were close to a few dozen ounces total. If he did, I'm sure he put it back after Elroy mentioned we were holding the drugs for Scott. A lie! Still, the confusion was my fault for not moving fast enough to get the crack to Tisha's.

Nevertheless, sleeping under the same roof with an untrustworthy, convicted murderer, who appeared to be a thief, was not my idea of home. I decided to leave my sister to deal with that mess on her own. She was as blind with Blue as I was with my entire life. All of this soon promoted Penny to make the necessary arrangements to get us into a townhouse in Essex, Maryland, before I would get myself killed.

As you all can see by now, I was a complete mess. I was never a thug or even a violent young man. I'm built pretty solid, specifically mentally and spiritually; never in the sense of a "tough guy," or one who would practice bullying or senseless violence. Throughout the years, I've been told I'm far too nice to sell drugs; too nice to the ladies. I was learning the hard way; selling drugs comes with so much more than what's initially expected. I was a peaceful guy who never cared to really harm anyone, yet, because I was making money illegally and living in a certain area, there were people who actually wanted me dead. This idea really concerned me whenever I took a break to reflect. I would never want anyone to be killed. I always saw us all as troubled; my approach to the black struggle was based on compassion, not anger. Disappointed; once I realized I was being referenced as one with the desire to participate in the violence, I made a small turn. I began to feel there was more to life, but I still was not equipped to know how to go after a more promising lifestyle. I continued to pray every night, hoping God would watch over me until the storm of despair would end. I also thanked God for Penny. She reappeared in my life at a very crucial time. As the idea of change began to form, I stood on the corners alongside my peers willingly adding to the destruction of society. Again, Penny was greater than even she believed. If it were not for her efforts, I would have likely stayed local longer. She had more of a sense of urgency than I. She made tremendous strides to get us all to an area where I could live long enough to possibly find the change I so desperately needed.

As McCabe Avenue was experiencing more and more heat, change would come my way whether I wanted it to or not. By the second month of our second union, Penny was pregnant again; by me this time. This would be her fourth child, and my very first. My sister Gina was also pregnant with her second child. The thought of having a child really scared me. The temperature was rising in the streets and at home. I felt I was not cut out to be anyone's father. The thought of fatherhood brought forth more of an urge to relocate. My business was still expanding out in the county. The unwanted attention from authorities increased on me and Elroy. Scott was experiencing similar pressures in west Baltimore which made him more determined to leave hustling behind altogether. As time moved on, he became more and more unavailable, despite the large sums of money we all made together. At this same time, I slowly began to feel uncomfortable on McCabe Avenue just as I did as a harmless teen. I could sense a spiritual shift within, but I was still lost and confused; not really sure if what I felt would produce better results.

As Penny awaited a return phone call from the rental office of Tidewater Village, located in Chase, Maryland just miles north of Essex, I sat on the steps of 731. I was selling drugs with Tareek, Dro, Rick, Elroy, and Bennett. It was around midnight and one of the guys had taken the liberty to, once again, shoot out the street lights, making it pretty dark where we were. Elroy and I were just about done with the $1500 worth of crack we had brought to the block throughout the night. We all were fortunate to experience a decrease in police activity on this night. Elroy and I were discussing our concerns about Scott relocating to the west coast to concentrate on establishing his very own music studio. We only had a couple of mediocre options to deal with as regular backups. The more solid or successful a kingpin, the harder it was to catch up to him regularly. We were unsuccessful in scoring from Scott before he left to set up his final move. I tried to catch up with him before he left, despite him not answering his cell phone. I drove west to Franklintown only for a guy to tell me Scott was about to leave town. The guy also told me Scott was cruising around town with a legendary rap star. He actually gave me a name of the famous rapper, but I'm not sure how authentic this accusation was. A clue? He was actually referring to a legendary, New York City rapper, but I can't say; sorry. I realize there are too many to pick from! This showed me just how serious Scott really was about moving on from dealing, and I must admit; I was impressed.

The six of us sat on those steps that night, for hours, taking turns selling drugs. I was leaning on the same pole I once faced with covered eyes as we played, "Hide 'N Seek." Now, with unrested eyes wide open, I was serving as a lookout for police who often liked to come from all angles in an attempted sweep. Elroy and I were finished for the night, but decided to stay until Bennett finished the remainder of his $500 stash. It was now Tareek's turn to make a sale. Soon, a white male quickly advanced towards us on a dirt bike. We knew this person was unfamiliar with the area, because he was riding the loud dirt bike up Alhambra; a one-way street in the opposite direction. As he approached on his Honda to buy drugs, he had no idea this was a very wrong turn; a turn to his final judgment here on earth, but neither did my close friends and I.

"I got this one," Tareek stated as he dug his hand into his pants to get his stash. Tareek then advanced to meet with the white male, dressed in a white tee-shirt and tan shorts, in the middle of the street. The rest of us waited for Tareek to return, just to hear how much the guy had purchased.

On average, white folks spent the most money buying drugs on McCabe Avenue, although none lived nearby. The neighborhood would usually get excited if whites came through, especially if they really gave off an appearance of being anything besides authority figures.

The meeting between Tareek and the white male appeared routine initially. What took place next totally caught everyone, besides Tareek's cousin Dro, off guard. In the blink of an eye, during the exchange between the two, the guy tried to snatch Tareek's entire stash from his grasp. The two struggled in the street as the dirt bike fell in between the legs of the addict. Tareek successfully regained total control of his baggie and violently kicked the man in the side of his head. A bit dazed and confused, the man shook his head, quickly pulled his bike up from the ground and took off. Tareek tried to grab the guy off of the bike, but the torque from the bike broke his grip. The back tire of the bike sped outward as the biker dashed forward. Once again, the man was driving up a one-way street; McCabe. He got about eight houses north of where we all were sitting, but just seconds later, he was down.

As the man quickly drove up McCabe Avenue, Dro hurried off of the steps and reached into his pants drawing a small automatic handgun. "D... D... Don't worry fellas!" he yelled, aimed, and giggled. "I... I got him!" Four shots followed those words. The rest of us were in total shock on the steps. We could not believe what had just transpired. We all witnessed large, red circles appear on the back of the man's white tee-shirt, causing him to spill off of the bike. "Oh shit!" Bennett yelled. "I'm going to go get the bike," Rick, who loved dirt bikes and pit bull terriers, insisted. I was speechless as Elroy said, "What da fuck?" The man was down, but we all were up quickly to watch Rick hurry towards the man. I was not sure if I was going to run in the house or simply run away. We all were stuck in shock as Dro took off running first. We all waited to hear what Rick had to say. He was the closest to the man and could see what kind of state he was in. He quickly grabbed the bike with its rear wheel still slightly spinning. Seconds later, he dropped the bike, kneeled closely to the injured man, looked down the street at us all, and yelled, "Yo, he's dead!"

We disbursed in groups, nearly as fast as the unwarranted bullets that now rested with the still body of the young male. Tareek and Rick all fled in the same direction as Dro. Myself, Bennett and Elroy all dashed towards Elroy's house. I didn't want anyone to see me turn around and run into my old home. The three of us crashed into Elroy's hallway floor in total disbelief about the sudden tragedy. Before we all could catch our collective breaths, we could see blue reflections on the walls from inside. The three of us peaked out of Elroy's front door window and watched dozens of police emerge, almost immediately. It was clear they were trying to quickly gather clues. I didn't hesitate to instruct Elroy to allow us to exit from the rear of his home. I wanted out of the house and the neighborhood.

Bennett immediately followed me out of the back door. "Those dudes are crazy O," Elroy whispered from his back porch. "Man, let me the hell out of here," I replied with anger. "I don't know about you son, but I'm about to be done with this fuckin' place buddy," I added. "That man didn't deserve to fuckin' die; not like that, and y'all know it," I passionately stated. Bennett added a nod in agreement. I turned and looked at Elroy from his backyard and just shook my head. "It's almost over here buddy. It's over!" I stated seriously. As I walked away with Bennett, Elroy called out. "O, I know that shit was crazy, but guess what though?" he asked with a smile. "What's up?" I replied. "My big brother Steve on his way home in a month, and Nardo will be home again soon too," he explained. "I forgot to tell y'all cus the money was comin too fast," Elroy added. Bennett dropped his head in reference to the timing of Elroy's statements. "I feel you, but your timing is crazy son!" I offered. "I mean, that would be a great thing buddy if they had somewhere to come back to, but it's still a good thing though," I replied casually as I continued away from the backyard. Both Steve and Nardo had been gone for awhile for various convictions. In just a few months the justice system was about to dump them, or allow them to come right back into this intoxicating, bloody mixture of violence, greed, and death.

I crept to my car, and Bennett made it to his own back door. I hardly slept on this night. I was already wondering where that guy's parents were, and how they may have felt once they learned of how and where their son had died. He appeared to be one of those white, drunken, free-spirited, Loyola College students or something. I don't recall ever seeing him prior to this incident. White folks are often seen traveling along York Road on the weekends, looking for a party at the few pubs located on the northern portion of the road. During the summer months, these students would casually walk by the harmless, top portion of McCabe Avenue. Most catch cabs up and down York Road, for safety reasons, and to avoid driving drunk. Taxi's await these young adults like limousines as they drink the night away, simultaneously shunning any black hand waving, desperately seeking a ride. Perhaps the individual who was murdered was too drunk, too bold; far too curious.

Over the years, I've always made sure I kept some sense of history. Although more study is needed, the history of my race has always been tremendously interesting and important to me. However, I'll never go militant with my approach as some often have. To me, that's racists as well. Besides, this method hardly seems to work today. My neighborhood was unique for many reasons; one being its location. Again, social economically, McCabe Avenue falls somewhere between lower-class and middle-class. The area has a middle-class energy, but the occupants are more consistent with those living in poverty. I've frequently existed in both settings; there's a difference. This difference allowed situations like this incident to happen regularly on McCabe Avenue.

Here, it hardly mattered whether one million blacks died, opposed to only 20 whites, the bottom line was PEOPLE were dying. They still are. Racial prejudice is one of the saddest ideas in the world, but today, society in America is far too diverse to charge an entire race for the actions of a past generation. This country is more diverse than ever; blacks, whites… deal with it. For us Black people, we first must examine why OUR people are killing one another for nothing at all, or senseless reasons. 'Nothing at all' here is referring to the love of money, sex or a woman's approval, materialism and ego. Hard times are a part of life, but killing one another certainly is not a viable solution. There's really no good excuse for that. It's stupid! I've been to hell and back, twice; I get being put through the fire. I've seen it all, and I get all of the things we've unjustifiably received for no reason in the past. I was dealt what most call, "a crappy hand" in life, but I refuse to primarily blame White people, law enforcement, wealthy folk or the world of politics for the detritus I experienced or endured in northeast Baltimore City.

Later that evening, at home I overheard a fragment of Penny's phone conversation involving the slain white man on the block. I never conversed with her about any of the details, despite the incident taking place directly in front of 731. However, Penny still shared a little good fortune with me. Her pregnancy was going well, and we received a move in date to relocate to our new townhome. Talks about the pregnancy were not always a peaceful topic. My sister's personal feelings and my immaturity had created an uncomfortable nervousness in me. I even asked Penny would she ever consider getting an abortion, due to the three other children she already had. She nearly killed me on that day. She said she did not believe in abortions; I had trouble buying that one. Although I felt guilty for asking her this, I didn't know of too many women concerned with these beliefs, but was not concerned much with health, practicing safe sex, or holding off until marriage. Strange! Nevertheless, I felt I cared for her enough to leave the topic alone.

A few days after the murder, police increased their efforts in making life for every dealer on McCabe Avenue a new living hell. While authorities struggled to pull information from uncooperative homeowners on McCabe, I was receiving a rude awakening on Homestead Street. One morning, I arose in my bed from loud knocking at the front door. I crept upstairs to get a closer look. I observed two men in expensive suits on the porch. I was staring at them through the peak hole in the front door. I started not to answer, but I figured these were agents; they were smart enough to see a shadow come and go from the small hole in the door. Besides, I thought, I personally didn't do anything to anyone. Well, besides sell some crack, and witness a senseless murder, but during this time that was pretty routine to us all. Dozens die in the drug game in these types of areas; there are tons of worms in those cans. Endless!

I opened the front door to greet the two white detectives. "Mr. Richardson?" one guy asked. "Yes," I replied with a calm grin. "Hi, we're with the FBI Homicide Unit. I'm Agent Watkins, and this is my partner, Agent Collins. We need to ask you a few questions about an incident; a homicide that took place on McCabe Avenue last night. Do you know anything about that?" he asked attentively. "No, I didn't hear anything about that one yet. There's always something going on there, it seems. That's why I'm leaving the city all together soon," I stated consecutively.

"Well, we would like to ask you a few questions down at the station," he asked firmly. "No problem. Let me get dressed. Come in," I offered. A lawyer was my best option, and I knew it, and although I had just lied to the feds, I still knew in my heart the murder was totally out of my control. Snitching was never an option, but I was going to assure the feds through my demeanor or personality, I had absolutely nothing to do with this homicide; that's the God's honest truth.

The feds questioned me from the time I got into their car, until the time I walked out of their office downtown. The closer we got to downtown, the more cocky or ignorant they became. I was asked, "Who killed the white man?" at least one hundred times. I was also asked, "Did you kill the white guy?" "Was the gun yours?" "How many of you were there?" and "Were you guys all trying to steal the guy's dirt bike?" Although dirt bikes are popular in the hood, I never learned how to operate one. Again, I stayed away from most of the things the guys in the streets preferred. I'm simply not very interested in a lot of the things many in my culture considered to be popular. I never cared for dirt bikes, smoking weed, drinking too much, four-wheelers, video games, clothing with labels exposed, shooting dice or gambling, guns; none of that. The feds asked me so many questions, I actually became sleepy. I shared nothing with the feds during this interview. I was allowed to leave the building two hours after my arrival. I was told not to go far by the feds. "I'm sure we'll be back to visit you soon son," one officer informed me. "Next time, bring a blanket or breakfast, or some chicken or something please," I stated. "I'm hungry!" Surprisingly, they all laughed loudly. However, the intense questioning was anything but funny. I quickly went home, packed up dozens of outfits, grabbed a few thousand bucks, rounded up Penny and left Homestead. The officers were sure I did not pull the trigger, but this may have been all they were sure of. Penny left the kids behind with her mother and we headed for the county to stay in multiple hotel suites. It was not hard to tell; it was time for me to lay low for a while.

Penny and I would experience several different hotels for weeks. This move proved to be a smart one on my behalf. The feds kept their word. I learned through talks on a land line with my sister, they indeed continued to come by the house. "What did you do?" Gina asked. "Nothing, it's a long story, but it's not my damn story. "I didn't write this one at all sister,"

I claimed passionately. "Don't worry sis, it's cool on my end," I assured my older sister. The good news was the police were mystified about my whereabouts. The bad news was much more plentiful. Two white, middle-class people had died on McCabe Avenue from gunshot wounds, and there were no suspects or arrests. At the same time, our business with Scott was becoming unglued. During the same week, a couple of guys attempted to kidnap, rob and likely kill Scott in west Baltimore. Two guys he once dealt with, held him at gun point as they all rode along with him in his Mercedes down Fayette Street. They faked a buy and instructed him to take them to his home at gunpoint. Scott's home had suddenly become his probable "executioner's chamber." Luckily for him, he somehow found room to jump out of his own car, while it was still moving. He did this right in front of a Baltimore City patrol car. His assailants recovered the driverless car and sped away. I got a chance to observe his mangled, left arm he sustained during this incident. This was all the evidence I needed to see. Scott informed me the next transaction we conducted would be our last with him. I was happy for Scott, but quite frustrated about my future ventures with purchasing crack. Our business ran almost flawless with Scott for a lengthy period. It was time for Elroy and I to find another connect we could trust. In the drug game during this time, these people seemed to be nearly extinct.

Elroy and I made our final move with Scott, while I resided at several county hotels with Penny. We purchased 15 ounces of crack and packaged it all up in $20 portions once again. Knowing this was our last move with Scott, we also decided to make the packages smaller, to increase our profits, and to hold on to the best product a little longer than normal. I'd asked Scott if there were any affiliates of his we could deal with in the future, but he declined. He said he did not want to get anyone unintentionally setup or killed. After his incident, he just wanted out. He didn't trust anyone. Not even us really. We managed to squeeze $33,000 worth of crack out of 15 ounces. Scott was serious about moving to L.A. I was equally as serious about moving to Essex. Hardly comparable, but we both realized, nothing stays the same in the drug game. I nearly accumulated the same amount of cash I possessed from my inheritance when I turned 18, but here no one really knew much. The duffle bag I hid very well in my sister's basement floor was evidence the drug game does have its financial benefits. The green bills could never display the pain connected with them. Staying clear of car payments to drive pricey vehicles, and excessive materialism like high-end fashion and jewelry allowed me to prosper financially. There were times I would buy half of an ounce of crack from a dealer, just to make sure he thought I was broke, or close to it. Dealers and many inner-city black males due to father absence, handle conflict, pressure or issues like females; they share in excessive ornamentation desires, and they talk poorly about others to feel more secure within themselves. I knew my small purchases would be spread in the streets. I did not care. In reference to cash, I knew I was doing fine. A lot better than most, and better than most believed, and I liked it that way.

The summer of 1994 entered with cooler temps than the previous year. The feds somehow discontinued their semantics and interrogation tactics to get someone to roll-over about the tragic death on the warm spring night. I struggled with the incident and all of the others, but I had to focus on my own survival. It really was everyone for himself on McCabe Avenue, and lots of people were losing their personal battles; the war within themselves to find a drop of decency in life. Elroy and I drew nearer to completing our last package from Scott in only two weeks. Police were becoming more aware of our success on the block. The undercover officers were focusing on my two pals and I. It had been two years since I attempted to run away from the cops and got myself arrested. Now more determined to never go down like this again, I paid closer attention to the authorities as well. I was very confident I would never go to jail. I was quietly sending the message out to the others; violence and impulsive behavior is never better than smarts and quiet money.

By the time we collected more than $25,000 cash from the crack we sold, the three of us were observed separately running from the authorities. To a certain extent, we all were very hot. The police wanted to arrest Elroy and I so badly, they even ran down on Bennett from all angles. Surprisingly enough, they did not arrest him for the $400 worth of crack he possessed. Instead, they took the stash from him and simply let him go. Police were hoping the rest of the hood would label Bennett as a snitch. It's just like planting a bomb. In most inner city neighborhoods, we've been taught by our parents never to talk or tell on someone. Now, these same instructors or role models are promoting snitching when it's concerning their own safety or welfare. Our parent's innocent little plan to instill toughness in us as kids has backfired. It's at home where kids are taught the concept of not telling or snitching, fighting back, and settling a score head on, on our own. Our parents said to us as kids, "You better not ever tell on anyone in your entire life about anything."

This stunt pulled by police was foreign to those on McCabe, but I possessed a wide social circle; this was commonplace further east. For us, no one had to tell on anyone. We were making our own bed here; we were hot on our own. Police understood Elroy and I were the guys making most of the money on the block. Genius and Etton were able to accumulate more once again, but those proceeds initially came from our product. They both had kingpin aspirations; Elroy may have as well, but I certainly did not. I was a part of a trio of guys who saw jail time as extremely "wack," lame, or trash. Elroy, Bennett and I, along with Tareek had not served any time in jail since we all started dealing. We believed the police felt if they used Bennett and make him appear to be a snitch, then the others would take him out and take us with him. Police likely believed this would bring violent perpetrators from the area out of hiding, to deal with those who snitch. Here, this did not work. With both of Elroy's big brothers back, we were prepared for all reactions, but I mentally passed the violence. Bennett was a decent person. Everyone believed his story enough to keep their fingers off of the triggers.

The scheme used by police did not promote more arrests, but it did force Bennett to think about quitting the game. I understood his position, but I was just getting started. I was too busy spending thousands of dollars on hotel rooms and on my car, again. While Penny and I began packing for our move to Essex, she mistakably crashed my car, then tried to lie about how the entire fender got dented. She told me the large dent was in the fender before I gave her the car to drive; crazy. I guess that's what I deserved for allowing an inexperienced, no licensed driver use my car. I only did so because I was hiding from the authorities. Luckily for me, I had MAACO body shop still in my corner. Paint jobs and body work cost me next to nothing during this time. I would hardly pay over $200 for any job.

After showing the police up in a foot race, twice, I decided it would be a good idea to never carry drugs on my person again, and to consider hiring a younger kid to sell drugs for me. Many older hustlers practice this. Initially, this questionable idea really rubbed me the wrong way. Low self-esteem and poor judgment allowed me to still try it once. Not only did the young teen get arrested for selling crack, I initially lost $700 in the deal. I was immediately finished with ever dragging someone else into my criminal misery. I felt horrible about playing a role in the teen's criminal background. He did manage to pay back the money he owed me over time. After receiving a final payment from the kid, I simply stated, "Sorry kid, I should have never given you those drugs anyway." Before he and his mom left the neighborhood, I encouraged him to never sell drugs again. I pray to God he took my advice.

Penny was now eight months pregnant. We finally settled into our two-bedroom townhome in Chase, Maryland, near Essex. I reluctantly spent less time in the streets and more time preparing for the birth of my first child, while also taking care of Penny and the others to the best of my abilities. In the midst of the dealing, I still believed I was a positive presence for Penny's other three kids. I was surprised how much I enjoyed looking after her kids. The innocent and carefree expressions they would give whenever I took them all out to eat, or out for toys, were priceless. For the first time in many years, I could sense feelings of real love. I could feel I had four-and-a-half individuals in my life who all genuinely loved me. Although I was not transformed enough to totally rid myself of all the negatives, I knew this was a way of life I could really be comfortable with one day.

The days to driving to Franklintown in west Baltimore to cop drugs in bulk were over. Scott was still around, but was gearing up to move to Los Angeles for good. Elroy and I soon began to conduct business with a childhood acquaintance named Pierce. He was a timid kid many of the bully kids picked on quite often when we all were younger. Due to his affiliations also in west Baltimore, Pierce climbed to above-average status in the streets. We felt he was one of the best guys to deal with and get our money's worth. Like Elroy and I, Pierce was no fan of violence, even more so. I also dealt with another guy from the Winston Avenue area, but like Scott, he was the best, but very hard to catch up with. I initially heard of Andrew through Old Man. Andrew and Hubert were great friends; I considered them both as good dudes. Sadly, Old Man overdosed not much longer afterwards. He was found dead sitting on his front porch. Despite confirmed new associates, we still were searching the overcrowded market for good drugs, right along with the rest of the city. Nothing in the streets felt stable at this time. The police were growing extremely frustrated with the entire area. Old York Road was always a problem, and I had a little girl on the way. My unborn daughter was positioning to enter this world full of pain and unpredictable ideas I was entrenched in.

Brandy Mone't Richardson entered this world on August 1st 1994. She weighed six pounds even. Brandy and I immediately shared a common bond. Just as the world and the devil apparently had a "noose around my neck," Penny's delivery did not go as well as planned. As my daughter made an exit from her mother's womb, the umbilical cord somehow closed tightly around my daughter's neck area. During this process, I read the doctor's expression and realized right away, there was trouble. I could also see just how tight the cord was around my baby's neck. The woman doctor struggled mightily to get a finger in between the cord and my daughter's throat area. Penny soon began to panic from above, just as the woman firmly gripped onto the cord. "What's wrong?" "Nothing," the doctor and I simultaneously stated quickly. The doctor grasped then pulled the cord over Brandy's head, but another problem arose. When the doctor removed the cord from around Brandy's neck, she was finally able to breathe freely for the first time ever. She immediately began to scream before she was fully clear of the womb. When her mouth opened wide to cry, fluids rushed down into her mouth, down into her trachea, and into her lungs. Brandy was finally out in the world, but not without complications. The complicated delivery caused Brandy to develop fluid in her lungs. I never panicked, but Penny grew very upset. I calmed her down and stayed optimistic. Brandy was forced to spend two extra days in the hospital until her lungs completely cleared. Things worked out fine! Praise God! By the third day, we were all in Chase, Maryland trying to start a new life with a new addition, but still with an old way of thinking on my part. On August 1stI became a new father, but I was not even close to being ready to become anyone's dad, or a real man.

Chase, Maryland was an easy place to settle into. The neighborhood was quieter than McCabe Avenue by far, but it was not quite the same as Towson, or the other surrounding counties I periodically operated in. I often stood outside of the front door, just to get a closer look at the people in the area. I immediately could see there were guys there from the same background as I. I watched their body language from afar and drew the conclusion pretty easily, drugs were being sold in the area. "There's money out here," I whispered to myself before re-entering the house.

I placed the idea of getting familiar with the drug business in Essex on the back burner as soon as I considered inquiring. I tried to make sure Penny and the kids had all they needed, including quality time from me. I was not as quick to run back to the city streets as in previous years. We had plenty of money saved and coming in. For the next few days, I would simply pace the floors, holding my newborn daughter in my arms until she would fall off asleep. I already had a little experience with changing diapers, making bottles, and bathing small children from helping out my sister with my niece Lia. Sometimes, I would just stare into my daughter's eyes in amazement. "WOW!" I would say to myself. I could not believe I had a child. At 22 years old, I was learning there is a lot more to life than what's happening in the streets. Having a child was not going to suddenly change it all. I knew that, but I wanted to be a good father to all of the kids I supported, yet deep inside I was still childlike myself. I stayed inside for a few weeks making sure the kids were fed and the house was clean. I could feel the pressure of being responsible for so many lives mounting inside of me. The pressure of responsibilities played a role in why I decided to sell drugs, but I was gradually learning to attack pressure, not flea from it. The streets I used to avoid real life, trained me how to deal with the worst forms of it. Basketball helped as well, but that was just a game. Hustling or drug dealing is often called, "the game," but it's no joke. I wanted to do whatever was needed to make sure my household remained stable. Whatever they needed or wanted, I was going to provide.

Before returning to McCabe I reunited with Evan. I wanted to get back into playing more basketball. I needed to clear my head, and basketball was the best way for me to do so. It had been some time since I sat down to write or sketch a portrait of my favorite superhero. The writing was compromised because I stopped expressing the emotions necessary to produce a good story. Again, in many ways, I stopped caring about matters of the heart. However, during a conversation with Vikki, after she learned of Penny's pregnancy, she reminded me of an extensive letter I had written to her when we were still in high school. "I still have that long love letter you wrote to me boy," she stated smiling. "It was the most passionate letter I've ever received. It was great," she stated with certainty. "Not just what you said, but how you said it," she added with a smile. "You good," she added with a nod. "Oh yeah, maybe I'll write more than. I like writing," I replied with a smile. A blank stare followed. This was the first time I told anyone how I felt about writing, and the first time anyone would compliment me on my writing. The letter I wrote to Vikki was eight pages long and powerful enough for her to talk about it almost five years later. I was impressed. I was very impressed with me.

Evan and I were turned on to an outside basketball court near Elkridge, Maryland, off of Dorsey Road (Route 176). This was one of the few outdoor ball courts in the state where we were allowed to play ball until 2 or 3:00 a.m. Most courts in the city and counties did not have long running lights at night. Dorsey Road did! With the scorching summer temps and the poor air quality, Dorsey Road became a second home for the two of us. Whenever we were not playing ball, or if I was not at home trying to become a good dad, I would be either on McCabe Avenue dealing, with Evan in his area selling, or in the Towson area doing the same. At this time, the desire to be on McCabe Avenue was slowly drifting away. I wanted to stay connected with Elroy, but he seemed to be too attached to the neighborhood. We were already a bit hot, yet he still made sure he was seen there often. My new plan was to solidify my outside operations in the county, check out the situation in Essex, and eventually pull myself and my friend away from McCabe Avenue for good. Bennett was already done dealing crack on McCabe. We still loved the place itself as home, but things were just too stupid there, and we were getting older. The money there was beginning to decrease anyway, and the senseless violence would elevate once again.

The birth of my daughter Brandy forced me to find moments of peace. Penny was never a morning person. She, pretty much, at the time, lived her life without ever holding a job. I had worked a couple of small jobs as a teen, therefore getting up early in the mornings when I did not feel like it was not a huge deal. I was never a fan of working, but I was still a morning person. Basketball and several of my prominent customers got me accustomed to waking up earlier than most. I regularly met one guy at his office to help him get a "jump-start" to his day. I loved waking up

4:00 a.m. to the screaming voice of my daughter. I've always had an "It's not where you start, but where you finish" attitude. Putting Brandy back to sleep by pacing back and forth, longer than she could cry, felt great. This consistent pacing said to Brandy, "Daddy is here." Do I need to say more? This also allowed me to be more patient. This was one of the first ideas that allowed me to see there's victory in patience. I was learning from within as the days progressed, but I was not growing in my outer life. No matter what good took place around me in the world I was still trapped inside of my own tainted mind.

After dropping Penny and the kids off at her mom's place in Patterson Park, the heart of southeast Baltimore, I ventured north to meet up with Elroy. We scored from Pierce and I was eager to see how well the product moved. I was hoping we had found a new connection which would allow us to do just as good as we had with Scott. However, as I entered onto the block, the thought quickly left my mind. As I slowly drove towards 731, all I could see were dozens of patrol vehicles. The police were everywhere. Surprisingly, all of the guys were out as well. It appeared to be a standoff of some sort, and Genius was smack in the center of it all. Something was about to happen; something wild and crazy, and I still had my ageless "front row seat."

I quickly parked my car around the corner and jogged to stand on my old porch. Guys were yelling out, "Fuck 5.0!" "The police suck!" and their favorite, an N.W.A classic, "Fuck the police!" As I stood and watched, Elroy and Bennett suddenly joined me. "O, some crazy shit about to kick off, the cops and niggas beefin," Elroy said while smiling. Apparently, Genius was seen placing a gun or a large stash of drugs in one of his seven vehicles; his Mercedes, to be exact. When he observed the officer, he quickly closed the door to the vehicle and locked it. Police decided to skip the red tape by attempting to force Genius to reopen his car door through probable cause. Backup was called and most, including Etton, rallied in support. An explosion was about to ensue between dozens of Baltimore City's boys in blue, and the dealers from McCabe Avenue.

Genius and one of the officers spent minutes cursing back and forth at one another. What made this situation so interesting was the police were not exactly there to arrest guys for dealing drugs. It appeared as if the police were actually there to square off or fist fight with the hustlers.

As the cursing continued, this officer took off his belt and handed his gun to another officer. A few other officers disconnected their armor as well, tossing their belts into their patrol cars. "Yeah come on," Genius said with a smile. "I'm going to beat the shit out of this cracka," he yelled with a devilish grin. "Oh yeah nigger, we'll see about that," the white officer replied as he quickly advanced forward. Although the 'n' word drew everyone's attention, the neighborhood appeared to be evenly divided. Some people were cheering the police on, and some were cheering for the guys. I believe the support was due to observing these young black males standing against something other than themselves. The scene was unbelievable. I giggled at the entire situation, in total disbelief. The Baltimore City Police Department momentarily replaced rival neighborhood Old York Road.

Soon, Genius and the huge officer began to wrestle in the middle of the block. The others wanted desperately to join in. Tareek, Etton, Mell, and Dro, were just a few. Days ago, Dro had struck an officer with a stolen car. He escaped before being identified. As the others closed in on the fight taking place, officers pulled out their nightsticks. The officer was attempting to retrieve Genius' keys as the two tussled in the center of the block. Genius was already headed to jail for violently resisting arrest and disorderly conduct. One officer told another, he actually did observe Genius making a sale and then hurrying to place the drugs inside of his car, once he saw police approaching. The officer in the scuffle was successful in getting closer to the keys Genius held. The officer's hand was partially on the keys causing many in the crowd to grow nervous. Several others were still yelling profanity at the officers. Then, the officer briefly retrieved the keys from Genius. "Get back!" "Get the fuck back!" other officers yelled. "Fuck you!" "Bitch ass niggas!" returned from the crowd. Genius had to act fast, and he did. In the blink of an eye, he broke free from another officer's grasp, snatched his keys back, and tossed them to Etton. The crowd cheered as Genius was simultaneously thrusted over the patrol car. He was nearly tackled and quickly subdued by four other officers. Now things would get really crazy!

The attention of the officers immediately would shift to Etton, who now had the keys to the Mercedes Benz. Etton circled around parked vehicles as cops swarmed and chased him. "Run! Run! Etton! Run!" the others yelled. Just before being grabbed and tackled himself, Etton heard a voice yell, "Over here E!" It was Ollan. He was the infamous and anonymous character involved with the domestic altercation, which resulted in Limon's death. He was waving his arms through the crowd for Etton to throw him the keys. He did. The crowd again cheered and burst into laughter. Ollan snatched the keys out of the air like a star wide receiver and dashed towards the alleyway. The entire neighborhood was clapping as if they were actually watching a movie or the Super Bowl. This was a scene possessing many different elements, just like an award winning film. There was drama, action, suspense, negativity, and most importantly, a social economic or ethnic twist. This was a moment in time where you could actually feel a togetherness between average citizens and drug dealers. Many of the officers were white and most of the crowd's response was consistent with racism. This was one of those situations where matters of race actually dominated the issue of justice.

After Ollan ran off with the car keys, the small riot would continue. An officer twisted Genius' arm so violently from behind, he screamed. This scream was followed by a powerful "horse kick" backwards into the officer's groin area. The officer fell to the ground, and even more cheers surfaced. Others watched Genius drop the officer and decided to join in. As the situation escalated, a few officers finally drew their weapons. Guys were hit in their heads with nightsticks, beaten, and arrested. A few managed to throw an officer or two around, but the momentum quickly shifted in the officers' favor. Tareek and his cousins managed to run away, but the others were not as lucky. In all, there were twelve arrests made, including Genius and Etton. It was very clear; things on McCabe Avenue were as unpredictable as ever. It was also clear my relatives still had the best seats in the house. We stood on my porch and watched this entire situation unfold. Elroy and Bennett giggled as we observed the officers violently throw a dazed guy into the transport van. I giggled religiously during this situation as well, but I was still focused enough to say to myself, "Damn, we're all hot as hell!"

Just when I thought all of the surprises were done for the day, Elroy told me he had offered Killer Kev a job to partner with us. "What?" I replied in shock. "O, he's cool, and we can use him for muscle," he added calmly. "Elroy, that's the point," I explained seriously. "Muscle for what?" I shouted. "He is cool, but he's more concerned with the violence than he is the money," I stated with certainty. "He's a problem. You know this! That's all we need at this point is for the police to link us up with him; of all people," I said with tremendous disappointment. "I guess you would be even more upset if I told you, I let him hold the Tech 9 as well?" he asked with uncertainty. I was speechless. I turned to Bennett. He instantly dropped his head as he would whenever one of us would make a poor decision. I gave Elroy a long, hard stare. Then, I turned away and left him standing on my porch without saying another word.

Elroy had apparently made quite a few poor decisions while I was caring for my newborn daughter. He allowed a very controversial individual to enter into our circle. Killer Kev was originally a "stick-up kid" or armed robber. I actually liked his personality whenever we talked about issues other than drugs, sex, and violence; not very often. All else we hardly agreed on. He relished in putting fear into people and using firearms. That simply was not my style at all. Dealing with guys like Kev could get you killed easily in the inner-city. He apparently rubbed too many people the wrong way over the years. Elroy was still my boy, but I was never able to look at him the same after he made this move, especially without letting me in on it. Killer Kev sensed the tension, but did his best to remain neutral. He knew we were making profits of five/six-figures per week, and he was desperately trying to impress a female; one I turned down multiple dates with. I believed she was a good person, just not good for me. I knew with Kev now as a partner, our time on McCabe Avenue had become shorter. I began to really analyze and keep a detailed count of how much money I actually made in the county per week. I was beginning to set up an out. I was lining myself up to leave the city and all "open air" or corner dealings behind permanently. I was totally losing the desire to affiliate, hang out, or sell drugs in Baltimore City.

Most of the guys in my city sold drugs to obtain a lifestyle they believed was too illusive to achieve solely through a blue collar job or a dream. Financial desperation was never the true motive behind my decision to sell drugs, although I played that role well. Dealing was something I gradually allowed myself to slip into because of low self-esteem and a lack of guidance. Negative and tragic circumstances compromised my thinking abilities, natural common sense, and stole away my zest for life. It became very hard for me to see a productive future for myself. Now, city life was beginning to take its toll, and I knew I needed a drastic change. I enjoyed the things I was able to purchase with the thousands I had made, but the negativity around it all really sucked. Moving forward, I began to pull away from city living as things deteriorated more.

Elroy's decision to recruit Killer Kev began to backfire almost immediately. With the actual dealing, the plan was always to bring back no less than $400 off of each $500 stash. Killer Kev hardly ever seemed to make this mark. He would usually have $300 or $350. Sometimes he would only make $275. He had a big problem with spending money off the top. Meaning, he would make personal purchases before meeting the mandatory set figure. Elroy's choice of partner was slowly chipping away at a very profitable operation. This was compounded by the weaker quality of product we had purchased from Pierce. This was all topped off by an ongoing feud that was coming to a head with me falling somewhere in between.

Weeks passed by, and I sat back and watched a five-figure operation spill gradually. I voiced my displeasure with Elroy, Killer Kev, and Pierce. Everyone in my neighborhood, with the exception of Bennett, was beginning to rub me the wrong way. Bennett grew frustrated long ago and was able to quit beforehand. The decision to stop dealing was much easier to pull off for Bennett. He hustled strictly for material purposes. He did not have the same severe emotional defects as I. He took his new job at Valley Motors, a luxury car dealership in Timonium, Maryland more seriously than he did selling any drug. After the incident he experienced with the narcotics officers, the decision was not a hard one. He began dealing a little weed on the side, but never gave a second thought to crack again.

Bennett and I still hung out together at the local bars and on the basketball courts. Our connection was fine, but I felt like I was back on the outside looking in with all of the others. I had a few arguments with Pierce about the quality of his product. I also had a disagreement with Tareek about a female I introduced him to named, Amanda. Amanda was one of Vikki's best friends. She was seen with Vikki often when she would come through McCabe looking for me in previous years. Tareek pleaded with me in the past to introduce him to other females outside of the neighborhood. Hesitantly, I decided to do him a favor. I'm not really into match-making, although it worked out great when I introduced a pal of mine named Ronnie to a female classmate he was afraid to approach. They married soon after we graduated high school and have one son together. However, that was high school, this was the "school of hard knocks." After promoting this connection, Amanda soon believed she was dealing with an irrational personality. I eventually became the middleman in this awkward situation. Life in the hood didn't have to be so rough, but for me, it truly was.

Even with the problems we all endured, Elroy and I concentrated on our financial situation on the block to see if we could produce some magic of old. Friction between Pierce and I remained evident. During a deal we made with him, I elected to pay for only half of the mediocre substance he sold us. I felt like the product was not worthy of the full price, at all. He agreed on the deal I set initially, but grew tired of the lengthy wait for the rest of the money. He knew we had the money, but he learned about other scores we had made with other connections during this same time. Andrew, a cool guy and friend of Hubert, also from Winston, was a much better connection though pretty hard to keep track of. This forced me to continue a business relationship with Pierce. A relationship which was turning bad, just as everything else was on McCabe Avenue.

Just when I thought things could not get any worse, I learned my aunt Marie was doing something we all dread about out in the streets. I learned from a pretty reliable source, my aunt was having sex with various guys in the neighborhood for drugs. When I asked for names, I was specifically told Tareek, Harold, and Big Bug. I suspected others; those closest to myself. I was devastated by the news, but kept it all inside with the rest of my garbage. I was hurt badly by the news. I was hurt for Shawn. I was tremendously frustrated with my peers, and my family situation, therefore I declined to speak with my aunt or the guys about the matter. I felt I would do something stupid and make digressing matters further complicated. However, I wanted to explode when in my aunt's presence. Instead, I would simply glare, speaking to her without ever saying a word. My aunt figured I knew, specifically or not. I love my aunty more than she knows, but back then she really needed lots of help. But we all did.

I did gain a bit of unrelated information from my aunt Marie once the shock of this news passed over. She learned of my new residence when she asked me about the well-being of my daughter. She told me a close friend of hers lived in the exact same complex as I, in Chase. I stored the information in my mind, thinking this individual could be my ticket to getting a new operation started out in Chase. I remembered seeing the familiar woman's face once or twice in the neighborhood. I recalled the woman having a son who nearly killed himself in an attempt to escape from police in a stolen, Nissan 300 ZX. It was said he was seen being dragged down the road outside of the car, faced down. He tried to jump out of the moving vehicle to escape, but forgot to do one thing; undo his seatbelt, OUCH!

There were many instances like these throughout the neighborhood; situations having nothing to do with me, drugs, or the feud. Everyone was a member of this society, full of despair and disappointments. I observed one of Tareek's little cousin's body sprawled on Northern Parkway near my old high school one evening. "Pop" and a friend decided to drive a motorcycle 100 miles per hour, on a winding road, without helmets. This decision killed them both, instantly. Guys were still going to prison for years, only to be released to do the same thing they were arrested for originally. There were next to no signs of constructive energy. Besides Tupac's elevation, there only seemed to be one other guy who dared to dream, or have enough confidence in himself to do better in life. I remember guys hurrying to observe this other young rapper display his talents. Guys would periodically say, "Hey y'all, Petey around the corner rappin." I was there, but I never paid much attention to the young, upstart rapper or his younger brother named, "Freeze." He would soon leave the McCabe Avenue area and the city altogether. He became a sensation from North Carolina named, Petey Pablo.

Tupac Shakur and Petey Pablo were doing their best to make their marks in our society through hip-hop, while the positive inner qualities within the rest of us fell dormant. We were living our lives through the culture of hip-hop, but failing to produce any positive results in life. Hip-Hop is a beautiful culture indeed. It's always been an unprecedented, urban creation, opening the doors for limitless possibilities. As for the rap music and its content; it does get a bit senseless and disturbing at times, especially for an outsider who lacks the knowledge about the truth of the streets. Ignorance is truth. I've noticed many of today's artists are not speaking very clearly. This makes it tough for me to digest the content. Brothers often rap about things they're already expected to do, but that is the reality of the young black male and the current culture of hip hop. However, I do understand it, but I'm not in alignment with a lot of it.

Overall, I still feel rappers are simply talking about the truth or what takes place within our culture. If you don't want to hear it, turn it off. Period! The music was more creatively balanced and more informative years ago; the talent is still there, just not as much. Buying cars, cribs, jewelry, and dealing with multiple women is not news; so what, but hey... whatever works, I guess. With this said, I still believe hip-hop is knowledge for the curious and the ignorant. In my opinion, it sounds very good! Let's not forget these guys could be doing things society does not care for. The decisions artists made to start music careers is a tremendous blessing for society. It's also very fun entertainment and street creativity on the highest urban level. I believe it gets unfairly judged at times by those who don't quite understand it or know its origin. On the other hand, it's also my belief the music is sometimes misleading and misunderstood by my own people. The consumers sometimes take the music far too seriously. They should keep an open mind when purchasing and listening to the music. This music often helped me feel a little better at the poorest times in my life, but it can drive your negative juices too if YOU let it. I love all music, but I don't live my life by it like so many of my people try to do. So please people, don't blame these hardworking performers for society's issues, because a lot of us are simply not responsible people. Don't get me wrong, the music does play a role, and it has the ability to encourage folks to be positive or negative, depending on the individual. I know; I was one of these people.

Unlike the world of hip-hop, I was experiencing more lows than highs on the city streets of Baltimore. My daughter represented the only part of my life with substance or purity to it. My relationship with Penny was going alright as well. It could have been much better if I was in control of my uncontrollable flirtatious ways. No matter how hard I tried to be a faithful boyfriend, I would always end up back in the presence of another beautiful sister. I would hardly even try most times. All I had to do was go out to any kind of social event. Shortly afterwards, I would always find myself at a movie theater, an amusement park, a mall, and ultimately a hotel suite with a gorgeous sister. Then, I would usually feel bad for a day or two afterwards, or just long enough to meet another beauty and follow the same routine. Sad but true, this was my life in the hood.

My life was a sad mess, but I actually felt alright at the time. I was making money, women were no problem to share time with, and I had a beautiful daughter who lit up at the sight of my face or the sound of my voice. As 1995 approached, I continued to stretch my time away from McCabe as long as I could. Elroy and I were still having problems with the authorities. We struggled to do a decent job at staying out of their sight. If the police were busy on the block at night, we concentrated on working throughout the days. We stayed out extra-late if the cops patrolled the days away, but they were still onto us both. To us, it really didn't matter, as long as we were producing thousands per week. Even though troubles were nearby, I actually believed I could not be arrested. I believed I was too smart. Everyone in the area, except me, seemed to get pinched every once in a while. I would stick and move like a prizefighter. However, there were many close calls. I was usually staggered, but never "knocked out," not yet.

There were a few incidents where my escape abilities were put through the test. One morning, after making nearly $1000 in less than two hours, I was approached by police. Two new agents were appointed to McCabe Avenue. Serge was no longer there to put fear into the hustlers on the block. Elroy was thrilled. He felt he had survived Serge's attempts to finish him up. However, his "victory dance" would be short-lived. It came to a halt when he was told by these new cops; he was still a top priority. Now, I was no exception. So there I sat on 731's steps one morning with several others. It was time to dance with the cops again.

Most of the guys seated on the steps of 731 were the same individuals from the night of the tragic shooting incident of the young white guy. Out of all of the guys here, I was the only one with just one arrest and no violent charges, but these two agents still had all eyes firmly planted on me. As they stared at me, I did the same back at them. I normally would have paid no attention to police, especially from my own porch, but this situation came with the same problem as the 1992 arrest. I "slept" again. I was "dirty." In my pocket was a stash of $400 worth of crack.

Apparently I was the only guy on the steps with drugs on my person. I really hardly ever carried drugs on me. If I had anything on me, it would usually be for no more than ten minutes or however long it would take me to get from "point A" to "point B." Officer Jacobs, one of these new agents, and his partner could sense the concentration and anticipation in my demeanor. The doors to their black, Pontiac Grand AM slowly opened after pulling up to the front of 731; now labeled as a "nuisance house" or a house folks believe affiliates with some form of trouble or illegal activity. I immediately stood as the officers drew closer. Their eyes seemed to never blink, staying fixated on me. As the two knifed through the others below, I slowly paced backwards. By the time the officers reached where I was sitting, I was staring at them, from inside, behind a closed door, through the diamond-shaped glass. I quickly turned the lock on the door knob. I sprinted upstairs as they watched through the small window. I quickly headed to a room to stash the drugs. I felt like I was in the clear, therefore I decided not to flush the drugs. I walked passed the empty toilet and placed the drugs in the room where my grandma once slept. The room was being occupied by my aunt Marie. Her son Jayson inherited my old room next door. I was very surprised to see pairs of my grandma's underwear still inside of the drawer. She had been dead for nearly three years. Perhaps it should not have been much of a surprise to me. All the curtains in the windows were also still the same. The biggest surprise, however, would come once I returned downstairs.

When I returned downstairs, I was shocked. I was face to face with the same two officers. My uncle BoBo was in one of his moods. BoBo was an easy person to get along with when he was drunk, which happened to be most of the time. However, whenever he was not, he would return to his old form of years ago. He would turn into a "citizen on patrol," a snitch. It hardly mattered if I was his nephew. He would assist authorities no matter who was involved. My uncle welcomed the agents inside, allowing them to search the entire home without a warrant. I was immediately instructed by police to sit on the couch. I was surrounded by three backup, uniformed officers. I went from being sure I was one step ahead, to being sure I was going to jail as I sat in our infamous living room. I was thinking all kinds of crazy thoughts. One of these uniformed officer's gun was at arms reach. I briefly thought of going for it, but as always, I tried to remain calm. That thought was not reality-based. It was based on the writer mindset I had yet to embrace. In my mind, I often see life or real life circumstances as a movie. This is a common approach for writers. I'm not crazy; this is a frequent lens we all see life through. As the officers searched relentlessly upstairs, my heart was pounding hard enough for me to feel it in my feet.

My uncle had assisted police in denting the armor of confidence I had built up since my first arrest. I can't lie. I was worried as hell.

After an hour of intense searching, the two officers slowly walked down the stairs. They were still piercing at me intensely. I was not sure if they were going to instruct the police to cuff me or allow me to stand up under my own will. The stare down lasted a few more seconds before I heard the words, "You're lucky this time son," come from Officer Jacob's mouth. "Let's go!" he instructed the other officers in the house. There were a total of seven of them inside of the house on this day. The police were unsuccessful in locating the crack I had placed under my grandma's bloomers. I guess it was fair to say she was still covering me, but this was not exactly the same as running to Mama as a kid for security. Not only did the officers not locate the drugs, they were totally in the wrong room. They never entered the room where the drugs were. I guess they assumed I still resided on McCabe. Jayson's room was nearly destroyed throughout. His room served as a decoy during this search. I smiled at the mess, as I took a quick glance at the old Reggie Lewis basketball poster left on the wall from years prior. I retrieved the drugs from the dresser drawer, surveyed the landscape outside from the front window, and proceeded with my hardheaded ways. I sprinted down to the back alleyway and stumbled across four addicts. I sold the infamous $400 stash in less than three minutes.

A similar close call returned later in the same week. This time I was forced to throw a smaller stash in the front porch window where Mama once sat. "Someone" had mysteriously locked the front door this time. I had to act fast. I pushed the window screen out and tossed the drugs inside of the house. Thankfully, Montell did not allow the cops to enter the house. He came through for me much better than my blood-relative had. He grabbed the stash off of the floor from inside. He picked it up so quickly, narcs were mystified when the use of their flashlights produced poor results. Obviously, I was very appreciative for the way my uncle handled things in this situation. During this time, I tried hard to stand clear of my family, for the most part, when it came to the actual dealing. They did not care for me to see them in the state they were in. I was also a little embarrassed to be seen by them as a drug dealer, something they never expected of me.

Over the years, I was pleased to be able to stay away from my drug-addicted relatives. However, in this situation I was so relieved about the outcome my uncle allowed me to experience; I regret it today, but gave him a few free bags. I never shared any of these experiences with Penny. I wanted her to feel secure with me as a boyfriend and father, despite my casual approach to being in a committed relationship.

The heat was definitely being turned up by police. They were really fed up with McCabe Avenue and everyone there. The Old York guys were also refocusing their attention back on McCabe. Nut was back up to his usual antics. So much so, Tareek swore to personally deal with him. After a situation where he and Miran drove through the block shooting a gun up in the air, startling Tareek, he yelled out, "That's it! I'm going to kill that little bastard, watch!" With the temperature rising in regards to violence, profits, and police activity, everyone here was a subject to experience more harm. Everyone was a target constantly staring at death, myself included.

*Chapter 17*

# A VISIT FROM
# THE REAPER

I began the year 1995 with trying to have a better outlook on the near future. Selling crack on city street corners was getting old; the risks and rewards were starting to balance out, and that's not good. My ability to branch out and accumulate profits in the surrounding counties was proving to be a much better fit. I was doing a decent job with staying away from the violence, but this was often easier said than done. The money still came relatively easy on the block, but the violence seemed to come easier. People were still getting seriously hurt in the streets. Thanks to a healthy dosage of snow for the start of the year, no one I knew was killed.

Gangster rap still dominating the sound waves throughout the neighborhood as the crack cocaine and heroin reached out to more lost souls. Despite heroin's infamous heroics really reaching the northeast, I continued to exclusively deal with crack cocaine. I stayed in motion while mentally shuffling the thought of a drastic change in my life. However, the connection I had made with the block over the last 15 years was surprisingly tough to break away from. Despite all of the inconsistencies, part of me wanted to be there. I knew I would soon have to leave the corner life behind, or give up on my life completely.

Summer approached, and despite my "open-air" dealings apparently drawing to its end, I was successful as ever. Avoiding the violence and fighting with the inability to obtain a steady connect was tough, but I was able to regularly possess product good enough to produce hefty profits once again. On top of this success, more expanding took place. Through my aunt's close friend, I eventually managed to develop another profitable situation in Essex. I began dealing with just two folks in Essex. I had 16 people in Towson and Hunt Valley, Maryland, to go along with my side dealings with Evan in his area near the city line. McCabe Avenue was certainly still profitable, but was becoming a liability. The plan was to get it to a point where I would never need the proceeds from the block. Folks were still making money around the way, but the corners were seemingly doing more harm than good. More arrests, more shootouts, guys were experiencing shorter runs on the block to only get handed longer sentences. The bad was consuming the celebration of quick profits. At 25, I believed it was time to do my own thing. I honestly believed I was getting too old to be around so many other dudes. I lived with the fear of not knowing what I would become, but I was not afraid of society itself.

In all, I was soon able to make a five-figure profit income each week by myself. Elroy and I were still partners, and he was doing well himself, but our time being seen together had lessened. We were growing apart; I liked this. However, my independent success would actually promote more flirtatious behavior. Again, I would rekindle an off and on relationship with Vikki. There were a few others as well, but she seemed to occupy most of my free time. Vikki and I were together so much, it was as if she was my girlfriend, and Penny was just a close friend. My unshakable feelings for Vikki kept me local more than I wanted to be. City life kept me closer to the pretty young ladies, where I wanted to be, but it also kept me around the police and the violence. It would only be a matter of time before they all would harshly mesh together.

One warm and sunny afternoon, I picked Vikki up from her home on Guilford Avenue located in east Baltimore. We decided to go to the mall and rent a nice hotel room at the Holiday Inn. Again, cheating became very easy for me despite the sadness I will feel afterwards. Penny, upset about what she was hearing in the streets about me, also practiced being unfaithful. She was trying to finish whatever drama my actions had started. One night, I arrived in her mom's neighborhood unannounced, and witnessed her exiting a new, black Nissan 300ZX with an unknown guy behind the wheel. She never saw me, and I never mentioned the situation. I called myself holding on to the dirt for insurance in case I was to ever get caught in the act myself one day. I rarely blew up when I learned a female I affiliated with was seeing someone else. If I did overreact, I would immediately wake up. I've always been a realist. I knew I deserved to be dumped or cheated on. This was a time where everyone wanted everything, and we all were doing whatever we felt was necessary to get it. I was not trying to deliberately hurt anyone, but I was living a lifestyle in an area where you did not have to try to mess up. It just happened! Mishaps came naturally. Again, infidelity, arrests, violence, or the possibility of getting killed was always just a small turn away.

Two minutes after picking Vikki up from her house where she lived with her mom and grandma, we sat at a traffic light on the corner of 22nd Street and Greenmount Avenue. Ironically, I was listening to a Tupac Shakur song titled, "My Block." At the song's end, the artist mentions the block, Cator Avenue; the street off of Old York Road. Vikki heard the song for the first time and was surprised by the lyrics. As we sat at the red light, she shared with me how the rap star, as a young teen, consistently flirted with her years ago in their old neighborhood. She said she would always decline his advances. "We all knew he was talented in many ways, but no one wanted to talk to him like that," she claimed. "Not my type!" Vikki stated. "You're something!" "Many of us were a bit rough around the edges back then," I offered. "For real though, he was always talented. He would act out little movie roles n' stuff; he would act like Rick James or somebody like that on the corner, and rap n' stuff, but no one wanted to talk to him in that way at all," she repeated. "Would you talk to him now?" I asked smiling while cutting my eyes over in her direction. "What do you think?" she replied with a grin. I smiled back at the beauty before I turned to watch the orange flashing hand, indicating a changing traffic light. I felt the question I had just asked Vikki annoyed her, due to the new silence which suddenly consumed the vehicle. I soon learned she was not mad at all, just scared, nearly to death.

Just as I began to grow impatient with the long red light, I felt two hard slaps on my right arm. A hasty, "Uh, Uh, Uh," came from Vikki's distorted tone. I turned, looked at Vikki, and read the fright in her expression. She frantically pointed out to her right and I too became alarmed. It was Nut. He was approaching my car while drawing a large revolver from his pants.

"Go! Go! Go!" Vikki finally yelled as an armed Nut got within 15 feet of us at the traffic light. I smashed the gas pedal and dashed through the red light just as it had turned green. Three loud shots soon followed the sound of my screeching tires. "Oh my God!" Vikki yelled while shaking and holding her head. "That was Emmanuel!" she added. This was Nut's birth name. Nut had just shot at us on a busy main street in broad daylight. I was beginning to grow just as tired of Nut as Tareek. This incident really annoyed me. Miraculously, there was only a single mark from where the bullet grazed the car just under the tail light on the passenger side. Vikki babbled repeatedly about how Nut was such a nice kid many years ago. My mind was already made up; drastic measures were needed. It was time for me to have a word with whoever was running things on Old York Road. Enough was enough!

After relieving stress and making sure Vikki and I celebrated life after our brush with death, we checked out of the Holiday Inn. I dropped her off about 2:30 p.m. the next day. We had a great evening thanks to Penny staying in town at her mom's house. She wanted to be closer to her family because of a tragic situation involving her relatives. They were dealing with a horrific situation with one of her older sisters and an older female cousin. Penny has three older sisters; Linda, Diana, and Leslie. Penny's sister, Linda was the sibling involved with this incident, along with her older cousin, Brenda. The two of them were being held at the Baltimore City Jail for an unspeakable crime which occurred a few days earlier. The two women, both heroin addicts, hopped in a Jimmy's county cab late one night. Desperate for money to score a fix, the women attempted to rob the driver, but killed the middle-aged white man instead. Penny's cousin shot the father of two, in the back of the head while he was still driving, causing the car to suddenly crash into a street pole. Delirious and hurt from the crash, the two women struggled to flee on foot. Minutes later, police were able to capture the two injured women. This was a very sad incident. Jimmy's cabs were usually instructed not to pick folks up from the streets, especially in the inner-city. The Baltimore County-based cab company only dispatches from the county, and operates solely by phone. These cabs did not come equipped with the bulletproof glass like many others in the city. The driver happened to be in the city after transporting a fair from the county. This man tried to simply help two women get out of the rain at night and safely to their destination, and his generosity cost him his life.

I consoled Penny when the incident occurred, but quickly grew tired of the negative vibe surrounding the events. After leaving Penny's mom's house it was time to deal with my own shooting ordeal. I did not hesitate to get to the bottom of my incident. Before even going up to McCabe after dropping Vikki off at home, I decided to drive through Old York Road. I no longer cared about what would happen or who was at fault for any particular incident. I needed answers, or to at least find out what was on the minds of these guys. Indeed, there was a chance I could have been killed by going there, but I was close to this outcome anyway. I was tired of being threatened, so I felt it was time to approach all of the guys from the other side. If they wanted me dead, they were about to get their chance. I was coming to them; weaponless.

I pulled onto Old York Road and immediately observed several guys gathered up against a wall to my left. I could see their attention shift towards my car as I advanced. I felt I had a moral victory, because no one ran or reacted to me as I slowly drew closer. I parallel parked directly in front of Jackson. He was Limon's understudy and one of his closest friends. Casper and Ward, along with three others, stood and intensely gazed down at me as I sat in my car. "Look fellows, we have to talk! This shit has to stop," I said with a serious expression. "I got fools shooting at me n' shit, at every turn, and I have never shot at anyone," I added firmly. After a stare and a one minute pause, Jackson slowly began to speak. "Look here Odell, I personally don't think you are involved with this shit, but this is a fuckin war!" Jackson yelled. "You know it!" "You fuck with those niggas O," he added passionately. "People got to watch their asses," he continued. "If you're with them, no one knows if something is going to pop off," he stated firmly. I nodded as he spoke, before replying. "I'll tell you what, I can promise you this; nothing will come from me personally," I stated with passion. "If y'all happen to see me with someone y'all have a problem with, I assure y'all, they will not make a move while I'm there." I added while making eye contact with all present. "If I'm not around, y'all on your own. I just don't want any more stupid shit coming my way. I be having women with me, kids; I don't have time for that shit. No more shooting at me or my fuckin' car, whether I'm in it or not," I said with a passion.

Make no mistake, the nervousness was trying to break through, but I was there. Whatever was going to happen was going to happen. "Yeah, alright, whatever, cool, but I can't control the actions of those younger dudes in the area. You on your own there, for real," Jackson shared. "They're on their own damn missions half the time. I don't promote it, but I'm not mad at em either," he added with a glance in Casper's direction. Casper observed intensely but never said a word. I followed with a look at the teen. "No dudes close to me will ever fire your way," Jackson added with certainty. "Cool," I replied while shifting my car to D (Drive). Just as I had known all along, Jackson proved to be a cool street guy. He's real! We shook hands before parting ways. Lets remember folks, this is real. This beef is noted as one of, if not the longest and bloodiest rivalries in Baltimore City's history. As I pulled away, I was aware I was only yards away from where Tray was killed; only feet away from where I first saw Limon on the block as a teen, and as I spoke, my car was precisely parked in the very same place where Jimmy's slain body rested on the day Evan and I were dropping Berry here. Three men dead, only separated by yards of where they all once stood.

Despite the intensity of the rivalry, these guys from Old York seemed to be more controlled on their set. I observed closely as I slowly left the group of guys. Many folks did not understand I was always a bit familiar with several guys from Old York Road stemming from my days in elementary school. This made this encounter different for me, more open-minded. That was the vibe I gathered from visiting the area all together, a feel of more stable-minded individuals. Around McCabe, Mater P's harsh lyrics blasting from a boom box had the entire block jumping up and down for hours, releasing stress. I guess the relaxed vibe on Old York Road came from most of the guys growing up together as kids. My palms met with at least three of these guys before I pulled off slowly. Casper was not one of them. I knew handshakes are not taken as seriously as they once were years ago, but I felt a lot better after approaching these guys. It was a start.

It's good to know you're not being viewed as a person several folks wanted dead. They had a good chance if they wanted to do so, and there was nothing I could have done about it, but die. I felt so comfortable after this brief meeting, I stopped ahead a block to socialize with another beauty from Old York. Jackson and the others observed as I stopped at the beauty.

I saw them all looking at me through my rearview mirror. Her name was Nena. Nena was another beauty I attended high school with. She and Vikki once petitioned for the same guy in school. The contest resulted in a tie. Nena, like so many females, hated Vikki. That explained the huge grin on her face when I pulled alongside of her. A week later, Nena and I were enjoying a walk in the park, followed by a movie.

I resurfaced around my way the following week and never spoke a word of the encounter I had with "the enemy." Their enemies, that is! I tried not to have many enemies. I was already my own worst enemy. I honestly can say, for the duration of my time dealing drugs, I never really disliked anyone. I had a problem with one guy; ME! I was doing a great job at hustling, yet I was unaware I was destroying my own life in every way. My ability to pray religiously was probably the only reason I was still standing. Nothing was for certain. Guys were still getting knocked off in the area by police or each other. I felt good about the progress I had made with Old York in reference to the violence. Sadly, after the meeting I had with Old York, there were moments I actually felt I stood a better chance of being shot on McCabe than I did by a person from another area, yet I still felt desire to be there.

However, a few weeks after I had the talk with Jackson and his crew, I learned my chances of getting shot or killed by the rival group still remained quite high. One night after another movie and dinner date with Nena, the third female I dated while I was with Penny, I headed towards Cator Avenue to drop her off at home. Nena lived on Belgian Avenue, a side street, just off of Old York Road near Cator. Genius' sidekick Nick, originally lived two doors to the left. Since the corner conference, I had been to Nena's house a handful of times without incident. I even parked my car right outside of her home several times, for hours. I grew pretty comfortable with being in the midst of the guys whom wanted to kill every guy I hustled alongside of. During these visits I never talked nor saw anyone from Old York, but it all appeared safe. This all would come to an end on this night after dinner. I pulled in front of Nena's home and we talked for a minute. Nena was easily one of the cutest girls I've ever met. After the small talk, she gave me a small kiss and then headed up several steps towards her porch. I enjoyed the view as she gracefully climbed each step. I kept my eyes glued on her until the final second. Before she entered the house, she turned and gave me an angelic stare and smile. Then, the dream was over. As soon as the door closed behind her, the shallow opening to my life nearly closed as well.

One second after Nena's front door closed, there was an explosion. It was my rear windshield. Glass flew everywhere and I immediately ducked downwards. My reaction was a hair late but the blast was slightly off to my right. I once again, smashed the gas pedal, creating a spinout. I was apparently threatened by a shotgun blast of some sort. The blast eliminated my entire rear windshield. Fragments also imploded my entire rearview mirror inside of the car. I hurried out of the area and appeared on McCabe, giving the others even more to talk about. I believe there were guys there who found humor in watching me get shot at repeatedly. Little did they realize, these shootings were from one likely source; Nut. I believed Jackson was keeping his word. Still, I felt the time had come for someone else's car to get messed up. Despite the discounts I received, I had already spent a couple thousand bucks on my car with filling bullet holes. Now, I was forced to purchase a new rear windshield. Before I even cleared the broken glass from the car, I went to Killer Kev and retrieved my Tech 9. Bam Bam, Donte, and LiL Bug instantly joined me to go down to Old York, specifically Cator Avenue. If putting holes in my car was a way to send messages or make statements, I was way ahead of everyone's count in terms of being hit. After resurfacing onto Old York with my headlights out, I located the Mercury Sable, Ward's mom's car, the one used in the previous post-club assault which resulted in the four holes I had repaired. It was parked on Cator Avenue. Ward had used this car during several violent encounters. I did not even touch a gun on this evening. I simply stood and watched the guys let off some steam, theirs and my own. The guys liked doing stuff like this. For them, it was recreational. For me, this one was personal. All three guys emptied their artillery simultaneously in the car's direction. They wrote a healthy warning paragraph to Old York on that evening. The hail of bullets pierced dozens of large holes into the entire side of Ward's mom's car.

That night was the only time I willfully allowed someone to discharge a firearm on my behalf, while in my presence. I immediately returned the weapon to Killer Kev, although I had no say in him originally acquiring it. "It's yours," I said to him. "Cool, how many dem' niggas you kill O?"

Kev stated sarcastically before giggling. We spent nearly three clips on the black Mercury Sable. I thought I would feel better after finally taking a stand and sending a message of my own, but I really didn't. Well, maybe a little. Someone else finally had more holes in their vehicle than I. However, being so close to gunfire is a bit intense. Although guns were not my thing, I was becoming too familiar with them. After the stunt I pulled on Ward's vehicle, I promised myself and God I would never carry or use another gun, ever, in my lifetime. I love to eat, but I'm not even a huge fan of the idea of hunting. Unfortunately, less than a week later, hunting would indeed be the theme, and I would find myself in close quarters with not one, but two more guns.

It was a warm, pre-summer night when I found myself on the corner of McCabe and Alhambra. I was talking to two guys I rarely spoke to at all. These were cool guys, but also the guys who struggled to find above average profitable schemes in the drug game on the block. All hoods have individuals who struggle to make a lot of money in an area full of it, but they're still constantly around. Like I said, I tried to be friendly with everyone, no matter who they were, or what my situation was. For me, the day went extremely well. I had just finished a $2000 stash and was set to leave the area for the night. I was able to accomplish this without any disruptions from any kind of violence, or disturbances from the police. However, I was unable to venture out to Towson on this night. I failed to make it to a rental car retailer, and my car was once again in the body shop from the shotgun incident near Nena's house. Besides the window, during daybreak, I came across more damage. I was vacuuming the car and noticed a bullet hole near my right rear tire. I gathered this damage went undetected from the shooting incident on Greenmount and 22nd a short while back. These findings were the direct result of why I was waiting on the corner of McCabe Avenue for a Yellow cab. I patiently leaned up against a parked vehicle, periodically looking up the darkened street. Again, the street lights had been shot out. I counted the $2300 I had made that day and placed the neatly folded stack in my sweats. I was done for the day, but I was not aware, I was well on my way to being done, forever.

I waited patiently for my cab while sharing a few laughs with the guys. I continued to glance to my right to check for a taxi sign on any approaching car's roof. I quickly turned left to observe all taking place throughout the block. Guys were doing their normal routine; gambling, interacting with the young ladies, and dealing. Everyone was outside jockeying for position to push their own products. I observed the busy street for a minute, thankful to be done for the evening. I noticed two figures exiting a familiar alleyway, but thought nothing of it. I turned back to my right to check for the cab I called almost 30 minutes prior. I rested back onto a parked vehicle with the arches of my feet on the edge of the curb. I was relaxed with both hands in my pockets; one on the large ball of money, the other on my door keys, I suddenly heard a resounding yell from close behind. "Don't move!"

Suddenly, life as I had known it was moving faster than ever, yet it was in slow motion. My pressure immediately elevated as I turned slowly. My eyes were open still, but it was as if the other guy standing with me vanished. I quickly found myself staring directly into the barrel of a shotgun. When I slowly turned back around, I observed another guy standing in front of me with, what appeared to be, a black 9mm handgun. "Y'all know what time it is!" he stated loudly. I quickly realized I was being held up on the same corner where I once danced for petty cash. Everything was happening very rapidly, so this explanation cannot be completely expressed or truly indicative of just how fast things happened. I was extremely nervous from knowing a gun was being pointed at the back of my head. I panicked. I was trapped in between two decisions; should I run or stay completely still. The thoughts were too fast for my body to process. The guy to my rear began to shout the phrase he yelled minutes ago, but this time, something inside of me was not trying to stick around to hear it. "Don't move!" was all I heard. I quickly ducked, turned to the left, and attempted to run. Things quickly fell apart immediately afterwards. In an attempt to flee, my left foot slipped, causing me to try and catch myself; I fell!

As I tried to regain my footing, I heard a loud blast; POW! I was down. My adrenaline was at an all time high, but my chances of surviving this incident were extremely low. I heard the blast, but surprisingly I was not aware if I had been shot or not. The mind spins in many directions when an assault such as this takes place. The shot sounded off too closely to my fall. Suddenly, I was faced down on the ground. I figured I had likely scraped a few body parts during the fall, but I somehow figured my assailants believed I was hit. Immediately, I could hear the guy who fired the shot yelling from above. "I dare you try to run!" he stated loudly. "You will end up just like that fucka over there," he threatened. I was trying to remain still and very calm. I knew the shooters figured me to be seriously hurt or dead, but I was not sure if I was hit. It was extremely dark on the corner, therefore I was able to wiggle my fingers and toes undetected. "Kick that shit out!" the shooter shouted towards the other guy. "What else you got?" he asked. "Yo, you try something Imma blast ya ass," apparently came from the holder of the shotgun. Nervous and still desperate, I believed I was in good enough shape physically to make a last-ditch move. This is Baltimore City. I knew once these guys refocused their attention back onto me and realized I had around $2300 and was still alive, that would be it. I would have been killed on the spot! I was not about to stay on the ground and let these maniacs fill me with bullets. I took a few deep breaths and quickly made my move.

As the drama continued to unfold from above, I was suddenly reminded of my teenage robbery experience downtown. I slowly planted my hands on the sidewalk in a push-up position, then, I quickly pushed upwards and forward. In a matter of seconds, I jumped up and took off running, all in one motion. I tried to immediately cut in between the other parked cars while ducking and covering my head area. I made it to the first car. Shots were immediately fired in my direction! I could hear others outside becoming alarmed. I'm sure the gunman also could sense this. I stayed very low as I ran around and behind, every other parked car. I was hurrying, making my way down the block. The neighborhood was in a state of panic from the sound of the ongoing blasts. People were running everywhere! I continued to use the parked cars as shields. Bullets crashed into every car I ran near. I desperately ran as fast as I could from a bent position. I soon drew near the alleyway where these guys came from. Thinking fast, I decided this was my only chance to really run for my life. I was across the street from the alley, and I had managed to get within a few houses of being parallel with the pathway. With shots still thrusting in my direction, I suddenly dashed across the street. To run as fast as possible, I could no longer place my arms up near my head area. Bullets were chasing with every quick step. When I reached the middle of the street, I experienced a truly frightening moment. I actually heard two bullets pass by, very closely, to my right ear. I slightly hunched while running as fast as I could during this very scary moment. As the shots proceeded, I remember wondering, "How long will these shots last?" I had finally made it to the alleyway, but my traumatic night was far from over.

Amazingly, the shots continued into the alley. I was soon able to pick up speed and stand a bit more erect. I never looked back, but I could hear the echoes from the shots being fired in the narrow passageway. I hustled across a dirt field and leaped out onto Beaumont Avenue. Just after my feet smacked hard against the blacktop, I heard three clicks. The shooter finally ran out of bullets! I never knew how many bullets a 9mm carried, but on this night it seemed as if there were at least one hundred bullets in that gun. I continued to run quickly towards the home of an old schoolmate. I kept a fast pace. I was not sure if the shooter had extra clips or if he was still on my heels. I finally slowed as I drew nearer to an old friend's house. I began to walk and realized my mouth was extremely dry. I also realized I was sweating more than I ever had on any ball court. I immediately became a bit light-headed as well. I felt as if I would pass out or faint. As I continued to walk, I was regaining my breath, but I could also feel an intense burning sensation in my left forearm. I lifted my arm to check things out, and that's when I saw nothing but blood and exposed tissue. My left ring finger was motionless. It was now clear to me, I had just been shot.

My eyes grew wider and I again began to sprint. Minutes later, I reached my pal's front door. I tried not to knock too loudly, but I was sure to be repetitious. To my dismay, my old schoolmate Dutch was not at home. Panic was resetting in as I constantly looked over my shoulder. Soon, his aunty answered the door, totally surprised. She had no clue who I was or what I wanted. "Who are you?" What's wrong?" she asked nervously. "I'm an old friend of Dutch's ma'am. My name is Odell. I was shot a minute ago, and I need help. I need you to call an ambulance please?" I explained without pausing. Hesitantly, the middle-aged woman allowed me to enter into her home. "Are the people still after you?" she asked in concern. "No ma'am. I don't think so," I answered right away. "I hope not," she stated with eyes widened as she quickly closed the door. "Why did they shoot you?" she asked curiously. "They were trying to rob me," I replied in a lower tone. The more I regained my breath, the more the pain intensified. Being shot is vey painful. It's so painful, you can't cry, scream, or ignore the discomfort. It is so painful you likely will not know what to do, if you have a chance to survive. "The paramedics are on the way," she informed gently. As I bled profusely from my arm, all I could do was think about my cousin Shawn. The hallway at Dutch's place was eerily similar to the one at 731. "Thank you very much," I said to the woman. "No problem, I wish you the best," she offered with compassion. "Tell Dutch I said hello please," I insisted in pain. This was not the way I preferred to say hello to Dutch after so many years. Thankfully, it would be possible for me to run across him at a later date. I managed to sit upright in the hallway of the house. I could hear the ambulance approaching. I was still extremely warm and in excruciating pain but very relieved. I did not know what the future held for me, but I was thrilled about the opportunity to possibly see another day.

By the time the paramedics arrived, I was walking out onto the front porch on Craig Avenue; this is an extension, but not the same intersecting street to McCabe. Police joined the scene. They asked the routine questions. "Do you know who shot you?" "Why would someone try to kill you?" or "Do you have any enemies?" I answered the questions "No," but that was not the truth. I really believed I recognized the guy who shot me. The other guy I never saw before. As for the other two questions, the best answers for these were directly linked to my decision to sell drugs. Drug dealers die every day in B'MORE; they die all around the country, some are reported while others are not. So yes! We all have enemies, even if we don't know exactly who they are. I was assisted into the ambulance and attended to. "What happened out there Odell?" the medic shouted. "Looks like a flesh wound," he stated with a grin. "You're very lucky son," he added with a smile of certainty. "We don't get many of these in this city at all." It was confirmed the 9mm bullet hit my left forearm and traveled straight through. There were two, quarter-sized holes in my left arm; an entrance and an exit wound. "You damaged a nerve, but a little therapy should correct your ring finger issue," he stated confidently. "You're going to be alright son," he stated. "I'm hot!" I stated slowly. "Can I get a drink of water?" I asked. "Oh no, not a good idea son," the medic stated adamantly. "If I give you a drink of water, this controllable situation may change drastically," he offered seriously. "You could actually bleed to death, very quickly." "Hold up!" I said while in pain. "I could bleed to death if I drink a glass of water from a gunshot wound to the arm?" The medic simply looked at me and said, "Without a doubt." Wow!

Before leaving the area in the ambulance, I noticed nearly all of the guys from McCabe were in the backdrop, making sure I was alright. Genius actually climbed into the emergency vehicle to speak with me. "Are you alright boy?" he said with look of concern. "Yeah, they almost took me out tonight Genius," I replied with a stare. "That's crazy man. We didn't even see those dudes," he whispered. "Well, as long as you're alright," he added while smiling yet shaking his head. Genius' presence was real for me. He and a few others were strapped on the scene, despite the many police officers present. They still had guns on them. I saw the handle of a gun pushing through the front of Genius' shirt. Despite our issues, he and a few others cared. My uncle BoBo also surfaced. He was extremely emotional, but was elated I was alright. That night, my sister Gina, Penny, Elroy, and my cousin Monnie all appeared at Union Memorial Hospital to support me with this scary ordeal. They all arrived in a panic. Somehow, a rumor about me getting shot in the head surfaced throughout the neighborhood before I even reached the hospital. My relatives were relieved when they observed me fully clothed, sitting upright when they reached the room I was in. Little did they all know, the rumor was nearly a reality. Man, were the sound of those close shots near my head scary! If one particular shot would have been an inch or so to my left, I would have been shot directly in the back of my head, smack in the middle of McCabe Avenue.

Everyone except Elroy stood around with tears in their eyes. He was giggling, as usual. "Man you're crazy. Do you really think this is funny too?" I asked in pain with an intense stare. "O, as long as you didn't get seriously hurt, it's funny as shit," he stated while smiling. "Whatever you say buddy," I replied while looking over my wounds. "Here, take this," I said with my off arm extended. I handed Elroy the $2300 cash I had made and nearly died for. Being shot took me back to several instances where many people did not receive the same outcome I was awarded. This was the exact same hospital my mom passed away in years ago. I was sure to thank God immediately for the grace I was granted. However, I still was a lost soul and allowed myself to believe there was something the guys could have done differently to prevent two, armed robbers from walking directly into a sea full of street soldiers, and nearly ending my life. Today, I often asks if I was set up by folk in my own hood. At the time, I looked at it as if we all simply "fell asleep' or slipped up. I felt the chances of something like this happening twice were next to impossible, but they actually were probable. Two days after I was nearly killed, I was back on the block, dealing again, cast and all.

On the block, I immediately had a run-in with Rickey. He was the guy on the corner with me during the night of the shooting. He questioned my decision making on that evening. He said I should not have run off. I disagreed. "If those guys would have robbed me for the twenty-three hundred, they would have simply finished the job," I stated boldly. "You know how small the city is!" I added loudly. I defended my decision and Rickey soon calmed down. "Man, those fools took my fifty bucks O," he said. "I hurried to get my own pump, but they were gone by the time I got back," he informed me. Ricky wanted the $50 back the robbers took from him. "It was everyone for themselves in my mind buddy," I stated passionately. "I'm happy as shit I did not let my life rest in the hands of those two assholes."

Over the next few weeks, I spent time at home with Penny and the kids. I may have been a bit course with Rickey, but I knew it was God who saved me here. I knew it was only HE who allowed me to see the very next day. The therapy with my left hand was going along much faster than diagnosed. In a week, I had regained 90% of the motion in my ring finger. The cast was removed and I was allowed to wear just a gauze wrap. The only painful experience was the cleaning. Cotton balls were placed on the entrance and exit wounds. After a while, the cotton would become attached to my flesh. Peeling cotton from flesh is really an irritating ordeal. After a while, I would instruct doctors to simply snatch both cotton balls from each hole, simultaneously. This would normally promote a fair amount of bleeding. Other than this, I felt I healed well enough to continue in the streets and on the basketball courts. I knew it was nearly time for me to leave McCabe Avenue, but I could not forget the last time I was there, I had made an easy $2300, well before 9 p.m. In other words, I needed to stop being greedy. The legendary KRS-One had already told all of us: "Love is going to get you!" But we were all sadly too busy glorifying the wrong aspects of the great song, instead of taking heed to its powerful warnings.

The Summer of 1995 was close by, and I was still unable to fully eliminate myself from my old, destroyed neighborhood. The feud between Old York and McCabe was amazingly still going back in forth. Tareek already began searching for a way to run down on Nut. He still promised to kill him. Meanwhile, the heat from police resurfaced since I was shot. Pierce and I still did not see eye to eye about the quality of product he offered. I soon learned, despite the reason for police on McCabe, I was not excluded from being sought after. Elroy and I were still being watched. I may have literally just dodged many bullets, but I still had plenty to run from.

For weeks to come, Elroy and I found ourselves doing one or two things constantly. We were constantly running from the police, or diving on the ground during consistent drive-by shootings. "I'm sick of this mess Elroy," I stated one night as we sat at a local restaurant. "What are you going to do buddy?" I asked. "What do you mean?" he replied. "This shit here is over man. Can't you see that? It's been over for a while now," I emphasized. "How is that?" "We made stacks this week O," he reminded with power. "That's not the point son. It's all about to be over," I added again. "The ease and comfort is gone," I reminded. "I'm about to take my share to the county," I stated with certainty. "The closest I'm going to come to the city is Evan's neck of the woods," I informed. "I don't have anywhere else to go O," he replied disgruntled. "There's always somewhere else man," I stated compassionately. "This crack shit doesn't have any boundaries D," I added softly. "I think we took this spot as far as it's going to go son," I said seriously. "Maybe I should buy a car and move around a bit," he stated with uncertainty. "I think that's a good idea," I replied with a nod. "To start, I'll give you a few of the people I deal with out in Towson," I suggested. "That's relatively close!" I added. "You can have the MAACO people too," I insisted. "They'll make you $500-$700 a week by themselves. "You can even walk from McCabe to see them during regular business hours up on York Road," I added. "They close at five, so catch them before then and that will save you a trip to the county," I explained. "Cool, but what about when I can't walk to the sales?" he said. "I don't have a driver's license like you." "Yeah, that is a problem!" I replied confused.

Elroy's inability to read well enough at the time handicapped his plan to leave the neighborhood and the street corners while driving a car of his own. He was not alone in the city with this issue. Driving in Baltimore County without a license is one of the worst things anyone could do, drug dealer or not. He had more than enough money and street smarts to purchase a nice car, but not enough book smarts to drive one legally at the time. I knew after our talk, we were slowly drifting apart as we tried to come up with a secondary safer plan. I was really getting fed up with the same neighborhood he really felt trapped in. However, if Elroy and I were going to part ways, I was going to do all I could to help my friend move on to something better as well.

It was actually my relationship with Elroy which promoted me not to rush and leave the block even faster. A little after the shooting, I had another $2000 worth of crack I decided to sell. The next package I scored was going to be sold in the other three places I had customers in. I now had at least ten people in Essex, thanks to my aunt's friend, Ms. Lorner. I also had access to Evan's neighborhood which was unknown to most. Most importantly, my Towson business had swelled to 20 people, including Martie, the 20 year retired veteran of Animal Control Facilities (Department of Agriculture) for Baltimore County and the State of Maryland. I set out to sell four $500 stashes before leaving the area. I did not have to sell it all there. McCabe was just the quickest way to get rid of the drugs; not the safest nor the smartest place to do it. Elroy and I were forced to get started in the early evening. Officer Jacobs and company patrolled the neighborhood religiously during the morning and afternoon hours. We believed we could sell most of the drugs overnight. It was a rainy night and we felt this increased our chances of getting the job done safely and quietly. I learned quickly, we could not have been more wrong.

Elroy and I, along with Pierce and a few others, all gathered on the corner of McCabe, in an attempt to make large amounts of money without any troubles from the police. Elroy and I were the center of attention with the authorities. I sort of felt my days were numbered on McCabe Avenue, but Elroy, greed, and a fear of the unknown also kept me in the area. The night began slowly, but we attributed this to the poor weather. It was nearly 3:00 a.m. and raining apparently to no end. Elroy was curled up in a corner on the only pay phone in the area. He was talking to Rica, an old friend of Vikki's who begged me to introduce her to my partner one night at a local 7 Eleven. He immediately fell for the feisty cutie. As the showers intensified, so did the sales for crack, finally. I stayed focused and made an impressive, $700 in less than an hour. Pierce cleared about the same although we hardly made eye contact that evening. I was on the block, but I was comfortable, because I believed I had found a safer plan. I hoped I could ride this new wave out until I completely left the area. With $360 worth of crack left to reach $1000 for the night, my optimism left me in a blink of an eye.

I stood with my back up against the brush near the last row house on the corner. I split time between watching rain drops fall from my hooded sweatshirt while staring at the side of Kizzie's old home for headlight glares. This method allowed me to see if a vehicle with occupants inside was approaching or observing. This was simply a precautionary method I used for safety at night to possibly get a jump on the police. I had a few close calls with these particular cops therefore, I was a bit paranoid. In the streets, feeling paranoid, nervous or anxious can get a person arrested or killed quickly, especially on McCabe Avenue. However, this feeling helped me stay focused and very alert during the wee hours of this early morning grind. On this night, it could have been my unstable gut feelings that actually may have saved my dim future.

By 4:00 a.m., it was raining so hard, I was forced to blow the water from off of my lips as it poured down my face. Surprisingly, the money and the drugs were the only items on my person not soaking wet. After observing each corner for customers or cops, I took a look at the wall in front of me. I could see a pair of lights approaching. I crept to the edge of the hedge and slowly peaked around the corner. Suddenly, my eyes opened wider as my jaw quickly dropped. I was shocked to realize I was watching the same two officers who had been on my trail for weeks. Both of them were slowly exiting the vehicle, just yards up the block. Their apparent plan was to ease down and ambush the entire corner, but they forgot to turn off the headlights to the car. I suspected they were planning to ambush us all as I glared at the officers for a few seconds. Moments later, I made eye contact with Officer Jacobs as he tried to fully exit the black Pontiac. "Motherfucker!" the officer yelled out violently. "Oh shit!" I yelled out. "5-0 y'all" I shouted as I began to run. I thought I was warning the others about the officers as they quickly approached the corner. Little did I know, they only had one person in mind here; me.

By the time the officers reached the spot where I first observed them, I could hear helicopters and sirens coming from all directions. I took off running down Alhambra, towards a familiar alleyway; one I understood well from my days as a playful kid. As I drew closer to this alleyway, a patrol car would suddenly turn in at the corner and stop in front of its entrance. With Officer Jacobs in hot pursuit, I had to think very fast. I was unable to run full speed. I was faced with poor traction and mediocre sneakers due to the bad weather. I ran as fast as I could in a ski-like motion. I got directly next to the right side of the hood of the patrol car, and jumped. "Freeze!" the driver yelled with his gun drawn. I ignored the officer's warning as I easily slid across the hood of his wet car. I was running frantically, but I knew the driver of the car returned to his seat to back the car away from the alley for his co-worker to pursue safely. I quickly headed down the dark alley. Perhaps the officer of the car would have fired a shot, but Mr. Jacobs was no more than a few paces behind. For a taller white man, he was fast. I was able to pick up speed with the change in the surface in the alleyway to gain a bit of separation. Not as much as I had hoped for on the taller-than-average officer. I continued to run my heart out as I headed for a hidden entrance to the next street over. I figured I could lose the officer in the busy dark alley. As I approached the secret passage, I could see the passageway had been covered. It was closed off by an eight-foot piece of ply-wood with sharp points on top. Officer Jacob was now close enough for me to hear him breathing in my ear. With stash in hand, I was headed for a dead end. I had nowhere else to run.

With only 25 yards to go before running out of real estate, my options were exhausted. My first thought was to attempt to run clear through the wood, but I knew I would stop completely and be easily arrested. So, the first move I made in the dark; I threw the drugs. As I approached the wooden wall, I quickly tossed the package to my right in someone's backyard. Next, I would act on instinct only. I jumped as hard as I could. It was as if I were attempting to pull off a difficult dunk. I wanted to get as much of my body over the wooden structure as possible. Again, the top of the wall had jagged edges like a picked fence, but sharper. The rough edges poked at my hands and in my stomach area as I struggled mightily to clear it. Officer Jacobs quickly grabbed a hold of my right pant leg. My left leg was already over the structure. "Come here you fuckin' bastard!"

he shouted as he tugged away. I violently snatched my leg from his grasp and profiled or flipped over the rest of the way. "Motherfucker!" the officer yelled out again as he banged violently against the barrier. "Go, go, go!" he yelled to his fellow officers who trailed, for them to go around. As the officer yelled profanity through the wooden structure, I was seated on the other side, holding onto my already injured left arm. The sharp- edged wooden wall managed to stick directly into the entrance wound I had from the shooting, instantly causing bloodshed. I hurried off the ground and ran away. I managed to gain a slight separation from police momentarily, but my night was far from over.

After hearing Officer Jacob's footsteps running away, I headed in the opposite direction. In excruciating pain, I fell back down to the ground, caught my breath, got up quickly, and entered into another dark alley. Choppers and several patrol cars flooded the area. I briefly hid underneath a known addict's back porch. I could see the search light from above and I saw the cars speeding by, down the street. I was amazed all of this attention seemed to be strictly for me. Suddenly, I was in a role similar to "John Rambo's," but I was far from a war hero. I was a loser, a drug dealer, and I was running for dear life, a life I was taking totally for granted.

It took me all of ten minutes to maneuver my way to a part of the block, away from where I first took off running. I knew McCabe Avenue like the back of my hand. By the time I showed my face, I was far away from the action. I then observed one of the many hacks in the neighborhood from a pathway. He was watching the cops every move from afar. "Hey, Neil, it's O, I need your help," I insisted from inside an alley. He nodded. "Get your truck and get me the hell out of here!" I instructed the 50 year old. He nodded for a second time. A minute or two later, I quickly ran and hopped into a silver, pickup truck. I was extremely muddy and a little bloody. I didn't have the knife with a compass, needle and tread like "Rambo," but I was still able to barely escape the authorities. "Is that mess for you?" Neil asked in reference to the sirens and lights. "Yeah, I believe so," I answered in pain. "Sorry about the mud buddy," I added. "Don't worry about that O. As long as you're alright," he assured. "I'm done with this corner shit Neil. It's over," I stated with certainty. At that instance, I truly felt I would never sell drugs on McCabe Avenue again. This incident, along with all the others, made this decision final, but it was not all up to me now. I was on my way to my sister's apartment on Homestead Street, but the drugs were still in the alley where I had tossed them. If Officer Jacobs and the others found the drugs, all of the running would have been for nothing. I still would be picked up later and charged with possession for a second time, but this charge would be a felony.

During the ride to Homestead Street, I asked Neil to give Elroy my car keys. I hurried home and immediately phoned my partner. I needed to know if he learned of any information about the stash I tossed during the chase. "Hello, Elroy. Did they find the stash?" I asked nervously. "I don't know O, but it does not look good for you buddy," he replied. "It's at least fifteen officers up here with flashlights, looking for your shit," he informed me. "Are the dogs there?" I asked. "Hold up I do see a couple of dogs yo." It was like I could see the vision through Elroy's words. Minutes passed as we waited in silence. "O, all I can say is the longer they're here, the better," Elroy stated. "They're starting to roll out now O," he said. "I can't tell if they found it or not," he added. "You'll know if they come for you with a warrant soon," he said with certainty. "Look, tomorrow come and get me. I need to go search for the shit myself," I stated directly. "Ok," he replied. "Please be here first thing in the morning Elroy!" I insisted. It was far too risky to go back to the area an hour after I had escaped it. As soon as the sun would crack the sky, I wanted to be at the place where I threw the drugs. If police found the stash I was already a convicted felon. If I were able to retrieve the drugs, I would have been able to close the chapter on my career as a dealer on any street corner.

I hardly slept the night after I was chased. I wasted no time in awakening Elroy to pick me up from my sister's apartment. Although he had no license, he had my car. I stayed up all night worrying and trying to explain an unexplainable situation to Penny. She was pissed because I had failed to come home on this night and a few nights prior. The cops, who so desperately wanted to see me go to prison, may have had more patience with me than Penny. The hustling lifestyle was chopping away at another promising relationship, and I was too involved to stop it. When Elroy pulled up to the front of the apartment, I was already on the porch. The ride to McCabe Avenue was nerve-racking, to say the least. We arrived to the spot minutes later. No one was outside. Elroy and I quickly exited the vehicle and began to search. The longer the search lasted, the more frustrated I became. There I stood; sigh after sigh, followed by a resounding, "Damn!" "O, I think we should go now. They got the shit," Elroy stated with disappointment. "I know," I replied while checking for oncomers. Elroy headed back to my vehicle. "We should get outta here before they come through," he insisted. I agreed.

I headed back towards the car as Elroy sat and waited. I took one last look over my right shoulder and noticed a glare from an object on the ground, which was reflecting off of the sun. I stopped, turned, and slowly walked back away from my car. As I drew closer to a plastic bag my pace quickened. "Damn," I whispered. There it sat; a plastic sandwich bag, partially opened with the exact same amount of crack in it as the night before. It was still there, all of it. I looked around wondering if this was some sort of "mousetrap" setup by police. Surprisingly, the stash was nowhere near the grassy area over a dozen officers had searched. It sat alone on the bright cement in someone's backyard. After recounting the contents inside of the baggie, I turned and watched Elroy's devilish smile and quickly entered the vehicle. We then sped off in a hurry. As we made our way out of the neighborhood, I looked over at Elroy and said, "That's it brother, I'm done here!" "As far as McCabe Avenue is concerned, I quit!" I offered.

Silence dominated the ride to Elroy's place. He knew I was serious about leaving the neighborhood hustle game alone. I immediately felt a weight lifted. I had stretched my luck as far as it could go on McCabe Avenue. Bennett and I were the only two dealers from McCabe to never be sentenced to jail time. We also were the only high school graduates in our age bracket. It was time to really try and reestablish myself as a better individual, and leaving the city streets would be my first step. I was still a drug dealer, and had no thoughts of quitting completely, but I was about to embark on a new way of life as a hustler. It was time for me to do things my way and by my rules only. I was about to disregard the steps dudes in the streets believe to be law while rising in the drug game. I still had a few loose ends to tie up on McCabe Avenue, but my days as a corner dealer there were over.

Plans to no longer hustle on a corner were cemented, but I figured I would be still seen in the neighborhood periodically. I had no issue with being in the hood. It was dealing in the hood I was done with. I actually wanted to show the others I had graduated, again, this time from McCabe Avenue and the foolishness it was known for. I was about to set out and use my own unique way to hustle. I did not care about who had the most or the best. I just needed to be more comfortable in my own skin. I wanted to be successful in the game, but only until I could find a better game to play in life for myself and my family. For the first time in years, I tried to look into the future. I still did not have a clear picture, but I was able to, at the very least, entertain a look ahead. I had escaped the snares of the grim reaper; for now. I was certainly glad to be out of the cage of McCabe Avenue, but I was still very much in the woods.

# Chapter 18

# UNCLEAN BREAK

The decision I had made to personally stop selling drugs on McCabe Avenue was final. No matter how much money I had an opportunity to personally profit, I was sure my run there was over for good. Elroy insisted on weathering the storm of defeat there. He felt the worst days there were nearly over in terms of the violence. We both could see the feud between Old York and McCabe was reaching its apex or boiling point, but there were more arrests. When this would happen, the violence normally slowed. The chance of things getting out of control always loomed. A specific plan to kidnap, torture, and murder Nut was finally executed, but did not go exactly how Tareek had hoped. He and Spoon silently crept down to the Old York Road area. They headed to Walter P. Carter Elementary School with the hopes of locating Nut. Several guys from Old York occasionally played basketball at the recreational center on weeknights. Tareek received news Nut was a regular at the facility. The two devised a plan to wait patiently in the brush until he exited the facility. Nut's reckless actions had everyone a bit unsettled for months, and guys felt it was time to totally eliminate him from the picture. They all agreed he had to go. McCabe Avenue wanted Nut dead!

Around 9:00 p.m. several local players began to file out of the recreational center. Tareek and Spoon hid and waited patiently to see if Nut would emerge from the building. Moments later, the two began to focus on a smaller kid named Mark. Mark was one of Nut's buddies. Mark was rarely seen by anyone from McCabe. I rarely ever saw the youngster, but Bennett was pretty familiar with him. They attended a few of the same classes together in elementary and middle school. The two hoped

Nut would surface soon afterwards, but he never did. Still, these two from McCabe saw an opportunity to get even with a familiar name from Old York, and they jumped at it; literally.

Moments after Mark exited the center, the two guys quickly exploded from the background and violently grabbed him. He immediately screamed in fear as loudly as he could. The others exiting the gym all scattered in a panic. Spoon, at nearly 300 pounds, easily handled the 130 pound teen. The two relentlessly pounded on the kid. Spoon then raised the youth's battered body above his head and slammed him with extreme force into the pavement. Mark was instantly knocked unconscious but the violent onslaught continued. The two repeatedly stomped and kicked the small boy as he lay dormant. Tareek would then jump as high as he could, landing down on the head of the helpless boy. He did this several times, often losing his own balance and falling over. The beating lasted for minutes after Mark was already out cold. Upon hearing police sirens in the area, the two quickly fled the scene, leaving the small teen for dead.

News of the endless beating flooded the area soon afterwards, but there was little authorities could do. The witnesses there on this night, "didn't see a thing." The police rarely solved anything throughout this entire feud. This incident was simply seen as a victory for McCabe Avenue. Miraculously, Mark did not die from the beating. However, his life was significantly altered forever. He was beaten so violently, he did not remember one bit of the incident. The trauma left Mark paralyzed from the waste down and his speech was heavily slurred initially. Mark had taken Nut's beating, and survived. I later spoke to Tareek about the situation. He was quite proud of his accomplishments. He even joked about how Mark's screams sounded "just like a little bitch," he claimed. I learned through Vikki just how furious the other side was about this incident. Retaliation was inevitable. Brief chats with Elroy and small visits with my aunt and uncle were the only times I would visit McCabe during this time. Although I still had a ways to go before making a better existence for myself, it was liberating to know McCabe Avenue no longer had a firm grip on my life.

This feeling allowed me to get out of the area a lot more. It felt great to be away from all of the foolishness. I tried to encourage Elroy and his older brother Steve, who had recently returned, to do the same. I would regularly give Steve a lift to his girlfriend's house on Wolfe Street, located in east Baltimore. He had only been home from prison a short while, and I did not want him to get involved with the stupidity. He was Benny's dearest friend, therefore I feared he may have felt obligated to represent for him in some way. I felt he may have tried to impress the others. I was sure to warn him several times during these rides, "down the hill."

Advising and encouraging while conversing with Steve was interesting; reflecting on earlier times where he would encourage or assist me with sound instructions, a pat on the head and some spare change. "Steve, make sure whatever you decide to do, you don't get caught up in this mess with Old York Road," I emphasized as I drove. "O, I'm not even worried about that shit. I'm just trying to make a little money and take care of these kids," he assured me. Steve had four kids; two boys and two girls. The young lady he lived with was a correctional officer he met through peers before he was released from prison. All of Steve's children were from another woman, but she fell victim and was struggling with an addiction to heroin. I was confident Steve would not hang out alongside any of the younger guys involved with the negativity. He was in his late-20s at the time. I knew Elroy would not affiliate with the beef, but I feared his unwillingness to leave the neighborhood would somehow catch him off guard. I called myself trying to show the others a "light" or a different path even while still hustling myself. I could finally see it, and I wanted others to join me, but I soon would learn, seeing something and obtaining it are two very different ideas.

A certain level of peace came with no longer being a hustler on McCabe Avenue. I felt great about finally being able to leave the place behind, although to many I would still be seen as a dealer from my old street. What I forgot to factor in was guys from Old York Road probably did not know I was pulling away from the area. Had they learned about my change, a few simply may not have cared. One sunny afternoon, I dropped Penny at her mom's house as usual. We were holding on, but barely. I headed towards my old neighborhood to join Genius and the others for a game or two of basketball. Mentally, I was able to separate the hustling from the recreational things I shared with the guys; specifically basketball. Anxious to land a spot on the first squad, I decided to take a shortcut through Clifton Park. Clifton Park is an east Baltimore popular park attraction near the former Lake Clifton Senior High School / Lake Clifton Eastern High School/ Heritage High School (Closed in 2021).

The school better known as "Lake" had its share of turmoil throughout the years, just as Northern High had. The park which serves as a boundary to the school is an area similar to Dewees Playfield. The alternative route I was traveling proved to be a poor idea on this sunny afternoon. I had forgotten school was letting out for the day, meaning, traffic would be severely backed up. Guys loved to circle the park and flirt with the high school females as they left for home. Lake Clifton High was known to have plenty of fine females from the city therefore being stuck in traffic was not all bad. I was now five years older than most high school seniors. However, the age gap was not large enough for me to rule out adding a cute senior passenger on board to possibly take to the court with me. Several very nice views passed by at eye-level. A few even turned and smiled, but I was way too close to Penny's mom's house to make a move in the area. I liked flirting, but I was never pressed, overly-aggressive or "hard-up." I was not going to be conducting myself like perverted stalker.

The sights were nice, but I decided to stick to watching only by not approaching any particular cutie. I finally drew close to the traffic light just passed the crowds of students. There was only one car ahead, therefore I continued to practice patience. This traffic signal does allow turns on red. However, the intersecting traffic was non-stop and moving too quickly, therefore waiting on the traffic signal seemed to be the only option. Suddenly, while waiting I noticed a female waving at me from across the street. Her name was Sherese. I remembered her because she was very cute. She was frantically jumping up and down. I noticed her, so I smiled, but I could also see an expression of fear and concern on her face. Sherese was Rick's ex-girlfriend. We never really conversed, but she still recognized me from earlier days. I would give Rick lifts to and from her house quite often. This took place before I began hustling. They were no longer dating. I never thought I would see her again, and I certainly never thought she would resurface just in time to possibly save my life.

After Sherese caught my attention, I realized she was not trying to get to know me better, but I still watched her gestures closely. The traffic signal was still red, but the "Don't Walk" light was flashing. Sherese was still hopping up and down, but pointing in the direction directly behind me.

I looked at the light situation for a second. Then I glanced in my driver's side, rearview mirror. I was shocked to see a guy called, "D-Train" from Old York Road. I knew him from middle school. He and another guy had just exited a black Toyota Camry. They were about five car lengths behind me. The two quickly began to creep alongside the other vehicles, one on each side, in an attempt to trap me inside of my own. It's very possible I may have been killed in cold blood, in the midst of moving traffic had I not spotted the two. D-Train had his right hand under a dark colored towel as he crouched over and began to advance. His partner approached in similar fashion. Before the two could get too close, the light would change. I quickly made a right turn and sped away, but not before glancing over at Sherese. I raised my right thumb through my sunroof and gave a slight grin while glancing back once more. I knew instantly, I owed this young lady so much more. The two guys would quickly retreat, but their chance was blown. Sherese and two other females celebrated on the corner by clapping, hugging each other, and smiling about this outcome.

As I drove away from the intense scene, I could see her in my rearview. She continued jumping and shouting with emotional excitement. She was proud of herself. I was proud of her also. I quickly thanked God for her presence by looking into the beautiful sky also through my sunroof. The thought of what may have happened to me without Sherese being present is scary. The thought still gives me the chills, even today.

When I first began dealing crack outside of McCabe Avenue, I believed I could still periodically hang out in the area. It was situations like these that were beginning to show me there was more to life. No longer selling drugs on the block was just a start. I was still learning the hard way. I needed to leave the area in every way. I needed to act as if the place where I was raised, had so much fun, and learned so much no longer existed at all. Over the next few weeks, I would learn leaving Baltimore City altogether may be the best decision I could make to save myself from being killed. I still housed internal issues, but I really did not want to die. There were moments earlier where I didn't care if I were to die or be killed, but that mindset had expired. My neighborhood was consumed with guys who may have had a death wish. For those who did not care for this new approach or outlook, friction surfaced; adding another component as to why I should exit my surroundings permanently.

Tareek, who I actually liked a lot, would become one of the guys I would ultimately clash with. As I said before, Tareek was the type of guy who would be your great friend one moment, and your true enemy the next. He was still very unpredictable. It was going to happen. It would only be a matter of time before we crossed paths negatively. I believed I always naturally had something Tareek always wanted; outgoing charm, wide-spread popularity, and diverse wit. To the young ladies, Tareek and the others were not as popular throughout the city. Although they were seen as attractive males, sisters felt they also lacked maturity, personality and character. There was seemingly a lacking of the basic ability to be charming or gentlemanly. These are not my words; the ladies often made these comments. Women classified the guys from McCabe as a group; individually they were unknown to most, and that's a minus within itself. At parties, salons, galas, which I attended occasionally, or just out having casual conversations, if a guy from around the way was ever mentioned around bombshells, their responses would not be very receptive at all. I would even ask them why, and they would simply say, "He's just a 'NO'!" These guys could have plenty of money, nice cars, and good looks, and yet, these women still gave most of them a resounding, "Thumbs Down!" With women, I believe money can only carry a guy so far. That's the scary part about dealing; most dudes hustle to get things to impress the women. That will work with a specific type of woman, or an immature young lady, but not the grown mature bombshell. If a dude is missing manly qualities, you are voided from being able to date the finer, more sophisticated females. I was able to interact with many because I was able to show the young ladies a young man, first, not a drug dealer. That was key, so hustlers, these women are NOT "stuck-up," they just see you as "stuck-down." So you hustle to impress them, possibly go to prison, or die, and STILL will be labeled as a "strikeout artist" with the bombshells. Wow! Again, you hustle hard to gain access with the ladies, maybe land a date or two, or a few sexual episodes, but if there are too many alpha qualities missing, she's still going to vanish sooner than later.

Most guys fail to realize, as you mature, hustling no longer appears tough, or even interesting to stable mature women. It looks weak; like there is something drastically wrong with the guy. This will discredit your resources; how you produced them. The women will still take your money, or even sleep with you; you make the money easily, for some sleeping with you for "one minute" is taking the money easily. They like to hustle as well, but it won't last. Not with a woman. They're too strong too deep. They see you as a liability in reference to the future. And if you sell drugs, you are just that; unreliable. This is why I always would relate with folks, especially women, from the inside/out. So I would not limit myself with things or limit myself to one group of folks. It's going to always come down to the unseen; charm, depth, personality, integrity, compassion, and love. These were always my favorite traits, even with the dealing. I'm from an era where money can only get you so far, especially with the women, and it still may not help you much to fit in with advanced or distinguished social crowds. For this, you need undeniable character!

Tareek and the others were from an era where materialism ruled most; your car and your money did all the talking for you. This was the reason I was asked repeatedly by Tareek and others, to introduce them to the young ladies from more privileged or different backgrounds; if not that, women whose beauty was seen as above-average. With all of this said, I decided to do this favor for a couple of the guys, and this decision proved to be another very huge mistake.

After setting Tareek up with Amanda, immediately, he became too attached. She enjoyed the gifts, but she was concerned. Every concern she shared with Vikki, Vikki shared with me. Tareek never hesitated to spend large amounts of cash on the beauty. He spent thousands on Amanda, on everything from leather jackets to handbags. Amanda was appreciative, but not very impressed. I personally knew guys Amanda had previously dated, and they made more money than most of the dealers on McCabe, myself included. She was already very comfortable with guys giving her large amounts of money for gifts, and for her company. I believe Tareek could sense his generosity was the norm for Amanda and grew a bit frustrated. Before the second month of their union kicked in, Elroy and I found ourselves smack in the middle of a domestic meltdown between the two. Taking a short break from dealing, Elroy and I picked Tareek up from his home and headed to Amanda's mom's house. The two were headed to a hotel in Towson and wanted a lift. Tareek was always cautious and discrete outside of the block, but here his emotions would interfere, and his conduct from the neighborhood again would surface before us all.

Tareek left his new Acura Legend with his son's mother to assure not being caught cheating, or in a compromising position with Old York Road alone in a hotel suite. Five minutes after the two were in the rear of my vehicle, an argument mysteriously ensued. I don't know where the quarrel stemmed, but it intensified as we drove by the prestigious Morgan State University (HBCU), a great university in northeast Baltimore. We were around the corner from the house where Genius and the others once portrayed black mafia figures. The house had been raided weeks earlier by police. Surprisingly, no drugs were found and police could not get any of the arrests to stick. Genius quickly moved back onto McCabe. Like 731, this house too was labeled as a "nuisance." This was exactly what Tareek was becoming to Amanda.

Ten minutes after we picked Amanda up from her mom's, she and Tareek were cursing like sailors at one another. "Fuck you bitch!" he yelled. "Fuck you too, asshole!" she replied loudly. "Yo, pull this muthafucka over O!" Tareek yelled. "I'm about to knock this bitch out!" he added frantically. "She don't know who she fuckin with!" he continued. "Pull over!" he repeated. "Come on man, that's a girl!" Elroy yelled. "I don't give a fuck yo!" He replied in anger. "I don't give a fuck either nigga!" Amanda yelled. We already knew this meant nothing to Tareek. The argument was becoming a repeat of the crazy incident involving Tareek and the middle-aged female addict. "Go ahead, pull this car over," Amanda stated calmly. Just like the older woman, Amanda was fearless, but also now angry. "Let me out of this fuckin' car Odell!" she yelled. Tareek, just as before, was very frustrated. They both hopped out of the car and immediately he raised his fists, and again, actually got into a puncher's stance. Elroy and I looked at each other, then him very strangely. We could see the seriousness in his expression. However, we should have been paying much more attention to Amanda. In the blink of an eye, she pointed forward and squeezed the trigger.

Amanda shot Tareek directly in the face! She was packing a small canister of mace. Tareek yelled as Amanda quickly pointed the device at Elroy and I to stay back. Our hands were fully raised as she threatened to spray us as well. "You bitch, I'm going to kill you watch!" Tareek yelled out in discomfort. Tareek was jumping around like a roach often does after being showered with insect spray. He soon would take off running, blind, in the same northbound direction we were headed in. Amanda left our company and headed back south on foot towards her neighborhood. We got back into the car and caught up to Tareek by driving slowly. He initially declined to re-enter the car. He felt the night air would help restore his vision quickly. "Damn son, she got you good," Elroy stated with a slight giggle from the passenger window. "Fuck you!" he replied loudly. Tareek was looking at us with his eyes 90% closed as we slowly cruised beside him. He said he could only see blurred images of us. He stopped and asked us to look into his eyes. "Are my eyes messed up?" he asked. "Nah, they're just very red," I replied. I allowed Tareek to use some of my sterile solution for contact lenses, which I now wore instead of glasses. I emptied the majority of the contents into Tareek's inflamed eyes. Moments later, we all stood and stared at each other, took it all in, and burst into laughter. However, this laughter and mood didn't last very long at all. In an attempt to reconcile, Tareek was harshly rejected by Amanda. The only thing wrong with her decision; she used my name to free herself. Amanda lied and told Tareek I persuaded her to no longer date him. She told him I said that he was "crazy." Tareek was not really crazy, but I knew of his attitude before I set the two up for a date. "Crazy," in my estimation was in regards to having heart in the hood; I knew his child's mom, and there was no evidence of wrongdoings domestically. I never knew what he was like with women really, nor did I care. I was just hooking a brother up. Heartbroken and upset Tareek came after me for answers. This is exactly why it's not cool to play matchmaker, especially in the ghetto. Too many unstable emotions.

Days later, Tareek and I discussed the matter. I told him I said nothing to Amanda about the incident or his character. We even tried to visit Amanda's place, and I watched her lie directly in front of me. I did speak to Vikki when she inquired, but I never made a personal opinion about Tareek's ability to date Amanda. That's called, "hating." Who hooks a person up then hates? Exactly! I was very emotion and angry about the mix up. Every issue involving all of us was a life or death issue during this time. I did what I could to try to restore the union, but Amanda feared for her safety and had made her mind up. Tareek was not receptive to this outcome. He blamed me for the breakup and challenged me to a fist fight. The offer surprised me a little. I've always believed fighting over a female was silly. This was really outrageous, considering I was not emotionally involved with Amanda at all. I guess Tareek was heartbroken and needed to "collect" for his pain and suffering. He wanted to collect from me, and I eventually granted his wish. I accepted the challenge to brawl!

Going to fight a guy you've known for years, for a female you hardly knew well at all, was weird for me. However, the challenge was no longer about the girl. It was more about my ability to hold on to a sister like Vikki, and his inability to get a tighter grip on her understudy. In the hood, sometimes you just have to fight, period! Elroy, Tareek and I headed to Dewees playground, but not for a game of hoops. The two picked me up from Homestead, and we were going to an open field to fight, for nothing really. The field was dark and no one other than Elroy was able to witness. The closer we came to actually squaring off, the more interested I became. I wanted to beat Tareek up! Ego, most know what I mean; "I am originally from McCabe, I'm older," I told myself. Soon, we found ourselves standing about four feet apart, in an intense staredown. Truth be told, again, I really like Tareek. I knew the hood had gotten the best of him. I saw him as myself had I gone too far. Outside of McCabe, I felt he would have been a hell of a guy. I didn't want to fight Tareek for reasons involving a female, but I was prepared to. Well, that was until he reached into his pants and retrieved a small, chrome automatic handgun and handed it to Elroy. It was here, I immediately realized a strong effort or victory in a fist fight could actually result in my demise.

Watching Tareek hand the guy who brought him to McCabe a gun confused me mightily, although Elroy and I were close as well. Still, there were feelings I was being set up in a remote place by two people I really did not trust. I was thinking they planned it all out while coming to pick me up. My sister had my car but I was not going to make that be an excuse. I could not say with all my heart, Elroy would have not allowed Tareek to shoot me after the fight. Elroy and I were not exactly the same since the hiring of Killer Kev, and the initial misuse of our Tech 9mm firearm. I was now even struggling to get myself to believe he would not pull the trigger himself. The gun, the same kind that killed my cousin Shawn, changed the entire complexion of the situation. I was 100% sure Tareek would have used the gun on me if I would have done to him what I felt I could. Not saying I could have easily won the brawl, but I feel confident about my efforts with any average man of similar size, barring a professional, during a fight. Still, I had no choice; we fought.

The fight lasted about ten minutes. It was mostly a wrestling match. We struggled upright. I could feel Tareek's strength and I knew I had two more gears in my own strength that may have overpowered him. I simply refused to shift! All I could picture was him shooting at me out in the open field at Dewees or him actually shooting and killing me. He briefly felt my power. He began to put his thumbs over my eyes and pushed inwards. That was a tough situation considering I was wearing contact lenses. For the duration of the struggle I stayed at a medium. I didn't allow myself to be hurt, but I also held back from trying to seriously hurt him. Honestly, I carried my own fight! I cheated myself and allowed him to slightly edge out the victory before Elroy stepped in. Was I hurt? No! I took blows, but in no vital areas in the face or head. I was fine. When it came to women, intellect, and social skills, I had much more moxie than Tareek and the others, and I believe they knew it. However, in this situation, that hardly mattered. Fighting, I was completely fine with at times, but this was all so simple; he truly was something I was not; a killer.

After the fight we actually followed an old school rule. We shook hands like men and headed back to population. I respected the idea of fighting and moving on. It would have been just like the days of old if the gun was not present. I got passed the fight relatively fast. It was almost like it never happened. I was a bit frustrated with Amanda, but I was cool. No one was seriously hurt. I did suffer a bruised hip when I fell to the ground for a few seconds, but there were no visible scars. The fight didn't prohibit my basketball abilities or sexual performance at home. The next day, I was still dunking and my jump shot was still on. My jumper was not the only thing I had going on later during the week. As Tareek got over Amanda, I got on with her. The little white lie she created could have cost me my life. Now, I felt I had to allow her to feel where I was coming from. I made up with Amanda too.

A week after the fight with Tareek, I returned to McCabe and noticed everyone was smiling. I had not seen this since the 80's, at the block party. I wondered what had taken place for this dark valley to be in such great spirits. I ran into Elroy and stated, "What's going on around here today?" "Oh, you don't know?" he replied with a grin. "That little bastard Nut was killed earlier today," he added. "Everyone's happy as shit about that," he stated with a smile of his own. "Who did it?" I asked in confusion. "Some crazy ass nigga shot him and Jackson up at Northern, right on school grounds," he explained. "It should be on the news at five." An entire black neighborhood was celebrating the death of another black teen. Nut had shot at me at least five times. He was now dead. This was what everyone on the block wanted, yet I still could not find room to feel anything but sorrow for the kid and his family.

In the midst of the dealing, whenever I was to myself or alone, I would secretly pray for us all to make it out of the game. This did not happen very often, but it happened. I hurried into the house to see the news broadcast at 5:00 p.m. and there he was. "Nut" or Emmanuel Jones, was on his backside in the grass, directly across from the front entrance of the school. He and Jackson had been shot several times by an unknown assailant. Jackson was seriously injured, but was still alive, while Nut rested forever in broad daylight on the property of a school he never attended. He was covered with a white sheet over 80% of his body. His legs were crossed. All that was visible were a pair of tan Timberland boots. I learned later, during the shooting, Nut tried to pretend as if he was not seriously hurt when he was hit in the chest. I was told he sat down slowly and crossed his legs to show the onlookers he was fine. He died minutes later in that very position. His death gave the indication; when we pass on, it's like we don't even know we're gone. Death truly is inevitable! Despite the inaccurate depiction given, I still felt for Nut's family. I listened to the reaction of his devastated relatives on the tube. Nut was the little brother of Romeo, Gina's ex from years earlier. Romeo was still dealing with addiction during the time of his younger brother's death. Today, he's much better. Amen. During his little brother's death, I watched the family praise their loved one as if he would not hurt a fly. They could not have been more wrong. Still, a prayer was sent to heaven from me, for him, to God. Nut was off to see The King as we remained in the street struggle for many reasons, but I understood; at the end of it all we are still family. We're still all God's children!

In spite of my personal feelings about Nut's death, I still realized his demise was possibly adding to my survival. I ignored the comments made by the guys on the street. Comments like "O, I know you glad that sucka got smoked," or "Now you don't have to worry about his ass no more

O." Nut was said to be killed by a disturbed individual named Bruce. Bruce was known in the streets as a no nonsense kid similar to Nut, but far more calculating. Everyone swore I knew the kid from playing ball, but his identification mystified me. Once Nut passed away, the senseless shootings slowed significantly. The "beef" had died down as well. Things seemed to be returning to normal. Well, that's if you call selling drugs all night and shooting out the street lights normal. "Killing the lights" was still a typical practice for the guys on McCabe. I could feel the change. I knew I was finished dealing on McCabe, but a guy there reached out to me, and for some stupid reason, I used it as an excuse to still be where I knew I should have been no longer.

A struggling heroin and crack addict named Chuck approached me with a desperate proposition. He asked me if I could help him make some money while it was calm in the hood. I felt Chuck was a cool person despite his addiction. He would often wash my car and run errands for Elroy and I. He asked me if I could periodically front him $100 worth of crack at a time. He only wanted $35 out of the $100. He said he desperately needed to get his rent money together and only had a couple of days to do it. While I continued to try and persuade Elroy to leave the block before the heat returned, I decided to help chuck out. I set the small deal at 60/40 for Chuck. I figured I can help this guy out, and talk Elroy out of leaving as well. Elroy was as stubborn with leaving the hood as I had been with him trying to get me to buy kilos when we were younger. So there we were, back on McCabe Avenue, and things were cool, but little did I know the heat was still right around the corner.

I stood on the front porch and watched over Chuck as he began to hustle up some extra change for me, and rent money for himself. All I had left was $100 worth of crack. He claimed he needed a total of $150 for his rent. With my help, he could have made most his rent money in an hour or so. I observed Chuck as he made a couple sales. "Are you alright?" I yelled from the porch. "Yeah, all I need is another thirty minutes O," he replied. Those 30 minutes never ended. Chuck would never finish the deal we made.

Five minutes after the brief chat I shared with Chuck, police ambushed the entire area. Mark's severe beating and the death of

Nut had authorities seemingly directing more focus at the guys from McCabe. Just when the tension seemed to calm down a bit, the cops were back on the beat stirring things up. This was a routine practice for the local police and the FBI, in their attempt to gain information involving recent homicides and violent crimes throughout the area. At the very least, these sweeps would break up the rhythm or the flow of drug trafficking in the area. Like many of these stings, no one was arrested on this day. Thirty-minutes after police combed through the area, they were gone. Just like mice, everyone resurfaced when the trouble left, and casually picked up where they had left off. The inner-city drug dealer scenario is sort of like roaches. I no longer sold drugs in the inner-city, therefore I was a rare brown roach in the suburbs, in the midst of the more discrete white roaches. Hood roaches, they're usually dark in color and only seem to appear in poverty stricken areas, looking for anything to feed on. When the noise and lights come, they flee. As soon as the darkness return, they're all right back, but in this case, a roach ventured off and never came back. Everyone except Chuck returned to the block after the cops left. He stayed gone.

I fronted Chuck the last of the crack I had left. I sat on my porch and watched everyone resurface except him. I didn't worry until about an hour passed. I grew frustrated after several more hours had come and gone. I took my mind off of the situation and helped Elroy and Killer Kev move product, simply by serving as a lookout. They did well, selling over $3000 worth of crack between the two of them. I never left the block on this evening, and surprisingly, police never returned. By nightfall, Chuck's presence was still unknown. I was done with watching out for police for Elroy by 11:00 p.m. I was visibly frustrated by Chuck's apparent decision to walk off with the drugs and the little cash he had made. Honestly speaking, $100 was not even enough cash for me to eat for a day. I was not worried about the money. "I was just trying to help this nigga out," I thought to myself. This was about principle! The ongoing dispute I had with Pierce, along with the disagreement I had with Tareek earlier, caused me to lose the patience I normally practiced. A part of me felt I needed to make a stand or send a message to everyone. The longer I stayed on the block, the more upset I became. By 2:00 a.m. I had made my mind up. I was not going to leave the area until I met back up with Chuck.

Not going home to Chase was becoming easier by the day. Penny and I were all but over, again, for my stupid decisions, but I tried to hold on to the union for the sake of my daughter. I told Penny I would not make it home. It actually felt good to tell her I had to take care of business and actually meant it. Usually, a female would be the reason for such an excuse or lie. I stayed outside with Elroy all night. Uncharacteristically, I carried a gun as I stood with him. We were standing on the same corner where I was shot awhile back. I grew tired around 4:00 a.m. and decided to take a nap on the couch in 731's infamous living room. I told the guys outside to send Chuck to the house, if or when he resurfaced. I awakened around 8:00 a.m. to the sound of my sister's second daughter, Kia. My aunt was babysitting for my sister for the weekend. I was unable to sleep off the frustration from Chuck, who apparently decided to steal from me. I reluctantly chose to make a move. I was going to go after Chuck to confront him about leaving with my product without any explanation. I was pissed off, so I got set to make a visit to his home.

After listening to the small footsteps of my second niece from above, I decided to take all of the bullets out of the gun and put it away. I slid the unloaded gun underneath the chair and headed out the door. Surprisingly, Elroy was still outside. He was playing his patented fart game and making fun out of everything. The one thing about Elroy; he believed life itself was funny, and no matter what took place in the hood, he returned us all to laughter. "O, I made $3000 for myself last night. That's close to the record for one day," he shouted while giggling. "I'm going to take a vacation," he stated while dancing. "Oh yeah," I stated while slightly shaking my head at Elroy's moves. Have any of y'all seen Chuck last night or this morning?" I asked. "Nah, it's like he vanished or something O," Elroy stated. "He did, and that's fine, but not with my stash," I replied while looking around. I was searching for a blunt object of any sort. I soon found a thick broom stick leaning up against a wall. I grabbed it. "I'll be right back!" I said while violently stomping the thick stick into two halves. I believed I could simply beat Chuck up in a fist fight, but he was an addict. I did not really want to risk getting any of his blood onto my person. "This should do," I mumbled with a nod in reference to the stick.

Fighting an addict makes the dealer appear weak. Junkies are typically viewed as less than, weak or damaged property; dealers are to not get their hands dirty messing around with them. If they come up short; crack them in the head with something. Anyone else may have been out to kill Chuck for $100, but again, I am not a killer. I quickly hopped in the car and drove towards York Road. I had around $2500 in my right pocket; in the front passenger area rested a thick wooden stick, from the floor to the headrest. I should not have had that much money with me, but I grew uncomfortable with leaving my money with Elroy. Nor did I want to leave the money in the car or inside of the house with my drug-addicted relatives. Elroy and I finally cut all ties with Tisha, who once held everything for us. She began asking for a raise every two days, and we knew greed had taken over her spirits as well. I drove a short ways up the road and pulled my car into a supermarket parking lot. I began to walk in the direction of Chuck's house. With stick in hand, I was headed to confront him at his doorstep.

Chuck lived with his girlfriend Mildred, who was also a heroin addict. I knew she possessed a loud personality therefore I was hoping to catch Chuck outside. Seconds later, as I drew closer to the home, surprisingly, I found myself staring at Chuck's backside. He was just exiting a Murry's Steakhouse food depot before I was close enough for him to notice. Just like that, he was right in front of me. Unfortunately, he was headed in the opposite direction, away from the area where he knew I was likely awaiting. He was carrying two shopping bags, one in each hand. The closer he drew to his home, the faster I walked. Suddenly, I was sprinting towards Chuck. My grip tightened on the stick and my pace steadily intensified. I was in no mood for conversation at this point. Chuck walking in the wrong direction gave me all the information I needed. He had left me hanging, and now it was my turn to do the same to him, my way.

By the time I got within ten feet of Chuck, I was running full speed with the stick held in a swinging position. I stopped, planted and swung the thick stick at Chuck's head with all the strength I had. The thick stick hit a sweet spot and snapped immediately, causing Chuck to immediately drop his groceries to grab his head with both hands. I honestly did not expect the stick to break so easily. He briefly screamed in disbelief as he turned. We instantly grabbed each other. No words were exchanged and we began to struggle on the busy road. Old women were screaming for us to stop, but we were well into a fight. We both fell to the ground and began to roll about. I had my hands around Chuck's neck as he tried to get on top of me. Suddenly, from the corner of my eye, I could see two uniformed officers approaching. The officers were likely exiting a local Dunkin' Donuts. Chuck was attempting to gain a favorable position, but I was momentarily in control. With police drawing nearer, it was time for me to break free. The two officers with a hand on their weapons were hurrying across a busy York Road. That was enough. I snatched away from Chuck and dashed into a near pathway. I had over $2000 in my pocket, and I had just struck an unarmed man in the back of his head. Depending on Chuck's mood, I could have faced some serious assault charges if apprehended. I did not want to chance it.

Minutes after striking Chuck with the stick, I felt horrible for making such an irrational decision. This was totally out of character for me, and now this seemingly small situation was growing out of control. I made my escape through a familiar alleyway to the backside of the main road. I realized right away, the police were not directly behind me. Still, this incident had similarities to the infamous escape I pulled off weeks prior. Once again, I was hearing sirens and a helicopter above. This time, I wondered how all this could be related to my impulsive move on Chuck. I jogged towards Dewees field, periodically looking over my shoulder. Going back to my car was not the best idea. It was parked on an opened busy lot, located on the same road where I had executed this assault. I desperately wanted to get out of the area for awhile. I was glad no one was on the quiet block I had made it to. I started to run further north when I noticed a black car to my right. As I passed, I quickly took a glance inside of the vehicle. Two guys were inside. I knew of them. From the minute I spotted the two, I knew I was home free and safe; so I believed.

The two guys were from the neighborhood. Tyran and Will were two guys from the area who were known for dealing, but were thought of as "nice guys" or chumps. I didn't know them well enough to place a label on them, but they were nice guys. "Nice guys" was the term used for dealers other hustlers believed should not even have been in the game. That was me actually, but these guys were heartless! I've always had heart! If you were from McCabe Avenue you had to have some measurement of toughness and fearlessness. I just felt other traits were more important to my strategy and longevity. Irrational behavior is viewed as tough in the streets, but it's usually the result of an emotional weakness. I know this, but during this situation, I messed up. I lost control emotionally. "What's up fellas?" I said while cautiously looking behind. "Hey O, What's up?" Tyran, the driver, asked. I leaned over to make eye contact with the two guys. "Look, I just smacked a guy in his fuckin head with a stick, and the police are all over the place. Look..., man get me out of here!" I insisted while already grabbing for the door handle. I should have suspected something. These two dudes were on a quiet block, sitting in the car, periodically checking in the rearview mirrors. I sensed hesitation in them, but they said nothing. They were afraid to.

McCabe Avenue had such a reputation, these guys refused to tell me "No," like they simply should have. "Alright, where are you headed?" Tyran asked nervously. "I don't know, anywhere north. Do not go towards McCabe!" I replied. I rested low in the back seat of the sedan as the two slowly pulled off. I did not want Chuck, who was now probably being questioned by police, to possibly observe me in the car. I didn't think he would snitch, but I was not sure. Only if Chuck still had the remainder of the package I fronted him, in his possession, would he probably tell police all of what took place. Minutes later, after sharing the details of the incident from the back seat, I noticed the car was slowing down. From this moment on, things would drastically shift, get really weird, stupid, and out of control.

I continued to chat about the incident from a lying position in the back of Tyran's vehicle. I noticed the more I spoke, the car would slow down further. Neither guy would reply much to my conversation. I could feel something was wrong at this point. I slowly raised my head. To my surprise, Tyran had taken me precisely where I instructed him not to. I was just around the corner from McCabe Avenue, near the group home, but I had greater issues. As I looked upwards, I found myself staring at about 12 police officers, all with weapons drawn. I immediately raised my hands and sat upright. I instantly was thinking, "All this for hitting someone with a broom stick?" I immediately tried to plea my case as I realized I had hopped inside of the wrong damn vehicle. I was nearly 100% sure the officers were not there for me this time around. I was violently yelled at by police as I tried to explain to them; I was just taking a ride in the car. "Shut up, keep your hands up, and get out of the car!" one officer yelled with his pistol pointed directly at me. Another police instructed us all to the ground. When I got down on the ground, I actually chuckled a bit. Although I was wrong for striking Chuck, I felt I had no reason to panic. I did not have any drugs on me at all, and I knew the police were not familiar with the striking incident. They were there due to the other two guys. This was a sting of some sort, and I was all mixed up in it, because I decided to do something very stupid.

You see, drug dealing is a very desperate and foolish act to take part in. It's never as simple as dollars and cents. After we decide to do this hopeless act, many other foolish decisions usually follow. Many hustlers are in jail today, not for the specific decision they made, but for simply being in the world of poor decisions. After several failed attempts to explain my presence, I grew irritated. I tried relentlessly to express my concerns to a familiar officer I recognized from a previous basketball session. He continuously ignored my call outs. The cops were all huddled together like a football team, as the three of us sat on the curb, cuffed, with our legs crossed. The officers were doing a great job at ignoring me, therefore I decided to focus my attention on the other two guys. They were still very quiet and quite nervous. I spent the next five minutes glancing back and forth between the cops and the guys. I grew in suspicion as I heard sirens approaching. Another officer arrived, but this unit had a K-9 inside. Officers immediately began to search.

I sat patiently, but panic was gradually setting in as more police units surfaced. I decided to ask Tyran and Will a tremendously important question. In a very light whisper, I leaned sideways closer to the two and asked, "Do y'all have anything in this car?" The two simultaneously, but reluctantly, looked over at me. After a slight nod from Tyran, Will quietly stated, "Yes! It's in between the back seat, near the trunk. My head fell downwards! Minutes later, "The bionic dog" found a small stash of cocaine. "Yeah, hey, look what we have here!" stated one officer. In a last ditch effort I tried to clear my name in this situation. I never made mention of the stash, I just shouted, "Hey, I was just taking a ride, I only been in the car for three or four minutes! "Shut up!" another officer shouted. I thought I was opening the door for the two to simply confirm my story, but they never said a word. Soon, we all were read our rights. I was in a tremendous state of disbelief. Although I was completely clean from possessing any drugs of my own, I was still being arrested, again, for "riding dirty."

Thirty minutes after exiting my own vehicle, I was on my way to Baltimore City Central Booking and Intake Center for drug possession. I was arrested for drugs without having any! NONE! I sat very uncomfortably in the rear of the police cruiser. I immediately began to display my frustrations towards the other two guys. "Y'all know what y'all have to do, right? I asked with anger. "Don't worry O, we're going to take care of it," Tyran whispered. "You suckas could have taken care of it out there," I violently shouted while shifting my head towards outside. "Calm down O, we're not going to let you go down for our shit," Will nervously added. "This mess is crazy!" I expressed loudly. The police confiscated the $2500 I had in my possession. My uncharacteristic move was allowing me to see how stupid I really was. For the first time ever, I really let my pride win me over. Every action I had made on this day was not my true character. I assaulted a person for money, and I trusted people I did not know very well. I was in a heap of trouble, all for a measly $100. At the time, I believed hitting Chuck would serve as compensation for the stolen wages and lack of respect shown. Ironically, these dudes had some drugs in the car that were not hidden very well. I overheard officers chatting as we were being put through a more extensive body search at the correctional facility. I was shocked to learn we all were being charged for possessing cocaine; ironically, a little more than $100 worth.

After being separated from the other two guys, I would have to spend a night in jail. The commissioner struggled to believe the drugs were not mine due to the amount of money the police had seized from me, along with the first arrest I had a few years earlier. However, I fluidly explained the entire situation to the middle-aged magistrate, and the truth did set me free. He actually laughed about it! I was released on my own recognizance for the second time in as many arrests. I was extremely frustrated and embarrassed by the entire situation. I housed regret for not leaving the area for good, weeks before. Now, I felt obligated to stay close, just to keep an eye on Tyran and Will. I initially took their word I would be cleared of all charges in this matter. I was even told by the police I would be cleared, and would likely only have to make a brief appearance in court to retrieve my $2500. By not leaving the hood when I should have, I would possibly lose this figure in just a few minutes. Principle is extremely costly in the hood! That was not all; I ran into Chuck as soon as I returned to the neighborhood. We fought at least three more times.

I was upset about all money I had momentarily lost, and Chuck was still fuming from being hit in the head with a stick. These fights were intense. Much better than the fight I had with Tareek. There was no gun present! Chuck was no slouch either. He was an addict, but he was not long released from prison. He was still muscular and in his prime. At 32 years of age and 220 pounds, he was a tough customer to handle. I was in my mid-20s, and weighed a little more than 170 pounds. These matches repeatedly ended in stalemates, until Bennett grew restless as he watched. I was not performing well enough for my pal. I guess I was taking too long. He dropped Chuck with one punch as we clinched.

Everything inside and outside of my life was still out of control. I was fighting Chuck while contemplating physically approaching Pierce, who I felt was not playing fair. He was selling less than mediocre product, again, for prices we felt were ridiculous. The beef was at an all time high as Elroy's brother Nardo, who recently returned home, attempted to take out a few guys from Old York Road. My old schoolmate Donny was one of these guys. My relationship was a mess as well, but I tried to do the best I could to hide my troubles. My daughter and the other kids were all that were sacred to me during this period. My life was a mess as I still struggled to permanently disconnect from an entire neighborhood which had fallen from grace.

The hood I grew up in was all but finished as I peeled myself away from it, but I was mentally in yet another place. Aside from McCabe Avenue, I actually felt a need to be out in the world making lots of illegal money. I was desperately shying away from the city, but I was still deeply involved with the street life. I was experiencing inner city living at its worst. Love it or hate it! I certainly sided more with the hatred division. However, I was simply still too weak to respond positively to make a productive change. Instead, I was trying to hunt down the guys I had run into trouble with. Still, I was not the only guy to have a run-in with the law. Genius was also approaching a date in court. He was apparently looking at serving jail time for a handgun violation, but he had something totally different in mind besides change. He wanted someone to deliberately hunt him down.

I clung closely to the neighborhood to try to catch up to Will and Tyran with hopes of sorting out the situation surrounding my arrest well before our court date. I was completely done with dealing with drugs in the inner city. My operations in Chase, Maryland, Evan's area near the city/county line, Towson and Hunt Valley, Maryland, along with White Marsh, Maryland were more than enough to keep things growing. I could use McCabe Avenue as just another "pit stop," I called them; places I selected to hang out as the money generated in these other locations. I'd often stop through to make up stories of struggle to throw off the gossipers. I would even buy smaller quantities of crack from the guys after scoring bulk packages from folks they were unfamiliar with. With the ongoing violence McCabe could have been left off this list, but I still wanted to hang out with Elroy. One evening, we all were hanging out on the corner sharing a few laughs like the days of old. I felt a lot more comfortable knowing I no longer had to run from the authorities. Genius suddenly entered the crowd and interrupted us all with an alarming request. "Hey, look man, I need one of y'all to shoot me?" he said calmly. Guys immediately began to laugh until they observed the look on Genius' face. "Get the hell out of here man!" Tareek said. "Are you serious?" Killer Kev replied while smiling. "Yeah, listen niggas, I'll be seriously dead if someone fucks this up. I don't want to be dead n' shit niggas," he explained with a smile. "Who can do this shit right?" "I got court in the morning, and I'm not going to be able to do it!" he offered seriously. "Not today, or tomorrow; fuck that!" "I'm looking at a little time, and I'm not ready to go yet," he added. In order to evade imprisonment, Genius was willing to take a slug to be granted another postponement. It did not take long at all for someone here to volunteer to do the shooting. We were on McCabe Avenue, where something like this was considered to be an honor, and lot of fun.

Tareek's cousin Rob immediately stepped up to the plate to assure Genius would miss court due to injury. We all walked around into an alleyway, and I watched Genius hand Rob the gun to shoot him with. He quickly instructed Rob to aim for his back area. "Look man! Don't shoot near my head or spinal cord. Try to shoot me in the butt or somewhere I'll bleed a lot," Genius instructed. About eight of us stood and watched Genius brace himself as Rob shot the .38 caliber at Genius' backside. "POW!" sounded from the blast. "Ahhhhhh!" came from Genius' mouth as the shot went off and entered the kingpin. "Shit!" he yelled. "Damn, this shit hurts!" he continued while on his knees. Rob had shot Genius, just above his right elbow. The pain was apparently excruciating, but Genius feared the shot was in the wrong location. He felt like a wound to the arm would not be sufficient enough to warrant a missed court date. "Do it again!" he mumbled as he stood upright once again. He was trembling and grumbled before bracing himself for a second time. "POW!" the second shot exploded and hit Genius' left butt cheek. This scream was much more disturbing. Genius fell to the ground, slightly rolled onto his chest and stuttered the words, "Go call the ambulance."

This instruction caused all of the onlookers to disband. Other folks were surfacing several yards away. Paramedics, ambulances and police are like bug repellant to hustlers, but magnets to regular folks. On the block, someone could just say the word "police," and one crowd would dissolve, and another one would form simultaneously. Hustlers are always around intense action, but your average citizens are not. They show up when the cops surface. For some, it's exciting for something crazy to happen in the neighborhood, here and there. It makes for good gossip. I was the last guy to observe Genius as the ambulance drew closer. "O, get the hell outta here before they come with a bunch of questions for you to answer n' shit," he said while gasping. Genius earned himself a reprieve from court with this desperate move. The craziness would continue as the summer progressed. All negative ideas were coming to a head. I had no inclination, just how literal this all was for my own life.

My pending court case was approaching and I was still was having trouble locating my two co-defendants. With the case only a week away, I began to worry. Knowing I was not guilty of possessing any drugs gave me enough confidence not to use my retainer. I had a lawyer, an awesome white defense attorney named Mr. Koles. This was the same defense attorney who assisted me with receiving a verdict of Probation Before Judgement (P.B.J) in 1992. Mr. Koles is a very fair and compassionate attorney. I really like Mr. Koles as a person. He is a good man, period. He does his job very well, but he also displays his true personal feelings about a poor decision made by a client. He's honest! I periodically would stop in to socialize with the young attorney whenever I was in the downtown area and his schedule allowed. We spoke briefly about the matter and I felt it was not necessary for me to alter his busy schedule for a case of this nature. Although I struggled to reconnect with Will and Tyran, I felt all I needed to do was show up to court, listen to the two clear my name, and collect my money the system was withholding. It was not until I had an encounter with Will's mom, I realized something could go very wrong.

Although the days of selling drugs in the city were over, I still struggled fully pulling myself away from my inner-city roots. People outside of the game will likely never understand the undying attachment a lost soul has with his stomping ground. Just two days before court, I ran across Will's mom. I was already familiar with the woman because she knew my aunt Marie. She too was an addict. Like many women in the area, heroin was her drug of choice, a drug I've never sold. Desperate for answers, I approached the woman as she exited her boyfriend's home on McCabe Avenue. I was careful and sure to be respectful as I spoke to the woman, but things quickly deteriorated. Before I could get two words out of my mouth, she exploded and blamed the entire mishap on me. Apparently Will ran and told mommy; my two co-defendants misled everyone into believing the drugs were actually mine. I was in the midst of being framed for someone else's petty possession drug charge, and I was too distracted to catch it.

From the very second I arrived at the woman's doorstep, she was yelling at me. "Don't come up here looking for my son!" Ms. Baker said. "What do you mean by that?" I yelled. "Your son and his friend are apparently dodging me, and it was their stuff in that car," I explained. "No it was not, it was your drugs!" she replied loudly. "What?" I screamed. "I did not have any drugs Miss! They know the drugs were theirs," I stated in frustration. "It was your shit and nothing better not happen to my son either," she stated in anger. "Do you think I'm going to let those two 'clowns' place their charge on me lady, do you?" I asked sarcastically. "I bet you better not do nothing to my son," she repeated. "I'm not arguing with you lady," I replied in frustration while walking away.

The surprising argument I found myself in should have served as a warning. Somehow, I felt I still had nothing to be concerned about. Besides, as far as possessing cocaine, I was innocent this time. Optimism can carry a person a long way, but in this case I was doomed from the start. When I arrived to the courthouse alone, I felt out of sorts, like something was not all well. I was right! I soon learned from the familiar arresting officer I'd known from the basketball court, the other two guys had separated themselves from me for the trial. I was not up on this legal move, period. Now, I knew I had trouble. When the officer spoke to me he was doing more than informing me of this disturbing news. He was also telling me; it would be in my best interest to admit guilt for the five bags of cocaine, and settle for probation. "It's two against one," the officer said. "They already gave their accounts of what happened," he followed. "It was your $2500 we recovered!" "Look, it was not my shit sir," I said in frustration. "I believe you, but I have to go with the facts available," he whispered. "Well, what about the truth sir?" "What about the truth?" I repeated again. "The drugs did not belong to me!"

All of the pleading in the world would not have changed this outcome. Without my lawyer by my side, I was in a bad way. I lacked the skills and education of the law during this time. In terms of the law, I WAS STUPID! NEVER go to any hearing of any type without some form of representation, and NEVER enter any criminal hearing without a respectable defense attorney, PERIOD! I slowly walked down the aisle towards the judge's bench minutes later. By then, Tyran and Will were probably in the hood celebrating their victory with being arrested with drugs belonging to them, but never convicted. Tremendously frustrated, I stood and listened to the judge read out fictitious information about what he thought may have taken place on the day of the arrest. My eyes slowly closed briefly. I glanced to my right and viewed the neatly spread of the $2500 cash. There was something in me that wanted to lash out in the courtroom and get my point across, but I held up. What was I supposed to say? "This is not my shit! I don't even sell powder cocaine! I sell crack!" For cracking Chuck in his head with a stick, I had to take my own lumps. For drugs belonging to others, I was found guilty and placed on probation once again. This time it would be for 18 months.

I shook my head in disbelief as the verdict and sentence were read. I quickly signed the documents stating the conditions of my probation and left the courtroom. I was fortunate not to have already been on probation. I had successfully finished up the sentence from my first charge. This could have been disastrous. I hurried pass the officer I spoke with minutes prior. "Hey, I hope nothing happens to either of those guys son," he said with a grin. I just looked at him with a glare which confirmed his ability to read my mind. I shook my head again and headed for the exit. My inability to completely leave the war zone I grew up in allowed me to add a second charge on my criminal record. I immediately drove through my co-defendants neck of the woods, but they were absent. I'm quite sure, at the time, I would have done something very stupid again. For the first few weeks, something inside of me needed to violently confront these individuals. I'd heard from reliable sources, they both separated and left the area. A part of me was glad they were gone so I would not attempt to seriously hurt them. The other part of me grew angry, because I knew these "clowns" won, and they were well aware they both deserved the punishment I received.

With large profits pouring in, and plenty of fun and games, I placed the incident with Chuck, Will and Tyran in the past. The $2500 was not a large issue, but I did not want to lose it, and gain a charge as well. I was making more money than all three of those guys, combined. I had too many demons to fight to be concentrating on my silly moves and the shaky actions of others. I've always believed in the philosophy of karma, "what goes around comes around." I knew somehow, whether from me or elsewhere, those guys would get what was coming to them one day. Thanks to the intense games of basketball, I was able to channel a lot of my inconsistencies and frustrations with the streets and myself somewhere more constructive.

Dealing drugs on the street corners was finally a thing of the past. While Elroy was still ducking from authorities for his half of the fortune, I was becoming one of the leading providers of crack for addicts in Chase, Maryland. Still, my Baltimore County business in Towson became the "bread and butter" of them all. The number of addicts I frequently hosted swelled to 25. These upper and middle-class professionals I had in the bag were continuing to allow me to profit just above five-figures weekly. The cash was coming in so easily, most days I would simply be driving around doing nothing more than enjoying the sights of Baltimore, Maryland. It was never a good feeling to know I was getting away with such a demoralizing way of life, whenever it rarely crossed my mind. I didn't like to think I was actually "getting away with murder," but some would say, that's exactly what I was doing. However, it was a comfort to know, no one knew just how successful I actually was.

I never wasted much time expressing how much money I made or how I made it. Guys in the game seemed to always require more than just the money. Hustlers seem to always need others to solidify or add validity to their doings out in the streets. It's almost like they all would get the entertainment business mixed up with the streets or the drug game. The two are actually totally opposite! "He's getting money!" or "That nigga doin it!" guys often say. Over the years, I've heard countless conversations about how much money a particular guy was worth on the streets. It's really a very silly topic. Lets just say a guy made $400,000 a year, hustling. Now, what if this same individual got arrested for dealing several times, and spent eight straight years of his life in prison? Now take a hard working guy making about $50,000 a year, throughout his entire adult life, and for the same eight years in which the hustler was incarcerated, he was working everyday. This is a guy who has never been to jail, kept his peace, raised his kids, had good credit, pension forthcoming, retirement, and got married to a stable loving woman. What about life insurance, or health insurance? Most drug dealers don't have either! One minute a guy is a kingpin, the next, his family is scraping up cash to bury him.

Attend the average dealer's funeral, and you will likely see, in most cases, he never really had much of anything. Guys have become very comfortable with playing the role of a kingpin or a person of financial success. Women do it too. Hell, the culture loves to pretend; they profess wealth as they work jobs they're willing to admit they detest. You hate the job, but you're rich doing it! Ok! Most slain drug dealers leave their moms the responsibility to fit the funeral bill, because there was never any substantial money saved or possessed by the dealer all along. So with the "worker vs. hustler" scenario, it's easy to see who would make the most money or make out best overall? Exactly, that's why for me at this time, having success hustling was not solely based on dollars and cents. My number one priority as a hustler was my ability to stay free, so I can wake the hell up. I was addicted to the street life for sure, but deep inside I realized my best life was dormant. Some guys spend so much time going in and out of jail; hell, a homeless person's career is more profitable in the long run. For me, it's always been about staying free, first.

Despite the two drug possession charges, I was doing a fairly decent job at staying free. Nearly all of my peers, including Elroy, were convicted felons. Most of the guys were working on their third or forth visits to prison. Elroy had already served eight months on a felony-drug charge, just prior to our partnership. He shared that info with me later, after we drew closer. I was amazed by this, and how he still felt comfortable with dealing on McCabe Avenue with the cops so hot on his trail. I was through with dealing drugs there, but I still dealt out dope lessons on the basketball court. I still enjoyed playing ball with Genius and the others, despite their 1991 Detroit Pistons' "Bad Boys" style of play. Guys were constantly leaving the court with sprained ankles, split lips and pulled muscles. I received a gash or two over both eyes, for penetrating too freely down the middle. Make no mistake about it, everyone's true feelings about themselves and one another came out on the basketball court. Guys were going down hard, but we still called it fun. During these moments, we had no inclination more darkness loomed. We all were able to get up when knocked down, but on one warm, early evening, another comrade would be put down forever.

I had just about gotten over the situation I endured with Will and Tyran. I slightly still wanted to seek revenge, but I was doing so well in Towson and Chase, I hardly had time for senseless foolishness. I was profiting over $2000 a week in Chase, Maryland; double that amount in Towson. The only time I spent on McCabe Avenue was in relation to these pick-up basketball games, creating false narratives for gossipers, or brief chats with Elroy. Evan and I toured throughout the city to hoop against much better talent, but we still loved the hard-nosed style of play we experienced in our neighborhood. I was feeling great about my ability to finally leave the illegal activities alone on the block. With the exception of Pierce, I was getting along well with all of the other guys. Pierce and I were still having disagreements about a few hundred dollars involving some less-than-mediocre, product he had sold us. We both displayed our feelings about the situation. I physically challenged the nearly, 300 pound, "pretty boy," at least three times. He declined! Pierce was viewed as soft and everyone knew it. Initially, I liked him despite the titles others used when referencing Pierce. However, times were changing and even those considered as punks were getting a little bolder. Somehow guys were beginning to believe a little money could actually make them into tougher guys. Hustling was once a package deal years prior when dealers were bred from the inside/out. One would at least be able to hold his head up at the sight of a physical threat of violence to be considered a little tough. The early to mid-90s were a far cry from the 80s. The streets were now filled with the so-called "tough guys," who possibly had never been in a single, one-on-one fist fight in their entire lives.

Aside from a couple of very stupid decisions, I was never one to seek out a fight or negativity, but I could name at least seven different guys I fought as a teen or young man. Most of the encounters I kept to myself, although I performed pretty well. I recall during school hours, I was brawling before the entire class. I got into a scuffle with a classmate from east Baltimore over a game we played often, but on this day, I didn't care to participate; this was all my fault. Tables and chairs were flying everywhere. I was so upset; I walked clear out of the school afterwards. Surprisingly, I was not suspended. This is no good, but that's how things were for us as kids. We fought! Yes, the scuffles were for silly reasons, and I regret 95% of these situations. The remaining 5% was the experience that I had no issue with gaining. Still, fighting and dealing with shaky characters was a thing of the past for me during the Summer of 1995. Despite my inability to choose the correct path, everything in my life was running on all cylinders. I was just driving "the wrong type of vehicle." Still, I moved with a classy sense of caution, staying out of the traps of the inner-city. I was cleaning up east and west of the city in the White Marsh or Belair area, Chase, and in the Towson area, where most dealers feared to go. I knew I was onto something when I truly realized how much money I was making, and how few people knew about it. Baltimore City has always been a place where everyone knows everything, about everybody. My decision to leave the inner city circle, where most others were comfortable, would prove to be the recipe for longevity I needed before locating a real life. With my profits increasing, I would be reminded of just how timely and smart my decision to finally leave McCabe Avenue really was.

Chapter 19

# END/THE BEGINNING

By mid-Summer, 1995, I was well on my way to being able to do, pretty much, whatever I wanted, whenever I wanted. Money was not an issue at all. Minus the mansions and exotic cars, I felt I was actually living like a star. I hung out with the cutest females and wore all the latest fashions. I stayed in the lane I created exclusively, and made it more interesting than the common lane chosen by most hustlers. In my head, this was not going to be the same movie theme where some black guy makes a billion dollars, only to get himself killed or thrown in prison for the duration of his prime years. This was my real life; taking the flare most glorified amongst one another in the hood, and enhanced or expanded it through diverse networking, communication skills and class. I stayed away from flashy jewelry and chrome wheels without question. I hardly cared to imitate the images of the hottest rap artists, as guys in the hood often tried to do. Instead, I unconsciously slid into a casual role of a dealer, who simply did not appear to be. By the society, drug dealers are not just guys who sell drugs; they're also often seen as ruthless thugs who will do anything if the price is right. I made sure my image was the total opposite. While violence was spiraling out of order on McCabe, I was drinking Moet at a cookout in Towson with several of my white associates. I had been discussing a venture or partnership opportunity with Mr. Allen, a 45 year old business owner. Mr. Allen owned his own landscaping business and was looking to re-open and expand, and so was I. I was really elevating my brand in the game in a unique way, but my comrades elsewhere were not having the same luck.

As I silently continued to polish my new hustling blueprint, I still made time to play ball with the others from the hood. I loved knowing no one knew a thing about my ventures away from the city. That was exciting! Being different! Evan and I were at Dewees one summer afternoon, along with Genius and the others, playing ball. I was so excited about the moves I was making in the surrounding counties, my game improved. Again, I loved not sharing any of this information with anyone. I knew I had one up on everyone. I was making so much money undetected, I was concerned the others would try to copy my routine or sabotage it. I pretended to be your average dealer, who just wanted a little money and no trouble. The "no trouble" aspect was accurate, but I was more than certain, I was more successful than 90% of the guys I knew. Their hustle was too basic and the violence had even compromised that. Speaking of such; playing ball at Dewees, which served as the platform that reminded us all of the despair I was successfully escaping.

As I stated, the excitement I was feeling from my success in dealing drugs had carried over onto the ball court. I spent most of that afternoon torching Genius and everyone else. There are not many emotions in life to compete with the one a basketball player feels when he simply cannot miss a shot. I'm no pro, but I've enjoyed that experience countless times. I was nailing so many jump shots, I was actually heading back in the opposite direction, taking my eyes away from the ball, while the shot was still in mid-flight. Often, I would only need to be a few feet pass half court to consistently sink a jump shot. I was equally impressive above the rim. Only my ball handling and decision making skills would still set me behind the city's elite players. Still, on this day I was unstoppable; hitting shot after shot. I was on fire, and there was little anyone could do about it. The sun soon began to hide behind the backdrop as we all slowed. Despite the tightness in my elbow, I was hitting so many shots I already was getting my ego together to brag at the court the following day. Not solely from hoops; awhile back, I took a hard fall one afternoon while running from police, slightly dislocating my right elbow; my shooting arm. For as many shots as I was able to knock down on this day, we were all about to learn about the most significant ones of the day.

We continued to play our last game of the evening before sundown. It was turning out to be the only game where I continuously fell short.

Guys were suddenly "cherrypicking" or hanging in the backcourt to get an advantage. As we finished up with the last few points, we all suddenly heard five pops from afar. It would only take a moment for panic to set in. Everyone knew the stakes were high and the beef was, again, at a boil. The ball immediately stopped bouncing and everyone took off running. Concerned about Elroy, I too ran off. "E, I'll catch you later!" I yelled in Evan's direction. "Alright O," he replied. Evan had left McCabe long before it became a living hell. At this time he would not have set foot on the block even if he was paid to do so. After hearing several gunshots from the court, we all took off running down the small, farmland's hill Dewees sat on top of. Everyone knew trouble loomed and somehow mustard up the energy to run their fastest, even after a hard day of competing on the court. Nine of us reached the bottom of the hill and, again, I noticed something peculiar. My uncle Frank was lying in the tall grass, giggling. Frank sometimes would walk up to the field, and simply lay in the grass. However, he would usually be very drunk, unconsciously impersonating some kind of friendly, free-spirited canine. Normally, I would indulge Frank, but there seemed to be a more serious situation taking place. I quickly glanced over at my uncle, but my grin only lasted for a second. I knew by the reaction of the others something was terribly wrong. I was just praying Elroy was not the latest recipient of the shots we heard. I was still attempting to get him to pull away from the corners, so the thought it would be too late was present.

All drenched in our own sweat, we landed on Alhambra Avenue. To our surprise, it was fairly peaceful on the block, therefore we quickly continued onto McCabe. After pausing, tensions resurfaced when we observed Elroy's sister, Rebbie quickly sprinting into the alleyway. This was the same passage I once dashed through as I ran for my own life. Screams and anxiousness followed Rebbie through the narrow path. All of the neighborhood players from the court, and most of the neighborhood followed. I was elated to see Elroy although he appeared to be just as worried as his older sister. I put two and two together and concluded either Steve or another guy from the neighborhood was involved in a bad situation. Rebbie, leading the way, came to a halt on Beaumont Avenue, the next street over, and there still was no sight of any foul play. The crowd had swelled to at least 25 people. The scene looked like the last miles of a marathon. We all continued to run as fast as we all could until we reached

Winston Avenue. Before getting to the corner of Winston, we all could see blinking blue and red lights. Somehow you could just feel these lights were connected to the five shots we heard minutes prior. The mob of around 30, myself included, meshed into another growing mass of onlookers. Rebbie quickly melted into the audience. I pushed through the crowd slowly. A scream followed, drowning out all of the other loud voices. I kept a very close eye on the back of Elroy's tee-shirt as I forced my way through the confusion. Seconds later, one of my worst fears was realized. I was staring at Steve; nearly motionless in the middle of the street. A couple of those five shots had found their way into Steve's chest.

The entire neighborhood watched Steve's body lay dead in the street before it was tended to and covered by paramedics. My heart stopped as I became dizzy from all of the commotion. Observing Elroy's mom jog to the crime scene, only to leave in total disbelief, was unreal. I could not believe I was experiencing another fallen pal. Steve, like Tray, had assured me he had no interest in participating in the warfare shared between the two neighborhoods. I wondered what kind of incident had taken place. We all discovered quickly; Steve's demise was, in fact, related to the feud.

In prior weeks, I pleaded with Steve not to get involved, but like Tray, he too allowed my warnings to fall on deaf ears. Everyone soon learned of the details surrounding Steve's death. He was not alone during this incident. He was accompanied by Tareek's little brother, Lamar. He was only 18, but he was still able to influence Steve, in his late-20s, to get involved with the feud. On the block, Lamar delivered all of the details surrounding the tragic event and everyone carefully listened. After taking in all of the information, the guys from McCabe would begin to implement a plan; a plan to kill.

B-Mack quickly learned of his friend's death from jail. He was devastated. Lamar had told everyone, he and Steve were on York Road and Winston Avenue trying to catch a flow of money coming through. Although they were not from Winston, it was not unusual for some of the guys from McCabe to venture onto other territories nearby to make their money. The surrounding areas were not likely to put up any resistance in these situations. The two waited for customers on that night. This is when Lamar spotted Nysheme in a black Ford Bronco with his girlfriend. Nysheme was Melody's ex from high school. His position in the rivalry was pretty similar to my own. We both interacted with the guys in the streets, but neither of us really cared to be a part of the foolishness. After Nysheme was pointed out by Lamar, it was said, the two advanced towards his parked vehicle. Steve then would try to pull Nysheme from his vehicle. As Steve pulled and the two violently swung across the frantic female, Nysheme reached underneath his driver's seat, drawing a large handgun. Lamar was heady enough to retreat and dodge behind the Bronco. Steve, coming off of a lengthy prison sentence, was not as sharp. He was caught directly in the line of fire. Nysheme nervously pointed and fired several shots, before pulling off leaving Steve to die in the street.

Retaliation was a certainty, but Nysheme decided to take another angle. He soon turned himself in, admitting to killing Steve in self-defense. He pleaded down to a lesser charge. While Nysheme struggled to quickly place the tragedy behind himself, the guys from McCabe were displaying tremendous amounts of anger. They all wanted to avenge Steve's untimely death. However, any kickback from the situation would be done without Nardo. He too learned of his older brother's situation from inside prison walls. Not long before Steve's murder, Nardo began serving a five-year jail sentence on a parole violation, only weeks after he was released from another charge. His broken voice via telephone helped produce more of a sense of urgency in the others to strike quickly. I attended Steve's funeral and burial. I had been to so many funeral services by this time, I felt like a teen again. I stood and stared over Steve's darkened corpse, wishing he had taken heed to my many warnings. Despite my pleas, he was oblivious to how badly the area had really digressed in the negative. Steve was only 27 years old, and soon to be engaged.

I was beginning to understand when many of the pastors said, "Death is a time to celebrate!" With all of the negativity our world has to offer, it was still hard for me to believe a guy like Steve was going to a bad place. He certainly was not headed for bigger and better things here. While everyone would become enraged at these funerals, I actually awakened a bit. I began to understand spirituality a bit more. I had never read a Bible before, but I was becoming more intrigued to learn about something more than what the naked eye could see. I was aware Steve's death was sad, but listening to the preacher's sermon made it quite difficult to feel the tragedy was solely a bad thing. It was clear to me at this point; the really bad instances were not in death, but still here on earth, while we're all still alive.

In the past, the time spent with loved ones after a funeral meant a lot more. It hardly mattered if this was the only time the entire family came together. But during Steve's repass things were much different. Although guys were sure to retaliate against Old York, they had no idea the momentum was still on their rival's side. Everyone gathered around Elroy's home, comforting his mom after losing one of her five boys. I stood in front of the home, due to the overcrowded porch. Of course, there was plenty of food to go along with the tears, but no one knew what was literally around the corner as the sun fell.

Despite Steve's passing, guys were still continuing with their normal routines. There were plenty of addicts and hustlers outside, still chasing and pushing their #1 product; crack. Once again, I found myself on the dimly lit block, surrounded by nothing but despair. I found myself gazing at the alleyway where the two armed robbers exited, nearly claiming my life that evening. I could picture 731 being consumed, once again, with grieving family members. I simply thanked God. I was thinking about how fortunate I was on that night, not to have had on the same $200 pair of slippery shoes I was standing in. I was also very gracious for not having an all too familiar sprained ankle. I would not have been able to run very fast if that were the case. I honestly believed I had made it pass all of the shootings and deaths. I was very wrong; almost dead wrong, again.

Seconds after observing the crowd on the porch, screams erupted. A late model sedan with its headlights out suddenly appeared, speeding down McCabe. A guy was shooting from outside of the driver side, rear window. By the time the vehicle reached 731's front, I was lying in the gutter, a few car lengths away, in a similar positon of my previous near-death experience. I managed to peak my head upwards, high enough to see the frantic crowds of people scattering. Everyone on Elroy's porch, including his mom, dropped for cover. I observed everyone disbanding with hopes everyone would escape unharmed. This was nearly true, until I observed Nee-Nee, a close friend of Penny's, frantically running towards her home as the car drew closer. Nee-Nee was screaming, "Ma! Ma! Open the door!" as she frantically hurried up the small grass hill to the front of her home. Shots were ringing out as the vehicle continued to advance. Suddenly, I observed a single splatter appear on her light-green, tee-shirt. She fell immediately, shocking the scared onlookers. She was struck once in the back. She fell hard in her front lawn as the shooter sped off towards York Road. This incident took the neighborhood over the top emotionally. Before Steve could even get comfortable in his new "Home," another person was shot. This time it was a female. Miraculously, Nee-Nee recovered successfully. However, the single slug to her back missed her spine by less than an inch.

After celebrating Nee-Nee's fortune of surviving her injury, I visited a grieving Elroy. Just afterwards, on the infamous corner of Alhambra and McCabe, I found myself in the midst of preparations for retaliation. Elroy's mom made sure he stayed inside. He hardly wanted to get involved with killing someone despite his brother's death. We were both realists, to an extent. We understood taking a life would never make us feel any better about a lost loved one. Although we felt trapped in the game, we understood our lifestyles left us more susceptible to experiencing grief, but neither of us were killers. We cared about things most hustlers don't, but we were too weak-minded to do anything about our situations or to make a positive change. No one pressured Elroy into joining the retaliation efforts, and they all certainly knew I was not participating. I viewed it all as stupid, and I could never forget Benny pleading with me over the years to never get involved. Even without his pleas, I still would not have participated. To many, I was viewed as sort of an "Old G," who was not older yet. I was not a part of the violence, but I was trusted. It was comfortable for all of the guys to share their experiences with me. That's why I found myself on the same corner I was assaulted on, listening to the plan to kill everyone they could from Old York Road.

On the corner, I huddled closely and heard everything. Tareek, Rob, Tockey, Killer Kev, Dro, Nick, and several others plotted how they would strike and finish off Old York Road for good. They felt this ambush would be so intense it would finally put an ending to this beef which lasted for decades. I stood and watched these predatory, pain and anger-filled individuals display their feelings towards the other side. I did not oppose any statements, nor did I make any. "Alright fellows, this is it," Nick calmly stated. "Let's do this shit!" Dro quietly mumbled. "Man, I hope ya'll not bluffin and shit!" Killer Kev shouted. "I'm going to kill every muthafucka down there, and I don't care who it is," he stated coarsely. "I'm ready," Tareek stated with a smile. "I don't care either, fuck all of them niggas," he added vibrantly. "I'm going to call my boys from the westside for some more fire power too," Kev stated with excitement. "Let's do it," Rob stated with a smile as well. "Hey, I have a stolen mini-van. It... it's around back," Dro whispered. "It's a dark blue one, so... so... so... we good fellas," he stuttered. "Yeah, that's cool, I'm sick of these niggas. This is it," Tareek vowed. "We just goin' roll up on these fools and kill all of them, that's all," he added with a hunch of his shoulders. The crowd soon would disband with plans to reunite a bit later, and I was sure NOT to be there. People were apparently about to die, and this simply was never my thing. In the publicized words of historic and legendary, yet controversial figure, Mike Tyson; "I'm crazy, but not crazy like that!"

As the plot for danger materialized, I shared the details with Elroy. Despite the death of his brother, he did not seem thrilled, at all, with the probability of more bloodshed. However, he was not at all interested in trying to stop the violence. He was more concerned about the $1000 Killer Kev still possessed from our digressing partnership. "O, go get the money from that dude please," Elroy stated. "Take your half and bring me the other five hundred," he instructed. "I told you to not give him any 'work' man." I stated. "He's a cool dude at times, but not for business," I added. "How much does he owe you altogether?" I asked. "Too much to count O," he replied. "Ok, I'll stop by his apartment to get the cash," I assured Elroy. "He's really going to need some money soon, or maybe he won't need any at all. Hell, he may not have it to give or keep, you know what I mean?" I said with a slight grin. I stared at Elroy as we were both talking about money owed by Kev, but that was small talk really. Emotions were evident in terms of Steve's death, but we were short on words. "Damn Steve," was all I could muster as I parted ways, leaving Elroy's bedroom. "Yeah, I know. Please get there before they go do that stupid shit," Elroy pleaded. I simply nodded as I continued through the door.

I hurried to Killer Kev's apartment to retrieve the $1000. He lived in the same complex as Evan, just a few buildings to the left. There was so much money coming in, even Kev managed to get a place of his own. This was an area once ran solely by Evan. Unfortunately for Evan and his peers, it would not be long before a group of dealers from Brooklyn, New York learned of the "gold mine." They managed to integrate or somewhat take the place over without any resistance. A "Takeover" usually involved some element of danger or death, but this came with none. This was not really

Baltimore City; it was just above the city line, relatively far away from the troubled hoods making this jux rather simple for the New Yorkers. This was not an agreed upon partnership. Evan and the others did not really want the New Yorkers there, but they just came in and set up shop. The Brooklyn natives were put onto the location by a junkie who was originally from up north. She placed a call back home, and here they were! I stood in the midst of them all; to be honest, it was a very weird dynamic. I asked Evan about it all, but he seemed too embarrassed to go into detail about it. He still made his money and that's all that mattered to him. I didn't care much for violence, but to have a group of out-of-towners suddenly take over your profitable drug strip, make lots of money, in your face, daily, was a bit extreme, even for me. I kept my nose out of it as much as possible. I was set with my own endeavors. Again, this was not in the city, but extremely close. Unconventional hustling styles were playing themselves out for myself and others outside of B'MORE City. I no longer needed the $500 or so a week I was able to make here with Evan, before the takeover. I knew to pull myself away from the area. I would have let the New Yorkers know what I thought of the situation. This possibly would have brought the city element a little further north. I knew no one really wanted that, not even I. We were in Baltimore County, barely, and Brooklyn, New York was winning, but it was none of my business. I was there to simply pick up $1000 from a guy who was getting set to go on a confirmed shooting spree.

I entered the building to Killer Kev's apartment and moderately knocked on the door. He never asked the question, "Who is it?" I knew he was at the door, but I refused to look for a shadow in his peep hole. A little while back a pal of mine, we once danced against, got into the game as well. He silently went to his own door to see who was on his porch after a few knocks. He pierced through the peep hole once. He's still alive today, but he only has one functioning eye, and a contorted face from a gunshot blast. "Boy, I didn't know who the hell you were," Kev offered as I entered his place. "Don't scare me like that son," he stated with a grin as he quickly opened and closed his door. "My bad," I replied smiling. "Let me guess," he stated with a giggle. "You're here for some money right?" he asked. "That's it man. It's supposed to be a 'g' ($1000) right?" "Yeah," I replied with a nod. "Boy, that's one thing bout you O, you don't play!" he shouted with a grin. "All you want is some money, a few bad bitches, and some peace ha?" Kev asked. "I guess you can put it like that Kev," I replied with a grin. "You should've picked another line of work then homie, especially for the peace shit, dontcha think?" he concluded with a smirk. "Tell me about it," I replied with a false grin. "Tell the truth O, all you really want is cash and a few bad bitches right?" he insisted. "What else is there?" I asked. "Oh, there's a lot more than that," Kev shared. "I will show you!"

During this time, it was all of our understanding; money and women were the grand rewards when hustling. Money, beautiful women, and possessions were a bit of an afterthought to Kev, I guess. He preferred the action. That explained why his apartment was still empty after living there for over six months. "O, don't wait in the living room. I have to hurry up! You already know why. Come back here. I'm working," he stated one after the other. I entered Kev's bedroom and was taken aback immediately. Talk about "working from your home."

When I entered Killer Kev's room, all I saw were guns and rounds of bullets. I observed a couple of 9mm automatic pistols, a 357 Magnum, a .38 Special revolver, a shotgun, a Desert Eagle, and our infamous Tech 9. Kev had disassembled all of these weapons. He was cleaning them with his own homemade solution; water, a little detergent, and rubbing alcohol. "What in the hell are you doing?" I asked loudly with a confused grin. "O, I'm cleaning my shit," he replied aggressively. "I'm really about to kill me a few muthafuckas O," he explained. "Do you understand me; I refuse to have any one of these hammers lock up on me," he added with a smile. "I'm going for it all on this one O buddy," he stated boldly. "I have to hurry up and put these bastards back together," he stated as he used a small bottle brush to clean the barrel of a gun. "O, you want some beer or Kool-Aid or something nigga?" he asked. "Yeah, Kool- Aid is cool," I replied while gazing at what Kev was doing. Killer Kev did have one thing going for him. He had a fresh, full, tall pitcher of cherry Kool-Aid. "O, you think this is something. I got two homies coming ova from the west side. Watch the shit they bring," he said excitingly. "Don't go anywhere buddy. You have to see this shit!" he emphasized. "I'll give you your money in a minute," he stated. I was beginning to see; watching Kev walk up and down York Road with a Tech-9 in a pouch, in broad daylight was just for starters. He was as excited about committing a drive-by as I would be about meeting or dating a fine sister. It never registered to me, at the time, someone was actually about to be shot or killed. All I understood was I was not going to be a part of any violent situations.

Killer Kev's pals arrived a few minutes later. He introduced me to the two guys but not by name. They both were younger than I and were very slight in their builds. Surprisingly, one guy really resembled someone from a dice game at Scott's grandma's house. The two guys both carried tall, green, lawn bags over their shoulders. Kev was acting out as if the guys had Christmas presents, but the contents in these bags were only called toys by personalities like his own. Simultaneously, the two guys dumped out the contents of the bags. Inside were four assault rifles; one being an M-16, and another being an AK-47. For the second time, I was observing strands of ammunition like Stallone wore in his blockbuster film, "Rambo." I once observed similar "ammo" at Skippy's years prior. "Ya'll crazy," I stated. "I told you O. We're going to really take all of them niggas out tonight O," he insisted. "Here O, you can go now," he stated while handing me a ball of cash. "It may be a little short, but I got you," he stated with a nod. "I'll catch you later. You get away now! You don't need to see any more of this shit. It's officially on now!" he explained violently as he stared at the firearms. I never counted the money Kev handed to me until I got back into my car. All I knew was Elroy was going to get the short end of this money. I was personally taking out a deduction for his decision with dealing with Killer Kev from the start. Kev gave me $920, surprisingly more than I expected. I knew as I pulled away from the complex, we would probably never receive the balance, nor see Kev ever again.